LAKE ERIE

GREENWOOD PRESS, PUBLISHERS
WESTPORT, CONNECTICUT

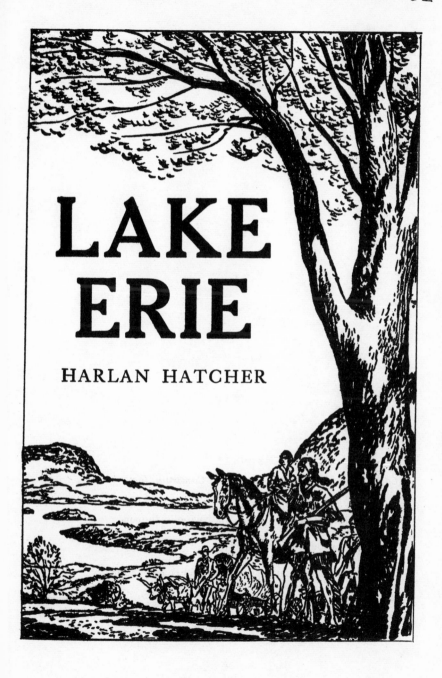

LAKE ERIE

HARLAN HATCHER

For
LINDA LESLIE HATCHER
AND
ANNE HUME VANCE

EDITORIAL INTRODUCTION

THE NAME OF Lake Erie preserves the memory of an ancient tragedy. In recent years Nazi Germany, reverting to the standards of primitive savagery, has converted civilized Europe into a charnel house. So, too, the tribes composing the Iroquois Confederacy 300 years ago suddenly ran amuck, conquering or destroying all their neighbors. Numbered among the victims was the Neutral nation living north of Lake Erie, whose memory is preserved in the name of Niagara, and the Erie nation whose homeland was the country south of the lake. When the work of death was ended both nations had vanished from the face of the earth. Of the country around Lake Erie the Iroquois had "made a solitude and called it peace." Although no white men were present to describe for posterity the golgotha of the Erie, in all essential respects it must have repeated the scenes which attended the earlier destruction of the Huron, and these were recorded by the Jesuit fathers with horrifying fidelity to reality.

In several respects Lake Erie differs markedly from its sisters in the chain of Great Lakes. Last to be discovered by the white man, it lies much farther south than the others. It is also much shallower, compelling the huge freighters which traverse its surface to follow definite, well-marked routes of travel. The same factor contributes to the agitation of the lake which, more than any other, is vexed by sudden gales. This was noted by the first Englishmen who ever ventured upon it. "There is no dependence on the Lake in the very best season," wrote Captain Donald Campbell, who accompanied Major Rogers' expedition to Detroit in the autumn of 1760, and the experience of thousands of subsequent navigators has abundantly confirmed his observation.

The favorable southerly location of Lake Erie gives to its hinterland a more genial climate and a more uniform distribution of agricultural wealth than the other lakes possess. Proximity to the industrial heart of the nation combines with the geological accident of Niagara to insure to Erie's many busy harbors the maximum exploitation of the wealth of forest and field and mine which flows down from the Upper Lakes; while the same favored location midway between the great seaboard cities and the industrial centers which crown the head of Lake Michigan has rimmed Lake Erie's shores with several of the nation's most important railways. Little wonder therefore that Ohio, tucked between Lake Erie and the Ohio River, ranks among the foremost states of the Union, both industrially and agriculturally; or that Erie's American shore is lined with busy cities from Buffalo on the east to Detroit on the west.

These and all other things in, upon and beside Lake Erie's waters are charmingly expounded by Harlan Hatcher in the chapters that follow. No reader of his book, we feel confident, will lay it down with any shadow of doubt over the editorial wisdom and good fortune involved in obtaining his consent to undertake the important task of relating the story of the great lake which borders his state. He is a native of Ohio and a graduate of its State University, and has been a member of its faculty almost from the day of his graduation. Although strongly inclined in his earlier years toward history as the field of his scholarly specialization, he finally settled upon literature, and for many years he has held the position of Professor of English in the Ohio State University. He returned from service in the United States Navy in 1944 to become Dean of the College of Arts and Sciences. He is the author of several books of fiction and of *The Buckeye Country,* a substantial characterization of his native state. He has traveled the Great Lakes and their adjacent shores from Kingston to Chicago and Duluth by freighter, passenger ship, automobile and airplane; and has written a comprehensive description of them all in his recently published book, *The Great Lakes.* His knowledge of Lake Erie is encyclopedic, and his mastery of literary art enables him to impart it in effective and entertaining language. Both editor and publishers will congratulate themselves if the authors of the books yet to be published in the *American Lakes Series* shall match the standard of historical and literary skill achieved by Dean Hatcher.

—M. M. Quaife,
Detroit Public Library.

TABLE OF CONTENTS

PART I

TABLE OF CONTENTS—*Continued*

PART III

LIST OF ILLUSTRATIONS

LIST OF ILLUSTRATIONS—*Continued*

Part I

Chapter 1

The Lake

LAKE ERIE is intimate and wayward. Of the five Great Lakes, Erie is fourth in size, for only Ontario is smaller. Cool, deep Lake Superior is the Amazonian one; Lake Huron, wild and island-studded, is next; and Lake Michigan with her gates of gold at Mackinac and the silver finger of Green Bay to break her regular coast line is third. Lake Erie is less than half the size of Lake Michigan— 9,940 square miles in area, or a little larger than the state of Vermont.

The long grain ships, loaded to the Plimsoll line with wheat from the elevators at Duluth, ease down the Livingstone Channel past Grosse Isle and out into the western corner of Lake Erie. They swing round at the Detroit River Lighthouse and head east-southeast through Canadian waters and keep between the buoys north of Ontario's Pelee Island. They usually have the wind behind them as they clear Point Pelee and Southeast Shoal Light and steer straight for Buffalo, about 200 miles away at the eastern corner. They are never far from land. At the widest point the Erie shores are only fifty-eight miles apart; at the narrowest they are separated by only twenty-eight miles. In her present state Lake Erie is shallow. Her thirty-foot-depth contour is regularly about a mile offshore. Her harbors were filled with sand which has had to be dredged out. Her deepest soundings are but 210 feet, 1,000 feet less than Superior's, and 660 feet less than Michigan's; and her mean depth is only ninety feet. That is one reason why Erie is vagrant and temperamental rather than brooding.

Erie's waters stir in this shallow bowl. Perhaps saucer is more accurate than bowl. Or, if we think of its shape as well as of its shallowness, it is more like a trencher of the era of Hawkins and Drake. The water from Lake Huron pours hurriedly under the International Bridge at Sarnia and Port Huron. It flows down the St. Clair River, widens lazily out into a lake in the St. Clair Flats, then gathers itself together again at Windmill Point to become the Detroit River. It

15

moves on down the twenty-eight-mile-long channel past Detroit and Windsor, flows around the islands in the river, and spreads imperceptibly into the long narrow basin that confines Lake Erie. At the Buffalo end it is channeled once more and funneled out through the Niagara River under the Peace Bridge past Squaw Island at the rate of 215,000 cubic feet each second. Then it runs rapidly down to spill over the Niagara Falls into Lake Ontario, about 330 feet below the level of Lake Erie.

The northern half of Lake Erie belongs to Canada, the southern half to the United States. The province of Ontario borders its entire north shore—all the way from Fort Erie at the entrance to the Niagara, and Port Colborne where the ships enter the Welland Canal, to Amherstburg and Windsor on the Detroit River. The province is shaped exactly like a big Indian arrowhead with its point aimed straight at Detroit. The Erie shore forms one edge of the point, the Huron shore the other; the Niagara escarpment is its southern barb, the Saugeen Peninsula the northern. Its neck is the narrow strip of land between Georgian Bay and the Hamilton wedge of Lake Ontario. Only a few small creeks and one fairly large river—the Grand—flow down from the north into Lake Erie. The Thames River is only a few miles away, but it runs parallel to the Lake Erie shore and empties into Lake St. Clair. The regular shore line is broken only by the jutting peninsulas of Point Pelee and Rondeau in the west and Long Point in the east.

The big port cities of the province are on Georgian Bay and Lake Ontario at the neck of the arrowhead. The Erie shore line on Canada's side is a bit lonely. There are no great cities, few roaring mills, no giant elevators, fine harbors, long wharves or railroad yards on the north coast. The smokestacks of the International Nickel Company's plants loom up against the sky at Port Colborne where they are clearly visible from the steamship lanes on Lake Erie. The stacks and brick walls of the mills at Amherstburg rise high above the texas houses of freighters going up the Amherstburg Channel in the Detroit River. Between them are beaches and summer resorts, quiet towns and fishing villages, marshes, forestry stations and provincial parks.

The proud cities with crowded harbors and teeming lake commerce are on the United States side. The recital of their names sounds like a Walt Whitman chant to the muscular new world whose sons and daughters have erected monuments fit for these states: Detroit, Toledo, Sandusky, Huron, Vermilion, Lorain, Cleveland, Fairport, Ashtabula, Conneaut, Erie, Dunkirk and Buffalo. These are the harbors where the great ships come and go. These cities receive the stupendous tonnage of ore and grain that flows in an ever-increasing river of red and gold from Duluth and Superior, Ashland and Marquette, Chicago and Milwaukee. And from seven of these cities flows back an equally stupendous tonnage in the unending black river of coal for the thriving cities of the Upper Lakes.

On this south shore Lake Erie belongs mostly to Ohio. It sweeps across 184 miles of the northern Ohio border: all the way from the port at Conneaut, past Cleveland and Sandusky Bay, to the busy city of Toledo and the crowed estuary of the Maumee. Of those thirteen important ports on the lake, whose names we have just recited, nine are in Ohio. Ever since the Civil War Lake Erie has pulled the center of population to the north away from the Ohio River. Ohio's pleasant and generally peaceful neighbor Michigan went to war with her in 1835 over the Maumee estuary. Michigan at that time had about 1500 miles of coast line on Lake Michigan, Lake Superior, Lake Huron, Lake St. Clair, and the not very profitable or important western shore of Lake Erie from Grosse Isle down to the present northern suburbs of Toledo. Michigan also claimed Toledo, and waged war for its possession, but that port was denied to her, as we shall see. Pennsylvania had a western water outlet at Pittsburgh, but she did not wish to be landlocked on the northwest. She coveted at least one port on Lake Erie. She did not have to go to war with her New York neighbor to reserve her narrow corridor to the sea. It extends only a few miles east and west of the port city of Erie. New York had already extended a long arm west from Albany up the Mohawk Valley to take in the entire southern shore of Lake Ontario. She also reached a thumb farther west to seize about one-fifth of the Erie coast, including the key terminal and transport city of Buffalo. With Ontario on the north shore, more states border Lake Erie than any other lake in the entire chain.

Lake Erie is also by many miles the most southerly of the system.

Its basin lies at a rakish angle from southwest to northeast. It freezes late and thaws early. On the average the ice does not close in until December 17, and it is open for navigation at Toledo and Sandusky by the end of March—a week earlier than Lake Huron and two weeks earlier than Lake Michigan. This shorter winter and temperate climate make the cluster of islands in western Lake Erie a favored spot for the vintners who have through the years made their wines world-famous. Twenty-four states of the republic are wholly or in part farther north than Cleveland and Toledo. The shore line between these two cities is farther south than northern California or Hartford, Connecticut, and all of the lake's surface is farther south than Milwaukee. Lake Erie, in fact, hangs like a jeweled pendant from the blue thread of the St. Lawrence on the northeast and the long thread of interconnecting rivers and lakes of the great waterway to the northwest.

The shallow basin and the position of Lake Erie also make it the most tempestuous and choppy of the Great Lakes. The wide frontal storms roaring down over Lake Huron from upper Canada and Hudson Bay strike Lake Erie with great force. The subtropical highs press in from the south. They engage in conflict over and around Lake Erie, and its shallow waters plunge and toss furiously. The winds can whip up tremendous seas on the surface almost without warning. The navigation charts are figured on a low-water datum of 570.5 feet above sea level. The actual level fluctuates widely from half a foot below this datum in winter to four feet above it in certain summers. And the wind alone, sweeping up from southwest to northeast along the axis of the lake, may lower the level at Toledo by eight or more feet, while the depth of the harbors at the east end may rise by several feet. Likewise a strong east wind lowers the water at Buffalo and has, at times, actually laid bare the rock bottom of the lake near Fort Erie.[1]

All through its maritime history Lake Erie has been unpredictable.

---

[1] There are many references to this phenomenon in the history of Lake Erie. Captain James Sloan recollected that in 1817 when he put his boat in at Point Abino, a few miles west of Buffalo, the water fell so rapidly that he could not move out fast enough. Within a few minutes his vessel was stranded on the sand and the captain walked around her on dry ground. The natives informed him that this was not an uncommon occurrence. At the other end of the lake the staff of the Franz Theodore Stone Laboratory at Put-in-Bay have walked across from Peach Point to Gibraltar Island on dry (or rather, muddy) land when the wind has been strong from the southwest.

Uncounted numbers of disasters, tragedies and shipwrecks have over-taken the men who have sailed over her blue surface. Time and again ships have put out from Buffalo under friendly skies only to be turned back or beaten to pieces by a raging sea before they reached Erie, Pennsylvania, or Long Point, Ontario. More voyagers have been seasick on Lake Erie than on Lake Superior.

But with all her moods and whims, Lake Erie remains the most intimate and happy of all the Great Lakes, ready alike for a gala week-end holiday and for the tremendous burden of bulk commerce of the workaday world that has brought to her shores such a concentration of the world's wealth and population.

Chapter 2

Shifting Shore Lines

LAKE ERIE, the last of the Great Lakes to be discovered, was the first to take form. In preglacial ages a mighty river flowed eastward through what is now the Lake Erie basin. When the ice sheet formed and moved south, it rammed one lobe along the axis of this stream. It gouged heavily into the soft Devonian shales to the east, and it carved deep grooves in the hard, resistant Devonian limestone at Sandusky Bay to the west. These grooves are conspicuous on the islands, especially on Kelleys Island, where one exposed section of this glacial sculpture has been made into a state park. The southwestern lobe of its basin, where the white pioneers found the Black Swamp, was first uncovered when the last of the ice sheets, known as the Wisconsin, began to melt back from the corner of present Ohio, Indiana and Michigan. The sun had beat upon the advancing front of this ice sheet, melting it down and releasing from its frozen grip the billions of tons of rock and gravel which were left piled up in terminal moraines 500 feet deep in places. The water filled in between the moraine and the receding ice sheet and discharged out of the Maumee lobe down the Wabash River. And when the water was extensive enough to be called a lake, Lake Erie had begun its metamorphosis to its present shore lines.

The process was a long one. The lake has gone through numerous stages and has stood at various levels. The earliest level was 200 feet higher than the present one, for the water, walled out of the Niagara River by the ice, had to rise over the watershed at the head of the Maumee River. The old beaches of the successive levels are clearly discernible as you ascend from the lake shore to the low watershed south of the lake. Highways follow their even contours from east to west. The level of the principal beaches and the geological names for Lake Erie as it went from one stage to another may be briefly indicated in this table as worked out by Leverett and Taylor:

Lake Maumee at an elevation of 785-795 feet (Lake Erie is now about 573 feet); Lake Whittlesey at 735-740 feet; Lake Warren at

680-685 feet; Lake Lundy at 615-620 feet; Lake Erie, in its Early Algonquin stage, 540-550 feet, and in its Nipissing stage, 560 feet.

The previous lake levels are so easily recognized that an unschooled English farmer, observing them while on tour in the 1820's before geology was a science, wrote, "There are ample proofs that the lakes and bodies of water in these extensive countries have covered a much larger space than they now occupy; for the Mountain as it is generally called, which runs by Queenston to Ancaster (and onward north-west) within a few miles of the south of the head of Lake Ontario . . . is evidently an original bank of Ontario. . . . How far this original bank has extended on the States' side, I have not the means of knowing. . . . In Canada it may be traced a considerable distance with the eye from the Lake."[1]

The Lake Erie shore line has always been, and still is, restless and unstable, and this characteristic, as we shall see in due course, has had a profound effect upon its history and its economy. Lake Superior lies secure and fixed in her hard, resistant bowl of pre-Cambrian rock. Her shore line has altered little in the centuries since she took shape in front of the retreating ice. But the Erie bowl is brittle at the edges and changes rapidly not only from century to century but from year to year. Between Toledo and Port Clinton the low-lying shore is weak, silty clay with no outcropping rock. Behind the barrier beach of this section are marshlands where migratory birds stop to feed. Some of the better land has been diked and drained for agriculture or, as at Reno Beach, for a building development. The Catawba Point-Marblehead peninsula is a low limestone cliff. Eastward, across Sandusky Bay, is the sand arm of Cedar Point. On toward Lorain the shore rises gently, never to great height; and between Lorain and Cleveland are cliffs of shale. From Cleveland eastward the shore line is now resistant glacial drift. On this 184-mile-long strip there are only about thirty-four miles of rock shore, and only eleven of rock that resists erosion. And so it is all round the lake. Except at Cedar Point, the mouth of Maumee Bay, a strip west of Camp Perry, Crystal Beach, Long Point, the popular Kingsville Beach, and a few other short stretches, there are no good sand beaches on the lake shore. The rivers coming into the lake from the south are short, but they wash sand, soil and gravel into the lake and

---

[1] Joseph Pickering, *Inquiries of an Immigrant* (London, 1832), p. 153.

construct bars at their mouths which must be cut through and dredged to provide harbors for ships. Despite its record shipping, Lake Erie did not have a single deep usable natural harbor when the white men came to her shores.

Confine a vast body of relatively shallow water in a bowl of this material, 240 miles long by thirty to fifty-eight miles wide, let the winds beat upon it, the waves attack it and the rains wash down into it, and alterations will occur at an astonishing rate. That is what has been happening to the shore line, and the problems created by it are acute. A half-million dollars' worth of land is bitten off the shore every year and strewn over the Lake Erie floor. The process was under way before the Connecticut men came into the Western Reserve, but it has accelerated since that time.

Judge James Kingsbury was probably the first settler to spend the winter in the Western Reserve. His cabin stood near the edge of the lake at Conneaut, and his child, the first white child born in the Reserve, died of starvation during the harsh winter. Seventy-five years later the site of Kingsbury's cabin was on the floor of Lake Erie, torn down by the ceaseless attack of the waves.

The boundary line between Pennsylvania and Ohio was first surveyed in 1786. It was resurveyed and marked in 1881. T. H. Langlois [2] saw the possibility of getting an exact measurement of the rate of recession of the Lake Erie shore at this point. On May 11, 1944, he visited the spot and found the markers of 1881 in place. The shore line along this portion of the lake is a fifty-seven-foot blue-clay cliff. The 1881 markers had been set 383 feet from the edge of the cliff. Langlois measured the distance in 1944; it was 255 feet. The waves of the lake had undercut the cliff, and in the sixty-three years had caused 128 feet of shore to topple down into the lake. That is slightly more than two feet each year—nearly 350 feet since Moses Cleaveland and his party passed westward to found settlements on the lake. This action goes right on unchecked. Huge chunks of good land are this minute crumbling into Lake Erie and the slope is slumping into ugly ruin. [3]

Mrs. Jameson noticed this action on the Ontario shore in the 1830's.

---

[2] Director of Franz Theodore Stone Laboratory and Chief of the Fish Management and Propagation Section of the Ohio Division of Conservation and Natural Resources.

[3] *The Ohio Conservation Bulletin* (August 1944).

During her visit to Colonel Talbot she wandered out to the cliff overlooking Lake Erie at the mouth of Talbot Creek. She saw a great tree hanging upside down over the cliff. It had been undercut by the waves and floods, and had crashed over. Its still green leaves were suspended near the water's edge, and its roots, still clinging to the soil, were exposed to the sun. The romantic visitor wept for the fallen monarch.

Lake Erie has made rapid advance in its attack on the shore east of Cleveland. Five houses directly north of Painesville, Ohio, once had a greensward of at least 150 feet rolling down to the lake. Now the lawns have disappeared, and in some places the houses themselves have been undermined. They are falling slowly into the lake. A fine old house on Catawba Island was built solidly on a rock overlooking the lake. But in geologic time a house on a rock on the Lake Erie shore is but little safer than one built upon the sand. This one is now undermined. Erie has assaulted the limestone cliff, has worn it away, and has now carved out a deep grotto beneath the house. The owner has shored up the overhanging cliff with pillars underneath the stone, but someday his house will fall into Lake Erie.

Eagle Island in Sandusky Bay, as an early record shows, was once listed on the tax duplicate as having an area of 149 acres. In 1944 there was about half an acre left; the rest of it has been worn away by action of the waves and deposited on the floor of the bay or carried out into the lake. One section of the south shore of Sandusky Bay is being cut back by waves as much as twenty feet per year. Not long ago a portion of the road along the bay was washed out, leaving a strip of water between the roadside fence and the remaining strip of pavement, with shrubbery awash in the water. The average annual loss here is twelve feet a year. On the south shore of Maumee Bay in the last ninety-six years the annual loss has been almost twelve feet; forty feet went into the water in the year 1930.[4] We shall see later on what all this action is doing to the fishing industry and the ship channels. For the present we have said enough to show how restless Lake Erie is and how impermanent are her shape and form. One might speculate on the fact that Lake Erie, like all the other lakes, but faster, is gradually filling up her bowl and converting herself

---

[4] George W. White, "Lake Erie Shore Erosion in Ohio," *Shore and Beach* (April 1944).

to a river; and that the time will come in the not too distant future when there will be no wharves at the lake-port cities, and when some future generation of farmers may till the soil which their fore-fathers permitted to wash out onto the bottom of the lake.

But we do not speculate long. Geologic drama is slow-paced. In the meantime an exciting human drama is in performance at a fast tempo on the lake and around its shifting shore, and we shall begin with its prologue.

Chapter 3

Discovery and First Sails

WHITE men had seen the other four Great Lakes before they looked upon Lake Erie. To Frenchmen went the honor—and the unimaginable hardships—of discovering all the Great Lakes. Jacques Cartier got only as far as Montreal in his famous pioneering voyage of 1534. From the heights of Mount Royal he looked off to the mysterious West beyond the glimmering rapids at Lachine, listened to the tales of the Indians who had been in those regions, and then returned to France. Seventy-four years went by before the empire-building Samuel de Champlain sailed up the St. Lawrence to Quebec in 1608. But it was not until the summer of 1615 that he was free to make his long-projected trip up to the lakes.[1] In July he toiled up the Ottawa River, through rapids and tangled forests and droves of mosquitoes, around waterfalls and obstructions to Lake Nipissing. Then he descended the French River, paddled down Georgian Bay and crossed over to Lake Simcoe. From there he went on with a party of Indians to Lake Ontario. He paddled over the eastern end of the lake to make war on the Iroquois (in which he was wounded and defeated). After reluctantly wintering around Simcoe, he returned the way he had come. It was a long way round. The great explorer never saw Niagara Falls or viewed the expanse of Lake Erie.

That extremely tortuous and difficult northern route by way of Ottawa, Lake Nipissing and the French River became the regular road for the Récollet friars and Jesuit missionaries on their journeys of ceremony and discovery to and fro through the wilderness. It was used by the Indian canoe trains that brought furs down to the French trading mart at Montreal. It was followed by the voyageurs who willingly went to live with the Indians in the stink and the fetid cabins of their cold villages. Nicolet followed it on his voyage to Green Bay in search of the Northwest Passage to Cathay in 1634, and he

---

[1] It is quite possible that Champlain's young scout Brulé saw Lake Erie that year and later, but the records are silent on this point.

died without knowing that Lake Erie existed. Father Allouez traveled that route when he went out to lonely Chequamegon Bay in 1665; Father Marquette toiled over it a few years later when he followed Allouez into the Lake Superior and Green Bay region. None of these famous men ever went down to Lake Erie.

Why not?

There were many reasons. Undoubtedly the most potent was that the formidable, highly organized and (for Indian warriors) well-disciplined Iroquois lived along the south shore of Lake Ontario and controlled the two Lower Lakes and the portages between them. Partly through ignorance, Champlain had made mortal enemies of them. They retaliated by raids on the St. Lawrence and up into Ontario, and at times threatened even the northern communication line. Neither Champlain nor any of that generation attempted to use the upper St. Lawrence River or to cross the Niagara Peninsula to the western water lane of Lake Erie. So Lake Erie lay for a longer time untroubled by white men, a happy fishing ground for the Ohio Indians who dwelt on its low-lying shores.

It was only a question of time, however, before Lake Erie would have to be linked to the expanding French empire in the New World. The architecture of that empire was grandiose. It was possible nowhere else on the globe. It hinged on a simple schoolboy fact of geography, but that does not make it any the less interesting. The mouth of the St. Lawrence is far up in the icy North Atlantic; the valley is almost a straight line due southwest all the way to Detroit. The barrier between the Great Lakes and the Mississippi River is only a few feet high and a few miles long. Except for a few portages, therefore, the French found a natural waterway from Newfoundland to New Orleans. This waterway, bending in a vast crescent through the heart of North America, was the central avenue of communication for New France, and Lake Erie was the keystone of the arch.

Roughly paralleling this crescent waterway and protecting it like a Westwall fortress was the chain of mountains extending from the St. Lawrence above New Hampshire and Vermont, down across New York, western Pennsylvania, Virginia and North Carolina into Georgia. The Dutch were in New York, but their days were to be brief. The English were France's only rivals. But they were busy on the Atlantic Coast and its hinterland. They faced the ocean and the British Isles, and for generations willingly turned their backs upon the forbidding mountains so far to the west of their interests. Conflict between the two empires seemed remote in the early days of settlement and colonization. That wall, however, was not so solid as it looked, nor the interests of the empires so harmonious. Straight through it in northern New York cut the Mohawk Valley, and at the head of that valley was Lake Erie. The British Americans were also interested in fur, and the rivalries of France and Britain that led so often to war in Europe had an unhappy way of expanding into world wars with battles on their meeting ground along the Ohio River and the lakes. We shall stow these facts away for the time being while we focus again on the undiscovered lake.

Lake Erie continued unmolested until the late summer of 1669. The first known white man to see it was young Louis Jolliet. He was born under the Rock at Quebec, son of a wagonmaker of the Lower Town. Intendant Talon commissioned Jolliet to go up by way of the Ottawa to the Lake Superior country to hunt for the copper mine that kept cropping up in the talk of the Indians who came to trade at Quebec and Montreal. Jolliet did not find the copper mine, but he did find Lake Erie. His Iroquois guide, whom he had picked up at the Sault, persuaded him to return by a southern route. They paddled down the St. Clair River, over the placid Lake St. Clair, down the Detroit River and out on Lake Erie. They kept close in to the north shore and followed the pleasant lake past Pelee and Long Point to the Grand River. But Jolliet's guide was afraid of encountering hostile Indians along the Niagara portage. To avoid them he led Jolliet across the Niagara Peninsula to the north and brought him down over the escarpment to a friendly Indian village in the vicinity of present Hamilton at the head of Lake Ontario. Jolliet, trained cartographer and explorer that he was, made a fairly accurate sketch of the lake.

Jolliet beat his twenty-five-year-old contemporary from ancient Rouen, René Robert Cavelier, Sieur de la Salle, by a few days to the honor of discovering Lake Erie. La Salle had come to Canada in 1666, his head buzzing with plans for exploring the West, making his fortune and opening a passage to Japan. He compiled all the information he could get about the West from friendly Indians whom he entertained at his house by the Lachine Rapids. It turned out that he had come at a favorable moment so far as the Lake Erie region was concerned. For the Marquis de Tracy had led a large force of soldiers into the Iroquois territory, had routed their warriors, burned their villages and dictated his own terms to their chieftains. This break in the tight hold of the Iroquois on the upper St. Lawrence and the route to Lake Erie made it possible for La Salle to attempt to enter the unknown region. He joined with two Sulpician fathers, Dollier de Casson and Galinée, who wanted to carry their religion to the heathen in the wilderness.

After what seemed to him interminable delays, La Salle set out on July 6, 1669, with some friendly Seneca, who had been his guests, to guide him. They dragged their canoes up the St. Lawrence rapids, where, as Galinée wrote, they were "not a finger's breadth but only the thickness of a few sheets of paper from death." On August 2 they reached Lake Ontario, which stretched westward "like a great sea with no land beyond it." They kept to the south shore of the lake and underwent the usual dangers, adventures and delays of journeys among the Indians. Finally, on September 4, they reached the end of Lake Ontario, a few miles north of present Hamilton. They said they heard the roar of the Falls as they passed the mouth of the Niagara River. They entered an Indian village where, after much feasting and Indian time-killing, the Indians encouraged La Salle to believe that less than two moons of traveling would bring him to the Beautiful River. He was also informed that another French traveler was in the next village. By a curious coincidence, that traveler was Louis Jolliet, whom La Salle had watched depart on his copper-hunting expedition many weeks before his own party could get ready to embark.

La Salle did not rejoice in the meeting with Jolliet. It was the confrontation of rivals rather than friends. Jolliet poured out an excited account of his discoveries into the eager ears of the Sulpicians. He copied his map for them and showed them the way to Lake Erie. He described this wonderful body of water and how it was connected with Lake Huron by the Detroit and St. Clair Rivers. He urged the willing priests to give up the idea of searching for the Beautiful River. He persuaded them to go instead among the Indians to the northwest whose language they knew and whose souls needed saving more than the Ohio needed discovery. And he told them where he had hidden his canoe at the head of the portage. The Sulpicians decided to seek the canoe and the lost souls.

La Salle listened in reserved silence while his party was split. He had been ill on the two months' journey—Galinée said it was because he had seen three rattlesnakes crawling over a rock in his path, but that is, of course, a gross slander or a bit of priestly humor. He did not disclose his own plans, but he did separate from Dollier and Galinée. These two priests followed Jolliet's directions. They went on to Lake Erie on the first of October. Their first glimpse of the lake was uninviting. Erie was not in one of her friendly moods. She frowned menacingly at the robed men of God, "tossing like an angry ocean." The priests did not go far. They paddled to Black Creek near Long Point, where Port Dover now stands, and built themselves a log hut. They were charmed by this spot, which Galinée called the "earthly paradise of Canada," and by the abundance of fruit and nuts which they found there that autumn. They spent the next five months and eleven days here. When spring arrived, they set up the usual cross, marked with the arms of France to signify that they had taken possession in the name of His Most Christian Majesty, King Louis XIV. A cairn now marks the site of their cabin, and a white marble cross has been erected where the wooden cross stood.

The two priests then ventured westward along the north shore to Point Pelee. There a misfortune befell them. They beached their canoes and piled their baggage and altar-service near by on the sands. During the night Erie stirred up one of her sudden storms, the seas ran high in the shallow basin, and the waves seized their belongings and destroyed them. The disconsolate priests paddled on to Detroit without provender and without their precious altar-service. On the riverbank they saw a large stone, daubed with paint, crudely shaped like a human figure. They were in no mood to endure such a heathenish object after what they had suffered. In a high and righteous rage Galinée devoted one of his precious axes to the demolition of this false deity. He attacked it and smashed it to pieces. Then he lashed the canoes side by side, carried the largest fragment out into the middle of the river and cast it under the waters where it would never be heard of again. Galinée says that in reward for this action, the true God sent them a deer and a bear which they slew and feasted upon that day. Rejoicing, they went on their way up to the Sault at Ste. Marie.[2]

This first east-to-west journey of white men on Lake Erie is a matter of record. But what of La Salle who was left standing near Hamilton, sick and with countenance wrapped in mysterious silence? Darkness and obscurity settle over the great explorer for the next few years. But some time later there appeared in Paris an anonymous memoir entitled *Histoire de Monsieur de la Salle*. It purported to be based on conversations which the author had had in Paris with La Salle. It says that La Salle, after separating from the Sulpicians, persuaded a few brave men in the party to continue the expedition with him. Instead of going on to Lake Erie, as he certainly would have done had he not met Jolliet, La Salle went round by way of Lake Onondaga in the company of a Seneca guide, and, keeping well to the south of Lake Erie, he descended the Ohio as far as the falls at Louisville. And the following year, 1670, the account says that La Salle made his way back to Lake Erie, embarked upon it, and himself passed up the Detroit River. It is more than probable that he did exactly that. For he certainly returned to France with irresistible plans for another journey to the West to enlarge the boundary of King Louis' domain. And he returned to New France with rope, sails, anchors, tools and skilled men to build a sailing ship on Lake Erie. He carried out every detail of his plans with the air of one who knew exactly where he was going and why.

Thus it came about that La Salle was back in January 1679, ready to build a ship for his impressive scheme for exploring the lakes and the Mississippi, for speeding up commerce on the lakes, and for reaching the Western Sea that would lead to Cathay. With infinite toil he overcame a series of heartbreaking obstacles, and got a party of thirty men across Lake Ontario, around the Falls and into a harbor on Cayuga Creek which empties into the Niagara River about four miles above the Falls. He selected a spot for his shipyard, and his men set to work to clear it and prepare the ways.

Over these artisans and workmen La Salle placed his two lieu-

---

[2] The journal of René de Bréhant de Galinée was translated and edited by James H. Coyne, Ontario Historical Society *Papers and Records*, Vol. IV.

By courtesy of T. H. Langlois

SUMMER AND WINTER ON THE ERIE SHORE

THE "IRVING S. OLDS" SHEATHED IN ICE

tenants. One was a French gentleman, La Motte de Lussière, whom he had recently met in France and invited to join his expedition. The other was Henri de Tonty, a one-handed, able man fanatically loyal to La Salle. The master carpenter was Moïse Hillaret; the contrary, disobedient pilot, who was always doing the wrong thing, was Luke; the blacksmith's name is lost in illegibility. Father Louis Hennepin was priest, and the crew was a motley of Flemings, Italians and Normans. They toiled in the bitter cold of winter, cutting trees, bending timbers, shaping the hull, and keeping close watch on unfriendly Indians. By the time spring came, energetic Tonty had the *Griffin* ready for launching. Father Louis said the blessing, the crew sang the *Te Deum,* and the new hull was rolled and slid into the Niagara River where she lay safe at anchor until her fittings were complete. Then Tonty tried to take her up to Lake Erie. He met with the same difficulty that many another ship's master was later to experience. The current in the upper Niagara was too swift and the east winds were too light and infrequent to sail a ship through. Father Louis, excitable and garrulous as usual, hastened down to Fort Frontenac to give the news to La Salle, but to assure him that the ship was safe. La Salle then hurried across Lake Ontario and up the Niagara to take personal command of his ship. He found her riding at anchor near Black Rock, only a couple of miles from "pleasant Lake Erie." He stowed her with gear, provisions and articles of trade for the Western Indians. He put a dozen men ashore with towropes. He made sail, a fortunate northeast wind blew up the river, and the combined sail and tow brought the *Griffin* up the swift current into the lake. They again sang the *Te Deum* in thankfulness. They were at last ready for the voyage.

On the morning of August 7, 1679, La Salle made sail and stood the *Griffin* out upon Lake Erie. At the age of thirty-five, having been in Canada for thirteen years, he had brought this far toward success the great enterprise upon which his ambition had so long been fixed. Had he or had he not already seen Lake Erie from the stern seat of a Shawnee canoe? There is no certainty, as we have said, but on that August day as he paced the quarter-deck of his own ship and whiffed the odor of fresh timber, pitch calking and hemp rope, he gave commands with the confidence of a master who knew at firsthand the geography of this lake.

The brave sight of that first ship on Lake Erie comes vividly to the imagination. Her two tall masts are crowded with square white sails, and she has a good east-northeast wind behind her. Her railed quarter-deck stands high and gives the master full view of her sixty-foot length. La Salle, in impressive seventeenth-century costume, paces his quarter-deck while his wheelsman steers west-southwest toward Long Point, and the leadsmen take soundings. The five new guns are shiny in the morning sunlight. She is of forty-five tons burden, and she rides smoothly in the blue water on her rounded hull that is modeled over the familiar lines of a Dutch merchant vessel. Above her beakhead is a reproduction of the half-eagle-half-lion, known to fable as a griffin, emblazoned on the arms of Count Frontenac. Above the quarter-deck is a gilded spread eagle. The master shifts his eyes from the Erie horizon to the details of his ship, and he hears the arguments of La Motte and Hennepin and the voiced fears of his crew below. For these men had listened to the endless rumor and Indian tall tales about danger lurking for them just over that deceptively gentle horizon.

La Salle had no fears as he sailed westward. Even if he had no personal knowledge of Lake Erie, he could rely on the information which Jolliet had given to him and Galinée, or upon the map which Jolliet had drawn for Frontenac in 1674. This map showed Lake Erie much larger than it proved to be, but the north shore from the Niagara to the Detroit is not badly drawn or too much out of scale. Long Point and Pelee are exaggerated, as might be expected from a canoeman geographer.

La Salle's account of the sailing is particularly interesting to the lake mariner, and it carries a curious insight into the complex character of the great explorer.[3] He speaks with assurance of two reefs in the lake and of the close call the *Griffin* had with one of them, on which "we should have wrecked had I taken every one's advice. It was night, and a thick fog hid the shore from which we were distant about ten leagues. I heard breakers about a league before us. Everybody believed it was a certain noise common on these lakes when the wind changes, which happens always on the side from which it is about to come, and the pilot wished to crowd the sails to gain anchorage before we were caught head-on. But as I knew these reefs

---

[3] See Frances Gaither, *The Fatal River* (New York, 1931), pp. 106ff.

went very far out [How did he know?] and as I believed myself very near that one which was indeed in front of us, in spite of everybody, I veered at once and steered northeast instead of west northwest." They eased along in this fog for an hour and a half with the ominous sound of water over reef still in their ears. The advisers aboard (for we gather from this account that everybody was talking and speculating and offering advice) still thought the noise was wind and not reef, but La Salle was certain that they were surrounded by the barrier on the north. "Indeed," the account continues, "one-half hour later, we found all at once only three fathoms of water. [Not uncommon on Lake Erie, by the way.] Every man sprang to the ropes and I tacked about and bore to the southwest, always sounding without finding bottom. [This is the deepest part of Lake Erie.] Finally when the fog lifted they all saw I had been right and they owed me the obligation of having saved them from this danger." An odd remark to come from the owner and master of a ship.

Thus did the first ship on Lake Erie sail westward around the dangers of Long Point. The *Griffin* crossed the 240 miles of Lake Erie in three days. She put into the mouth of the Detroit at the head of the lake on the morning of the fourth day. Tonty had gone ahead as La Salle's emissary to prepare the way against his coming. He had pitched camp near Grosse Isle to await the *Griffin*. It was a morning of rejoicing when, with dawn breaking, he lifted the sails of the ship. He set three fires to serve as buoys to guide La Salle in, and paddled alongside to welcome the ship. The first voyage over the route that was to become one of the most traveled in all the world was successfully completed.

The *Griffin* sailed north up the Detroit River. La Salle and his men were entranced with the prospect, as Cadillac and others who came after them were also to be. The ebullient Father Hennepin was recording the sentiment of all aboard the ship when he wrote:

This streight is finer than that of Niagara, being 30 leagues long, and everywhere one league broad, except in the middle which is wider, forming the Lake we have named St. Claire. The navigation is easy on both sides, the coast being low and even. It runs directly from North to South. The country between these two lakes is very well situated and the soil very fertile. The banks of the Streight are vast meadows, and the Prospect is terminated with some hills covered with vineyards, trees bearing good fruit, groves and forests so well disposed that one would think Nature alone could not have made, without the help of Art so charming a prospect. The country is stocked with stags, wild goats, and bears which are good for food, and not fierce as in other countries."

And he added a characteristic touch of self-praise and admonition to posterity: "Those who shall be so happy as to inhabit that noble Country cannot but remember with gratitude those who have discovered the way, by venturing to sail upon an unknown Lake for above 100 leagues."

La Salle's men hunted along these idyllic shores, and filled the ship's galley with game. Wild turkeys slipped back into the forest of oak, chestnut and walnut, and flocks of swans gathered nervously about the ship with the white sails. The *Griffin* moved cautiously across Lake St. Clair while the leadsmen took soundings. She hit adverse winds in the St. Clair River, and the men had to go ashore and drag her upstream with ropes. Battered by a Lake Huron storm, she sailed on to St. Ignace on the Straits of Mackinac, and then westward to Green Bay. There La Salle put aboard a cargo of fur, and dispatched her back to the trade mart of Montreal to satisfy his creditors. The *Griffin* vanished on her homeward-bound voyage somewhere on the Upper Lakes, leaving no clue whatever to the mystery of her fate. But the *Griffin* had done her part for Lake Erie. The lake was now known with certainty to navigators, and it had become a central sea lane in King Louis' new empire.

Chapter 4

Gateway Forts

A FTER La Salle bade Godspeed to his ill-omened ship laden with fortune at Green Bay, he pressed on over the Great Lakes watershed into the Illinois River and at last floated on the Mississippi itself. On April 9, 1682, he reached the far-off Gulf of Mexico; and, following the ceremonial pageantry of his day, he planted there the arms of his King and claimed the heart of the continent for the empire of France.

One glance at the map of this territory, holding the British colonies of the seaboard in the arc of its sickle, showed that Lake Erie was the key to the bastion doors between the two halves of this empire. On that point the farseeing and long-suffering La Salle was eternally right, and the loss of the *Griffin* with all hands and without trace did not alter the fundamental geographic fact. The great master doors with their bottleneck passageways were at both ends of the lake—one at Niagara and one at Detroit. Forts at those two points would command the entrance and the exit. And since the low watershed of the Lake Erie bowl lay so near to the lake shore on the south, it was easy for the French to slip their canoes out of Lake Erie at Presque Isle, Sandusky, or up the Maumee, and portage over to the upper streams of the Ohio which took them by short cut into the Ohio and the Mississippi and down to Louisiana.

The British colonists on the seaboard began to take notice of this encirclement. After all, now, their title extended from the Atlantic Coast all the way back across the continent to the next ocean. It did not halt at the mountains or the Mississippi. The French, in the English view, were encroaching on their American rivers and lakes and inciting the Indians to hatred and hostility against them. On their side the French looked upon the British as interlopers whose grandiose claims were ridiculous and spurious, and they tried to wall them out of the Mississippi, the Great Lakes and the St. Lawrence Valley. Decisive conflict was inevitable and only a matter of time.

The live issue, of course, was not this vast wilderness for its own territorial sake, but for the lucrative fur trade which it supported. The French and English merchants were interested solely in the beaver pelts which they could buy from the Great Lakes Indians for a trinket or a few gills of alcohol and sell at a big profit to the furriers in Paris and London. The French had centered their western trading post at the Straits of Mackinac on the direct canoe-and-portage route across Lake Huron and Georgian Bay, up the French River, over Lake Nipissing and down the Ottawa River to Montreal. They did not use the Lake Erie-Lake Ontario-St. Lawrence route to the south. It was left wide open to their rivals, the British. They pushed westward to Lake Erie from their post at Albany and tapped this rich area. The Indians of Ohio and Michigan found it easier to trade with the British down on Lake Erie than to make the hard journey from the beaver streams around Detroit to the French post at St. Ignace. Moreover, the British brought with them kegs of good rum which the Indians found more interesting if less enduring than the knives, beads and blankets in the packs of the French.

The shadows of decisive conflict were thus lengthening over Lake Erie. The French trade at the Straits of Mackinac fell off, and the alarmed merchants on the St. Lawrence complained vigorously to the Paris government. The encroaching British must be expelled from this French territory.

So the French now hastened to build their forts and trading posts down on Lake Erie. The man who provided the vision, the plans and the energy was the temperamental Gascon gentleman, Antoine de la Mothe Cadillac. He had come over from France as one of Count Frontenac's young officers. Frontenac had placed him in command at Mackinac in 1694. His quick, empire-sweeping mind had rather quickly grasped the situation of the French on the Great Lakes. His patience was short with the Jesuits at his post who objected to his civil and military authority and to his policy of trading brandy to the Indians. He approved of brandy not only as a good article of trade with the Indians, but also on therapeutic grounds; "a little brandy after the meal," he contended, "seems necessary to cook the bilious meats and the crudities they leave in the stomach." And when Father Carheil, the Jesuit Superior, opposed him on this issue, Cadillac replied "that his talk smelt of sedition a hundred yards off, and begged that he would amend it. He told me that I gave myself airs that did not belong to me, holding his fist before my nose at the same time. I confess I almost forgot that he was a priest, and felt for a moment like knocking his jaw out of joint; but, thank God, I contented myself with taking him by the arm, pushing him out, and ordering him not to come back."

Cadillac saw that Mackinac might be a good field for the priests who labored with such devotion and zeal to save the doubtful souls of the Indians, and that it was strategically placed at the northern gateway to the Upper Lakes and the Nipissing-Ottawa route; but it was too far from the increasingly vital Lake Erie and the enterprising British traders. So he turned his eyes toward the Detroit River. It was quite obvious to him that the portentous future lay to the south and not to the north, and that Detroit, not Mackinac, lay squarely athwart the central communication system. A strong French post on the Detroit River would be a bulwark against the British traders, it would be a center of influence among the Indians of the Northwest, and it would be a key bastion in the chain of forts from Quebec to the lower Mississippi. With characteristic energy he set his plans afoot.

The Jesuits were opposed to the project because they feared it would have a demoralizing effect upon the Indians; Cadillac overrode them. The merchants at Montreal were doubtful of Cadillac himself and suspicious of his designs; he scornfully dismissed them as little and inconsequential men who, only a short time ago, were blacking their masters' boots. He went straight to Paris, over all the provincial heads, and won his case before Minister Pontchartrain. Clothed with proper authority, he returned to Canada to erect a fort and plant a colony at Detroit. He assembled a caravan of twenty-five large canoes at Montreal in the summer of 1701, and set forth on the long northern journey on June 5. In his party were fifty French soldiers in blue uniforms, two Récollet fathers in gray habits with pointed hoods, fifty Canadian woodsmen to cut timber and plant gardens for the colony, and a few Indians to act as guides and interpreters. They toiled up the tough paddle-and-portage Ottawa during the hot mosquito season, across Lake Nipissing and down the French River into Georgian Bay, and followed the Lake Huron shore into the mouth of the St. Clair River. So remote was

Detroit in 1701 by this route that it took this caravan of vigorous men forty-nine days to make the trip.

With Cadillac at the head of the procession they paddled the flotilla across Lake St. Clair, rounded Windmill Point and entered the Detroit River at Peach Island. They had arrived at a good time. It was July 24, and the weather over southern Michigan and Ontario was idyllic, the growing season luxurious after abundant rains. Cadillac studied the terrain as they floated down the beautiful, gently curving river past Belle Isle, past the River Rouge, past the marshy length of narrow Fighting Island to Grosse Isle where they camped for the night. Tough, realistic, hard-driving Cadillac was reduced to near sentimentality when he tried to describe the beauties of this favored river and the shore line past which it flows. The great city that now spreads along the mile-wide river and extends far back into the countryside does not entirely obscure the prospect.

Along the green shore where the rich now have their great houses among the trees and their fine boat slips in their front lawns, and where the vast acreage of the Ford, Chrysler, U. S. Rubber and Cadillac industrial plants roll out the machines of our rubber-tired culture, Cadillac saw fruit trees bending with fruit, heavy clusters of grapes and ten species of forest trees of prodigious size. Where Detroit's tall Fisher Building, the Penobscot Observation Tower and the Book-Cadillac Hotel now rise high into the smoke haze of the city's sky, he saw deer and fawns wandering romantically among the trees, and squirrels collecting apples and plums on the ground. And where the ships go by at the rate of one every ten or fifteen minutes, where the buoys rock gently in the two-miles-an-hour current, and the millions of lights glitter on the water, he saw quantities of golden pheasants, quail, doves and woodcocks; and the geese and swans on the river were so thick that "they draw up in lines to let the boats pass through."

This sweet prospect, so remote on that July day from the carnage that would eventually stain its soil, inspired Cadillac and his men with confidence in their project. Having surveyed the river, their problem was to select a site for their fort somewhere along its twenty-eight miles of wooded shore line. Wisely they chose the spot below Belle Isle on the north bank where the river was narrow and unobstructed, and where it circled in a great arc from east to west to almost due south. A creek meandered through the woods, almost paralleling the river along Congress Street, and curved round a low bluff near the foot of First Street in present-day Detroit. The river and this creek formed a natural moat around three sides of the bluff, and the bluff itself, facing the river toward Windsor, would easily command the vital passage between the lakes. Crowded Jefferson Avenue with its heavy truck traffic now crosses the spot and the Detroit-Windsor Tunnel debouches near by.

Cadillac beached his canoes, made camp and ordered his men to proceed with their operations. They cleared the top of the bluff, and trimmed and hewed logs for cabins, a church and a stockade. They enclosed about an acre of ground with a heavy protective palisade about a dozen feet high, built of logs driven into the ground, and entered by three gates. Cadillac named the fort for his patron, Minister Pontchartrain. At each of the four corners they erected stout bastions from which the soldiers with their brass cannon could command the approaches to the fort. A narrow street bisected the enclosure, and fronting on it were the twenty-nine log huts of the soldiers and settlers, equipped with rude furniture fashioned from the woods. Like all good Frenchmen of that age, they next built a chapel and dedicated it to Ste. Anne. From that day to this the bells of Ste. Anne have sounded over the harbor and city of Detroit. Cadillac next had constructed a storeroom for their provisions and a magazine for their precious powder, and the fort guarding the west end of Lake Erie was completed.

With characteristic French industry the colony cleared away the forest in the immediate vicinity and planted wheat for the next season's harvest. The Indians of the region were disturbed by the news of all these French activities. They gathered at the river to see what was going on. Cadillac assured them that he had come in peace, that he was their friend and protector, that he wished to trade with them and that he hoped they would move their wigwams to Detroit. His overtures were well received by the Indians, and Cadillac was extremely gratified when they decided to trade at his new post instead of taking their furs up to Mackinac. Part of his pleasure was his triumph over his Jesuit enemy, Father Carheil. He wrote exultantly that only twenty-five Huron went up the straits in 1703, and added, "I hope that in the autumn I shall pluck this last feather from his wing; and I am convinced that this obstinate priest will die in his parish without one parishioner to bury him."

Cadillac clearly intended this colony, so auspiciously begun, to grow into a key center of New France. In the autumn his wife and six-year-old son, and the wife of Alphonse de Tonty, captain of the garrison, came up to Detroit over the very route—Niagara and Lake Erie—which the fort was designed in part to safeguard. It was a great moment in the history of the settlement to see these distinguished women in the fastnes of the wilderness interior. No white woman had ever ventured so far, and their coming was an act of courage and confidence. The masculine colony, which had seen only Indian squaws, met the Frenchwomen at the river, fired salutes in their honor and escorted them with fitting ceremony up the bluff to the fort.

Though others were slow in coming, the post gradually expanded, chiefly as a trading center. Cadillac imported three horses and ten oxen to cultivate the soil around the stockade. He freely traded brandy to the Indians for beaver, and lured them into the vicinity of the fort. Some 6,000 of them pitched their tents near by. The Huron established a small village under the shadow of the fort. The Ottawa congregated on the south bank across the river from Detroit. The Miami to the southwest, on the Maumee-Wabash watershed, came up to the fort for barter. The Sauk up around Saginaw Bay and the Iroquois at the east end of Lake Erie were— and remained—hostile to the white encroachments. These tribes formed the nucleus for the intertribal warfare and for resistance to the French, the British and the Americans, as each in turn seemed to present the most serious threats to their interests. The British took immediate advantage of the Iroquois hostility to acquire from them by treaty the entire Great Lakes territory as far north as Lake Superior in return for their protection of the Five Nations against the French. This conveyance, made at Albany in 1701, became the legal ground for the claims which Britain later made on France in the Great Lakes, and particularly in the Lake Erie region.

Overt conflict was still in the future, however, and while the dragon's seeds were sprouting at their leisure, the colony at Detroit went on its tortuous way. Since profits were the sole concern of the company which controlled the Detroit colony, the frictions inevitable in a new colonial venture were intensified. This kind of trading post, with a garrison of soldiers, was expensive. Those who bore the cost complained about the income; they wanted more profits. Those who were not in the company protested their exclusion, though they wanted to share the income without becoming responsible for the expense. Cadillac was not one to placate the disaffected. He maneuvered successfully against the company and forced them to sell out their interests to him in 1706. But the hostility which he had created in the company and among the missionaries moved his powerful enemies to overthrow him. He was removed from Detroit in 1710, and sent to the south end of the crescent empire as governor of Louisiana. But his post at Detroit was firmly enough planted on a strategic spot to survive the intrigues and vicissitudes of its first decade under his management, and the next score of years of poor government, discord and uncertain direction; of Indian attack and British scheming.

The other and more important gateway to Lake Erie was the Niagara River on the east. The mountain wall separating British America from New France was breached by the Mohawk Valley and the lowlands westward to Niagara and Lake Erie. The portage around the Falls made Niagara a tight bottleneck between Lake Ontario and Lake Erie on the waterway from Quebec to Louisiana. The French had already tried to secure the foot of Lake Ontario and the entrance to the St. Lawrence River by erecting Fort Frontenac. Now if they also had a strong fort at Niagara, they could seal off Lake Ontario, they could guard the approaches to Lake Erie, and they could confront the English and their Iroquois allies on the Mohawk. La Salle had seen this necessity. One of the first things he did when he started west to build the *Griffin* was to order La Motte to build a stronghold a few miles up the Niagara River from Lake Ontario. It had been maintained, after a fashion, since La Salle's expedition in 1679. It served its purpose, but it was no longer a bulwark against the rising dangers of the early eighteenth century. In 1720, therefore, the French proceeded in earnest to fortify this Niagara gateway. For it was obvious that the long-impending conflict with the British would eventually be drawn in this danger zone of contact on the edge of the Iroquois country.

The French used all their diplomatic wiles to gain consent of the Indians and to erect their fort without arousing their suspicions or resentment. They suggested innocently that they would like permission to put up a bark house near present Lewiston to store their furs and their supplies. Under proper oral safeguards the Indians gave their consent. The French did not feel bound to explain that the flimsy house was to be converted into a fortress of stone, but when they began to build a stone wall, they had ready a guileless excuse: furs and food and powder kept better in a stone house than in one of bark. It was built under the supervision of Chevalier Chaussegros de Léry, an expert engineer imported for the purpose. On his advice the site was shifted to the mouth of the Niagara. Its structure was so solid that it is still standing and is annually visited by thousands of people from the United States and Canada as a monument to the continued peace on these waters which has made further fortification unnecessary.

The forts at Detroit and Niagara anchored the line of defense and closed off the gateways, but they did not protect Lake Erie from a flank attack, as the French soon learned. For British traders were slipping into the forbidden territory through the mountain passes of western Pennsylvania and Virginia, and they were having great success in spreading disaffection among the Indians. The French had done little to placate the Indian tribes since Cadillac's first conference with them at Detroit. They maintained a post with no military significance near present Fort Wayne in the heart of the Miami tribal lands. They also had a trading post at Sandusky. These stations were supposed to facilitate trade, to discourage English adventurers and to protect the canoe passages out of Lake Erie over the Wabash and the Miami River routes into the Ohio and Mississippi.

The Indians at the western end of Lake Erie felt that the monopolistic French were defrauding them by driving sharp bargains in the fur trade. They worked themselves up to hot resentment against the French. The antagonism, always keen among the Miami, spread to the Huron, Wyandot and other tribes. They were quite ready to renounce or attack the French, and their unrest offered the British an opportune opening. The British invited their chiefs to conference in Philadelphia to consider trade agreements and an alliance against the French in Ohio and along Lake Erie. One of their most capable agents, the wily Irishman George Croghan, came out from

Pennsylvania to Ohio in the 1740's to forward the negotiations. He was skilled in the Indian languages and customs, and he knew how to get the most in return for his presents of cloth, trinkets and kegs of rum. He succeeded in undermining French prestige and in diverting the fur trade to the British. He convinced the Indians of the advantages of British protection and British markets. He soon had a post at the mouth of the Cuyahoga, and camped among the Huron at Sandusky, right under the nose of the French at Detroit. When three Huron, smarting under the conviction that they had been cheated, killed five Frenchmen near the fort at Detroit, they sent their stock of furs with a French scalp to the post at Sandusky, and asked for a trade agreement with the English. Croghan was there. He transmitted the request from "these Ingans That has thire Dwelling on the borders of Lake Arey."

That was in 1747. The following season another Pennsylvania agent was sent over to continue the negotiations. He was Conrad Weiser, likewise schooled in the Indian tongues and an able diplomat. He met the hospitable chiefs near present Pittsburgh. He doled out rum and rolls of tobacco and in a spirit of complete accord he counseled them against the French. The temper of the meeting is revealed in the grimly humorous speech which Weiser made to the Indians on September 17, 1748, as he himself recorded it in his priceless journal of the proceedings: "Brethren: Some of You have been in Philadelphia last Fall & acquainted us that You had taken up the English Hatchet, and that You had already made use of it against the French, & that the French had very hard heads, & your Country afforded nothing but Sticks & Hickorys which was not sufficient to break them. You desir'd your Brethren wou'd assist You with some Weapons sufficient to do it." To assist in this undertaking was precisely what the British desired to do, and the conference was a great success.

These incidents alarmed the French. Their fort at Niagara was no protection against assault from the Ohio Valley. They would have to extend their bastions along this gap in the mountain wall. They erected, therefore, a chain of forts from Erie across northwestern Pennsylvania to Pittsburgh. And in 1749 they sent Céleron de Blainville to circle the Lake Erie and Ohio Valley territory and warn the British traders to stay out. With an impressive retinue of 250 men and a flotilla of canoes, Céleron left Lachine on June 15. The company went up the St. Lawrence River, paddled around Lake Ontario to the Niagara, paddled and portaged into Lake Erie and followed the Erie shore to Chautauqua Creek. They crossed Lake Chautauqua, continued down Conewango Creek, and reached the Allegheny near present Warren. Paddling down the beautiful Ohio, they stopped at intervals to erect a cross and nail to a tree a sheet of tin decorated with the arms of France, to remind all intruders that this favored land belonged to His Most Christian Majesty, Louis XV. And they buried lead plates, about the size of a piece of typewriter paper, bearing an elaborate inscription to the effect that the French were renewing their possession of all this territory on both sides of the Ohio River as far as the sources of the streams which empty into it.

Céleron went down the Ohio to the mouth of the Great Miami River, then turned north up that river to Pickawillany, crossed to the Maumee and paddled back eastward along the Lake Erie shore to Niagara, having circled, as it were, the moat around the disputed region. He reached Lachine on October 10, just 118 days after his departure. He might have saved himself the trouble of this 3,000-mile journey. His signboards had no deterring effect whatever on the British. He was hardly out of sight before Christopher Gist, surveyor for the Ohio Land Company and "better stamp trader" from Baltimore, set out to make a sweep around the same country. He paid no attention to Céleron's tin signs and he planted no lead plates, but he was uniformly successful in winning Indian friendship. When he reached Pickawillany, an Indian village under Chief La Demoiselle, he found a delegation of French traders there trying to win favor. Gist persuaded the chief to accept the English. La Demoiselle spurned the French with the words, "We have been taken by the hand of our brothers, the English." He was given the name "Old Britain" for this act of loyalty, but he paid for it with his life a little later on when he was captured, killed, boiled in a pot and eaten by tribesmen who remained under the protection of the French.

These skirmishes and intrigues involving dozens of sordid frontier episodes were Lake Erie's part in the conflict between England and France known as King George's War (for George II). They settled nothing, but they did point up the growing danger. The serious crisis came in the next phase of the century-long wars for empire, the Seven Years' War (1756-1763). When it came, all this fort-building and sign-posting brought small profit to the French. They would have been in much better position, perhaps, if they had taken Governor Gallissonière's advice and sent over from France 10,000 peasants to settle in the Ohio Valley.

They did succeed, however, in holding the British out of the Lake Erie country. They forced the Huron back into peace, or at least restrained hostility, and they retook the fort at Sandusky from the British agents and their allies. John Mitchell's map of the lake in 1755 bears under the name of "Sandoski" the arresting notation, "Usurped by the French 1751." The usurper was Céleron himself, who stopped there on his way across the lake to take command of Detroit shortly after his tour of the region. It was not much of a fort. Joseph Gaspard Chaussegros de Léry, son of the builder of Fort Niagara, on his expedition to Detroit, beached his twenty-seven canoes at "lac Ostankoské" on Sunday, August 4, 1754. In his journal he records that "I imagined that some vestiges still remained of the fort the French built in 1751 and which was afterwards evacuated. To find it I followed the shore on the north side of the said lake which runs east and west. After proceeding about 3 leagues, I found a clearing where I landed at noon and discovered the ruins of the old fort." The site was near present Port Clinton. In that same year the French erected Fort Junundat on the east shore of Sandusky Bay as a further bulwark against the British traders. They also sent their forces to intercept General Braddock's threatening march toward this region through the mountain passes.

But these efforts, as it turned out, were all peripheral. The center of the danger was along the St. Lawrence, around Lake Ontario and at Niagara. For the entire chain of western forts was dependent upon that vital communication line. If it held, the posts in the West could stand firm; if it were strangled, they must wither and die. The British proceeded to cut it to pieces. Colonel Bradstreet slipped up to Fort Frontenac one August night in 1758, encircled it and took it with astonishing ease. The following spring General Prideaux and Sir William Johnson led a force of 2,300 men up Lake Ontario from Oswego and invested Fort Niagara. It did not fall so easily. The brave and gallant Captain Pouchot, in command of the fort, held out valiantly while he awaited reinforcements. The French hastily summoned all the officers and men they could muster throughout the Upper Lakes; they recruited Indian warriors; and they sent them down Lake Erie to relieve Pouchot. The British were waiting for them below the Niagara portage. Along the portage road, a couple of miles from the fort, the British engaged them, taking a heavy toll of French officers and routing the Indians in panic. They never reached Fort Niagara. Most of the French officers were either killed or captured, and their men fled back toward Lake Erie, hotly pursued by the British. The few who escaped crossed the lake and took refuge at Detroit. With this last hope gone, Pouchot surrendered the fort on July 25, 1759. Just forty-nine days later, Wolfe took Quebec. And the following year, almost on the anniversary of the fall of Quebec, Montreal capitulated.

With that keystone pulled out, the whole crescent empire crumbled to pieces. The remaining forts on Lake Erie and in the West were officially surrendered at Montreal. But the gateway at Detroit was remote by many weeks of hard traveling time from the action which changed its destiny. Not until the British boats rowed up the river to the fort in late November to take possession did the French at Detroit learn that their two centuries of dominance were ended. The messenger was the celebrated Robert Rogers, commander of the Rangers, then at the height of his fame.

Chapter 5

Three Flags over Detroit

THE surrender of Detroit was a melancholy pageant for the fallen French. It took Rogers, now Major Rogers, and his 200 Rangers seventy-six days to get there from Montreal. He departed on September 13, 1760, just five days after the fall of the city. He led his column of fifteen whaleboats up the obstructed St. Lawrence River, crossed along the north shore of Lake Ontario and reached the Niagara portage after seventeen days of hard traveling. He spread the news of the English victory among the tribesmen, and recorded in his journal that the Indians "seemed to be well pleased with the news we brought them of the surrender of Canada." At Buffalo Creek they pushed their flotilla into Lake Erie. The weather was bad with October storms and the lake was rough. They kept close in to the south shore. They paddled by day and encamped on the beach at night. At Presque Isle they bivouacked while Rogers made a quick detour by way of the line of French forts at Le Boeuf and Venango to Fort Pitt. Then they continued to the mouth of the Cuyahoga River where later Moses Cleaveland and his surveying party camped and selected the site for the great city that bears his name—with a slightly simplified spelling. George Croghan, who had traded here with the Indians, was in Rogers' party as Indian interpreter. He left an interesting, matter-of-fact record of this journey.

Ottawa Chief Pontiac, one of the few organizing minds in Indian annals, stopped the Rangers' captain at the Cuyahoga and blocked his advance. For twenty-four hours, so Rogers later reported, the issue hung in balance. Rogers says of this critical meeting, which he dressed up, no doubt, in his account written long afterward, that "Ponteack" demanded to know what business Rogers had in his country, and how he happened to enter it without leave. Rogers, with that tactful but decisive manner which he always used in Indian councils, replied that "it was not with any design against the Indians that I came, but to remove the French out of his country, who had

47

been an obstacle in our way to mutual peace and commerce, and acquainted him with my instructions for that purpose."

Pontiac went away for the night without an answer, but he did supply Rogers "with several bags of parched corn, and some other necessaries." A night of meditation persuaded Pontiac to accept Rogers in friendship and become a brother to the British. He smoked a pipe with him, and said "that I might pass thro' his country unmolested, and relieve the French garrison; and that he would protect me and my party from any insults that might be offered by the Indians; and, as an earnest of his friendship, he sent one hundred warriors to protect and assist us in driving one hundred fat cattle, which we had brought for the use of the detachment from Pittsburg, by way of Presque Isle. He likewise sent to the several Indian towns on the south-side and west-end of Lake Erie, to inform them that I had his consent to come into the country. He attended me constantly after this interview till I arrived at Detroit, and while I remained in the country, and was the means of preserving the detachment from the fury of the Indians, who had assembled at the mouth of the strait with an intent to cut us off." Thus attended, Rogers and his men went on around the south shore, hampered by stormy weather, and reached Detroit on November 29.[1]

As they rowed their whaleboats round the gently curving bend in the river above Fighting Island, they got their first glimpse of Detroit, with the French flag still fluttering in the light wind over the fort. A pleasant sight greeted Rogers' eyes. The colony had grown in the sixty years since Cadillac landed there. The stockade had been greatly enlarged. Five hundred souls were living there, besides the itinerant traders and many Indians. Their cabins overflowed the stockade and spread out around present Jefferson Avenue from the river to Cadillac Square. Women and children thronged the settlement, and there were 160 horses and many cattle. Cabins and farms also lined the Windsor side of the river. And the fur trade had become so lucrative that the British found a half-million dollars' worth of peltry in the stores when they took over.

These fruits of more than a half-century of French toil were

---

[1] Rogers left his own narrative of this expedition in his *Concise Account of North America*. It was published in London in 1765. He did not record the dramatic Pontiac episode in his Journal, and it is probably embroidered in the *Concise Account*.

now to pass under the control of the victorious British-Americans.

Rogers beached his boats, formed his Rangers and made camp on the cleared land a half-mile from the fort. Then, with a few officers and men and with his ensign flying, he marched in well-planned style suitable to the occasion toward the French fort. Commandant Belêtre made a final bid for time by asking to see a copy of the Canadian governor's surrender. He was naturally determined not to yield to Rogers, but when he read the terms of surrender as signed at Montreal, he capitulated. A large crowd of astonished Indians gathered round the stockade to witness the ceremony of a few quiet Englishmen in full dress who, without firing a shot or brandishing a sword or even butchering a single enemy, were receiving the surrender of an entire garrison of French warriors. It was stupefying. The garrison was formed and paraded before Rogers. They came to attention, and while the drums ruffled, the white flag with the lilies of France was slowly struck and the British ensign bearing the red cross of St. George was smartly hoisted to the peak. The British took complete control of Lake Erie.

Their experience on Lake Ontario had already taught them the vital importance of ships in the control of the lakes. They had none, of course, on Lake Erie. In fact, no British force had even been on the lake until Rogers made this trip to Detroit. The French had built no more ships on it since the *Griffin* disaster. In the century following La Salle they had been content to travel and transport their goods by canoes, bateaux and whaleboats.

Now British traders swarmed into the new territory. They came over the mountains to Pittsburgh or up to Presque Isle, and they came across from the Mohawk to Lake Erie, eager for the fur trade opened to them through the fall of New France. Pontiac and his tribesmen viewed with deepening dismay this influx of Englishmen with their sharp trade practices. Their enmity smoldered for three years after the surrender of Detroit. Then it flamed into war on western Lake Erie and around the fort at Detroit in the year 1763. The episode is known as Pontiac's War, and Francis Parkman devoted a brilliant volume to it.

Pontiac had received Rogers in friendship because he thought that the Indians would fare better in trade with the British than with the French. They did not. Two years of disillusioning experience taught

Pontiac that British policy did not live up to the promises of British traders, and he came to dislike the British more than the French. Unrest spread among the Indians of the region, and they began to talk about resistance to the British. The French in Illinois aroused them with glib promises of aid if they would revolt. Pontiac put the suggestion into action at the key fort at Detroit. He established his headquarters on Peach Island. He organized the Huron and Ottawa along the river. Tribesmen in small groups drifted in to swell the encampment without arousing too much suspicion. Pontiac rehearsed them in his stratagem for seizing the fort. A company of selected men would file off the barrels of their guns, conceal them under their blankets and gain entrance to the fort for an audience with the commandant, Major Gladwin. Then, on signal from the chief, they would rise, shoot and slay the garrison, open the gates to the waiting warriors outside, and slaughter the British. The plan was Pontiac's parallel to the famous ruse of the lacrosse game by which his allies at Mackinac later gained entrance to that fort and massacred the British. Gladwin, however, was an able commander. Learning of Pontiac's plan in advance, he was prepared to meet it. He admitted the chief and sixty warriors, but when they came into the hall, Gladwin had his soldiers in readiness and fully armed. Flanked by these men, Gladwin, in a dramatic scene, exposed Pontiac's treachery to his face. He threw aside the blanket of one of the braves and pointed to the sawed-off gun. Pontiac did not accept the challenge. Instead he protested against Gladwin's suspicious attitude and with great dignity withdrew.

From that moment the siege was on. It is a tribute to Gladwin's leadership that with only a small force (about 100 soldiers at the outset) he held the fort through six harrowing months against more than 1,500 Indians. The Indians murdered and scalped the British settlers outside the protection of the stockade. They landed on the west end of Belle Isle, where they killed Mrs. James Fisher and some soldiers who were working on the farm maintained by the garrison. They seized and killed Sir Robert Davers, who was with Captain Robertson's lake-survey party at Port Huron. They ambushed Captain Dalyell and his 250 men who had been sent to the relief of Detroit; twenty-three were killed and thirty-four wounded. But Gladwin held on to the fort against all odds from May 1 to October

31 until the Indians were exhausted and the British were able to bring arms and diplomacy to bear for a settlement. Pontiac, watching his warriors melt away to hunt food for their families, asked for peace.

Gladwin's defense was heroic, but it was British naval strength on Lake Erie that finally saved Detroit. The British had sent ship-wrights from their yards at Oswego in 1761 to build two vessels above the Falls in the Niagara River. They chopped down timber, sawed it by hand, and by the opening of the season of 1763, two eighty-ton schooners—each sixty feet long with a fourteen-foot beam, a seven-foot hold and armed with cannon port, starboard and bow— were launched on the Niagara. They were christened the *Huron* and the *Michigan.* Like the *Griffin,* they were towed up the swift current and made sail on Lake Erie, loaded with supplies for the Detroit colony. During Pontiac's attempted blockade these two ships kept open the supply route from Niagara. The Indians attacked them by ruse, by ambush, by fire rafts and with rifleshot, and even boarded one of them, but the schooners always got through.

Other lake-borne expeditions did not. Lieutenant Cuyler set out in whaleboats from Niagara with ninety-six men and a load of supplies. They chose to follow close to the north shore. When they camped at Point Pelee, with boats drawn up on the beach, the Indians ambushed the detachment. They killed or captured sixty men, and the others barely escaped in two overcrowded whaleboats.

Major Wilkins suffered an even more serious disaster at the hands of capricious Lake Erie herself. He started for Detroit from Niagara in whaleboats with 600 men and a quantity of ammunition. He chose the south shore. The high seas capsized the boats, and broke many of them on the rocks. Wilkins lost all his stores and seventy of his men. He never got to Detroit.

Colonel Bradstreet learned nothing from these tragedies; in fact, he recklessly brought one of equal severity upon himself. He did get to Detroit in whaleboats in the summer of 1764, but his arro-gance and general bull-headedness defeated his negotiations with the Indians. He returned to Sandusky. In late October, when Lake Erie is most capricious and treacherous, he suddenly ordered his men to break camp and proceed eastward to Niagara. That night he foolishly camped on the exposed shore when he could have harbored in the mouth of a quiet river not far away. He was not weatherwise. A devastating storm kicked up the waves of shallow Erie. It hit the whaleboats, destroyed half of them outright, with all the stores, baggage and ammunition, including six precious cannon. For three days and nights the storm battered them. One hundred and fifty men, deprived of their boats, had to fight their way through the northern Ohio, Pennsylvania and New York wilderness to get to Niagara. Many died of hunger and disease; others perished from exposure and exhaustion.

Experiences like these, contrasted with the speed and comparative ease with which the schooners plied back and forth,[2] dramatized the need of the British for more ships on the Upper Lakes. The need became acute as goods piled up at the east end of the lake to await transport. The British built at least fifteen more ships, rigged as schooners, snows, brigs and sloops, for service on Lake Erie in the time between Pontiac's War and the evacuation of Detroit in 1796. In addition to this provincial marine, they also built at least seven commercial ships on Lake Erie between 1785 and 1792. Some of these ships were built in the Niagara above the Falls, and about a dozen were launched from the flourishing new shipyard at Detroit. By the time the British and the Americans came into conflict over this region, the British had a substantial marine in operation on the lakes which gave them a marked advantage.

The thunder of the American Revolution echoed faintly on Lake Erie, but it did echo, and we must listen to it for a few paragraphs. Independence Hall, the Lexington Green and the rude bridge arching the flood at Concord were a long, long way from the Detroit colony. So were Valley Forge and Yorktown. But the virus of war has a diabolical propensity for spreading itself. General Henry Hamilton, the new commandant of the post at the head of the lake, was no democrat. He read of the treasonous conduct of the British colonists in Pennsylvania in 1776. As a loyal subject of his king, he treated the revolutionists with scorn. He stirred up his Indians against them in the Lake Erie-Ohio River region and offered a fair price for rebel scalps and prisoners. He reported in July 1777 that he had sent out fifteen raiding parties. The Indians were scarcely in need of encouragement. The infiltration of the whites into their

---

2 Despite the loss of the *Michigan* on the north Erie shore after three years of service.

hunting grounds was sufficient provocation, and they raided far and wide. The Americans were, of course, incensed. They referred to these marauders as "scalping parties." Their indignation ran high. Benjamin Franklin struck off on his private press at Passy a *Supplement to the Boston Independent Chronicle,* complete with masthead and advertisements, in which he printed an imaginary account of the results of these scalpings. A Seneca chief, it said, had sent to the British governor general in one shipment eight packages containing 954 scalps of soldiers, farmers, women, children and infants, "cured, dried, hooped, and painted, with all the Indian triumphal Marks." And with them was a letter saying, "Father, we send you herewith many Scalps, that you may see we are not idle Friends. . . . We wish you to send these Scalps over the Water to the great King, that he may regard them and be refreshed; and that he may see our faithfulness in destroying his Enemies, and be convinced that his Presents have not been made to ungrateful people."

Franklin sent copies of this paper to Charles W. F. Dumas with a letter in which he said that the paper "places in a striking light, the English barbarities in America, particularly those committed by the savages at their instigation. The *Form* may perhaps not be genuine, but the *substance* is truth; the number of our people of all kinds and ages, murdered and scalped by them being known to exceed that of the envoice." This canard expressed the belief and the sentiment of the Americans during the war, and it was widely circulated and accepted as fact.

The Indians were, in general, on the side of the British during the Revolutionary War. One of their most distinguished leaders was the Mohawk Thayendanegea, known to history as Joseph Brant. He was the friend and brother-in-law of Sir William Johnson, noted British Indian agent. (Sir William had married Brant's sister.) Sir William sent Brant to school at Lebanon, Connecticut, where he sat under the instruction of Eleazar Wheelock, later founder of Dartmouth College. He helped translate parts of the New Testament into Mohawk. He accompanied Johnson to Detroit to negotiate with the Indians at the close of Pontiac's War. He became an international figure with his natural Indian poise and his intelligent absorption of English culture. On a visit to England in 1775 he was a sensation at court, he was made much of by the nobility, he met Boswell and

Sheridan, and got his portrait painted by no less an artist than George Romney. He returned to the Lake Erie frontier in time to lead his people against the Colonists, and to make his name hated and feared by the Americans. He was with the Loyalist John Butler when Butler's Rangers made their raids on his home neighborhood at Wyoming, Pennsylvania, and at Cherry Valley, New York, in 1778, massacring old men, women and children and carrying away captives. The Americans were so much incensed by the Indian raids that they went back into the Mohawk country later in the Revolution and laid waste their villages and lands to Niagara and Lake Erie.

The British treated Brant and the Indians as noble allies who had suffered and sacrificed themselves for the English cause. They solemnly set apart a fine tract of land extending six miles on each side of the Grand River from Lake Erie "to the head of said river" for the "Mohawk Nation and such other of the Six Nations Indians as wish to settle in that quarter . . . which they and their posterity are to enjoy forever." Brant himself received a liberal grant at Burlington. He lived there in lordly style at spacious Brant House, served by Negro slaves whom he had captured during the wars. This relationship between the British and the American Indians was to have further important consequences to Lake Erie, as we shall soon see.

The other significant repercussion of the Revolution on Lake Erie concerned the Loyalists. The Colonists were not at all united in their rebellion against the mother country. Thousands of them from Boston to Charleston considered the uprising as treasonous conduct on the part of mean and worthless fellows which would soon be put down by His Majesty's arms. Many of them were mobbed, tarred and feathered, or jostled out of the community astride a rail. Their loyalty to their King led them to abandon their homes and property and to take up arms against the Americans. Some 20,000 of them fought on the English side. Thirty corps were organized under such significant designations as King's Rangers, Queen's Rangers, Royal Fencible Americans, Prince of Wales's American Volunteers. The great Colonel John Graves Simcoe, later the governor general of Upper Canada, whose name is written large and memorialized in place names along the north shore of Lake Erie, led the Queen's Rangers in battle against the Americans—"persevering, rapacious and ambitious People," he called them. His leadership was inspired by his fixed belief that the rich and vital West would face a serious threat, and might pass out of British control, if the Americans succeeded in forming their more perfect Union.

But the rebellious Americans did succeed, and the West was threatened. The Loyalists, of course, were ruined. They had gathered in large numbers around or near the eastern end of Lake Erie. Niagara was their stronghold. Both Niagara and Detroit remained unmolested in Loyalist hands throughout the Revolution, largely because the Colonists could not get at them. It was just as well. As Detroit had fallen to the British without a battle when Montreal was surrendered by the French, so both Detroit and Niagara passed to the Americans without assault when the seaboard was taken. When the Treaty of Paris was signed in September 1783, Lake Erie was split to form the northern boundary between our two countries, and Detroit and Niagara became, theoretically, American territory. That is to say, Britain agreed to give possession "with all convenient speed."

Britain had good reasons to find speed inconvenient. She had an earnest concern for these thousands of Loyalists who had lost their property and could not return to their homes. Britain wrote into the treaty an agreement pledging the Americans to restore Loyalist property, or give compensation for its loss. The Americans also agreed to pay their outstanding debts to British merchants. "Creditors on either side," the pledge read, "shall meet with no lawful impediment to the recovery of the full value in sterling money, of all bona fide debts heretofore contracted." This part of the bargain was equally inconvenient to the Americans. Britain had to assume large responsibility for the Loyalists. She compensated them with a total of some $18,000,000 and 3,000,000 acres of land. Many of them settled permanently in Ontario, along the Grand River, and along the north shore of Lake Erie. Their descendants are to this day the aristocrats of the region and proudly refer to themselves as the U.E.L.—United Empire Loyalists. They have the same fierce satisfaction in their origin and lineage as the F.F.V. and the descendants of passengers on the *Mayflower*. We should add that there were also a good many Canadians who sympathized with the Colonists and suffered for their cause; and that a big tract of some of the best land in Ohio just east of Columbus, known as the Refugee Tract, was set aside for their use to compensate them for their sacrifice.

Remembering all the bitterness and hatred which is stirred up and magnified by war, and which rankles in men's hearts after formal peace has been signed, we can find small cause for wonder that all was not well on the Lake Erie frontier at the close of the Revolution. Britain was reluctant to surrender the border posts—particularly Detroit, because its possession was a form of security, or a kind of mortgage to protect her interests and ambitions. For that settlement, now almost a century old, was not only the military key to the West, but it was also at this period a thriving colony. Its fur trade was booming. The British were dispensing nearly 20,000 gallons of rum each year to facilitate the Indian trade. So they stayed on. The Americans made threats and protests, but they did not immediately attempt to force the British back across the Detroit River, and Britain's flag flew over the fort until July 11, 1796.

Those thirteen years were dark and evil around the western end of Lake Erie. A given quota of intrigue, strife, bloodshed and cruel frontier warfare were required to bring a final settlement and a lasting peace. The details of this conflict are as devious and complicated as human cunning, but the basic pattern is as simple as human greed. We must examine this pattern and recount a few of the episodes that impinged harshly on Lake Erie.

For the Americans one of the fruits of the victorious Revolution was the opening of Ohio and the Northwest to white settlement. The young states on the seaboard paid off their debts to officers and men with grants of land in the territory claimed by them west of the mountains. Settlers streamed through the passes and down into the Ohio Valley. They erected forts and planted settlements on favored land at the mouth of the rivers, squarely in the midst of the finest hunting grounds of the Indians. At the same time, but more slowly and with less obvious intent, the British were moving west across Ontario and planting themselves firmly on the Detroit River. Their primary concern during this period, however, was not to settle but to trade.

The Indians were caught between the pincers of this twin westward movement of the whites. They could not be sure in which direction they should turn. The British encouraged them to believe

that they were the children of the King of England, who would protect them against the inroads of the Americans. English agents went
among them to dispense bounty, to present gifts in trade and to stir
them up against the settlers in Ohio and Indiana. Some of these
agents became notorious on the western Lake Erie frontier. Simon
Girty, known to the Americans by the ugly name of renegade, served
the British among the Indians in the most expert and barbarous
fashion. He had been captured by the Indians at the age of fifteen
after Braddock's defeat in Pennsylvania, and adopted by the Seneca
tribe. He had seen his stepfather tortured with hot gun barrels,
scalped alive and given the *coup de grace* by a small boy with a
hatchet. He learned the cunning and cruelty of Indian ways, and
added refinements out of his own superior brain. He became a leader
in the British cause among the disturbed Indians. He roamed the
region from Pittsburgh to Louisville and up to Detroit. He took
part in the torture and death at the stake of Colonel William Crawford, who was captured while leading an expedition against the
Ohio Indians. His very name was a terror to the whole region. With
such men to foment their resentment against the Americans, the Indians were led to believe that their interests lay more with the British
than with the Americans, and in choosing between two evils they
accepted British leadership.

We must bear in mind, however, that there was no nation or
combination of tribes of Indians in the Ohio or Lake Erie country
comparable to the organized Iroquois between Niagara and the Hudson. The Erie who had hunted and fished in what became the
Western Reserve were refugees from the East with no power to
resist their enemies. They had been exterminated by the Iroquois
in 1655. Farther west, on Lake Erie between Sandusky and Detroit,
the Wyandot were stronger and more strategically placed. The other
tribes in Ohio, Indiana, Michigan, Illinois and Ontario were only
loosely associated with them, and firm coalitions were difficult to
form and maintain. It was equally difficult to get them all bound
together in the same treaty. The Americans made attempt after
attempt to bring their representatives into a common meeting in
order to work out an agreement. A few always came, a few always
signed, and the negotiators always ended the powwow with the Mu-
nich hope that a final treaty was signed and war averted. But the

ink was hardly dry on these agreements before other tribes, and factions within the represented tribes who had refused to gather, protested and disavowed the terms and intensified their resistance to white encroachment.

Neither the Americans nor the British wanted to risk war with each other over this western frontier. The Americans were trying hard to get the British to move out of Detroit, but they were using diplomatic pressure and avoiding force of arms. The British wished to discourage and harass American infiltration in the region, but they did not care to provoke war. Their natural alternative, therefore, was to aid and abet the Indians in resisting white settlement between the Ohio River and Lake Erie. For the Indians as a group claimed, all partial and contrary agreements aside, that they had never yielded to the whites any right to any territory north of the Ohio River.

The field for conflict was obviously most fertile. The Indians watched with genuine alarm the rush of white settlers into their homeland on the rich and pleasant Ohio-Erie territory. Many of these settlers were mean customers, as the Indians learned, who could shoot a "savage" as readily as an Indian could hack off the scalp of a Pennsylvania trader. The Lake Erie frontier during the years following the Revolution became, therefore, a region of terror. The terror was not allayed by the intrigues of the British at Detroit nor by the partial measures taken by our inexperienced young government to reduce it. And these general observations bring us to the episodes which made a chapter in the history of Lake Erie.

In a period of seven years preceding 1790, more than 1,500 settlers in the Ohio Valley had been killed and scalped by the enraged and resisting Indians. The Congress got disturbed. It authorized George Washington to call up militia from Virginia, western Pennsylvania and Kentucky to crush the tribes. Washington was concerned lest the British think—as they did—that the expedition was aimed against them at Detroit. He ordered Governor St. Clair of the Northwest Territory to assure the commandant at Detroit that "the expedition about to be undertaken is not intended against the post you have the honor to command, nor any other place at present in the possession of the troops of his Britannic Majesty, but is on foot with the sole design of humbling and chastizing some of the savage tribes, whose depredations have become intolerable and whose cruelties have of late become an outrage, not only to the people of America, but on humanity." General Josiah Harmar of Philadelphia, veteran of the Revolution and friend of General Washington, as commander of the first United States Army, led this force of about 1,450 men. Only 320 of them were regulars; the rest were unruly frontiersmen, boys and old men, with no regard for discipline or military precision. The supplies were meager; they lacked everything from clothing to kettles and axes; and the communication lines were chaotic. After the most rudimentary training, this motley force moved from Fort Washington (Cincinnati) up the Miami River into the Maumee Valley. The Indians simply vanished before them like wolves in a forest. Harmar's men burned a few villages of Indian wigwams and plundered the autumn harvests of corn. Near the present site of Fort Wayne, however, the Indians met a detachment of Harmar's men and routed them. Some of the militia never fired a shot; they disobeyed orders, and they broke and ran in wild disorder back to the Ohio River. A second force of 400 chosen men who attempted to retrieve the disgrace were lured into ambush and cut to pieces. The expedition ended in worse than failure; 200 officers and men were killed outright, many were wounded and others had deserted. Harmar demanded a court of inquiry to clear his name of charges of drunkenness and incompetence; he was personally exonerated, but the victorious Indians were encouraged and incited to further action.

At that point General Arthur St. Clair was given command of a force larger than General Harmar's to redeem American honor and scourge the savages. It too was foredoomed. His men were just as undisciplined and inexperienced as Harmar's, and just as temperamental in obeying orders. There was no finer gentleman in the country than Arthur St. Clair, but he was ill, so crippled with arthritis in his knee joints that he had to be lifted into his saddle, and he was without experience in fighting Indians from tree to tree. His supplies were poor and his scouting completely inadequate. In 1791 he moved northward toward Lake Erie, building a chain of forts as he went. He was on the east fork of the Wabash on the morning of November 4, with his mob army greatly reduced by illness, necessary discharges and outright desertion to 1,400 effectives.

There the Indians led by Chief Little Turtle of the Miami tribe struck him in a surprise attack at dawn. Many of his men, like Harmar's, fled in a panic when the first bullets came at them. The rest were surrounded and overwhelmed. St. Clair exhorted and commanded and exposed himself in desperate attempts to rally his militia. Three horses were shot from under him and his clothing was shot full of holes, but by a miracle he escaped injury. It was all hopeless. A few fragments of his troops managed to cut their way through Little Turtle's tribesmen and escape. Two-thirds of the army were casualties: 632 killed and 264 wounded. The disaster was the worst ever sustained by troops of the United States. Panic reigned through the region as St. Clair and the stragglers fell back upon Fort Washington. The way seemed open for overwhelming Indian invasion from the north.

Then came Mad Anthony Wayne. President Washington gave him command of the United States Army and placed him in charge of the Indian wars in the spring of 1792. There were to be no more half measures. This campaign must wipe out the bitter memory of these disasters, and it had to succeed. Brilliant, dashing, considered rash and erratic by many, General Wayne was one of the greatest officers and Indian fighters developed in all the American frontier wars. The British minister to the United States, George Hammond, wrote to Lieutenant Governor Simcoe that "General Wayne is unquestionably the most active, vigilant, and enterprising Officer in the American Service, and will be tempted to use every exertion to justify the expectations of his countrymen and to efface the Stain which the late defeat has cast upon the American Arms."

Wayne had a few simple military principles: prepare every detail in advance, never sleep in Indian country and strike at the right moment quickly and with crushing force. The army was enlarged from two to five regiments. He recruited 2,500 men in the vicinity of Pittsburgh, and then moved slowly down the Ohio, training as he went, to Fort Washington in the spring of 1793. On the first terrace above the river there at Cincinnati he organized and drilled and practiced his army. He spent weeks and months on end training the wayward Kentucky volunteer woodsmen in the elementary military tactics of scouting, eternal vigilance in the woods, how to advance rapidly and safely, how to obey orders and how to shoot

Indians. And while Wayne drilled and made ready, and his fame spread north toward Lake Erie and Detroit, Washington tried once more to negotiate with the Indians.

The Indians gathered along Swan Creek in the suburbs of present Toledo. Some 3,000 warriors, the chiefs of the Confederated Tribes of the Northwest and of twenty-seven tribes of Canada met for conference with American representatives under the watchful eye of the British and under the protection of the British fort at Detroit. The conference broke down. Another one held at the rapids of the Maumee also failed. The Indians claimed their right to the territory, the Americans refused to recognize their claim, and no peaceful means of resolving the conflict could be found. Wayne began his ominous march north from Cincinnati against the Indians. Chief Little Turtle urged appeasement. He knew the prowess of Mad Anthony. In his speech to his fellow chiefs at the conference, he said:

"We have beaten the enemy twice under separate commanders. We cannot expect the same good fortune always. The Americans are now led by a chief who never sleeps. The night and the day are alike to him, and during all the time that he has been marching on our villages, notwithstanding the watchfulness of our young men, we have never been able to surprise him. Think well of it. There is something whispers to me that it would be prudent to listen to his offers of peace."

Little Turtle's view seemed cowardly to his fellows, and his counsel was not followed. The Indians prepared to meet Wayne. Wayne moved against them as methodically as General MacArthur fought his way back from Australia to the Philippines. Reaching Greenville, eighty miles from Cincinnati, in November, he decided to go into winter quarters on this central Ohio prairie and make it an advance base for the campaign of the next season. He built a stockade, protected it with a ditch and put up log huts for a camp. On the site of St. Clair's resounding defeat Wayne erected Fort Recovery. Despite sickness among his troops, he continued to whip them into a fighting unit during the winter. And in the spring of 1794, reinforced by more volunteers from Kentucky under Major General

Scott, he marched right on into the enemy territory on the Maumee where he built a fort and provocatively named it Fort Defiance.

The British were alarmed. They were certain that this mad general was headed toward Detroit itself, which, of course, they still found it unprofitable to relinquish. In April, while Wayne was still over a hundred miles away at Greenville, Lieutenant Governor Simcoe himself, accompanied by a staff of expert agents, engineers and military officers, sailed down from Detroit across Lake Erie and up the Maumee, past the site of Toledo, a dozen miles to the rapids in the river at present Perrysburg. There on the north bank of the river, near the ruins of an old British fort abandoned at the close of the Revolution, where the British agent Alexander McKee maintained a trading post, Simcoe ordered a fort built and manned to block Wayne's advance and to protect Detroit. It was built with a great effort during the summer of 1794, and called Fort Miamis.[3] It did not matter, in such an emergency, that this was on land definitely given up by the British by the Treaty of Paris. Excuses are always handy and easy to come by.

By the time Wayne reached Defiance in July and constructed his fort, the British were well entrenched at Fort Miamis as a base and support, less for their own arms than for the Indians whom they were encouraging to give battle. Wayne once more called for negotiations, but his overtures were again rejected. The two forces then moved toward battle. On August 20, 1794, Wayne marched on down the Maumee. The Indians, led by Blue Jacket instead of Little Turtle, moved up from Fort Miamis. They met a short distance above the rapids in a wilderness where a tornado had uprooted trees and twisted them into a chaotic barrier that seemed ideal for Indian warfare. Here Wayne's long and earnest months of monotonous preparation yielded high dividends. There was no separation of forces as under Harmar, and no surprise attack like the one which destroyed St. Clair's army. Wayne kept his right flank close to the river, and protected his left with his cavalry under Colonel Hamtramck. His infantry, trained for just this contingency, advanced steadily and in order. Some of them turned the Indian left flank and cut in from the rear. The main body used the natural cover of the

---

[3] F. Clever Bald, "Fort Miamis, Outpost of Empire," *Northwest Ohio Quarterly* (April 1944).

RECONSTRUCTION OF THE "NIAGARA," 1913

ON THE DECK OF THE REBUILT "NIAGARA"

fallen timber and fired only at close quarters. These tactics terrified the Indians. They were routed with heavy losses and fled back upon Fort Miamis, pursued by Wayne's men who pressed forward to the slaughter. In less than an hour Wayne had won the most decisive battle on the western frontier.

This Battle of Fallen Timbers virtually ended the Indian wars in the Lake Erie region. The British withdrew to Detroit, and on July 11, 1796, abandoned Fort Miamis, which had cost them so heavily in men and money. In the meantime Wayne gathered up the fruit of his victory. He summoned the chieftains to council and persuaded them to sign the Treaty of Greenville in August 1795. The treaty removed the menace of Indian attack and opened southern and eastern Ohio to an influx of settlers pressing in from the postwar dislocations east of the mountains. New Englanders began to leave their rocky farms and seacoast villages to follow the American dream westward toward Lake Erie.

The following summer (July 11, 1796) the British surrendered Detroit. The ceremony was somewhat reminiscent of the scene enacted over thirty-five years earlier when France yielded to the British. Two ships hired by the Americans sailed up the Detroit River on that July morning. Colonel Richard England, his troops, the citizens of Detroit and many visiting spectators were expecting them. Among the visitors were two familiar figures. Chief Little Turtle, with a big ring in his nose, silver rings in his ears, and garbed in a quaint costume of Indian and British garments, towered over his band of Miami who had come in friendship. (He died at Fort Wayne at peace with the Americans.) Simon Girty was there, wild and defiant as ever. Legend has it that when Girty saw the sails approaching, he rode his horse into the river and forced it across to Windsor while he swam behind, holding onto its tail. (Later pensioned by the British, he settled on his bounty lands at present Amherstburg where he died in 1818.) The approaching ships landed at the foot of Shelby Street. A company of Wayne's soldiers under Captain Moses Porter marched up to the fort. Colonel England hauled down the British flag; Captain Porter smartly hoisted the American ensign; salutes were fired; and for the second time the fort changed hands. The British retired to Fort Malden at Amherstburg which became their strong base for the War of 1812, and hundreds of British and Loyalist citizens of Detroit deserted the city and settled in Ontario.

Late in 1796 General Wayne sailed back across Lake Erie aboard a small schooner on his way to Philadelphia. He died en route at Erie, Pennsylvania. He was buried there at the blockhouse under the flagpole. Patriotic Christian Schultz visited the grave in 1807. He wept when he saw that the palings around the grave were rotted away, and that the only marker for this great American hero was "a misshapen stone, picked out of the rubbish of the fort, with A.W., the initials of the general's name, scratched with a nail!" Schultz took out his penknife and carved boldly in the rock under the initials, "Shame on my country."

In 1809 Anthony Wayne's son drove to Erie in a two-wheeled cart to gather up the remains of his father and carry them back to his home in Chester, Pennsylvania, to rest among his people. When they opened the grave, they found the body well preserved. They followed the old Indian custom of placing the body in a large kettle and boiling the flesh from the bones. Wayne's son took the bones away in his cart; the kettle was emptied back into the grave. All trace of the Erie blockhouse and burial place was lost with the years, but two generations later Dr. Germer dug up the coffin and found the plate marked A.W. and dated December 15, 1796. The kettle is still preserved at Erie.

Chapter 6

Settlements

WARRIORS returning from the West brought back descriptions of the land around Lake Erie. Their severe experiences along its shores did not blind their sharp, westward-focused, American eyes to the potential richness of the region. Their reports infiltrated among ambitious men in the East. A little time, a few settlers, a bit of foresight and hard work, and somebody would certainly get rich in the territory bordering Lake Erie. Detroit was already booming as a shipyard, trading post and commercial center on one of the most important links in the chain of lakes. But there was little except swamp and wilderness between Detroit and Niagara Falls until after Wayne's final swift victory over the Indians.

In the meantime the stream of settlement was far to the south: around the mountain wall by the Wilderness Road, and down the beautiful Ohio. Towns like Marietta and Cincinnati were flourishing along the river before the Lake Erie country was even surveyed. When the Northwest Territory was formed, the center of population and government was the Ohio River. The lakes were hinterland separated from civilization by miles upon miles of forest with only a few rivers and Indian trails for communication lines. Governor St. Clair wore himself out and got arthritis in his knee joints on punishing horseback journeys through the Territory. Delegates from the Territory on their way to Cincinnati would ride for days through timberland without sighting so much civilization as a squatter's cabin.

This condition would be changed in an extraordinarily short space of time by settlers from Connecticut. They would take possession of the Lake Erie shore as the Virginians took over the Ohio River. As you travel north across Ohio in the present day from Chillicothe on the Scioto to Painesville on Lake Erie, you feel that you have been transported from Virginia into Connecticut. You leave the Jeffersonian Greco-Roman brick houses with two-story southern porches along the back wing; you enter a region distinguished by its village greens with graceful white church belfries lifted above the trees, with matching town halls near by, and green-shuttered white colonial houses spaced neatly around the square. Along the lake itself you come upon villages whose white houses on the shore and sailing craft in the harbors remind you of some of the villages on Long Island Sound. They have names that reinforce your feeling: New Haven, New London, Norwalk, Ridgefield, Greenwich, Danbury. They might have been transplanted without alteration from New England.

In a sense they were.

Connecticut's charter, granted to her in 1662 by Charles II, grandiosely—and imaginatively—extended the border of the state to the Western Sea, or to the South Sea. The sea turned out to be the Mississippi River. When the Northwest Territory was being formed, Connecticut in 1786 relinquished her claims to the back country except for about 3,000,000 acres in Ohio which she frugally and speculatively reserved. This Reserve by good fortune extended 120 miles along the Lake Erie shore.

The people of Connecticut suffered heavily in the Revolutionary War. Nearly 2,000 of them had their property burned or destroyed by the British. Connecticut gave these people 500,000 acres of land along Lake Erie in the western end of the Reserve. They called the tract "the Sufferers' Lands." People in Ohio call it "the Firelands." The beautiful Wine Islands of Lake Erie were included in the grant.

Connecticut, therefore, had a rich lake-shore territory all ready for her postwar expansion as soon as Wayne's victory made it safe to enter and a succession of treaties with the Indians opened it to settlement. Although the lake itself was a ready-made highway for the Colonists, it was not so convenient as the Ohio River to the south. There were no gales or high seas on the river, and the three-mile-an-hour current floated immigrants to their destination with a minimum of effort. Lake Erie, on the other hand, was wild, treacherous and temperamental. There was no friendly current to carry a man and his family and his goods on a flatboat to the West. They had to go on foot or horseback along the shore, or fight their way forward against wind and rain in open boats, or traverse the ice in winter on sleighs. The region behind the shore line was thick, stubborn wilderness.

The first Connecticut settlers along Lake Erie faced hardships as great as any that confronted their forefathers on the seaboard. The prospect did not daunt them.

They were relatively late in coming. Moses Cleaveland led the first party of fifty, including two women, with thirteen horses and some cattle, to the Reserve in 1796. The beach of the lake was their road. In that same year, by contrast, 20,000 settlers in 1,000 boats went down the Ohio River from Pittsburgh. General Cleaveland, that short, energetic, somber, Yale man ('77), soldier and Connecticut lawyer, who was often mistaken for a New England divine, brought most of his party from Schenectady up the Mohawk, down to Oswego, up Lake Ontario and around Niagara to Buffalo Creek, and then west around the Lake Erie shore to Conneaut Creek just inside the Reserve. It was July 4, and they fired salutes to Independence. They made speeches in the form of toasts, and then, as Cleaveland recorded in his diary, "drank several pails of grog, supped, and retired in remarkable good order." Next day they built a log cabin which they christened "Stowe's Castle" in honor of the commissary of the party.

That was the beginning of the first settlement in the Western Reserve. The harbor at Conneaut now receives more ore for the steel mills than any other port on the lake.

Moses Cleaveland then went on around the shore in a small boat. At the mouth of the Ashtabula River, where twenty big lake freighters now dock simultaneously, two members of the party became so enamored of the prospect that they stayed there and founded the town of Ashtabula. Cleaveland continued his voyage to the mouth of the Cuyahoga River, just halfway across the Reserve. As he stood on the terrace overlooking the flat, narrow flood plain and gorge of the river and the broad expanse of Lake Erie, the wily surveyor, bitten by mosquitoes and tormented by wood flies, knew nonetheless that he had found the spot which he had come so far to seek. He blocked out a central square, after the custom of his country, built a storehouse and some cabins and laid the foundation for the great city of Cleveland. Then, having done his duty, he left a few settlers on the spot to suffer after him with dysentery and intermittent fever, and returned to the East to await the slow developments.

A ridge and watershed runs across Ohio, roughly paralleling the Reserve along its southern edge fifty to seventy-five miles from the lake. More than a score of rivers and large creeks run from this divide down to the shallow Lake Erie bowl. The first settlements were made at the mouths of these rivers. Sand bars lay across the harbors, giving them a draft of only three or four feet at normal lake levels. One of the first public undertakings of these New Englanders in Ohio was the improvement of Fairport Harbor on the Grand River below Painesville in order that ships might come into that port. Settlers for the Reserve landed here and worked their way inland, cutting away enough timber to build cabins and plant gardens.

They came slowly at first, generally keeping to the lake shore, just as the pioneers to the south remained near the banks of the Ohio River. One by one their villages were laid out and gradually took on a New England character. Mentor, where James A. Garfield used to live, was founded in 1799; Huron on the Huron River in 1805; Vermilion on the Vermilion River in 1808; Lorain on the Black River in 1810; Sandusky on the bay in 1816; Norwalk, Milan and New London in the Firelands, with Huron and Vermilion as outlet ports, also in 1816. Toledo on the Maumee was not yet thought of. Over at Erie, Pennsylvania, were at that time two taverns and a few houses overlooking the sand arm of Presque Isle. The villages, though officially plotted and named, were only small clusters of cabins, sparsely settled and widely scattered, with no interconnecting roads except the lake and the shore. The whole lake-shore region in both the United States and Canada was wild and lonely until several years after the War of 1812.

Detroit on her river was advancing satisfactorily. Her old-fashioned fort, manned by a garrison of only ninety-four men, looked not too menacingly down the river toward its British neighbor at Malden some fifteen miles away. The British fleet, based here at Fort Malden or Amherstburg, as the settlement was called, maintained complete control of the lake.

Down at the lower end the British had Fort Erie on the Niagara

River and a way station at Long Point, which juts several miles east into the lake from Ontario.

Buffalo was just getting under way. Detroit had placed a full century of stirring history behind her under French and British flags before Buffalo was planned. There were good reasons.

Fort Erie in Ontario across the Niagara River and the naval shipyards at Black Rock represented the spirit of apprehension which first brought men to this part of the lake. Between Lake Erie and the Hudson lay the wilderness and danger of the Mohawk Valley. Until the beginning of the nineteenth century the Buffalo region was menacing. A colony of Seneca lived near Buffalo Creek, within the modern city limits, at the time of the Revolution. But enterprising real-estate men soon pressed right on in. The Holland Company of Amsterdam bought a huge acreage known as the Holland Purchase, and sent Joseph Ellicott there to plan a town. He tramped westward around the lake from Black Rock on the Niagara. The mouth of Buffalo Creek, with the basin which it formed in Lake Erie, seemed to him a favorable site for a village. He surveyed the low terrace above the lake to the east of the creek and laid out the town which was to become Buffalo. Four years later, in 1803, he opened his plot for sale.

The map design was pleasing. It was modeled on the plan for the national capital. Viewed from the air over the present busy sprawling city, this old downtown section, a short distance from Erie Basin, looks like a neat cobweb. The center is a public square, now featuring the monument to President McKinley who was assassinated on the Pan-American Exposition grounds some distance to the east on September 6, 1901. The corners of the square are bisected by two arterial cross streets: Niagara, running northwest to southeast, and Genesee, northeast to southwest. Three other streets also radiate from the center as they do on Capitol Hill. Not many people hastened to buy Ellicott's lots, but 500 settlers had come by 1812, and there were many troops mustered near by confronting the British fort across the Niagara.

About the same time that Ellicott was developing Buffalo, General Peter B. Porter was promoting a rival settlement at Black Rock. We shall take notice of the rivalry a little later on. This settlement overlooked a fine protected harbor, but it was not so artistically planned, and it was two miles down the swift Niagara current. Ships could seldom get to Lake Erie against this current unless they had a good east wind, or were towed by men and oxen on shore. Ferry service was in operation here by 1796. It did a smart business carrying people and teams and transporting salt over to Canada where more and more settlers were moving into the Niagara and the Ontario Peninsulas and clearing farms and building houses. The village of Black Rock, now a part of Buffalo, took its name from a low, black rock about 100 feet broad that lay on the riverbank. Teams entered the ferry from it. Ironically enough, it was blown up and the harbor destroyed in the reconstruction of the Erie Canal which Black Rock fought so hard to bring into this harbor instead of Buffalo. Much of the shipbuilding in the early years was centered here at Black Rock.

There were no important villages on the Canadian shore between Fort Erie and Amherstburg, but Talbot and other promoters were gradually opening up the rich agricultural lands north of the lake shore. There were many farmhouses and mills springing up in this wilderness, and enough farms and men in Old Ontario to make it a military objective in the War of 1812, as we shall see.

This was the kind of preliminary activity going on around Lake Erie in the second decade of the last century when Great Britain and America once more allowed their interests to clash, to drift into a crisis and lead them into war. And this time, unfortunately, not the mere echo of the thunder but the lightning itself would strike on Lake Erie.

Chapter 7

September 10, 1813

THE War of 1812 was a melancholy affair. It was largely the result of these world-wide conflicts which have been disturbing us on Lake Erie. The hatreds and wounds of these wars were not easily healed. The peace that followed the Revolution, as in other postwar periods, was more of a truce than a settlement. Incidents which might have been settled by negotiations were aggravated by the tensions and the residue of fierce antagonisms. Impressment of American seamen was serious business of an inflammatory nature. War is also a serious business, but Britain and America permitted their relations to deteriorate steadily and to drift into armed conflict. Britain resented American aid to Napoleon and had the sea power to prevent it. Americans resented the British blockade, but with only fifteen ships against a thousand they were helpless to prevent it. Britain thought that the Americans were taking advantage of her life-or-death struggle with Bonaparte to seize the best part of Canada along the Great Lakes and the St. Lawrence. That view was not without foundation, and it is still held by our neighbors north of Lake Erie. Many Americans in the East shared this opinion and protested against the war mood of the West. But in the circumstances the war mood transcended sectional differences and became a wave which engulfed the country.

War was declared on June 18, 1812.

The brilliant individual actions of American frigates on the Atlantic, and the overwhelming force with which Britain sealed up American ports and drove American shipping from the high seas are no part of our story. But this war reached a bloody hand directly into Lake Erie, and brought it for the first time prominently to international attention. Among its peaceful western islands, under an idyllic September noonday sky, the Americans gained one of their few victories, and a decisive one, in a war notable for its blunders on both sides.

In 1812 the British in Canada, like the French before them, were

71

extremely vulnerable. In all that vast territory they had less than
5,000 regular troops, concentrated around widely separated forts
from Quebec to Malden and Mackinac. General Sir Isaac Brock had
330 of these regulars and about 400 militiamen at Fort Malden, to
which the British had withdrawn when they retired from Detroit.
They had also built a shipyard and naval base at Malden on the
widening Detroit River from which they could control Lake Erie.
They were heavily dependent upon the Great Lakes and the St.
Lawrence River for communication and supplies. Such makeshift
roads as existed across the Ontario arrowhead were incapable of
bearing supplies for this post. General Brock had foreseen his vul-
nerability. He wrote succinctly, "Should the communications between Montreal and Kingston be cut off, the fate of the troops in this
part of the province would be decided." It seemed like a simple
operation for the Americans to drive across the border and cut this
line wherever they chose: Montreal, Kingston, Niagara, Buffalo or
Detroit. Henry Clay boasted that the Kentucky militia alone could
do it. It is not improbable that with proper planning they might
have done so, but they did not. With overwhelming numbers of men
at their disposal, they failed in the relatively easy task of lopping off
the branch and gathering up the Lake Erie spoils at their leisure.
For the Americans were blunderingly led, and they lacked naval
power on Lake Erie—two disadvantages which cost them dearly.

The chief reason for their early failures on Lake Erie was their
disregard for British sea power on the lakes. The British, in addition
to their small commercial schooners, had three warships based at
Malden: the seventeen-gun frigate *Queen Charlotte,* the thirteen-gun
schooner *Lady Prevost* and the eight-gun brig *General Hunter.* (All
three of these ships were opposed to Perry in 1813.) The Americans
had only a small transport schooner, the *Cuyahoga,* in service, and
the brig *Adams,* undergoing extensive repairs and refitting at Detroit and unfit for service when the war broke out. The British were
able to seize both of these ships and a small sloop and add them
to their Lake Erie navy at the very outset of hostilities. The sloop
became the three-gun cutter *Little Belt,* the schooner became the one-
gun *Chippewa,* and both were in the Battle of Lake Erie. The *Adams*
became the *Detroit,* but it was retaken and destroyed. (The nineteen-
gun *Detroit,* Barclay's flagship in the battle, was a new vessel—

the only one built by the British while the Americans were constructing their fleet at Black Rock and at Presque Isle.)

The Americans, apparently unaware of the primary importance of these British warships at the head of Lake Erie, launched a land campaign against the British by way of Detroit. Its failure is one of the sorriest paragraphs in our military or Lake Erie history. It was led by General Hull, Governor of the Territory of Michigan. His name still bore the luster which it had acquired during the Revolutionary War, when he fought gallantly beside Anthony Wayne at Stony Point. He was praised before his troops by Governor Meigs of Ohio when the general took over the command at Dayton. The governor said they were honored to be under the leadership of this able hero, this superintendent of Indian Affairs and governor of Michigan, who was so well fitted to conduct them to speedy and complete victory. The general responded with a fine speech about the hallowed ground over which they were about to march, and about the British "system of oppression and injustice which that nation has continually practiced, and which the spirit of an indignant people can no longer endure."

The eloquent words were well spoken, the enthusiasm of the troops was high, and the young officers, among whom were Duncan McArthur, Lewis Cass and James Findlay, all colonels and all later distinguished, were optimistic. But General Hull, unfortunately, had seen his best days. He was heavy and fat in body and sluggish and confused in mind and spirit. His actions were poorly planned and indecisive. And these qualities came to the forefront as the 1,900 troops moved toward Detroit.

Their progress was slow and hazardous. There were no roads but sodden trails. Much of the region north of Urbana was forest and swamp. The army had to hack its way through the wilderness and wade through the miasmic marshes. Chills, fever and ague smote the men and many fell by the way. The animals in the supply train died on the road or collapsed at the Maumee. The ill-trained and undisciplined men became stupid and quarrelsome with fatigue. A solid month of such marching brought them to the Maumee Rapids above Toledo. There the general, who seems to have given no thought whatever to the necessity of naval support to help solve his acute supply problem, ordered his stores and baggage and many of the sick aboard the little schooner *Cuyahoga* to be sailed up to Detroit. The schooner proceeded down the Maumee and across the western end of Lake Erie. Quite naturally she never got to Detroit. The British of course seized her and brought her in. Besides Hull's supplies, they found aboard the schooner his papers and plans for the campaign which they promptly sent on to General Brock.

Hull and his men continued their weary march around the lake and finally reached Detroit on July 5, thirty-five days after they left Dayton. Military opinion is generally agreed that if Hull had shown the slightest daring and had struck the British at Fort Malden promptly and with all his force, he might have won a quick and decisive victory. He did cross the river, and he seemed ready to smite Malden with his vastly superior force. But instead of striking, he hesitated. He worried because he was afraid, he said, that the assault would cost too many lives. The Indians might rise and massacre the white citizens in the region. Perhaps the liberty-loving Canadians would rise to the appeal he had made to them and join the Americans against the British. So he hesitated and finally withdrew to Detroit without making an attack. In the meantime General Brock had ample time to bring up more troops and supplies, and to rouse the great Tecumseh and the Indians against the Americans. Knowing Hull's plans, knowing that every day drained away more of his food and resources, and seeing his indecision, Brock was able to move against him at Detroit. Brock's troops arrived at Amherstburg on August 13. He reached Sandwich on the fifteenth, and the next morning, after lobbing shot over into the fort, crossed the river to Spring Wells. The bewildered Hull surrendered Detroit to the British without firing a single shot in its defense.

It was a stunning disaster. Hull's men and officers were furious over the disgrace. Nathanl [sic] Adams, one of Hull's soldiers, expressed their attitude in a letter to his brother written from Detroit on August 19, 1812.

"My Dear Brother,

"I have only time to inform you that our army surrendered to the British under Gen [Isaac] Brock on the 16th. We could have whipped hell out of the rascals but Gen. Hull has proved himself a traitor and a coward. On the 12th of July, we crossed the river at this place and encamped at Sandwitch [sic] in Canada, with the object of driving the red coated devils away from Malden. . . . Gen. Hull was informed there that Fort Mackinaw above Detroit had surrendered to the British and Indians, who were rushing down the river in numbers sufficient to crush our people. Old Gen. Hull became panic Struck, and in spite of the entreaties of his officers and private Soldiers run us back to this place where we were made to submit to the most shameful surrender that ever took place in the world. Our brave Capt. Harry James cursed and swore like a pirate, and cried like his heart would break."[1]

Colonel Cass himself preferred charges against the General. Hull was relieved of his command and condemned by a court-martial, but the British again held Detroit and the plight of the Americans on Lake Erie was serious. Indeed it went from bad to worse as the Indians committed all sorts of depredations against the white settlers along the river. The British and Indians proceeded to Frenchtown, now Monroe, about halfway down the western edge of Lake Erie on the River Raisin, and built a stockade commanding the land approach to Detroit.

Meantime General James Winchester was sent out to Fort Wayne to take command of a new army being raised by General William Henry Harrison to go to the relief of Detroit. Winchester, also a Revolutionary War veteran, was no improvement upon Hull. He too was elderly and fat, and had lost such competence as he may have possessed by his thirty years of retirement on his Tennessee farm. He was, in addition, irritatingly pompous. Yet he was selected over Harrison who had already established himself as a skilled fighter and leader at Tippecanoe the year before. With the same disregard for primary military strategy which Hull had displayed before him, Winchester marched through winter weather around the west end of the lake to relieve the settlers at Frenchtown. There he was promptly surprised in his comfortable bed by the British and Indians, who attacked his force about five o'clock in the morning on January 22, 1813. Winchester and most of his officers and troops were taken prisoners. The Indians massacred a hundred or more

---

[1] Quoted from William T. Utter, *The Frontier State*, Vol. II of the *History of the State of Ohio* (Columbus, 1942), p. 89.

of the Americans by batting holes in their skulls with tomahawks in an orgy of scalping and bloodletting.

These two disastrous defeats within the space of a few months finally aroused the Americans to some understanding of the seriousness of this war on the lake. They decided to do what they should have done at the outset if they were to fight successfully in this region. That was to get a competent military commander, build a fleet and destroy British dominance on the lake. And that is where General Harrison took charge of the land forces, and where young Oliver Hazard Perry, whose towering monument at Put-in-Bay gleams in the September sunshine, steps on the Lake Erie stage as one of its greatest heroes.

It was no light undertaking to challenge British sea power on this lake. The lake is about 330 feet above Lake Ontario, and in those days there was no Welland Canal. Our fine shipyards at Sackets Harbor, Oswego and Niagara were of no use to operations on Lake Erie. That was an independent undertaking, and a major one. The young American ports were not yet equipped for extensive shipbuilding. There were no supplies handy and no experienced men to draw from. We would have to start from scratch, and we would have to build a fleet superior to that of the British. That would mean ten ships on Lake Erie. To get them built, armed and manned was young Perry's formidable assignment.

Perry's job was lightened somewhat by the daring exploit of an almost forgotten naval lieutenant, Jesse D. Elliott. In early September 1812 he began to build a navy yard behind the protection of Squaw Island on the Niagara about three miles below Buffalo. A few weeks later the British brig *Detroit* and the schooner *Caledonia* sailed down Lake Erie and anchored under the protection of Fort Erie. Elliott determined to slip over at night and get them. With about 100 men he embarked in two boats from Buffalo at one o'clock in the morning. By three o'clock Elliott and his men in one boat were alongside the *Detroit*. They scrambled up the sides and within ten minutes had possession of that fine brig. Only one of the men had been killed and one wounded. Sailing Master George Watts and his men in the second boat boarded the *Caledonia* and took her. Then Watts cut her cables, worked her over to the American shore and beached her. She not only lived to fight under Perry in his famous battle, but she also had aboard a $200,000 cargo of fur. Elliott labored hard to bring the *Detroit* across also, but the wind and current resisted. He was swept straight toward the Canadian shore, and was forced to drop anchor under the guns of Fort Erie. When the morning dawned, the fort began to shell him. He fired all his ammunition, then cut his cable and drifted across to Squaw Island. He and his men escaped with their prisoners in the ship's boats, while the shore batteries made a wreck of the *Detroit*.

That exploit helped, but the guns of Fort Erie still commanded the channel between Black Rock and Lake Erie. Until they were silenced, the little American fleet under construction at Black Rock would be effectively bottled up. The shipbuilders, as a matter of fact, were so close to the British guns that they were interrupted in their work by the shots lobbed over from the fort. The fort would have to be taken. That feat was carried out the following spring when the Army and Navy in a combined assault and landing forced the British to abandon the entire Niagara peninsula. Thus the way was opened for Oliver Hazard Perry's critical, crucial mission.

Five of his projected ten ships were at Black Rock. With the guns of Fort Erie silenced, these ships could be moved. The Niagara flows with a three-knot current from Lake Erie past Black Rock. The prevailing winds are with the current. It is seldom possible, therefore, to sail a ship up the river to the lake. Perry bent lines from the ships to yokes of oxen onshore and towed this section of his fleet up to Buffalo Creek. It consisted of the captured *Caledonia,* the schooners *Somers* and *Tigress,* the supply ship *Ohio* and the sixty-ton sloop *Trippe*. This squadron carried a total of seven guns.

The other ships were under construction out at Erie, Pennsylvania, under the protection of the long breakwater sand bar of Presque Isle. This difficult operation was in charge of two picturesque characters by the Dickens-like names of Sailing Master Daniel Dobbins and Master Shipwright Noah Brown. Dobbins had been a freshwater captain, and had done very well as a trader on the lake. He was at Mackinac with the schooner *Salina* in 1812 when that post was seized by the British. He was at Detroit when it was surrendered by Hull, and he was taken prisoner by the British. Dobbins escaped during one of those sudden, severe and most convenient Lake Erie thunderstorms. He seized an old canoe, and crossed the choppy lake to the United States shore. There he abandoned the canoe for a horse which he stole without compunction and made his way to Erie, his home port. After reporting to General Meade, he hastened on to Washington with the sad news of the disaster in the West.

It took these humiliating reverses to shock President Madison into a realization of the inadequate American naval power on the lakes. He pounded his White House desk with both fists and demanded vengeance. Then the shrewd old sailing master suggested to the Commander in Chief that we must have more warships on Lake Erie. The President forthwith gave him a commission and some funds, and sent him out to Presque Isle harbor to build them. Master Ship-wright Noah Brown joined him there on the last day of February 1813. Brown was a New York carpenter and shipbuilder of twenty years' experience. With his brother Adam he had built the frigate *New York* and many gunboats for the Navy, and had repaired dam-aged ships in the Brooklyn Navy Yard. Brown, now aged forty-three, hurried out to Erie, through heavy storms and through very deep snow, making the trip in ten days. He brought with him a small gang of men while his brother attempted to round up more.

The achievement of Dobbins and Brown in building the ships at Erie was surpassed only by that of Perry in fighting them. Erie was only a small village port on the edge of a wilderness. It had no ship-yard, no workers, and few supplies of any kind except the forest. It was some 400 miles away from the supply base of the Atlantic seaboard. In April these five ships were still trees in a virgin, snow-swept forest; in August they were in formation off Sandusky, manned, equipped and ready for a decisive battle. The simple bald facts of time and result are eloquent testimony to the driving energy of these men which overcame well-nigh insuperable obstacles.

Brown and his first handful of men began immediately to get out timber and frame the five vessels. The hands rounded up by Adam Brown arrived in April after a five weeks' journey across the snows. That made in all a force of about 200 men to build the fleet. They combed over the forest to select the ships' timbers. They chose trunks and limbs that forked at just the right angle to make a "natural knee" for the ribs between each frame. They cut these out with care and fitted them into the hull to give it maximum strength. They cut black-oak timber, fourteen by eighteen inches, for the keels of the *Lawrence* and the *Niagara*. The ship's planking was made of three-inch oak. They hewed the stanchions from white pine, red cedar and black walnut. The hull was secured by wooden pins, or "tree-nails," and by wrought-iron spikes. Iron, oakum and pitch were very scarce. Fortunately there was a British schooner frozen in the lake. Dobbins, Brown and their men boarded her and got, according to Brown's own statement, "about twenty barrels of pork and a quantity of rigging and cables. We made oakum of them, and burned the schooner and got her iron. It helped us with the gunboats, and I rode all around to the neighboring towns and bought of all the merchants every bar of iron I could find. The Government was to send iron, pitch and oakum, but the roads were so bad that I had almost finished the fleet before any arrival at Erie." Brown used lead for most of the calking of the *Niagara;* when that sturdy ship was raised and refitted for the centennial celebration in 1913, after lying for eighty years on the floor of Misery Bay at Erie, some of this lead was still secure and tight in her seams. When supplies and equipment did arrive, they were brought, most of them, by wagon across Pennsylvania from Philadelphia and Washington to Pittsburgh, and then towed by barge up the winding Allegheny River to the narrow divide on the rim of the Lake Erie bowl, only about a dozen miles from the shore at this point. Powder was hauled in a Conestoga wagon, drawn by six horses and guarded by four United States cavalrymen, across Pennsylvania to Erie. The cannon balls were cast at a little furnace near Steubenville.

Other supplies were equally hard to come by in this wilderness. Brown sent his agents all through the frontier settlements to get provisions for his men. They had to pay high prices for poor and meager fare. Brown recorded

". . . my men several times raised and declared they would work no longer if they could not have better fare; I satisfied them by giving them liberty to go and buy all the cattle and other provisions they could find. Several were gone four or five days, and when they came back their report satisfied them all, so I had very little trouble afterwards. I did all that man could do to procure the best the country afforded. We, all this time, were driving the vessels as fast as possible. It appeared that every man was engaged as if he was on a strife—the enemy often appeared before our harbor and several times came to anchor within three miles of us.

"Our men drew arms and volunteered to protect the ship yard, but the enemy did not venture to land, and we were as willing they should not land as they; so we had no use for our arms. We had completed our vessels by the middle of June, as follows: Three gunboats [*Porcupine, Scorpion* and *Tigress*] armed and fitted for sea; two brigs [*Lawrence* and *Niagara*] and one sharp schooner for a dispatch vessel, and to look out, as she could outsail anything in the English fleet. [This schooner, the *Ariel,* led the fleet into battle three months later.] All the above vessels were built by me,[2] and furnished with all materials, and we did not receive any funds from Government till March, 1814, when Commodore Chauncey came to New York and signed our bills. . . . Whole tonnage of the above vessels . . . 1,239.[25]/[95]."

Thanks to the heroic work of Dobbins and Brown and their men, the Presque Isle elements of the Lake Erie squadron were well along by the time Oliver Hazard Perry arrived to take command. There was probably no better man in all the United States Navy of 1813 for this difficult and crucial mission. He was born on August 23, 1785, in Rhode Island, to a family of an illustrious naval background. He went to sea at the age of fourteen. He served as a lieutenant in the war against the Barbary pirates in the Mediterranean, and as a lieutenant commander under Commodore Rodgers on the U.S.S. *Revenge.* He had already served with distinction in the War of 1812 as commander of a flotilla of gunboats stationed at Newport. The gunboats were ineffective, and Perry was chafing over his time-marking assignment at Newport when the lakes offered such a challenge. He felt that the war was passing him by. He applied for change of duty, and was overjoyed to receive orders to Lake Erie to take command of the new fleet that was certain to meet the British in action. His orders came on February 18; that same day he sent off fifty men to the lake front, and within a few days he had dispatched another 150. He himself set out with his thirteen-year-old brother on February 22.

---

[2] Brown's own statement, preserved by his family, and reprinted in *Journal of American History,* Vol. III, No. 1. Other accounts indicate that the *Tigress* was part of the squadron at Black Rock.

After a brief stopover at Sackets Harbor, he proceeded to Buffalo, and then by sleigh around Lake Erie to Presque Isle. When he arrived on March 27, he found his fleet rapidly taking shape under Dobbins and Brown. Perry's job was to fit it out, to procure supplies and men and to train his seamen. He was a flame of energy. Bold and daring in the grand manner, he believed in preparing to the limit of his time and resources, and then risking all in a dashing win-or-lose action. He was aggressive and dramatic. He had the John Paul Jones quality of infecting reluctant seamen with his own eagerness and audacity. He knew how to plan, to improvise and to do wonders with too little. And he certainly had need of all these qualities, plus luck and the flip of fortune, to succeed in this venture.

The ships at Erie were built in record time. Even then the speed with which the determined Americans got things done surprised the British. One after another the new ships were launched and fitted. There were two 480-ton brigs: the *Niagara,* and the *Lawrence* which Perry chose as his flagship and named in honor of the great captain who had died so heroically a few months earlier in the battle off the Boston coast. There were three small schooners, the *Ariel,* the *Scorpion* and the *Porcupine,* ranging from 83 to 112 tons.

The British in the meantime had added only one ship, the *Detroit,* to their force at Malden. Their fleet was under the command of Captain R. H. Barclay. Just why Captain Barclay ever permitted Perry to build and launch these ships is one of the mysteries. He knew they were on the ways, he had a superior force, and he did actually blockade the Erie harbor for a time. But he did not take positive action and he did not destroy his enemy. Perry outguessed and outmaneuvered him at every turn, and Perry had the hairbreadth luck that often draws the line between victory and defeat.

Perry's first good fortune befell him when he determined to join the Buffalo unit of his fleet with the Erie squadron. Barclay lay between the two anchorages. With a little dash he could have fallen upon them separately and annihilated them. Perry knew the risk he ran, but he was not deterred thereby. He sailed his five ships out of Buffalo and ran them up the lake. He was never required to disclose what he intended to do if Barclay fell upon him. One of those heavy quick ground fogs formed over the lake like a mantle of protection for Perry. He slipped past Barclay and joined his squadrons at Erie. So far, so good; in fact, it could hardly be better.

One more hazardous obstacle was still to be overcome. The Erie harbor is protected by a sand bar. That July the water was so low that the sand bar across the entrance was only five feet below the surface. The schooners and the sloops were light-draft and could sail across, but the brigs drew too much water. They would have to be hauled across. If Barclay should descend upon them while they were dragging bottom on the bar there would be catastrophe.

Barclay did not descend.

Perry unloaded all the ships' stores, dismounted the guns and removed the ammunition. When he had lightened them as much as possible, he ordered them taken across. It was Sunday, the first day of August, and as fine and clear a morning as you would care to see on Lake Erie. All day Sunday, all Sunday night, Monday and Monday night, Tuesday and Tuesday night they pulled and hauled and labored with the brigs. On the following day the last ship was over the bar, ready for reloading, refitting and the coming fight.

Barclay had disappeared. With an inadequate and improvised crew, Perry sailed forth to stalk him and seek a favorable moment for battle. He was at no time unaware of the importance of his mission. All during August he cruised the lake, training, instructing his men, instilling within them the will to conflict and the confidence of preparation and drill. General Harrison came aboard at Sandusky to talk with Perry and inspect the fleet. More important, he sent Perry a hundred sharpshooters to pick off the enemy when the ships should finally close, and it was their marksmanship that helped turn the battle from defeat to victory when it was finally joined. Perry chose Put-in-Bay among the Erie islands as his stalking base athwart the British supply lane where he could blockade Malden and keep a watch for Barclay. Eventually Barclay would be compelled to sail out and give battle.

He came out at last on the morning of September 10, 1813.

In his letter to his superior officer, Sir James Yeo, Barclay explained why he risked the battle. "Sir," he wrote on September 12, "the last letter I had the honor of writing to you, dated the 6th instant, I informed you, that unless certain intimation was received of more seamen being on their way to Amherstburg, I should be obliged to sail with the squadron, deplorably manned as it was, to fight the enemy, (who blockaded the port,) to enable us to get supplies of provisions and stores of every description. So perfectly destitute of provisions was the port, that there was not a day's flour in store, and the crews of the squadron under my command were on half allowance of many things, and when that was done there was no more. Such were the motives which induced Major-General Proctor . . . to concur in the necessity of a battle being risked, under the many disadvantages, which I laboured; and it now remains to me, the most melancholy task, to relate to you the unfortunate issue of the battle. . . ."

The sky was clear; the wind was gentle and southwest. Barclay's sortie was a fine sight on Lake Erie in the September dawn. Six ships with all sail set moved in formation toward the islands. The 70-ton schooner *Chippewa* was in the van. She was followed by the new 490-ton ship *Detroit,* the 180-ton brig *General Hunter,* the 400-ton ship *Queen Charlotte,* the 230-ton schooner *Lady Prevost* and the 90-ton sloop *Little Belt*—the fleet enumerated in Perry's famous dispatch to General Harrison: "two ships, two brigs, one schooner, and one sloop." The fleet was freshly painted in orange and black, acres of sail shone in the bright sun, and all battle flags were flying.

Perry was ready. He had called his officers to final conference the night before. He was sick and flushed with the fever that had been dogging him for months and at times forced him to his bed. But he was also on fire with eagerness to attack. He explained again that the United States fleet must keep in close formation and press in for action so that the short-range guns could be brought to bear. Then with his fine flare for décor he brought out a new blue flag on which was sewn in muslin letters the words of dying Lawrence: DON'T GIVE UP THE SHIP. "When this flag shall be hoisted to the main royal masthead," Perry charged his officers, "it shall be your signal for going into action."

Perry beat against the wind out of the harbor, formed his line and stood down on Barclay's advancing fleet. He ran up the blue flag signal while the men of the fleet cheered. The maneuvers were slow in the light breeze. Not until 11:45 did they close to firing range somewhere near Middle Sister Island. Then the *Detroit* opened up with her long guns. Five minutes later she scored her first hit with a shot that roared through the wooden sides of Perry's flagship and began the slaughter. Another five minutes elapsed before Perry's ships could get their guns within range, and ten more minutes before the *Lawrence* could reach the *Detroit*. In the meantime she had to withstand a murdering fire. By 2:30 the *Lawrence* was completely out of action. Perry's own report said, "Every brace and bowline being shot away, she became unmanageable, not withstanding the great exertions of the sailing master. In this situation she sustained the action upwards of two hours within cannister distance [250 yards], while every gun was rendered useless, and the greater part of her crew [83 out of 103] killed or wounded." Besides this damage to the flagship, one of the *Scorpion's* two guns had blown down the hatch, killing several of the crew, and one of the *Ariel's* four guns had burst with even more disastrous casualties. It was the dark moment of the battle.

Perry then made his dramatic dash through shot and shell to the *Niagara*. He lowered the only undamaged boat from the port side of the *Lawrence,* gathered his blue battle flag in his arms and was rowed by four sailors to the lagging *Niagara*. He boarded his new flagship at 2:40. Five minutes later he was pressing the *Niagara* forward toward Barclay's line. But Barclay's *Detroit* was now a complete wreck. He himself was sorely wounded, and had been carried below. Perry began a devastating broadside fire and his men raked Barclay's ship with rifles and pistols. The British stood this fire for ten minutes, but could endure no more.

Barclay reported that "every officer commanding vessels, and their seconds, were killed, or wounded so severely, as to be unable to keep the deck." This loss was particularly disastrous, he said, because the squadron was manned "with not more than 50 British seamen, the rest a mixed crew of Canadians and soldiers, and who were totally unacquainted with such service." Barclay lowered his flags and all guns ceased firing. Perry received the surrender on the littered and blood-soaked quarter-deck of the *Lawrence*. He permitted all the captains to retain their swords. He buried the dead sailors in the lake off Middle Sister Island. He took the captured fleet into Put-in-Bay, and cared attentively for the officers and men, the sick and the wounded. The dead officers were buried with special ceremonies.

Perry scribbled a note to Harrison on the back of an envelope: "We have met the enemy and they are ours." He controlled Lake Erie.

Chapter 8

Epilogue to Perry's Victory

T HE epilogue to Perry's victory was in two parts. The first was the successful turn of the war in the West. The island region is a distinct section of Lake Erie. The archipelago lying between Marblehead and Cedar Point on the south and Point Pelee on the north cuts it off from the open lake to the east. From the top of Perry's monument on South Bass at Put-in-Bay you can see most of the area. Just below you is Gibraltar Island, sheltering the handsome bay; there, on the high rocky point of the island facing Malden, Perry kept a lookout to give warning when Barclay's fleet left its base. Far to the north the Ontario shore is an indistinct line on the horizon blending almost imperceptibly with the sky. If you happen to be up on the monument when clouds are flying, or when squalls blow over the lake, you may catch a sunburst over the ship channel between Detroit River Lighthouse and Point Pelee which will light up the coast and sharply define its contours. Middle Sister Island, near which the battle was fought, is a low green oasis on the lake surface. Catawba Point, Sandusky and Port Clinton are clearly outlined on the shore to the south. The battle arena was visible from these shores, and people gathered to glimpse the action, to see the smoke of the ships' guns, and to hear the booming of the cannon. They knew full well that the fate of the West hung on the outcome of that three-hour struggle for the control of Lake Erie.

On the south shore at Sandusky, General William Henry Harrison anxiously awaited the issue. He knew that his future course of action was being determined by Perry's ships and men. Harrison had taken command of the army in the West shortly before General Winchester marched into humiliation and defeat at the River Raisin. With all the Northwest lying open to attack, he had recruited and drilled an army to prevent an invasion of Ohio from Detroit and Malden. While Perry was constructing his fleet and training his sailors, Harrison had built Fort Meigs at the falls on the Maumee just above the old British Fort Miamis, and had centered there his military stores

85

for his proposed campaign against Detroit and Ontario. During the winter, while Dobbins and Brown were driving their men at Presque Isle, Harrison had organized a select corps to cross Lake Erie on the ice, surprise the garrison at Malden and burn the stores and the ships which were frozen in and immobilized there. If that plan had succeeded, Perry's battle would have been unnecessary. This special force did cross to the Bass Islands, but the hazardous Lake Erie weather interfered, the ice on the lake between Middle Sister and Malden broke up and the expedition was forced to return.

General Procter had tried to destroy Harrison's army and its stores when the spring thaw permitted the British fleet to sail. With their British soldiers and Indian warriors, probably 2,500 in number, the general and Tecumseh marched round the head of Lake Erie and sailed across from Amherstburg to reduce Fort Meigs. General Harrison and his men withstood their bombardment and siege from April 28 to May 9, and finally sent them back in despondency and failure. Procter tried again in July and again failed. He then diverted his expedition against the weakly held Fort Stephenson which Harrison had erected on the present site of Fremont, Ohio. He was held off, defeated and turned back by a twenty-one-year-old Kentucky officer, Major George Croghan, and a handful of men in one of the most amazing military exploits of the American forces in the entire war. Young Croghan had only one cannon with which to defend the vulnerable post. Harrison was so certain that it could not be held that he sent an order to Croghan to abandon it, destroy his stores and hasten to the protection of Harrison's own headquarters at Fort Seneca, nine miles farther up the Sandusky River. But the couriers got lost on the way, and by the time they got the order to Croghan it was too late to carry it out. The British and Indians were already upon him. The intrepid officer chose to fight. He moved his one cannon from port to port, firing in different directions to conceal from the enemy his extreme weakness. The British laid down a heavy bombardment on the flimsy fort, and then attempted to take it by storm. Croghan moved his cannon into position facing the direction of their charge, loaded it with grape and fired pointblank into the advancing British regulars and their Indian allies. They recoiled, hesitated, then re-formed and charged again. Another blast from Croghan's cannon blew them back. Again they hesitated, then broke and fled. Procter once more accepted defeat, and withdrew to Malden; Croghan was lifted to fame, Congress gave him a gold medal and he was promoted to a lieutenant colonel.

These were some of the experiences fresh in Harrison's mind as he watched Perry's ships make sail out of Put-in-Bay to meet Barclay's fleet on that September 10. If Perry could dispose of British naval power on the lake, Harrison could move against Procter. He waited anxiously.

On the Ontario shore was another party of witnesses, perhaps even more concerned. As Barclay's fleet hoisted sail at dawn and stood out for what was certain to be a critical battle, the Indians, the troops, and the citizens of Amherstburg, with Procter and Tecumseh at their head, gathered on the Ontario shore of Lake Erie. Revolving through Procter's mind, no doubt, was the recollection of these past defeats in his attempts to dislodge Harrison from the south shore. He knew all too well that if Perry destroyed the British naval squadron, Detroit and Malden would lie open to attack, and that without the Lake Erie communication line he could not supply his men or withstand Harrison's certain invasion. For Harrison would have overwhelming man power and absolute command of the lake.

From the strand near Bar Point the squat and worried British general saw Barclay's ships sail out into Lake Erie toward the islands, saw the glistening sails of Perry's ships approach from the Bass Islands, saw them join issue, heard the cannon roar across the water and watched the smoke rise from the guns and the burning ships. The results of the action were not immediately discernible from the Ontario shore. But as the afternoon lengthened, the firing ceased and the ships sailed off toward Put-in-Bay instead of returning to Malden. Procter knew that the worst had befallen. His life line was cut; Lake Erie was controlled by the American Navy. Within a few hours, he knew, Harrison would be preparing to move against Detroit and Malden by land and by sea. He had but one thought: he must retreat as soon as possible.

Procter returned to Amherstburg and ordered the evacuation of Fort Malden. Chief Tecumseh sensed Procter's plans. He observed the stores being moved northward. He feared that the British General, in spite of all his solemn pledges, was about to abandon his

Indian allies. He was angry and perturbed because Procter had not taken him into his confidence. He demanded of Procter a declaration of his intentions. In the graphic and eloquent language so characteristic of the great Indians, he said:

"Father, listen! our fleet has gone out; we know they have fought; we have heard the great guns; but we know nothing of what has happened to our father with one arm. Our ships have gone one way, and we are much astonished to see our father tying up everything and preparing to run away the other without letting his red children know what his intentions are. You always told us to remain here and take care of our lands; it made our hearts glad to hear that was your wish. Our great father, the king, is the head, and you represent him. You always told us you would never draw your foot off British ground; but now, father, we see that you are drawing back, and we are sorry to see our father doing so without seeing the enemy. We must compare our father's conduct to a fat dog, that carries his tail on its back, and, when affrighted, drops it between its legs and runs off.

"Father, listen! the Americans have not yet defeated us by land; neither are we sure that they have done so by water; we, therefore, wish to remain here and fight our enemy, should they make their appearance. If they defeat us, we will then retreat with our father. . . .

"Father, you have got the arms and ammunition which our great father sent for his red children. If you have an idea of going away, give them to us, and you may go and welcome, for us. Our lives are in the hands of the Great Spirit. We are determined to defend our lands, and if it be his will we wish to leave our bones upon them."

General Procter did not share Tecumseh's desire to fight or to leave his bones on hallowed Indian ground. He loaded his stores and equipment on every available craft that would float, and sent them up the Detroit River, across Lake St. Clair and up the River Thames. What he could not carry away he burned. Then, on September 26, the corpulent general with the red face and bushy whiskers retreated in a cart overland toward Chatham with his troops. Tecumseh, disgusted and angry, withdrew along with him. The force at Detroit set fire to the fort, threw broken guns, cannon balls, rubbish and garbage into the well, damaged the town and joined Procter's evacuation.

In the meantime General Harrison was energetically disposing his forces for the invasion of Canada. The minute he received Perry's laconic scribble that he had taken Barclay's fleet, Harrison sent three vessels and all the boats he could spare up the Maumee River to Fort Meigs to load troops, cannon, gun carriages, ammunition, flints, and all the flour, biscuits and salt provisions that could be transported on these boats. He ordered General McArthur to join him at once, marching the men who could not be crowded into the ships. He summoned Governor Isaac Shelby of Kentucky with his militia, and they came to Port Clinton a few days later 3,500 strong. The Ohio Indians, sensing the turn of events, joined Harrison's force. Perry, having buried with honor the British and American dead, hurriedly repaired his ships to follow up his great victory. Within ten days the expedition was ready to attack Ontario. The land unit under Colonel R. M. Johnson marched round the head of the lake toward Detroit. "Remember the River Raisin!" was their battle cry. Harrison assembled the main body, numbering about 5,000 men, at Put-in-Bay, then crossed to tiny Middle Sister Island where they bivouacked while Perry in the *Ariel* scouted the region around Bar Point and the fort at Malden. Finding that Procter had already departed, General Harrison on September 27 moved his men in Perry's fleet of sixteen vessels and a vast flotilla of small boats across the fifteen miles of open water between Middle Sister and Bar Point. Without opposition he landed his forces and marched into Amherstburg. The fleet moved on up the river while Harrison's army continued up the coast to Sandwich, and Johnson's force kept pace on the American shore.

They reached Detroit at the end of September. Perry sent several of his ships in pursuit of Procter's boats across Lake St. Clair, but they had already entered the safety of the shallow Thames. Harrison pressed on in pursuit of Procter. He caught up with him near Chatham on the Thames, about sixty miles by modern highway east of Detroit, where Procter's Indians made a brief stand. Procter retreated a few more miles eastward to a favorable terrain where his flanks were protected by the river on one side and a swamp on the other. Here was fought the Battle of the Thames. The decisive action lasted about five minutes. General Harrison, Lewis Cass and Captain Perry looked on from the high bank of the river. The American force, led by cavalry, charged and broke the British line. Procter and his staff fled to waiting carriages and escaped to the east. Mighty Tecumseh lay slain on the battlefield. After darkening the victory with a raid on the harmless and defenseless Moravian settlement near the scene of the battle, seizing their food, pillaging their gardens, burning all the houses and figuratively sowing the earth with salt, the troops were withdrawn to Detroit and Amherstburg in the second week of October. Most of them were disbanded and sent back to their homes. A considerable garrison camped in the ravaged and starving town while the weary war was finished and closed in the theaters to the east.

The second part of the epilogue is more inspiring to record. The war was formally ended on December 24, 1814. Both sides saw how necessary it was to find a means for settling outstanding disputes and keeping the peace between such close neighbors and brothers. In this mood Britain and America softened their demands into a workable compromise. The Americans quieted their yearning for the rich arrowhead of Ontario; the British came no more with arms across the established border. Each recognized the folly as well as the provocation of maintaining forts and warships on the lake. A century of warfare was quite enough. It was time to make rules for peaceful development of the land and friendly use of the common waterway. The Rush-Bagot agreement of 1817 provided the necessary framework for co-operation and outlawed war and men-of-war on the lakes forever. The agreement has been kept for nearly a century and a half while so many treaties and agreements have been discarded and wars have been fought in other parts of the stricken world. And no man of either allegiance can watch the great freighters of both nations moving side by side through the narrow channels of the Detroit River, or drive his car across the Buffalo-Fort Erie International Bridge, the Ambassador Bridge, or pass through the Detroit-Windsor Tunnel without a lift of his heart at the thought of how two powerful peoples have found their way out of separation through armed conflict into union through peaceful commerce and co-operation.

Chapter 9

Talbot and the North Shore

THE War of 1812 left many scars. The British crossed over the Niagara River and burned Buffalo in 1813. The 500 citizens fled for their lives, but most of them returned after the war to the seared ruins to make a new beginning. A few miles west of Presque Isle the citizens took pride in showing where the British squadron, captured during the late war, was "sunk for preservation."

The Canadian settlers on the north shore of Lake Erie were also hard hit. Tilly Buttrick, Jr., that irrepressible wanderer from Westford, Massachusetts, had started for Detroit in the summer of 1812. He traveled to Buffalo in a "pleasure wagon" drawn by two horses. He took the Black Rock ferry to Fort Erie, expecting to go overland across Ontario to Detroit because the north-shore land route was only 300 miles while the south shore was 400 miles long and the roads were terrible. He got over to Canada just in time to see a messenger ride up to the door with the news of the declaration of war. He was immediately taken into custody. Across the river at Black Rock, Buttrick could see American sentries stopping Canadians who were trying to get back home. The Niagara River ferry ceased to run. He was held for seventeen days. He heard the cannon at Black Rock firing salutes on the Fourth of July. He saw the distressed pioneers, fleeing from the plunder of the Indians, come pouring in to the protection of the fort—men, women and children, on foot, on horseback, in wagons. Many of the men were immediately seized by the Army and pressed into military service, and their horses were commandeered. Even so, Buttrick observed, it was better than staying in the woods to be pillaged and murdered by the savages.

Buttrick was finally released and permitted to cross back over to the American shore, but he had to leave his horses and his property because the only ship available for transport had sailed away. He returned to the East. But he came back again after the war in 1818 and completed his journey across Ontario. His account is brief but sufficient to describe the effects of the war on that region. "On my

91

way back to Detroit, I was most sensibly struck with the devastation which had been made by the late war: beautiful farms, formerly in high cultivation, now laid waste; houses entirely evacuated or forsaken; provisions of all kinds very scarce; and where once peace and prosperity abounded, poverty and destruction now stalked the land."

The savages mentioned by Buttrick were not the only raiders. Duncan McArthur, one of the great men of Ohio, marched a company up the Thames River Valley on a plundering expedition. They burned houses and mills and carried off grain and livestock. They closed in on Lord Selkirk's Baldoon settlement, took his foodstuffs, and drove away his prize flock of Merino sheep which he had imported at great expense from England to improve the Ontario flocks. Colonel Campbell sailed 800 men in six schooners from Erie across the lake to the Long Point settlements in 1814. They ravaged Port Dover and Port Ryerse and burned twenty dwellings, three flour mills, three sawmills, three distilleries, twelve barns and various other buildings. The raid was in reprisal for the burning of Buffalo. The colonel was tried before a court of inquiry and censured for burning the dwellings; the mills, however, were considered military objectives. John Dixon led a mob of former residents of Long Point, ten Americans, an Englishman, an Irishman and a Canadian half-breed to the Ontario shore to capture Colonel Talbot. They failed to find the colonel, but they caught and killed Captain William Francis and burned his house over his body.

Raids of this sort were made doubly repugnant to the Canadians by the arrogant published desire and intention of many Americans to take over the rich lands on the north shore of Lake Erie. Buttrick did not exaggerate the devastation or the misery of our pioneer neighbors across the lake. Their grain was all gone, their mills were burned or in ruins and the good citizens were in desperate distress. Singleton Gardiner, one of these hard-pressed settlers at Port Talbot, wrote a pathetic letter to his brother in October 1816. He had crossed from Port Talbot to Buffalo in an open boat to get flour for his family. He had spent ten days navigating the 150 miles. "God only knows whether I will get home or not," he wrote, "for the lake is so dangerous at this season of the year. . . . It is a great undertaking, but I must either do it or my family suffer for want of bread. . . . Many persons here [Port Talbot], I believe, have not tasted bread for two months; for they do not have the grain, and if they had, they could not have it ground."[1]

Despite these harrowing setbacks, however, the north shore developed steadily. Its growth was not spectacular like that of the American shore. Every traveler to Old Ontario during the next thirty years remarked on the sharp contrast between the American and the Canadian sides of the border. Joseph Pickering crossed over into Canada at Black Rock in June 1825. He had been greatly annoyed by the Americans who, though civil and friendly, boasted of their prowess in the "late puny war," and assumed as a self-evident fact that they were superior to all others "in virtue, wisdom, valour, liberty, government, and every other excellence!" Annoyed though he was, he did admire their energy and enterprise and regretted the apathy of his own countrymen.

"On the United States' side large towns springing up; the numerous shipping, with piers to protect them in harbor, coaches rattling along the road, and trade evidenced by wagons, carts and horses, and people on foot, in various directions. On the Canadian side, although in the immediate vicinity, an older settlement, and apparently better land, there are only two or three stores, a tavern or two, a natural harbor without piers, but few vessels, and two temporary landing places."

Mrs. Jameson came to the east end of Lake Erie just a dozen years later.[2] Her impression was the same as Pickering's, except that American energy had still further heightened the contrast. The Yankees were running a steamboat from Buffalo down the Niagara River to Chippawa above the Falls, and they had built a railroad from Lewiston to Buffalo. Mrs. Jameson took the train, the engine "snorting, shrieking like fifty tortured animals." She was astounded to find that Buffalo, "about ten years old," had 20,000 inhabitants, long rows of magnificent brick and stone houses, and "the largest and most splendid hotel I have ever seen, except in Frankfort." Crowds of people were "buying, selling, talking, bawling; the Indians lounging by in their blankets, the men looking so dark, and

---

[1] Jesse Edgar Middleton and Fred Landon, "Talbot Lands After the War," *The Province of Ontario* (Toronto, 1927), I, 289.

[2] Mrs. [Anna] Jameson, *Winter Studies and Summer Rambles* (London, 1839), 2 vols.

indifferent, and lazy; the women so busy, care-worn, and eager; and the quantities of sturdy children, squalling, frisking among the feet of busy sailors."

She counted fifty vessels in the Buffalo harbor—sloops, schooners and steamboats. She saw the *Michigan* lying in the harbor, ready for a voyage to Chicago. She went aboard and marveled at the "magnificent" arrangements of this steamer, "one of the three great steamboats navigating the Upper Lakes, which are from five to seven hundred tons burthen, and there are forty smaller ones coasting Lake Erie, between Buffalo and Detroit, besides schooners." All this activity was in marked contrast to the sleepy Canadian shore "where a lethargic spell seems to bind up the energies of the people." And she noted sorrowfully and homiletically that *"we* have [in 1837] on this lake two little ill-constructed steamers, which go puffing up and down like two little teakettles, in proportion to the gigantic American boats; and unfortunately, till our side of the lake is better peopled and cultivated, we have no want of them."

We should be in no hurry to conclude from these reports that Old Ontario was fast in apathetic slumber. Far from it. There was never to be a Buffalo, a Cleveland or a Detroit on the north shore, of course, but there was growth. Some of this growth was along the Niagara River. The Canadians did build the Welland Canal up the Niagara escarpment and later developed Port Colborne far enough from the American border to insure safety. Some of the activity was farther round the shore at Long Point. There was timber on the land, there was fair soil for tilling, the beach made a usable road and the lake was a seaway. There was also bog-iron ore in the region, and enough hardwood to make charcoal to smelt it. Samuel Mason came here in 1818 and set up the first successful iron smelter and foundry in Upper Canada. The Van Norman family later bought him out. Joseph Van Norman set up a furnace near present Normandale, seven miles west around the lake from Port Dover. Iron ore, dug from the bogs, was hauled to the furnace in wagons, just as furnacemen were doing in Pennsylvania, Ohio and Kentucky. It was smelted and cast into articles and implements for the pioneers of Ontario. Van Norman shipped stoves, plows, pots and kettles by boat on the lake to the little settlements all the way from Fort Erie to Amherstburg, some to Buffalo, and some to Detroit and Chicago.

THE RECONDITIONED "MICHIGAN" ("WOLVERINE") C. 1913,
AND PERRY'S MONUMENT AT PRESQUE ISLE

ANTHONY WAYNE'S FIRST BURIAL PLACE AT FORT ERIE

A WELCH VINEYARD AT HARVEST TIME

A WINE PRESS IN AN ISLAND WINERY

He made a small fortune. The ore ran out in 1847, and the furnace was closed. Pickering bought two cast-iron plows, cast at Long Point Furnace, at two pounds each; and he reported in the spring of 1826: "A new iron furnace, and forge, establishing on Otter Creek, forty miles below here, where good hands get thirteen dollars wages per month and board now, and fifteen dollars offered for the summer, payable chiefly in their casting ware."

But the settlers moving into Ontario were not seeking bog ore; they wanted land. And the man who controlled the best of it along Lake Erie was Colonel Talbot. His seat was about six miles up the lake from Port Stanley—about sixty-five miles from Long Point and almost exactly halfway between Buffalo and Detroit, or, as the colonel would have said, between Fort Erie and Amherstburg. It was the center of the most extensive and famous settlement along the lake in the years following the war, and Talbot was lord and master of both. He was the man whom Pickering was journeying west to see, for Pickering, like thousands of other men of the time, wanted a plot of ground, and Talbot had absolute authority to grant or withhold.

His journey is worth following. Pickering worked westward round the lake from Fort Erie. It was July 4 and people were putting up hay. He passed cherry orchards loaded with red fruit; and every passer-by was expected to take all he could eat without let or hindrance. He saw currants and wild gooseberries thick near the woods, and grapevines heavy with clusters, but not yet ripe. He came upon dead fish of up to twenty pounds' weight lying along the beach where they had been cast up by high seas and dashed against the rocks on the beach. He saw a shell-back duck with thirty-five young ones feeding on the fishes. A cool breeze came over the lake, and he could hear the Americans firing guns and cannon to celebrate their independence.

Pickering found some comfort in being on the Canadian side of Lake Erie. The walking was good along the sandy beach. He saw women doing the family wash on the shore. In dry seasons their husbands yoked up the oxen and hauled a washing tub and pot on a sled down to the soft lake water. He noted the many Dutch, "sturdy, old fashioned, and honest," most of them from the States, who had settled on this northeastern shore. Their houses were miserable. One

Dutchman had paid $800 for his farm by selling muskrat skins from the marshes at 2*s*. 3*d*. per skin. The high sandy shore line was covered with pines and junipers; much of the land was swamp; but behind the swamps was rich black soil on limestone. Near Grand River he saw some old vessels of war sunk and rotting at the naval depot. Cannon and cannon balls were still strewn on the beach. Gull Island near by was a refuge for ships, "one of the few places on this lake shipping can run into in safety for anchorage in bad weather."

He passed on through indifferent farming sections to the Long Point settlements. Everybody was busy cradling grain and getting in the harvest. A good hand got 3*s*. 4*d*. and board per day. There were quantities of sunflowers for poultry food and oil. Several miles beyond Long Point he came to "Talbot-Street," a clearing through the woods back of the lake that ran for miles through the section which Colonel Talbot was developing.

The eastern end of this wilderness road was sandy and barren. "Three parts of the houses are empty, the inhabitants having 'cleared out' for better land." He walked on through the new and thriving village of St. Thomas on Kettle Creek, and then down through the woods to Colonel Talbot's house a little way beyond. It was, says Pickering, "situated on the banks of the lake, upward of one hundred feet high, and commands a fine view of the banks and shore of Lake Erie for twenty miles down, and also the Colonel's Creek, winding through the 'flats' below."

The colonel was not at home, but he soon returned and gave Pickering a list of strip farms or lots to look at, thirty miles farther up the lake. That is all the practical-minded emigrant has to say about the lord of this region. He was more interested in the physical details of the farm and the opportunities in the settlement.

But the shrewd, volatile, observing Mrs. Jameson, who arrived a decade later, brightens up the picture with a few feminine strokes of her pen. She had come with almost incredible hardship overland to Port Talbot from Hamilton. She stopped at Brantford, named in honor of Chief Brant (she spells it Brandt) of the Six Nations who, as we have seen, were allies of the British against the Colonists in the Revolutionary War. Seven or eight thousand of them had settled here in 1783, but they had dwindled to 2,500 by 1837. Their best lands had "lately been purchased back from them by the British

Government and settled by thriving English farmers." The town was just above the head of navigation on the Grand River.

From Brantford, Mrs. Jameson traveled by wagon to London and then down to Port Talbot. She heard all sorts of rumor, legend and gossip about the great man which heightened her interest as she approached his estate. The Indians styled him the "Big Chief." Others called him the hermit-lord of the forest, absolute sovereign of a settlement so immense that it was known as "the Talbot country." She liked his road over which she drove in the late evening from his namesake town of St. Thomas. It was, she said, "the finest in the province." She had the right to speak, for she had been passing over roads where the wreckage of wagons, of wheels and axletrees, was strewn around bottomless pits of mud and quagmire, where her driver often had to stop, cut branches from trees and fill up the bogs to provide a bottom on which they could cross. Night fell before she drove up to the colonel's door. Lights were gleaming from the windows of his house on the Lake Erie shore.

To her great surprise the old curmudgeon himself emerged to welcome her; he was "not only cordial, but courtly." He took her by the arm, escorted her to a chair by a long wooden table "in front of a capacious chimney," and then, seeing that his guest was worn out, "with courteous solicitude, he ushered me himself to the door of a comfortable, well furnished bedroom, where a fire blazed cheerfully, where female hands had evidently presided to arrange my toilet, and where female aid awaited me—so much had the good Colonel been calumniated!"

The next morning she had a look at the house and grounds and the lake. The colonel had built his house, "like the eagle his eyry, on a bold high cliff overhanging the lake." On the east there was "a precipitous descent into a wild woody ravine, along the bottom of which winds a gentle stream, till it steals into the lake: this stream is in winter a raging torrent." The château itself, in this wild setting, was most impressive.

"It is a long wooden building, chiefly of rough logs, with a covered porch running along the south side. Here I found suspended, among sundry implements of husbandry, one of those ferocious animals of the feline kind, called here the cat-a-mountain, and by some the American tiger, or panther, which it more resembles. This one, which had been killed in its attack on the fold or poultry-yard, was at least four feet in length, and glared on me from the rafters above, ghastly and horrible. The interior of the house contains several comfortable lodging-rooms; and one really handsome one, the dining room. There is a large kitchen with a tremendously hospitable chimney, and underground are cellars for storing wine, milk and provisions. Around the house stands a vast variety of out-buildings, of all imaginable shapes and sizes, and disposed without the slightest regard to order or symmetry. One of these is the very log-hut which the Colonel erected for shelter when he first 'sat down in the bush,' four-and-thirty years ago, and which he is naturally unwilling to remove. Many of these outbuildings are to shelter the geese and poultry, of which he rears an innumerable quantity. Beyond these is the cliff, looking over the wide blue lake, on which I have counted six schooners at a time with their white sails; on the left is Port Stanley. Behind the house lies an open tract of land, prettily broken and varied, where large flocks of sheep and cattle were feeding— the whole enclosed by beautiful and luxuriant woods, through which runs the little creek or river abovementioned."

Behind this house was an orchard of sixteen acres bearing apples, pears, plums and cherries in abundance; and near by was a rose garden that delighted Mrs. Jameson "beyond everything else." The colonel took her to see it. It covered more than two acres, it was neatly laid out and enclosed, and the roses, which he had imported from England, were in bloom. He gathered some of the most beautiful buds and presented them to his guest. They then sat down on "a pretty seat under a tree, where he told me he often came to meditate."

But before we consider him personally and his meditation, we must have one more look at the place. And for this we return to Pickering. He had walked on westward to look at the land along the lake, but finding no lot to his liking, he came back to Talbot's estate and got a job as "foreman or overseer," during the seasons of 1825-1826. Talbot put his 150 sheep in a pen at night to preserve them from the wolves. He had twenty-five milch cows, four yoke of oxen "besides one yoke killed this fall," fifty or sixty head of young cattle which ran in the woods, twenty-three weanling calves, four horses "of the nag kind, with long uncut tails," four sows with pigs which got their living on nuts in the woods, and forty-two fattened hogs. Flocks of wild turkeys came into the farmyard where the men shot them. Great clouds of pigeons flew over; people caught them in nets, taking several hundred a day, and salted them down in barrels. The garden itself, which so enraptured Mrs. Jameson, failed to impress Pickering, though perhaps it had been improved in the ten years that had passed between their visits. Pickering only said that it was exceptional for America, "yet not like a good common one in England."

The farming methods were crude but energetic. Pickering kept a diary on the daily and seasonal round of activity: planting, cultivating, harvesting. He thought there was room for much improvement. He took Talbot's horses over to St. Thomas to be shod; one shoeing lasted the year "as the roads do not wear them out quick." He also went to the village for the whisky. Distillery grain was trodden out by horses and oxen, but flour grain was flailed by hand. In May 1826, Talbot sent "200 bushels of wheat to the 'still' to have seven quarts of whisky per bushel for it." In the spring they made maple sugar. They kept a seine in the lake to supply the household with fish. In April Pickering caught "nine maskinonge from five to thirty pounds each." He listened to the ice breaking up on the lake in the spring; "the noise caused by its breaking, when driven by a south wind on the shore, is like the various noises arising from the rattling of carriages, and the bustle of a large town on approaching it." He noted how the mid-May winds blew off the land by day and off the lake by night, and he exclaimed over the "millions of flies (called May flies in England, but here June flies) along the lake shore, and to half a mile distance, smothering everything." On June 6 he watched some vessels sail up the lake "for the first time this season."

He noted also the pioneers who were coming here to seek land, and the nature and habits of those who were already settled. He was particularly impressed by "some smart lasses" who came into a tavern where he was stopping one evening. "Most of them took a *smoke* with the landlord and the landlady, passing the short black pipe from one to another! Disgusting. . . . A girl of eighteen or nineteen, smart and lively, but without stockings, came in for a pound of tobacco (some of the landlord's own raising) to learn to smoke, she said."

And the master of all this north-shore region and its settlers?

His gravestone in St. Peter's Churchyard, Tyrconnell, a few miles west of his old estate on Lake Erie, tells us only that he was FOUNDER OF THE TALBOT SETTLEMENT. That terse statement was meant, no doubt, in the grim manner of old tombstones to commemorate a full half-century of labor to build in the Ontario wilderness a thriving colony.

Thomas Talbot was the well-born son of the Talbots of Malahide, a family whose barony had passed from father to son for 600 years. In 1790, at the age of nineteen, he came to Canada as a lieutenant in the garrison regiment at Quebec. The following year he joined the staff of the lieutenant governor of Upper Canada, the great John Graves Simcoe, and he spent three years with Simcoe traveling about Old Ontario. He went as far west as Detroit in 1793, very carefully noting the lay and the quality of the land north of Lake Erie. He was much taken with the Kettle Creek region. Legend has it that when the party encamped here in the bush Talbot exclaimed to Simcoe, in standard eighteenth-century diction, "Here will I roost and will soon make the forests tremble under the wings of the flocks I will invite by my warblings around me."

But the French Revolution interfered, and the young lieutenant had six years of hard service to perform before he could contemplate 'roosting' or 'warbling' on the Lake Erie shore. He rose to lieutenant colonel, and then resigned and sold his commission in 1800 in order to return to Canada. His service entitled him to a grant of 5,000 acres of land. He exercised his right and in 1803 went back into the bush on Kettle Creek.

This undertaking seemed so wild and unusual that people speculated and gossiped about it for half a century. Why, they asked, should "a man of noble birth, high in the army, young and handsome, and eminently qualified to shine in society . . . voluntarily banish himself from all intercourse with the civilized world, and submit, not for a temporary frolic, but for long tedious years, to the most horrible privations of every kind . . . ?" Mrs. Jameson put that question to the eccentric gentleman in 1837 and got a courtly, facetious reply: " 'Charlevoix,' said he, 'was, I believe, the true cause of my coming to this place. You know he calls this the "Paradise of the Hurons." Now I was resolved to get to paradise by hook or by crook, and so I came here.'" But he was not like Shelley, Wordsworth, Blennerhassett and his other contemporary idealists hunting for a Rousseauistic democratic and natural paradise in the land of the noble savages. He was lordly-minded, feudal in social outlook, and he wanted to be master of his own domain. The north shore of this lake seemed to offer him that opportunity.

Talbot found no paradise. Hard, unremitting toil, loneliness and conflict were his lot. Mrs. Jameson waxed sentimental about his hardships. "For sixteen years," she wrote, "he saw scarce a human being, except the few boors and blacks employed in clearing and logging his land: he himself assumed the blanket-coat and axe, slept upon the bare earth, cooked three meals a day for twenty woodsmen, cleaned his own boots, washed his own linen, milked his cows, churned the butter, and made and baked the bread. . . . He has passed his life in worse than solitude."

Despite all the obstacles, however, he persevered for a full half-century in building up his vast settlement. His plan was as ingenious as it was autocratic. He filed at York (Toronto) for his 5,000 acres, but he went right over the heads of the colonial administrators to the court of George III to get more. This was a regular practice of Talbot. Who were these functioners at York that he, a Talbot of Malahide, should be a suppliant before them? He got what he wanted.

That was the right to select the people who could have land in his country, to place them wherever he pleased and to get a suitable reward for the transaction. So he picked out his own demesne on the high, fertile, wooded and well-drained land around Fort Talbot; and he got authority to divide his 5,000 acres into fifty-acre plots, and for each settler on one of these plots he was to have for himself 200 acres somewhere else in the district. Talbot interpreted this neat arrangement in his own way. He actually accumulated about 60,000 acres for himself, and he kept his settlers at a distance.

His colonial procedure was, in fact, quite singular. He never actually promoted settlement; he engaged no agents, and he offered no inducements. He sat in his eyrie and waited for people to come. A dozen or so Irish families from Pennsylvania had come in the years just preceding the War of 1812. They were ambitious and thrifty, and they brought cattle and grain and looms. These and other

Irish who came after the war were welcomed by Talbot. The settlement on the lake shore west of Port Talbot was known as "Little
Ireland." The Scots were likewise welcome. Highlanders came
after the war in large numbers from Argyllshire. To this day the
north shore of the lake is dotted with communities bearing good
Scotch names like Port Bruce, Wallacetown, New Glasgow, Tyrconnell, Fingal and Campbellton. Immigrants came almost daily to
his door high on his Lake Erie cliff, and he selected lots for them.
He had a map of his country, rather carefully prepared by the
great surveyor Mahlon Burwell. On this map he simply penciled in
the name of the chosen settler, and the settler moved onto the strip
and began to clear a few acres for farming. If he lived on his land,
built a road in front of his holding and paid his dues, Talbot in due
course gave him a certificate and he could apply for a patent. If he
"cleared out," Talbot merely erased his name, and if he sold to
someone else, he added the name of the newcomer.

This arbitrary method of selection or rejection, which seemed so
right to the aristocratic master, caused much difficulty. All sorts of
strange men came to his door. Mrs. Jameson noted them standing
about the house, "ragged, black-bearded, gaunt, travel-worn and toil-
worn emigrants, Irish, Scotch, and American, come to offer themselves as settlers. These he used to call his land-pirates; and curious,
and characteristic, and dramatic beyond description, were the scenes
which used to take place between this grand bashaw of the wilderness
and his hungry, importunate clients."

Legend has preserved some of these dramatic scenes. It tells that
the Scots pioneer Duncan Patterson asked for land in a good location and that Talbot refused. That dour and determined Scottish
pioneer grabbed the proud descendant of Malahide, threw him to the
ground and held him there until Talbot promised him the land he
wanted. To avoid such unpleasantness Talbot devised a new technique to deal with supplicants. He constructed a sliding window to
separate him from the client. His faithful lackey, Jeffrey Hunter,
would keep a lookout for the "land-pirates." When he saw one coming, he told the colonel and the colonel got behind his protecting
partition. The customer was placed on one side of the wall, then
up popped the stern visage of the Lord of the Talbot Country to
demand, "What do you want?" If the colonel decided that the

prospect was fit and worthy, he would assign him land somewhere in the district. The pioneer was expected to take what he was given. If the colonel did not like his looks, or think well of his prospects, or if he should argue with the Lord, Talbot, it is said, would bang the shutter close and have Jeffrey sick the dogs on the offender to drive him away. Nonetheless, earnest men kept coming on. By 1822 Talbot claimed that he had "at least twelve thousand souls" in his settlement. In 1826 he boasted of 20,000; and if his figures are correct, about 2,000 a year were streaming through his house onto his land. They formed, he said, "an uninterrupted communication between the eastern and western extremeties of Lake Erie, and the settlements to the northward."

They were not a community, however, with all the advantages of schools, churches and social outlet which a community might have enjoyed. They were scattered and isolated, and their life was primitive and circumscribed. The great lord wanted no democratic nonsense in his country. A reform group had the audacity to hold a meeting in his town of St. Thomas, the town to which he went once a year to receive homage and accept a bouquet in his honor. He ordered his men to break up this opposition meeting, and he exulted when they "routed the rascals at all points, and drove them out of the village like sheep, numbers with broken heads, leaving their hats behind them, the glorious work of old Colonel Hickory." But he did understand the importance of a road, and he saw to it that every settler did his part. His plan of compulsory road building made possible the famous "Talbot-Street" which we have already glimpsed. Every traveler commented enthusiastically on the Talbot road. It ran for more than fifty miles through this wilderness about six miles north of the lake shore.

Over that road came in time the tremendous influx of settlers from the Old World who were determined to build a new one. And not even the aging eccentric of Port Talbot could impose his wishes upon them or hold them down indefinitely. He reaped the reward of his own despotism and contempt for his inferiors. He summed up his fifty years in Old Ontario in a pregnant sentence to Mrs. Jameson, possibly while they sat on the bench under a tree in his rose garden: "I would not, if any one was to offer me the universe, go through again the horrors I have undergone in forming this settlement."

Chapter 10

South Shore and *Walk-in-the-Water*

THE long era of peace and prosperous commerce got under way rather promptly after the interruption of the War of 1812. Lake Erie, with Buffalo at its foot and Detroit at its head, became the center of activity on the Great Lakes. Part of the activity was ships and shipping, stimulated by the westward movement of immigrants, by the opening up of the land in Ohio and Michigan and by the growth of the fur trade. Most of this trade was now diverted from the Nipissing-Ottawa route to the Lower Lakes and the St. Lawrence. Astor's company set up headquarters at Mackinac, with a branch office at Detroit and with posts scattered all over the Great Lakes region. The trade required a large quantity of shipping, for the western posts were not self-supporting. Ships had to carry flour and rum and clothing to them from the East, and they had to bring up all the bulky articles such as hatchets, axes, knives, traps, guns, pots and blankets for barter with the Indians. So they had a two-way load: peltry coming down, provisions going back. And though the shores of Lake Erie were only a minor trapping region in this era, the lake was then, as now, the arterial waterway between the East and the West.

There was also a rapidly expanding local trade on Lake Erie as the settlers continued to arrive, to hew out the forests and plant farms, homes and villages along the lake shore. There were the little settlements on the Sandusky River and Bay, for example. Our peripatetic friend Tilly Buttrick, Jr., came there in 1817, having journeyed up from the Ohio River. As he crossed the ridge between the river and the lake he noted herds of Kentucky cattle driven up there to graze and wax fat on the six-foot-high grass on the open savannas. At Venice, three miles west of Sandusky (now a region of lagoons overgrown with swamp grass and inhabited by fishermen), he found a community of some twenty to thirty log houses, two large frame stores, two wharves and some very sickly inhabitants. Fair-sized vessels were already coming up here, six miles

104

from the bay, to lay down supplies and take on produce from the farms up the little river. Incidentally, he was there when President Monroe passed through on his inspection trip to the West that took him all the way to Detroit.

Buttrick was back in April 1819 for a stay of some months at the near-by community of Portland, now Sandusky, on the bay. He found it "a pleasant village" containing about twenty-five houses, three large stores, and three wharves "of considerable length" where vessels in the lake service came in to discharge cargo. Its rate of growth is indicated by the report of another traveler, James Flint, who passed through this same town in October 1820. He found thirty houses, four warehouses, four wharves, and a ten-and-a-half-ton ship that had been built in Connecticut, hauled over the portages on the Mohawk, launched on Lake Erie, and was now engaged in the salt trade out of Sandusky. He heard people talking about the proposed canal system that would soon open up the country with waterways to New York and New Orleans. This keen-eyed observer also saw a portent for the future in the womanhood of this new westland. Some of them, he said, were elegant. "I have often seen among the inhabitants of the log-houses of America, females with dresses composed of the muslin of Britain, the silks of India, and the crapes of China."

The ports in the Western Reserve and eastward were increasingly busy and prosperous after the war. Most of them had their own shipyards and their village schooners. Huron's *Huron,* Vermilion's *Ranger,* Lorain's *Dread,* Painesville's *Widow's Son,* Ashtabula's *Zephyr,* Conneaut's *Salem Packet,* Erie's *Erie Packet,* Dunkirk's *Dunkirk,* Silver Creek's *Fayette Packet,* Cattaraugus' *Fire Fly*—all these small vessels spread their white sails on Lake Erie before 1820 and carried passengers, pork, butter, whisky and salt from one port to another: up to Detroit or down to Buffalo and the markets of the East.

The optimistic Moses Cleaveland had declared with pride that he had laid out a town on the bank of Lake Erie "which was called by my name, and I believe the child is now born that may live to see that place as large as Old Windham." His city outgrew Old Windham soon enough for a Connecticut child to go there as a young man after the War of 1812 and see it rise to a place of dominance in

the Reserve. The town had four schooners of its own registry—
Neptune, American Eagle, Fairplay and *Aurora*—and was agitating
for a canal to the Ohio River in 1818. Boats to take General Harrison's troops to Detroit for the Battle of the Thames were built at
thriving Painesville. Erie was a small but an important port of call
and outlet to Pittsburgh from the lake.

Buffalo was beginning to thrive as a beachhead for traffic from
New York. James Flint, one of the many indefatigable and journal-
keeping travelers of the period, also foresaw its future when he visited
it in 1820. He saw the coaches coming and going from Albany and
New York, and observed that "when the great canal between Hudson River and New York is completed, Buffalo must become a place
of considerable importance."

Detroit was already important though the war had damaged the
city. It had burned down in 1805, but that was not entirely a misfortune. The Americans had rebuilt it with neater houses over a
better city plan. For some years settlers tended to avoid it on the
strength of Surveyor General Tiffin's mysterious report that the land
adjoining the town was not suitable for farming—a report in as-
tounding conflict with Cadillac's enthusiastic prospectus. The able
work of Governor Cass, that great statesman of Detroit, Michigan
and the Northwest Territory, soon corrected this error. Cass made
Detroit his capital, and after 1818 a steady stream of people came in
from the East through Buffalo and up from the Ohio Valley. It, too,
was ready for the postwar expansion.

Ships, and not flatboats or bateaux, were especially important to
Lake Erie. As we have seen, the Ohio River was the first highway
and population center of the West. It was freed from the Indian
menace and it was removed from the wars that raged round the international borders of Lake Erie. Perhaps even more significant was
the natural propulsive power of the river itself. Its two-or-three-
miles-an-hour current carried downstream with a minimum of effort
anything that would float. Almost any enterprising farmer could
build a barge or flatboat, load it with produce and engage the river
to carry it down to market at Cincinnati or New Orleans. Immigrants could buy a skiff at Pittsburgh and float with the stream to
their destination. And there were no sudden, death-dealing storms.

Rowing and paddling on Lake Erie were toilsome and strenuous and the storms were devastating. Tilly Buttrick, Jr., found out all about that, too. He boarded a small sail-and-row boat at Sandusky Bay in 1817 to make the short trip up to Detroit. They sailed at noon with a fair wind, and by sunset had made about twenty miles, keeping well inshore. They had just taken shelter for the night at a creek mouth when one of Erie's violent, unannounced storms, with high winds and torrential rain, struck them. All night and most of the next day the storm raged while the little party of four men, one woman and three children huddled disconsolate and hungry on the shore. The lake "appeared more like the Atlantic than like an inland navigation, the waves running so high that it was impossible for us to venture out." They got off toward evening. There was no wind, and they rowed all night. At daybreak they sighted Malden six miles ahead. They got food there at the British settlement. Then they rowed from ten in the morning until two o'clock the following morning up the eighteen miles of river to Detroit, making a little more than a mile an hour against the current.

Obviously Erie was not a lake for rowboats. It needed seaworthy sails and the new steam engines to drive ships across her alternately still and storm-tossed waters. The *Walk-in-the-Water* was the first attempt to meet that need on Lake Erie. She was built in 1818 at Black Rock in the Niagara River for the Lake Erie Steamboat Company by the New York naval architect, Noah Brown, and his imported company of thirty ship carpenters. She was a trim, schooner-rigged, two-master with two giant, awkward-looking paddle wheels port and starboard amidships, and an incongruous smokestack forward. It is something of a question whether the sails were to augment the steam engine, or whether the steam was auxiliary to the sails. At any rate her schooner rig and her square foresail gave her a skimming speed before a good wind, and her engines failed to save her in her last big Erie storm.

Her maiden voyage was a sensation around Lake Erie. She was, indeed, an elegant ship. She carried on her taffrail a row of heavy carved work brightly painted in white, green and gold. Her figurehead was a bust of Commodore Oliver Hazard Perry. In good weather she carried a smart awning over the main and quarter-deck. She had no upper deck, but her quarter-deck was five feet above the main deck, and a companion door opened into the gentlemen's cabin. The mainmast ran down through this cabin, and was decorated with mirrors. Folding doors separated the gentlemen from the ladies' cabin aft. This cabin was lighted by six stern windows and a skylight. The below-deck space was too shallow to accommodate the boiler; about one-fourth of it extended above the main deck.

On Sunday, August 23, 1818, this fine ship was towed up the Niagara from Black Rock, with her engines running, by sixteen or twenty yoke of oxen.[1] She could not put in at the Buffalo wharf because her eight-and-a-half-foot hold drew too much water for the shallow harbor. She stood outside at anchor and was tended by small boats. She took on sacks of mail and twenty-nine passengers for this first voyage, at a fare of $15 to Cleveland and $24 from Buffalo to Detroit. These fares were soon reduced to $10 and $15. Among the passengers were the Earl of Selkirk and Lady Selkirk, who were developing their estate and colony in Old Ontario. On August 23, 1818, with Job Fish as her master, she steamed westward, making leisurely stops outside the harbors at Dunkirk, Erie, Cleveland and Sandusky to discharge passengers by lighter and to take on firewood for her boilers. Two days later, at nightfall, she triumphantly reached Fighting Island in the Detroit River. She lay there overnight so that she could be properly welcomed to Detroit in daylight. She was met at the island by the mayor, his official family, and distinguished citizens. Then she steamed up the river lined with spectators, and with great ceremony came alongside the new wharf as her safe arrival was hailed by the firing of a gun. The wharf was jammed with welcoming citizens who looked on admiringly while Job Fish, megaphone in hand, stood on the fifteen-foot paddle box and directed the landing. Her voyage was a great success.

For three years she sailed on schedule back and forth across the lake, making money for her owners and carrying passengers speedily to the West. She made a few voyages also with United States troops and excursionists to Mackinac Island, and one voyage to Green Bay. James Flint took passage on her from Sandusky to Buffalo in October 1820, just a year almost to the day before she was lost in a storm

---

[1] Accounts vary. Mary A. W. Palmer, a passenger on this first trip as well as on the last, says sixteen. (*Publications Buffalo Historical Society,* V, 319.)

that struck her off Point Abino. He left a graphic description of his trip.

"On the 14th I went on board the American steam-boat *Walk-in-the-Water,* a fine vessel of 330 tons burden, with two masts, and rigged, for taking advantage of the winds in the manner of sea-craft. The interior of this vessel is elegant, and the entertainment is luxurious. There were twelve cabin passengers of genteel and polite manners, and about an equal number of persons in the steerage; the whole indicating a degree of intercourse and refinement which I did not expect to see on Lake Erie.

"During the afternoon, and a part of the night, we experienced the most severe gale our mariners had felt on the lake. The swell rose to a great height, and occasionally immersed one of the wheels deeply, while the other was almost entirely out of the water, causing the vessel to heave and flounce very disagreeably. Most of the passengers were affected by the same kind of sickness, similar to that which prevails at sea . . . the water appeared to be green, showing that its depth is considerable. . . . Altogether, the lake presents much of the phenomena of the ocean."

On the last day of October 1821 the *Walk-in-the-Water* sailed as usual from Buffalo in the late afternoon and with a good list of passengers aboard. The weather was dirty but not formidable. A storm came on and quickly increased to a gale. The big paddle wheels forced the ship on against the wind, but the seas rolled up angrily as evening fell. She was off Point Abino, a few miles from Buffalo, when the buffeting grew too severe for her light timbers to withstand. She lost headway and shipped water. The night was dark and the rain violent. The primitive boiler could not supply enough steam to run both the engine and the pumps at the same time.

Captain Rogers tried to turn around and head back to Buffalo. The storm whipped him off course and he lost his bearing. He dropped three anchors, but these only pulled his ship apart and let in more water. At four o'clock in the morning he called all passengers and told them he was about to run onshore. He then slipped the chain cable, cut the two ropes to the other anchors, and let his ship go with the gale. As she hit the beach on a swell the sound of breaking china and glass could be heard above the surf. Another swell fixed her in the sand not far from the mouth of Buffalo Creek. A sailor got ashore with a hawser which he secured from the ship to a tree. The passengers were then removed in the ship's boats. All were saved, but the ship, except for her engine, was a total loss. The engine was salvaged and used again in the *Superior*, which was soon running over the route inaugurated by the *Walk-in-the-Water*.[2]

Mrs. Thomas Palmer of Detroit, one of the passengers aboard the *Walk-in-the-Water* on that nerve-racking night, visited the wreck a few days later. She said that it lay broadside on, and that she "could almost walk around it dry shod, the sand had been deposited around it to such an extent. The oakum had worked out of the seams in the deck for yards, and the panel-work had become disjointed in many places." It was a pitiful ending for the first proud sailing steamer on the lake, but she was only one in a long list of ships that failed to survive the hazards of Lake Erie, as we shall have occasion to see.

---

[2] The main cylinder of that engine was still in use in 1865 as a blowing cylinder in Shepard & Company's steam-engine works in Buffalo. (*Pub. Buf. Hist. Soc.*, V, 318.)

Chapter 11

Canals Through the Barriers

ALL this tentative progress pointed toward two salient facts: Lake Erie, with all its potentialities as a seaway, was landlocked in her basin behind the Niagara escarpment on the east; and it was cut off from the Ohio River on the south by the ridge that formed the rim of her bowl. These barriers would have to be broken through before commerce could flow in and out in sufficient volume and at low enough cost to bring prosperity to the region.

Consider what it meant to get a load of goods from New York City to the hold of a vessel on Lake Erie in 1820. The goods were boated up the Hudson River to the Mohawk; they were then transshipped up the Mohawk in bateaux or Durham boats, taken through the Utica and Rome canal, then down Wood Creek, over Lake Oneida, down the Oneida River, down the Seneca and the Oswego and around the Oswego Falls to Lake Ontario. Then they were hauled in boats up the Ontario shore to Lewiston, unloaded, portaged with teams around Niagara Falls, again loaded into boats and taken up to Black Rock and there stowed into the hold of a waiting lake ship. Finally the ship was towed up the Niagara into Lake Erie for her voyage westward with the much-handled goods. A portion of the traffic came on up the Mohawk Valley in wide-tired wagons. It was slow and costly transportation. Ships often lay for days in the Buffalo or Black Rock harbors waiting for enough goods to arrive from the East to complete a profitable cargo. Impatient captains would meet the stagecoaches to inquire whether the driver had passed any of these wagon trains with his cargo.

In the 1820's the only possible solution for this impasse was a system of canals that would link Lake Erie with Lake Ontario and with New York City and New Orleans. Timid and unimaginative men called the proposals wild and fantastic dreams. But men like Clinton of New York looked beyond the obstacles to the reality. The geography of the region made it relatively easy to build canals. Even an ordinary layman traveler like James Flint could see the pos-

111

sibility. In the summer of 1820 he was traveling toward Lake Erie along the trail that passed for a road north of Mansfield. This road, he observed, was crossing a ridge. He stopped to examine the terrain. The ridge was only sixty to eighty feet in breadth. It was, he estimated, eight feet higher than the plain spreading northward before him toward the lake, and six feet above the flat ground sloping away behind him to the south. Flint accurately deduced the fact that he was standing on the watershed divide between the lake and the Ohio River. He looked to east and west over the panorama. He saw that the ridge kept a level line paralleling the lake shore all the way, and he wrote down in his journal, "A doubt of this having been once the margin of the lake can scarcely be entertained." And he noted how well favored this terrain was for constructing a canal that would open up the interior of Ohio and connect Lake Erie with the Ohio and Mississippi Rivers. He poked a little good-natured fun at the Ohio Legislature, which refused to authorize the Ohio-Erie canals but sent memorials to Congress asking about the practicability of a canal between the Gulf of Mexico and the Pacific! The only question in Flint's mind was how enough water could be provided to service a canal on this height of land.

Agitation for canals began immediately after the War of 1812. Internal improvement was in the air. The troops who had struggled up the Mohawk to Niagara, Black Rock and Buffalo; the statesmen and businessmen who sensed the oncoming westward march of America; the Connecticut shipbuilders who hauled their vessels up the Mohawk Valley to float them on Lake Erie—almost everybody, in fact, saw that a system of canals heading into Lake Erie was the next step for the nation on its way to greatness. New York had already made a preliminary survey before the war. With that unfortunate interruption out of the way, Governor DeWitt Clinton pushed the project forward, and a new survey was made in 1816. Nature herself, and the age-old process by which the lakes themselves were formed, had predetermined the main route by cutting the Mohawk Valley. The plans were rapidly completed, and our liberty-loving forefathers chose hallowed July 4 as the day to begin so notable a construction. With fitting ground-breaking ceremony at Rome the work was begun in 1817.

The canal was speeded along in sections under many separate

contracts. The famous haul between Rome and Utica, dug by Irish muscle, was opened to traffic just two years later. By 1825 the entire ditch, 363 miles of waterway, was complete, with locks, bridges and towpaths. The advertisements proclaimed it "only 120 hours long," and New York assumed its title of the Empire State.

That year of 1825 was memorable in the growth of the nation, particularly in and around Lake Erie. The great canal-builder DeWitt Clinton was kept busy traveling and celebrating. On the Fourth of July, while the finishing touches were being placed on his New York canal, he went to Ohio to spade the first earth for the construction of the Ohio-Erie Canal. The Ohio Legislature had postponed the building of the Panama Canal in order to dig one across the state to Lake Erie from Portsmouth to Cleveland.

It had been urged into the project by the energetic and imaginative young Cleveland lawyer, Alfred Kelley, of whom we shall have more to say in a later chapter. He was a zealot for internal improvement. In 1810, when he was twenty years old, he had come out to Cleveland to grow up with the country and make his way. On his twenty-first birthday he was made prosecuting attorney at Cleveland, and when he was twenty-four he was sent to the Ohio House of Representatives, then meeting at Chillicothe. He was the youngest, but one of the ablest, members of that assembly. One of his colleagues wrote that "he was the master spirit, whether in or out of the Legislature, of our canal policy. He urged it as a necessary means of developing the resources of the State, and to the extent that he advocated and aided it, it was eminently a success." He knew that the Lake Erie port fortunate enough to become the terminus of the canal would have an overwhelming advantage over its rivals, but he was equally sure that Cleveland was the natural outlet. He worked to that end and he was powerful enough to achieve it. Thin-faced, wide-browed, short, and so compactly built that he looked like "a man carved out of a block of marble," he inspired confidence and enthusiasm wherever he went or spoke. Ohioans were convinced that so vast an undertaking as he proposed could not be completed within their lifetimes, but they adopted the statutes which he framed to guide and govern the work, they made him canal commissioner and they placed upon his shoulders the heavy burden of arranging the finances. He accepted full responsibility and pressed forward the project.

The surveys were made, co-operation of the Federal government was secured, and now on July 4, 1825, thanks to Alfred Kelley, the work was actually to begin. Governor Clinton accepted a flowery invitation to come to Newark, Ohio, for the occasion.

The opening was celebrated in the grand manner. Clinton with his party came down through the Western Reserve in carriages. He was met on the road by Governor Morrow of Ohio and a guard of honor. He was paraded around the spacious courthouse square in Newark where flags flew and the band played. Then the procession was formed for the seven-mile pilgrimage to Licking Summit on the canal route. A large body of cavalry, followed by companies of artillery and light infantry, led the way for Governors Clinton and Morrow, Senator Ewing, distinguished veterans of Mad Anthony Wayne's campaign, Kelley, the canal commissioners and other important citizens.

Eight thousand people gathered to witness the drama, and those near the flag-draped platform listened to the speeches by Senator Ewing and DeWitt Clinton. They were eloquent, polysyllabic and prolonged, but keenly aware of the meaning of the occasion. Senator Ewing stressed the smothered marketing situation. It was expensive to drive cattle over the mountains from the Ohio feeding grounds to the markets of the East. Feed was expensive on the way, and the cattle lost weight. New Orleans was a most unsatisfactory outlet port for the region. Farmers had to wait for the spring rains to raise the level of the rivers and streams of Ohio to float out their produce. The market was, therefore, flooded at certain seasons, and it languished at others. The great intercommunicating system now beginning would open the interior, join Lake Erie to the Ohio, and make New York available for western shipping.

The senator talked so long that Governor Clinton found it unnecessary to speak at length. But with deep emotion the guest of honor said:

"You will now have, not only the market of New Orleans and New York but of Philadelphia, Baltimore and Montreal. The canals of New York, in their connection with the Susquehanna and Lake Ontario, which must speedily be formed, will furnish almost all these vast accommodations."

The peroration was right in the spirit of the times. Clinton let his voice out to full volume and declared:

"This great work will also confirm your patriotism and make you proud of your country. Every man of Ohio will say, not in a tone of rodomontade, but in a spirit of temperate encomium: see what my country has done in her juvenile state! And if she has achieved this gigantic enterprise in infancy, what will she not effect in the maturity of her strength, when her population becomes exuberant and her whole territory in full cultivation."

As the two governors stepped down from the platform, each was handed a spade. They lifted some earth into a wheelbarrow and the construction of the canal was under way. Then the governors crossed over to the Miami River and repeated the ritual a few days later for the Miami-Erie canal that would link Cincinnati to Lake Erie at the Maumee Bay.

In the meantime the Erie Canal was made ready for opening. The village of Black Rock fought valiantly to become the western terminal of the waterway. It had the ferry to Canada, it had a shipyard and a fine harbor, and it had built a long new pier to protect vessels at its wharves. But it was nearly three miles down the fast current of the Niagara River and the job of towing ships up to the lake was difficult. Buffalo was a more favorable site for the union of the canal with the lake, but the basin was shallow. For ages Buffalo Creek had deposited silt and sand in the harbor until a rather formidable sand bar practically blocked the entrance to the basin. The Buffalo citizens, however, agreed to remedy this if the canal were brought to their port. They raised funds, went to work, dredged a channel to the lake, built a breakwater, and the canal was extended to the streets just below the city square. From that moment the greatness of Buffalo was assured, and in due time Black Rock became a Polish suburb of the towering, spreading city.

The much-traveled Governor Clinton, after performing the rituals in Ohio, returned to Buffalo for the gala opening of his own canal on October 26. Its pageantry surpassed anything of its kind yet attempted. The *Seneca Chief,* specially built of Lake Erie cedar, bore the governor and his party at the head of the procession. It was decorated with a painting of a canalboat leaving Buffalo Harbor and one of Governor Clinton in the attitude of Hercules after his labors were over. It was towed majestically by four gray horses down the canal toward Albany while the crowds cheered. Fifth in the pageant was *Noah's Ark,* bearing two Indian boys and various fish and live animals from the West. On November 4 the party reached New York Harbor where the governor, after the tradition of the Doges of Venice, poured some Erie water into the Atlantic. The enthusiasm of the day was expressed by a spectator: "Never before was there such a fleet collected and so superbly decorated; and it is very possible that a display so grand, so beautiful, and we may even add, sublime, will never again be witnessed."

The response of commerce was immediate. Men and goods began to move westward in ever-increasing quantity. Land values at Buffalo rose, new houses sprang up like mushrooms, hotels were crowded to overflowing and goods of all kinds piled up on her wharves and in her warehouses. For Buffalo was the gateway city on Lake Erie.

While Clinton's pageant was making its festive progress, with much drinking, banqueting and oratory, down the Mohawk and the Hudson, the plain hard work of ditch-digging was proceeding to the south of Cleveland. Nature had gone a long way toward simplifying the work. The southern shore of Lake Erie, as Flint (and many other people) had noticed, was once fifteen to thirty miles nearer the Ohio River than it is now. The melting edges of the old glaciers had dropped their earth, sand and rocks and piled up a ridge across western New York, the panhandle of Pennsylvania and the whole state of Ohio. It forms the narrow, sharply defined watershed between the lake and the river. At one point the roof of a barn is the dividing line, and a drop of water splitting on its ridgepole will go half to the river and half to the lake. Just north of Marion the separation is so slight that the headwaters actually meet in time of heavy rains and floods. At Akron and Bellefontaine the ridge is high, but in no place was it a formidable barrier to the canalbuilders.

The river systems dictated the general plan of the canals. The Ohio Indians had used them as easy highways through the forests from north to south. The Cuyahoga reaches from Cleveland up to Akron. A short portage over the Akron hill led to the Portage

Lakes at the head of the Muskingum River. The Maumee was also connected by a portage with the Miami, and the Sandusky with the Scioto. The highest point on these routes was the Akron summit, and it was only 499 feet above the level of the Ohio River. Only forty-nine rather easy locks, therefore, were needed to lift and lower the boats from Lake Erie into the Ohio 307 miles away, and there were several stretches of seven miles without locks. A few dams thrown across streams at strategic points dispelled Flint's worry by creating great reservoir lakes to feed the channel. Some freedom-wary Ohioans still "viewed with alarm" the prospect of "a menacing utility that not only defied nature but tended to centralize wealth and tyranny, and to strangle liberty." But most people cheered the enterprise. Rival villages even fought each other in pitched battles over the location of the canal. The fortunate ones prospered and land values soared. Those that were by-passed went into bankruptcy or languished until they were revived by the railroads and highways. The bidding for section contracts was heavy and furious. Over 6,000 applicants placed bids for contracts on the job south of Akron. Immigrants swarmed in, seeking work for cash wages. The fighting Irish from the Mohawk Valley moved west to dig the Ohio and Erie and Miami and Erie ditches. Farmers along the route hired out themselves, their teams, their women and even their children. Mosquitoes buzzed in clouds over the bogs, swamps and stagnant waters, mowing the workers down with "canal chills" and "canal fever." Thousands died and were buried in shallow graves along the canal.

Alfred Kelley was here, there and everywhere. His friend Judge Alfred Yaple wrote in his *Reminiscences of Alfred Kelley* that he "abandoned his profession, sacrificed his health by exposure to the wet and malaria of the valleys, and accomplished the work. And the work was well done." He took up quarters in a cabin along the route and personally inspected the construction. He discovered that a few dishonest contractors were felling trees on the embankments, covering them over with dirt and then charging for them at a good rate per cubic yard. Kelley would walk along the banks with a long iron rod and probe into the loose dirt to expose their fraud. On one of his tours he discovered a pile of brush jammed in the gates of one of the canal locks. He got the division inspector and demanded to know why the debris had not been removed. The inspector replied that he had not been able to get anybody to clear it away. With characteristic spirit Kelley plunged into the muck and water and cleared the lock. Then he said to the inspector, "My name is Alfred Kelley; some political influence secured your appointment to this position, but we shall have no further use for your services. I will send another man to fill your place immediately." And when, a few years later, the financial plight of Ohio and of the canal was desperate and on the verge of bankruptcy, Kelley raised funds in New York by pledging his personal word and honor and his private means as security.

So the ditch was dug. It was only forty feet wide at the top, twenty-six feet at the bottom, and four feet deep, but it met the pressing need for fast, cheap movement of men and goods from the interior. The section between Cleveland and Akron, or Portage Summit, as it was called, was rushed to completion in two years. It was only thirty-eight miles long, but it cut across the center of the Western Reserve, and it made Cleveland the outlet port for a rich hinterland. Cleveland staged a jubilant celebration of the opening that was a near rival of the New York pageant, on the same model and with the same décor. A fine canalboat had been built and named the *State of Ohio*. It was lavishly decorated with flags and drawn, not by four stylish grays like Clinton's, but more modestly by one handsome horse that walked along the soft earth towpath at a four-mile-an-hour pace. Governor Allen Trimble and Alfred Kelley, accompanied by the commissioners and a few distinguished guests, were aboard. They waved and bowed to the citizens gathered along the yellow banks of the ditch to see the phenomenon of a boat being lowered in a stone lock and to cheer the procession on to Cleveland. At the village of Boston they were joined by the *Allen Trimble*, crowded with passengers going down to the celebration. A few miles down the old Lake Erie beach, the *Pioneer* fell in behind these two boats.

This epoch-making caravan, symbol of the industry and high hopes of the young state, floated into the basin at Cleveland on July 3, 1827. It should have waited another day, but it did give the enthusiastic populace two holidays instead of one. Cleveland was gaily decorated. As the *State of Ohio* drew up to the wharf, cannons fired salutes and the people shouted and cheered. If the Erie steamers in the mouth of the Cuyahoga had had whistles, they would have blown a welcome to these little boats that were ready to trade cargoes with them at the Cleveland wharves.

The governor and his party disembarked and marched to "an arbor in the public square" of the village, as the Cleveland *Herald* reported, for speechmaking. That evening a banquet was held at the Belden Tavern. Everybody was there. They drank toasts and listened to more speeches by the governor and Alfred Kelley. They finished off the festival, as the *Herald* wrote, with a "splendid Ball in Belden's Assembly Room."

The rest of the canal was completed in 1833; the cost had been $4,695,000. The flow of passengers and produce began immediately. The lake-port cities put on another spurt of rapid growth. New color was added to life in the region with masters fighting for first place at the locks and wharves, with passengers on deck dodging low bridges by day and by night sleeping on shelves erected against the sides below, with the boats stopping at nine o'clock in the morning and at two in the afternoon to feed the horses and cook meals for the passengers. The volume of traffic was immense. Formerly it had cost $125 per ton to move freight from the East to the interior; the canals reduced this at once to $25, and the rate was steadily lowered.

Toledo, still a few clumps of houses on the Maumee and not yet distinguished by its old Spanish name, was brought to life by the canals farther west. The first section of the Miami Canal was dug, quite naturally, to serve the Queen City of Cincinnati. The canal did not reach the Maumee River until 1845. In the meantime the Lake Erie canal fever had swept on into Indiana. The Maumee River almost met the headwaters of the Wabash. Obviously a canal across Indiana would also link it directly with the lake at Toledo and with the Ohio at Evansville and give the languishing state easy access to its share of the opening markets. Indiana got ambitiously busy to join in the procession. She passed what she called the "Mammoth Internal Improvement Bill" calling for three canals, two railroads and miles of highway. The Congress granted lands to help with the revenue. Governor Noble signed the bill in 1836, and the most ambitious canal program yet undertaken was launched at Fort Wayne, where the St. Marys and St. Joseph Rivers join to form the northwestward-flowing Maumee. This important section of the Wabash and Erie Canal was completed from Lafayette to Toledo in 1843. It joined the Miami and Erie at Defiance and came into Toledo at Swan Creek. It reached Terre Haute in 1849 and Evansville in April 1853. That made a total length of 460 miles of canal—eighty in Ohio and 380 down and across Indiana.

It was getting a little late in the Century of Progress, however, for any more profitable canals. Transportation on them was cheap, but slow. Their fate was already sealed by the time the first boat reached Evansville. The first railroad cars almost beat the canalboat to the Ohio River. There was as much celebration at the dedication of the new union depot at Indianapolis as at Evansville that year of the opening of the canal. The canal as a whole never prospered. It almost bankrupted Indiana. But Toledo flourished. It became one of the great outlet and transshipping ports on the lake. Flour, grain, butter, pork and some lumber came pouring into Toledo for shipment. It promptly jumped in population from a few languishing villages into a town with a good name and 4,000 people in 1850. Five years later it had increased to nearly 12,000. Fine houses went up on the bluffs overlooking the river, and hotels, stores, a customhouse and a post office were erected. The town advertised that portions of Kentucky, Tennessee, Missouri, and even Iowa, as well as Ohio and Indiana, "find Toledo the cheapest and most expeditious lake-port for the interchange and transfer of their products and merchandise." And by the mid-fifties the 373-ton steamer *Arrow* and the 297-ton steamer *Dart* were making daily runs across Lake Erie to Detroit, just seventy miles away.

Still another canal linked and cross-linked Lake Erie with the Ohio. That was the 136-mile Erie Extension Canal from Erie to Beaver, a few miles below Pittsburgh. This canal was joined to the Ohio-Erie by the Cross-cut Beaver Canal, as it was known, from Akron, Ohio, to Newcastle, Pennsylvania—the branch over which young Garfield drove mules on the towpath from log cabin to White House.

In the meantime the Canadians had not been idle. They did not wish to see all the Lake Erie traffic drained off through American canals to American ports because of the Niagara Falls barrier. They had certain natural advantages on their side. The distance across the Niagara peninsula was short. Ice jams at Buffalo generally delayed the opening of navigation for three weeks after Ontario's Grand River was free for shipping. A canal that would by-pass Buffalo-Fort Erie and allow vessels to go directly to Montreal would be an advantage.

The Provincial Parliament authorized a survey of the route in 1821. Members of the Canadian committee visited and inspected the Erie Canal and consulted with New York's canal commissioners. The Welland Canal Company was formed in 1824, and in 1825—the wonder year of American canals—the work was begun. The first route selected for the canal was the easiest to construct. It left Lake Ontario at Port Dalhousie, followed Twelve Mile Creek up the Niagara escarpment through forty locks, and was connected by a channel across the divide to the Chippawa River which drained into the Niagara River above the Falls. Vessels were to be towed by oxen up the river to Lake Erie. A feeder canal brought water from the Grand River to the escarpment. Our friend Joseph Pickering walked out seven miles from Chippawa on July 13, 1827, to see the Deep Cut. "Several hundreds of people were excavating for the canal," he wrote; "hands are in request to get through as soon as possible; good wages are offered, and the work is not extreme by any means; 2 1. 15s. to 3 1. 15s. per month, and board, is given according to the abilities of the workman, and to those having horses and oxen more in proportion; work from sunrise to sunset; this is general in all kinds of work, both here and in the United States." He had heard so much about the magnitude of the canal which would admit schooners that he was disappointed "to find it but very little wider than the Grand Junction boat canal in England." It was, as a matter of fact, sixty feet wide at the top, forty feet at the bottom and seven feet deep, with locks 110 by twenty-two by eight feet. It was opened in November 1829, and two eighty-five-ton schooners, the Canadian *Jane and Anne* and the American *W. H. Boughton,* immediately locked through—the first ships to go directly into Lake Erie from Lake Ontario.

Four years later, as the Ohio-Erie was opened, the Welland Canal was completed between Port Robinson on the Chippawa River and Port Colborne on Lake Erie, thus eliminating the "horned breeze" on the Niagara River, and avoiding the delay of the ice jams at Fort Erie in the early spring. Since that time it has been regularly widened, deepened and improved, right on down to the 1930's when the big Welland Ship Canal was completed and opened to receive the largest lake freighters. It is now almost twenty-eight miles long, 200 feet wide at the bottom, and with only eight giant locks, 820 by eighty by thirty feet to lift or lower the ships over the once formidable barrier.

These six canals with their interconnections, together with the short rivers on the American side and the then navigable Grand and Thames Rivers in Ontario, made a spiderweb of outlets from Lake Erie and gave the lake direct connections with the world. The canals were soon supplanted by the railroads, but they served their purpose admirably in their day. And two of them, the Welland and the Erie Barge Canals, are still of vital importance to Lake Erie commerce.

Chapter 12

Steamers

A GROWING fleet of sailing ships and steamers went into service to handle the booming commerce on the lake. There was hardly a village at the mouths of the rivers on Lake Erie that did not hear the pounding of hammers and calking mallets and smell the drums of pitch and cordage of rope laid down on the docks for the new industry. Sloops, schooners, barques and brigantines brightened the blue-green water with their white sails, but the steamers with their thin plume of milky-colored wood smoke were the objects of attention. We shall look at them first.

Buffalo, Cleveland and Detroit on the American shore, Chippawa, Port Dover and Chatham in Ontario, began to slide steamers down the shipways. At least thirty steamers were built at Buffalo between the breakup of the *Walk-in-the-Water* and the launching of the *City of Buffalo* in 1857. Black Rock launched nine between *Walk-in-the-Water* in 1818 and the *Union* in 1843. Cleveland built the 250-ton *Enterprise* in 1826, the 1,136-ton *Empire* in 1844, the 1,106-ton *North Star* in 1854, and six others ranging from the 308-ton *Robert Fulton* to the 1,224-ton *Buckeye State*. Detroit built sixteen, from the 100-ton *General Brady* of 1832 to the 926-ton *Illinois* in 1854. Erie launched seven during the same period, Sandusky five, Chippawa three, Port Dover one, and Chatham eight small ones, from the 60-ton *Little Western* to the 450-ton *Ploughboy,* for service to Detroit and Sarnia. They all carried both passengers and freight.

Every steamer on the lakes has had its own individuality and its own saga. By the time the engine of *Walk-in-the-Water* was salvaged and transported back to the shipyard below Buffalo, the Lake Erie Steamboat Company had the *Superior* ready to receive it. This new vessel steamed out of Buffalo on the twenty-third of April 1822, on her maiden voyage. She was a sturdier ship than her predecessor, more spacious, more elegantly fitted and faster. For years she carried without mishap an ever-increasing number of new settlers for Ohio, Michigan and northern Illinois. Two seasons after her launching

123

she was joined out of the same shipyard by the *Henry Clay,* likewise especially fitted for the immigrant trade. Since it was the custom in those days for the immigrants to provide and serve their own meals, the owners built in shelves and set up stoves and tables forward in the steerage for their convenience. This arrangement kept the cost of passage down to a minimum.

Two other ships were soon added to the company's line—the *Niagara* and *William Penn;* and three rival steamers—the *Pioneer,* the *Chippewa* and the *Enterprise,* all named for legended earlier sailing ships—competed for the trade on Lake Erie. These fine fleets made daily runs from Buffalo to Detroit.

The *Superior* and *Henry Clay* had one historic adventure. When the Black Hawk War broke out in Illinois in 1832, Lewis Cass, then Secretary of War for President Jackson, ordered General Winfield Scott to the scene with soldiers from the East. The general—Old Fuss and Feathers to his detractors, the Great Pacificator to his admirers— brought 950 regular troops and some West Point officers out to Black Rock and Buffalo. There he chartered four steamships, the *Henry Clay* and the *Superior,* and also the *Sheldon Thompson* and *William Penn,* to transport his troops around the lakes to Chicago. He loaded the *Superior* and the *William Penn* with supplies and a few troops, and jammed the *Henry Clay* with three companies of artillery and two or three of infantry under Colonel Twiggs. The general and his staff and 220 men embarked on the *Sheldon Thompson*[1] and the squadron steamed out of Buffalo across Lake Erie in early July 1832.

But an enemy far more potent than Black Hawk's warriors had also come aboard unseen. For 1832 was the black year of the cholera scourge on Lake Erie. It had leaped out of its breeding ground in Hindustan, had raced through Moscow and St. Petersburg, had crossed into Hungary and Germany and had ravaged Paris and London, leaving 200,000 corpses in its wake. At Quebec in June 1832 germ-carrying rats ran down the ropes of a ship just in from Europe, and scattered the plague on the wharf and through the Lower Town. It spread like a forest fire up the St. Lawrence to the lake cities. It was devastating Buffalo when General Scott mustered his soldiers. They picked it up and carried it aboard the troopships. As they

---

[1] Built at Huron, Ohio, at a cost of $16,000.

steamed up the lake toward Detroit, the epidemic struck and spread through the *Sheldon Thompson* and the *Henry Clay*. Soldiers sickened and died, and the steamers became mad and stricken plague ships. Panic hit them. General Scott wrote that "the only surgeon on board, in a panic, gulped down half a bottle of wine; went to bed, sick, and ought to have died."

General Scott sailed on from Detroit to Chicago aboard the *Sheldon Thompson*. Accounts of the voyage vary. Augustus Walker, master of the ship, records that death struck again when they had passed the Manitou Islands. The corpse was weighted and thrown overboard. "In like manner 12 others were also thrown overboard before the rest of the troops were landed in Chicago." The ship dropped anchor off Chicago "on the evening of the 8th of July, 1832, being six days and over making the passage. . . . Before landing the troops next morning we were under the painful necessity of committing three more to the deep who died during the night, making in all 16 who were thus buried." The three bodies were visible in the clear water. The sight was too much for the crew to bear, and Captain Walker changed his anchorage. Other ships in the harbor spread sail and fled from the plague-smitten *Sheldon Thompson*. During the following day and night, eighteen more died and were buried on a rise of ground near the lighthouse. Wrapped only in their blankets as winding sheets, they were left "without sign of remembrance or a stone to mark their resting-place. During the four days we remained at Chicago, 54 more died, making an aggregate of 88. The scenes of horror occasioned by this singular disease . . . it would be difficult to describe."[2]

The scene aboard the *Henry Clay* was frightful. Nearly every man of the 400 was stricken, and those who escaped the cholera were sick with fear. They jumped overboard in the Detroit River and ran to the woods. When the ship docked at Fort Gratiot at the head of the St. Clair River and removed its sick and dead, the 400 were reduced to 150 survivors. Deserters, already infected, streamed back along the shore toward Detroit, spreading the plague along the way. Many never reached the town. One of the officers wrote: "The dead bodies of the deserters are literally strewed along the road between here and Detroit. No one dares give them relief, not even a cup of

---

2 *Pub. Buf. Hist. Soc.*, V, 311-312.

water. A person on his way from Detroit here, passed six lying groaning with the agonies of cholera, under one tree, and saw one corpse, by the road side, half eaten by the hogs!"

The ships spread the epidemic from Buffalo to Chicago and it scourged and ravaged the entire lake region. On the edge of Sandusky is a well-kept cemetery where the victims in that district of Lake Erie were carried out and buried by the score in nameless graves. The Ontario coast, though less densely populated, was likewise scourged. At Turkey Point, where Fort Norfolk stood during the War of 1812 on the high bank overlooking Long Point Bay, a hospital was built to care for those stricken during the epidemic of 1832.[3]

The cholera took its toll and passed, and more ships brought more and more people to the lake ports. In 1833 there were eleven steamers crossing Lake Erie; in that single year they carried 50,000 passengers westward from Buffalo. Between March 15 and November 28, 1835, 1,900 vessels docked at Cleveland. The big new steamer *United States* came alongside the Detroit wharf in May 1836 with 700 people crowded aboard. Ninety ships steamed past Fighting Island in that single month going to or from Detroit. By 1839 a sixteen-day trip between Buffalo and Chicago was in operation. Despite storms, collisions, burnings and boiler explosions, the ships sailed on regular schedule.

The *Peacock* won the tragic distinction of having the first explosion on Lake Erie. While she was tied up to the Buffalo wharf in 1830, the water ran low in the boiler. Some inexperienced boiler-tender let in a full flow of cold water. The boiler blew up, killing fifteen men. Those were the days before tin safety plugs and hollow boiler tubes were invented, and the serious accident toll from exploding steamers on inland waters was alarming. It was always much worse on the rivers, however, than on the lakes.

The famous steamer *Great Western* began her long and faithful career on the lake in 1838. She was built at Huron, Ohio. She was especially designed for the immigrant traffic from Buffalo to the West. She was a beautiful ship. Across the enormous paddle boxes on both sides was painted in six-foot block letters: GREAT WESTERN. Two big smokestacks forward of amidships marred her trim appear-

---

[3] Only a cairn in memory of Fort Norfolk now remains on this beautiful bit of Lake Erie shore.

FISHING OFF PUT-IN-BAY
The equipment changes with the season.

TOLEDO ON THE MAUMEE
Anthony Wayne Bridge and coal loading docks in foreground.

ance somewhat, but they were subdued by her three tall masts and her outer jib sail. A long white pennant fluttered from the foremast emblazoned with the legend: GREAT WESTERN. She was the first lake steamer with cabins above the main deck. She had two tiers of them, like an Ohio River packet, with two promenade decks encircling them. Among the thousands of passengers carried by this ship was the philosophical Concord maid, Margaret Fuller, friend of Emerson and Thoreau, who toured the lake country in 1843 and wrote a nice book about it. She was impressed by the narrow, crowded Detroit streets with wooden planks laid on the mud for sidewalks, and by the hordes of Irish and German immigrants "working their way into the back country." As she steamed down the lovely river she heard a band playing, and saw the city decked with flags and the harbor lined with crowds of people. They had come to launch the *Wisconsin*. From the wheelhouse deck of the *Great Western,* Margaret Fuller watched the new ship slide down the ways to join the ever-expanding fleet of Lake Erie vessels.

The *City of Cleveland* (one of several steamers of that name) was for years a notable ship because she had the first steam whistle on the lakes, and people at Dunkirk, Conneaut and Fairport would turn at the mellow sound of her whistle to see if the big white vessel was putting in or passing by. The *Vandalia,* a 138-ton steam sloop, built down at Oswego in 1841, made history on the lakes. She was the first commercial steamer in the world to abandon the exposed side paddle wheels for Ericsson's new underwater screw propeller, and the first to place her engines aft. These innovations revolutionized ship design on the lakes. The seventeen-foot-six-inch screw on the *Irving S. Olds* is its lineal descendant. The *Vandalia* passed up the Welland Canal and sailed on Lake Erie. For decades after her successful run, ships with the Ericsson screw were known as "Propellers" to distinguish them from "Steamers." They were especially popular while wood was used for fuel. Their engines could be placed compactly aft and they required less wood. The 275-ton propeller *Hercules,* built in 1843, housed her 50-horsepower engine in a space only six feet square, and she could run all day on ten cords of wood as against the two cords every hour required for the normal-sized steamer. She not only saved about $60 a day in fuel, but also avoided some of the delays at the lake wharves while cordwood was loaded

on the vessels. Later improvements in marine steam engines overcame the disadvantages of the side-wheelers, however, and at the
present time the largest and fastest passenger vessels on the lake, such
as the *Greater Detroit,* are propelled by side paddle wheels. In shallow water they have better balance, less drag and higher speed. But
in the middle of last century the propellers were serious rivals of the
steamers. Lloyd's *Steamboat Directory* of 1856 lists 120 steamers and
118 propellers on the lakes, in addition to 40 barques, 211 brigs, 608
schooners and 290 sloops and scows: a total of 1,387 ships of all types.

Two of the Lake Erie steamers are remembered because of the
newsworthy passengers they carried. Maximilian, Prince of Wied,
sailed on the *Oliver Newberry* in June 1834. After going down the
Ohio River from Pittsburgh, he returned to Portsmouth and crossed
Ohio over the new Ohio-Erie Canal that passed through Newark and
Akron and reached the lake at Cleveland. He was deeply impressed
by the country and Lake Erie and left a vivid account of his passage.
"The sea-like expanse of Lake Erie was very striking when emerg-
ing from the wooded valleys, and the sight of it reminded me of my
approaching voyage to my native country. The dark blue lake
stretches to the far horizon like the ocean; the eye is attracted by the
white sails and the smoke of the steamboats; while the finest weather
and the purest atmosphere favored the illusion."

That was the Prince's first view of Lake Erie. He saw numerous
canalboats assembled in the basin in the Flats, many schooners, and
steamers going and coming. He noted the breakwater, "a long mole,"
as he called it, and the two lighthouses erected to guide the ships into
the harbor. From the starboard deck of the *Oliver Newberry* he
leaned on the rail at noon, admired the fine prospect of the Cleveland
waterfront, and speculated on its future greatness now that the canals
had linked it with the ocean and the Mississippi. The ship touched
at Fairport, Ashtabula and Salem "where great numbers of bats were
hovering over the entrance to the port."

They reached Dunkirk the next morning after losing time because
of engine trouble. The Prince wondered why this Dutch-like village
was not mentioned in the *Ohio Gazetteer* of 1833, not knowing that
he had crossed a part of Pennsylvania and was now in New York.
They lifted the town of Buffalo at eleven o'clock that morning and

watched two steamers in the familiar sport of racing for the basin. The *Oliver Newberry* docked at noon in the steamer-jammed Buffalo Harbor. The Prince was impressed by this gateway town of 1,000 houses and 12,000 inhabitants. "When we consider the shortness of the time, the sudden improvement of the town, which is now of such importance, really seems incredible; and perhaps there is no other country in the world where such a sudden rise would be possible."

He visited the remains of the Seneca tribe, once so powerful among the Five Nations of this region, on their reservation (still reserved) on the edge of the city. They showed him their Bibles and prayer books in the Indian language. He bought specimens of their work "adorned with porcupine and other dyed quills, and likewise bows and arrows." Then he stood on the ridge at the top of the gentle slope of Buffalo. He noted how, in the lower part of the town, the water of the lake and the canal had been conducted into the very streets, forming small harbors where numerous ships lay in safety. He lifted his eyes to admire again "the bright mirror of Lake Erie, which vanishes in the misty distance" toward Canada. Regretfully he turned away from this lake and city and traveled on to Niagara, the East and the Old World.

Not so with the other famous and distinguished man whose novelist-trained eye and heart should have seen even more than the Prince of Wied. He was Charles Dickens. He sailed Lake Erie in 1842, just eight years later. He too had gone down the Ohio River from Pittsburgh. He too had crossed the state of Ohio, from Cincinnati through Columbus to Sandusky; but he traveled in bad temper and wielded a satiric and vitriolic pen. He boarded a steamer at Sandusky. Of this thriving town on its beautiful bay, Dickens wrote only one sentence: "The town, which was sluggish and uninteresting enough, was something like the back of an English watering-place out of season." He did not designate the steamer's name, but it was the handsome ship with the name of one of Humphries' finest Navy frigates, the *Constellation*. Even Dickens warmed up enough to say that "she was a large vessel of 500 tons, and handsomely fitted up," but he added in the next breath that her high-pressure engines "conveyed that kind of feeling to me, which I should be likely to experience, I think, if I had lodgings on the first floor of a powder mill."

She carried a cargo of flour in the hold and an overflow of barrels on the deck. The captain sat astride one of the barrels and whittled at its staves while he talked to Dickens.

There is mischievous pleasure in recording that Dickens was very sick on the passage. "It's all very fine talking about Lake Erie," he wrote, "but it won't do for persons who are liable to seasickness. . . . It is almost as bad in that respect as the Atlantic. The waves are very short and horribly constant." He was able, however, to observe the "low dams stretching out into the lake, whereon were stumpy light-houses, like windmills without sails, the whole looking like a Dutch vignette." They arrived at Cleveland at midnight. The mayor of the city came down next morning to pay his respects. Dickens refused to see him because an editor of a Cleveland paper had written that Britain must be "whipped again," and had promised all true Americans that within two years they should sing *"Yankee-Doodle* in Hyde Park and *Hail Columbia* in the scarlet courts of Westminster." So Dickens sat behind the closed door of his cabin while the mayor coolly retired to the top of the wharf with a big stick and a knife and whittled. Dickens did not see the beautiful prospect of Cleveland as his ship steamed away toward Erie.

Early next morning he reached Buffalo. He did not see the future greatness of the city, or marvel at its growth in the wilderness. He did not visit the Seneca or buy examples of their art. He did not climb the terrace to see the bright mirror of Lake Erie, or the thriving commerce in the basin. He had his breakfast and then, "being too near the Great Falls to wait patiently anywhere else, we set off by the train, the same morning at nine o'clock, to Niagara."

Two years after Dickens snubbed the mayor of Cleveland, that city celebrated the launching of the 1,136-ton *Empire* in the yards on the Cuyahoga River. She was 260 feet long, the longest ship yet built on the lakes, and even then, her builders said, they were limited only by the tangents in that curving inlet. For several years the *Empire* was the pride of Lake Erie. Her cabin space ran almost the full length of the ship. She had separate saloons for ladies and gentlemen and large dormitory space below for the immigrants. Her 230-feet-long dining room was luxurious; and in these spacious quarters the passengers were served breakfast (at any time between seven and eleven), lunch, afternoon dinner, tea and ten-o'clock supper. She carried a band for entertainment and dancing. In the first year of her career on Lake Erie, during which 20,244 passengers went from Buffalo to Cleveland, thousands of immigrants boarded the *Empire* for their journey to the pineries and the wheat fields of the West, and she also did a profitable business in cargoes of flour and package freight.

The mass rush of immigrants to the West at the height of the canal era in the 1840's and 1850's and the increasing number of tourists and businessmen going out to Detroit or Chicago from Buffalo boosted the passenger trade on the steamers to higher and higher levels. The steamship companies responded by outdoing one another in building ever-larger, faster and more luxurious ships. The wonder steamer of one season was surpassed by a new leviathan the next. The competition was keen. Even the new railroad companies entered into it. The Michigan Central established a steamship line of its own across Lake Erie from Buffalo to Monroe, Michigan, in 1848 to bring passengers and freight to its railroad. In the mid-1850's it was advertising its daily service between the foot of Erie Street, Buffalo, and the Detroit docks, connecting with its trains for Chicago. The 2,000-ton *Plymouth,* the 1,830-ton *Mississippi* and the 2,000-ton *Western World* were announced as the newest and largest class of steamers on Lake Erie, fitted up and furnished for the convenience of passengers "in a style of comfort and luxury entirely unequalled." In all respects, the company assured its patrons, these were "the safest and most desirable steamers that sail upon the Western waters." And they were commanded by "gentlemen and officers of great experience and ability."

At the same time the Michigan Southern was advertising its rival line of "new and popular" steamships offering daily service over the same route, the *Southern Michigan* leaving the foot of Main Street, Buffalo, on Wednesday and Saturday, the *Western Metropolis* on Monday and Thursday, and the big 2,200-ton *City of Buffalo* on Tuesday and Friday.

The Chicago, Cleveland & Cincinnati Railroad Line ran two fine ships between Buffalo and Cleveland: the *Crescent City* and the *Queen of the West.* One of these left Buffalo each evening at eight o'clock. All eight of these railroad-line steamers were built between 1853 and 1857.

Other companies ran their ships all the way to Superior City and popularized summer excursions to Mackinac, the Sault and the Pictured Rocks of Lake Superior after the Sault Canal was opened in 1855. The Cleveland, Detroit & Lake Superior Line in 1857 advertised their propellers: the *Iron City,* a new boat, one of "the fastest on the lake," and the *Manhattan,* thoroughly reconditioned, "a sound, staunch boat in every particular." The steamer *North Star,* "so well appointed and furnished as to make her a PALACE HOME to the pleasure traveller," was advertised for an eight-day trip from Cleveland to Superior City. McKnight's Lake Superior Line ran the *Illinois* out of Cleveland on the same route.

The most seductive of the advertisements induced pleasure-seekers to sail on the steamer *Planet:* "New, 1,200 tons burden, low-pressure engine of 1,000 horse power; has an upper cabin 210 feet long, and splendid accommodations for 300 passengers, but on these trips, that they may be in fact, as well as in name, Pleasure Excursions, the number will be limited to 175. A good band will be in attendance to enliven the scene, and no expense will be spared to make these excursions the most agreeable that have been made to Lake Superior." The fare was $40 from Cleveland, $36 from Detroit.

Active service was also maintained between Cleveland and Detroit. It began in 1850 when Captain Arthur Edwards placed the steamers *Southerner* and *Baltimore* in operation. During the next three years the *Forest City,* the *St. Louis,* the *Sam Ward,* the *Cleveland* and the *May Queen* were added. Six more were built for this route between 1856 and 1878.

The shipbuilding boom led to overexpansion just as the railroads were banding Lake Erie on both the Canadian and American shores and a dozen outlet roads were stemming in and out of Buffalo, Cleveland, Toledo, Detroit and Windsor. The inevitable crash followed after a panic in lake transportation which began in 1857. The Michigan Central's three big steamers were hit by the competition of other lines and by the popularity of the new railroads. When the outbreak of the Civil War further dislocated traffic, they suspended operations and tied up their ships at Detroit for several seasons. The *Mississippi* had been in service only four years, the *Plymouth* and the *Western World* only three. After the war they were decommissioned, their engines were removed, and the palatial, rosewood-finished ships, already outdated, were used as humble docks at Buffalo, Cleveland and Bay City.

But that does not mean that passenger and package-freight service disappeared from Lake Erie. Far from it. It merely settled back to an adequate, instead of a surplus, fleet. The Detroit & Cleveland Navigation Company, incorporated in Michigan in 1868, went right on with its business. In 1878 it added the *City of Detroit I,* and in 1880 a new *City of Cleveland,* both handsome steamers built on iron hulls. For several seasons they operated on the Mackinac run, but from 1885 to 1889 they sailed between Detroit and Cleveland. In 1889 the *City of Detroit II* was added at a cost of $350,000—$100,000 more than the outmoded *Western World.* When the Cleveland and Buffalo Company was organized in September 1892, it acquired this fleet. It added new steamers from time to time, and made regular trips not only to Buffalo and Detroit, but also to Toledo, Cedar Point and Port Stanley. It continued to operate until 1938. But the railroads, and the big new highways, motorcars and trucking companies were too successful as competitors, and in 1939 the company began the process of liquidation which continued through the early 1940's. The *City of Buffalo* was destroyed by fire on March 20, 1938. The *Goodtime* (formerly *City of Detroit II*) was sold for scrap in 1940, and the *City of Erie* for the same purpose in 1941 after almost a half-century of service.

Old-timers on Lake Erie saw the passing of the *City of Erie* with regret and the revival of stirring memories of June 4, 1901. The steel-hulled *Erie* was three years old then—a proud, fast side-wheeler of 2,498 tons, 324 feet long and 76 feet wide. Her chief rival was the streamlined *Tashmoo* of Detroit. A race was arranged between these two vessels, officially known as the greatest race of Great Lakes ships. The course was the ninety-four miles from Cleveland Harbor to Erie, Pennsylvania. The *Tashmoo* won the toss and chose the outside, or deeper-water, course. This placed a handicap on the heavier-draft *City of Erie.* In the shallow water off Fairport the *City of Erie* lost speed and fell behind. But as soon as she reached the deeper draft beyond Ashtabula she began to inch up on the *Tashmoo.* As the steamers neared Erie, the *City of Erie* pulled alongside, and began to pass her rival. And in a final burst of speed, witnessed by thousands onshore and from steamers and tugs on the lake, she ran forward to finish forty-five seconds ahead of the *Tashmoo*. That year 1901, by the way, was the most prosperous and successful of the C. & B. Line's half-century of operation.

The most celebrated ship of this line, and the most famous on Lake Erie, had a more heroic future ahead of her. She was the giant *Seeandbee*. She deserves our attention and tribute. She was built at Detroit in 1912-1913 by the Detroit Shipbuilding Company and Frank E. Kirby, noted designer of side-wheel ships, at a cost of over $1,500,000. The model was tried out in a testing tank with the co-operation of the University of Michigan. As a result the plans were altered to widen her another three feet at an additional cost of $57,630. Her over-all width was 97.5 feet, her length 500 feet, and her depth 22 feet, 10 inches. Her seven decks had room to carry 6,000 persons in addition to a trainload of freight. Her giant paddle wheels were 33 feet in diameter and weighed 100 tons. Her four enormous smokestacks were 9 feet in diameter. Her 12,000-horsepower engines gave her 2,000 horsepower more than any other side-wheel steamer on the Great Lakes. Her guaranteed speed was twenty-two miles per hour and she sailed regularly at eighteen and a half miles per hour. Her 510 staterooms and 24 parlors were examples of the finest cabinetwork. They could not now be duplicated at any cost.

The company invited the public to name the new leviathan, and offered $100 in prizes for the most suitable name. They announced the choice on the day of launching. It was *Seeandbee*. On June 18, 1913, the *State of Ohio* left Cleveland for Detroit with officials and invited guests to receive the new ship. The next day the *Seeandbee* was brought down to Cleveland and opened to the public for inspection. Then she was turned over to the Cleveland Chamber of Commerce for their exclusive use on a special round trip to Buffalo. After all this ceremony and publicity she went into service.

It was not a prosperous period for passenger ships on the lakes. An unprecedented number of marine disasters culminated in the frightful tragedy of the Cleveland-built *Eastland,* which overturned in the Chicago River on the morning of July 24, 1915, with the loss of 812 lives. This steamer had been popular on Lake Erie prior to 1914; she operated between Cleveland and Cedar Point, and made special moonlight excursion trips. Thousands of people who had sailed on her read of this disaster and remembered "There but for the grace of God, go I." The notoriety and adverse publicity, in addition to restrictive legislation and unfavorable weather, caused the passenger trade to fall away alarmingly. World War I prolonged the depression. The *State of Ohio* became obsolete after lying at the dock for two years. The *Seeandbee,* however, continued to operate on the Buffalo division, and gradually picked up trade as the popularity of lake travel revived in the 1920's.

Throughout the 1930's this splendid steamer, showing no signs of age, was a familiar sight on Lake Erie and at the wharves of the big cities. But the war clouds of Europe again spread over Lake Erie. Ships of all kinds were needed desperately. The United States Government bought the *Seeandbee* in 1941 and the American Ship Building Company converted her into a graceful aircraft carrier for the training of naval aviators at Great Lakes. The Navy inspectors who watched her perform on her trial runs marveled at her speed and the perfection of the performance of her thirty-year-old engines. Her riveting was perfect to the point of artistry. There was not a ripple in her hull. With her staterooms and cabinetwork torn away, and her orlop and top tank deck replaced with a flat-top landing deck, *Seeandbee,* now the *U.S.S. Wolverine,* steamed out of Lake Erie to Chicago to do her brilliant part in World War II. Thousands of young aviators who had never seen her in all her glory on a moonlight night on Lake Erie remembered her only as a floating landing field on tossing Lake Michigan where they were trained to carry battle among Japanese Zeros in the skies above the islands of Japan.

The liquidation of the C. & B. Line left the passenger traffic on Lake Erie largely in the hands of the Detroit and Cleveland Navigation Company. They carry on the great tradition. One of their largest ships, the *Greater Buffalo,* was taken over by the United States Government. Like the *Seeandbee,* she was converted into an aircraft-carrier training ship for Great Lakes. She was rechristened the *Sable.* A sister ship, the *Greater Detroit,* and the *Eastern States* still sail nightly across the length of Lake Erie. One leaves Detroit and the other leaves Buffalo at 5:30 each evening throughout the season, each arriving at the opposite port at 9:00 in the morning. They generally carry a large passenger list of tourists and a few businessmen who prefer a quiet evening on Lake Erie to a night on the crowded sleepers. They transported capacity loads of private automobiles during the gasoline shortage. A tourist could stow his car aboard at Buffalo,[4] enjoy the lake trip, then cross over into Canada, draw his Canadian tourist allotment of gasoline, and make a pleasant tour along the north shore back to Buffalo. It was a popular wartime vacation.

The D. & C. Lake Lines also operate the *City of Detroit III* and the *City of Cleveland III* on overnight sailings between their two name ports, but service between Buffalo and Cleveland has been suspended.

There are also several smaller excursion steamers which ply between Buffalo and the Ontario pleasure beaches, from Cleveland or Detroit (sometimes from Toledo) to Put-in-Bay and Cedar Point. And there are small boats in service between Sandusky and Kingsville, Ontario, via the Lake Erie Islands, and from the islands to the mainland.

Voyages across Lake Erie on the big steamers are still memorable experiences. The giant elevators and the tall buildings of Buffalo take the sun in the evening across the wake of the departing steamer with the same magic light that fell on the tall masts of the schooners in the harbor in the days when Harriet Martineau sailed west to Detroit. Night falls and the lighthouses begin to flash as the steamer nears Long Point. The same moon rises over Dunkirk and paves a path of gold straight across the tossing lake to the big side paddle wheels at the feet of loungers on the deck above. Day begins to break near Point Pelee, and Southeast Shoal Light becomes a flashing part of the dawn. In the fresh morning the steamer turns into the Amherstburg Channel at Detroit River Lighthouse, joins the procession of ships in the crowded river, passes the slower, heavy freighters, and runs into the old and weathered dock at the foot of Main Street, imposing for a brief instant an air of tradition and romance upon that dreary structure quivering on its rotting piles.

---

[4] Gasoline is no longer removed from passenger cars going aboard.

Chapter 13

Sloops, Brigs and Schooners

THERE was never any doubt that the future would belong to the steamers. Though new and bigger and faster steamers and propellers appeared on Lake Erie every year or two, it took them nearly eight decades to drive the sailing ships from this waterway. The era of those sails is still one of the most picturesque in the history of the lakes.

Steamships were expensive and laborious to build. After the designers had drawn the plans and the shipwrights had fashioned the timbers in the early days, a marine engine and boilers had to be imported from the East or sent over from England and transported to the shipyards on Lake Erie. At first they burned quantities of wood from the timberlands back of the American and Canadian port towns. Jonathan Olmstead cut timber on the Indian Reservation behind Buffalo and shipped it by scow down to Black Rock to feed *Walk-in-the-Water*. Other contractors at the various ports supplied wood to the steamers in this same fashion. Later on the steamers consumed quantities of coal. Whether they used wood or coal, much good cargo space was filled with engines, boilers and fuel. They required large and regular pay loads for quick transit in order to show a profit.

During the years before the era of overwhelming bulk cargoes of iron, coal and grain came to the lakes, however, much of the traffic was carried in small lots from one settlement to another or over the lake to Detroit or Buffalo. For this service, where the hauls were short and speed was immaterial, the sails could easily compete with steam. A sailing ship could be built at almost any port where there was good timber. Every harbor of any consequence was also a shipyard. With little capital a man could build his sailing vessel at modest cost and to any size from a ten-ton sloop to a three-masted schooner. Its only fuel was the wind, and the wind was free. The captain-owner and his sons or his nephews or the neighbor boys could sail her down from Port Talbot to Buffalo with a cargo of lumber, or out of Huron

137

with a few tons of grain, or up to Detroit with butter and wheat and hardware. The operating cost was a trifle. Captain Alva Bradley and other famous men who later became millionaires began their business precisely in that way.

The beginning of the sailing fleets, therefore, was modest. The first American vessel built on the lakes was launched at Presque Isle in 1797. The first schooner was the twenty-five-ton *Surprise* built at Buffalo in 1804. She was followed in the same year by the small schooner *Mary,* built at Erie for Thomas Wilson. She sailed produce down the coast to Dunkirk, Silver Creek and Buffalo.

The schooner *Cuyahoga* was in service when the War of 1812 broke out. General William Hull commandeered her for his march on Detroit. In his somewhat blundering way he loaded her in the Maumee River with supplies for use at Detroit and sent her without escort across the west end of the lake and into the Detroit River. There, of course, she was the easiest possible prize for English naval power and land guns at Fort Malden. She was taken in the narrow channel between Bois Blanc Island and Fort Malden with all her cargo—including hospital supplies, the muster roll of the army and other documents.

The forty-five-ton *Zephyr* was one of the first ships launched at Cleveland. She was built on the high ground above the Cuyahoga River in 1808 and hauled down to the launching ways on the bank by yoked oxen. Ships of that tonnage were found to be best suited to the lake trade during the first decades of the century. A ninety-six-ton brig was laid up for a season because she was too large for profitable business on Lake Erie in 1814.

When Augustus Walker came to Buffalo as a lad in 1817, he found nineteen of these small American merchant vessels on Lake Erie.[1] Five of them (three schooners, a sloop and a brig) were at Black Rock, where they had lain during the winter. The ice continued to flow down the Niagara River through May, and these vessels were unable to leave port until early in June 1817—an unusually late season. This inconvenient harbor at Black Rock was the only safe haven for ships at the lower end of the lake until the extensive improvements were begun at Buffalo in the 1820's. The sand had drifted across the mouth of Buffalo Creek, making it so sluggish and shal-

---

[1] *Pub. Buf. Hist. Soc.,* V, 287ff.

low that a man could easily walk across it in dry weather, or when the east wind blew hard. Even in 1825, under the pressure of the wind, the water in this creek fell three feet, partly capsizing the *Abigail* and spilling her cargo of salt into the water.

The ships, therefore, went on down the Niagara to Black Rock, and then faced the hazards of getting back into Lake Erie. Unless by some miracle they were favored by a ten-knot wind from the east, they had to be towed. Captain Sheldon Thompson, for whom one of the steamers in General Scott's expedition was named, operated the towing service. It was known to sailors as the "horned breeze." The captain was an expert in the niceties of the technique. It was not so simple as it looked. From eight to fourteen yoke of oxen were hitched to a four or six-inch hawser. This hawser, from 200 to 300 fathoms in length, was made fast to the masthead and buoyed up by small boats, fifty feet apart, between the ship and the shore. Then the long team of oxen hauled on the line and dragged the ship up the current. At Brace's Ferry the vessel had to be shear-boarded out into the stream around a shoals, an operation that required good judgment and experience. When the vessel was well out of the current near the present Buffalo Harbor, the towline was cast off, hauled ashore, coiled in boats and taken back down to Black Rock. The ships dropped anchor in six fathoms of water out in Buffalo Harbor, and all goods and passengers were ferried out in scows by Winthrop Fox's lightering service. Then the vessels made sail and headed up the lake. Most of these early ships were dull sailers. Some of them, records Captain Walker who sailed them, "could hardly claw off shore under canvas." And in bad weather they had to run for safety to the nearest shelter.

The proper construction and rigging of sailing ships for these lakes became an acute problem. The first ones were crude affairs. Captain James Sloan's ships of 1815 were long, shallow, open and flat-bottomed. They sailed abominably. But he was able to haul stone from the Canadian shore to Buffalo in the heroic years when the citizens of that village were building their breakwater in order to get the Erie Canal to terminate there. His boats were built so they could sail close in for loading stone at the beach. He "loaded light and manned strong." Sometimes he had to cast overboard his cargo and run for shelter when a squall struck. And his boats had to get across the shallow water at the mouth of Buffalo Creek. In fact, one of the serious difficulties was these sand bars near the ports, and the channel in the Detroit River which was, in places, only five or six feet deep. Then as now the shipbuilders were forced to build their vessels according to the available draft in the rivers and harbors.

Lake-ship designers experimented earnestly to develop a vessel of light draft that could sail steadily and carry a good cargo. They devised leeboards which could be lowered over the side of the vessel. The fifty-three-ton schooner *Red Jacket,* built at Black Rock in 1820, was fitted with this device. She was seventy feet long, seventeen feet beam, and only four feet eleven inches deep in the hold. Captain Walker, master of *Red Jacket* on Lake Erie for seven years, described her as a "periauger, carrying immense leeboards, fan-shaped, and so arranged on the sides of the vessel that they could be hoisted or lowered away, as the case might be. . . . These leeboards . . . were necessarily elevated on entering port, where they extended several feet above the main rail, giving the ship a novel and somewhat unnatural appearance."

Red Jacket also had another innovation that soon became standard on Lake Erie ships. All the earlier models, including Stanard & Bidwell's fine seventy-seven-ton schooner *Erie,* built in 1816, the fastest sail on the lakes in her day, had open unprotected decks. They were wet, uncomfortable and hazardous for the sailors. *Red Jacket* was so shallow that she had little side above water when loaded. Her builders, therefore, constructed a "bulwark" around her deck, instead of the usual open rail and stanchions, to prevent seas from breaking free over her.

At the same time Fairbanks Church and Augustus Jones in their yards at Huron and Lorain were experimenting with the arrangement of masts and rigs. From 1825 on they designed and launched vessels with a graceful, swanlike appearance heretofore not seen on Lake Erie. They were broader in proportion to their length, and though their holds were still shallow (as they had to be to enter the harbors) they could carry more tonnage and sail better than other models. The secret lay, in large part, in placing the foremast nearer the bow and the mainmast farther aft. This separation permitted greater spread to the foresail on these fore-and-aft-rigged schooners which made them easier to haul upon the wind.

The awkward leeboards were never popular. The three-masted schooner *Lizzie A. Law* of Port Huron demonstrated their short-comings. She was caught in a storm with heavy weather. The seas carried away her leeboards and left her wallowing about. She was all but lost before her captain could haul her into shelter. But the centerboard and drop keel proved to be more effective. The center-board was a simple device to increase the area of resistance under-water and thus prevent leeway. A firm oak board from ten to fifteen feet long and six to ten feet wide was fitted into a watertight box or casing between the keel and the deck. It was pivoted at the forward lower corner; the after end could be raised or lowered with a tackle from the deck. If a schooner were entering the shallow harbor at Cleveland or Buffalo, or were passing into the canal or basin, up came the centerboard. But when she cleared the harbor and spread all her canvas for the run across the lake, the centerboard was dropped and shallow draft was overcome. The drop keel was the same device except for the pivot; the entire board was lowered.

With these basic difficulties overcome, the sailing ships lengthened, widened and improved as the channels and harbors were deepened and the volume of traffic increased through the years. In 1856, the year before the panic, there were 40 barques, 211 brigs, 608 schooners, and 290 sloops and scows on the lakes with a total tonnage of 325,293, or an average of about 280 tons per ship[2]—less than the tonnage of the Pickands, Mather & Company 1944 fleet, one of 210 companies now operating ships on the lakes.

The construction of these 1,149 sailing ships kept the yards busy and made fortunes for the builders. Captain Sam Ward, at one time the owner of the largest fleet on the lakes and one of the powerful men behind the building of the Sault Canal, began by building the twenty-seven-ton schooner *Salem* in his yards at Conneaut in 1818 for trade between the frontier villages on Lake Erie. He moved on west and established a shipyard at the mouth of Belle River above Detroit. Here he built the twenty-eight-ton schooner *St. Clair* which became famous as the first lake vessel to sail out of Lake Erie at Buffalo and down the Erie Canal and the Hudson River to New York in 1825. For the enterprising Sam Ward had arranged her masts so they could be unshipped when the *St. Clair* entered the canal and reset

---

[2] Lloyd's *Steamboat Directory*, 1856.

when she came out into the Hudson. He also built four other schooners in the next eight years, ranging in size from the twenty-ton *Albatross* to the 115-ton *General Harrison*. After 1833 he gave up building sailing ships and became part owner, with Oliver Newberry, of the steamship *Michigan*, and began building passenger steamers for the westward tide of immigration.

His partner Oliver Newberry was one of the characters on Lake Erie and at Detroit. He once ran a grocery store at the corner of Main and Seneca Streets in Buffalo, and did a brisk business in furs. He was conspicuous on the Buffalo streets in winter because he always wore a vivid Indian blanket coat. In 1820 he moved to Detroit to build ships and deal in fish and fur which he carried in his own bottoms. In 1834 he bought a strip of Detroit water front for his shipyard. Those cannon by the steps of the Detroit City Hall, mounted on stone with the legend "PERRY'S VICTORY—LAKE ERIE—September 10th 1813" carved deep in them, were recovered from the mud on Newberry's frontage. They had been brought from Erie to the old Government Depot on Woodbridge Street where the Detroit River silted them over and buried them. For a time after their resurrection they were used on the docks as snubbing posts for boat lines, but in 1872 they were removed and given their present place of honor.[3]

In this Detroit yard which he operated for thirty-five years the enterprising and eccentric Mr. Newberry built a fleet of sailing ships. He named his schooners after men and battles made legendary by the Napoleonic wars. He launched the *Marengo, Alma, Marshal Ney, Austerlitz, Lodi* and—the *Napoleon*.[4] Incidentally this inordinate fondness for Europe's conqueror and England's mortal enemy greatly annoyed Newberry's rival across the river, the Scotch shipowner at Windsor, Angus MacIntosh. The dour Scotchman in the early 1830's built himself a full-rigged ship, one of the rarest types in commercial service on the lakes, and proudly named her *Wellington* in honor of the Iron Duke who conquered the Emperor. He took deep satisfaction in seeing her twenty-four sails all set and the wind driving her with dukely grace toward Pelee Passage as the seven-sail schooner *Napoleon* beat up toward Bar Point.

The rivalry extended from individuals to port towns. We have

---

[3] George B. Catlin, *The Story of Detroit* (Detroit, 1923).
[4] *Pub. Buf. Hist. Soc.*, V, 307.

mentioned Black Rock and Buffalo. The same jealousy spurred Sandusky and Huron. Vessels often refused to call at Huron because, so they said, it was unsafe to enter that exposed and shallow bay. They went on to Sandusky—and even there the steamers and some of the sails often anchored off Cunningham's (Kelleys) Island and lightered passengers to the mainland in a small sailboat kept expressly for that purpose. Then the passengers bound for Huron had to travel back overland ten miles to reach their destination. Captain Walker of Buffalo, however, took his schooner *Lady of the Lake* in to Huron and captured most of the trade at this port. He joined with ambitious citizens of the Western Reserve towns at Huron, Milan, Norwalk and Vermilion who resented Sandusky's prominent position, and erected a shipyard at Huron. They built the *Huron* and many other sailing ships, and the steamer *Sheldon Thompson*.

All the other ports were just as active as Huron, Vermilion, Cleveland or Erie. Lorain not only launched her own fleet, but she cut lumber in the Black River forest and fashioned the timbers for John Jacob Astor's fur-trading schooner, the *John Jacob Astor,* in 1834. The prefabricated timbers were then shipped to the Sault to be put together above the St. Marys River falls for service on Lake Superior. Captain C. C. Stanard sailed her on that lake until 1842. On one of his voyages he discovered the dangerous rock shoal that lies nearly twenty-four miles off the Superior coast between Whitefish Point and Keweenaw. The great Stanard Lighthouse rising 102 feet above the lake, on this shoal, honors his name.

The number of these sailing ships and their variety in size and rigs delighted the eyes of all visitors to the lakes and brought excited comment from all the literary travelers. Many of them were quite sentimental about the white sails in the sun above the green water as the wind spread the canvas of barques, schooners and brigantines in the harbor at Buffalo, and as they floated effortlessly along before a good breeze past Port Talbot, or converged in the narrow channels at Point Pelee and off Bar Point.

They were picturesque enough, but they were too often subjected to costly delay by the vagaries of winds and storms. Take the log of one not unusual voyage. The hermaphrodite brig *Union,* Master James Beard, was towed by twelve yoke of oxen from Black Rock to Lake Erie. With a light wind she made Cleveland on the second day. She cast anchor out in deep water while the captain and a few passengers took a yawl in to the shore. Thirty barrels of pork were lightered out and stowed aboard. During the night the wind increased to a gale. It raged for two days and nights. On the second night one hawser cable parted, and the brig began to drag onshore. The mate quickly stood her out to sea and let her run fifty-five miles west to the Erie Islands where she found refuge in Put-in-Bay. Here the ship's crew made repairs to the mast, and on the next day, with a wind shift from east to south, the *Union* sailed back to her original anchorage at the edge of the Cuyahoga sand bar. She finished loading her cargo of 700 to 800 barrels of pork, and got under way for Long Point. She lay off Long Point for nearly two weeks, beating off and on from the mainland, while small boats and scows came out alongside at night to discharge the cargo. The *Union's* voyage from Buffalo to Cleveland and back had consumed four weeks. Yet this little ninety-four-ton brig made a clear profit of $6,000 during the season of 1816, according to Captain James Beard.

The sailing ships also generally had to be towed through the Detroit River, across the St. Clair Flats and along the St. Clair River from Lake Erie to Lake Huron. If the wind was favorable, which was seldom enough, they might sail through. But if it was light, or head-on, or broadside, the ship might be delayed for days, run aground, or even block the channel. The *Milwaukee,* in which Harriet Martineau sailed from Chicago for Detroit in 1836, never got her there. The ship hit head winds as she came into the St. Clair, grounded, was carried along with the current, bumping alternately bow and stern, and finally stuck fast a few miles above Detroit. After some days' delay, Miss Martineau and other passengers were transferred to a lumber ship and taken in to the city.[5]

The answer to such hazards of navigation was the steam tug. The towing business flourished at Detroit as it did at Black Rock. At the height of the sailing era near the mid-century there were about fifty tugs busy in these connecting channels between the lakes. The schooners would beat their way up to Bar Point and gather at the mouth of the river. Three or more—sometimes as many as six or seven—were secured one behind the other by long hawsers, with

---

[5] Harriet Martineau, *Society in America* (London, 1837).

another hawser bent to the tug. The steam tug then pulled them in graceful procession up the channel to Detroit—or perhaps all the way to Lake Huron. Photographs of Sarnia Bay in 1870, when sails were most common, confirm the memories of old lake men that twenty or more ore schooners often lay at anchor there, waiting to be towed down the rivers and across the flats. The bay was a forest of tall masts. If the wind was right, the schooners kept their sails spread to ease the burden on the tug and increase the speed. One of the most frequently reproduced pictures of the 1860's shows the steam tug *Champion* towing a fleet of six schooners in tandem down the Detroit River. The first three ships have their foresails and jibs set to catch a quartering wind; the sails on the last three are all furled.

It was always a big moment in the voyage when the ships finally cleared the Detroit River and could sail free on Lake Erie. A few old sailors still remember those days. Walter Waitt of Lorain, who retired in 1939 after nearly sixty years on the Great Lakes, remembers them. He tells of the fleet of schooners built in the 1870's for the coal and grain trade between Buffalo and Chicago or Milwaukee. It was known as the Blue Bottom fleet because each of the trim sleek hulls was painted a light blue. The schooners made the round trip in twenty-five to thirty days. Rivalry between crews on the Blue Bottoms became a tradition. Loaded with grain, five or six of them were towed by a Detroit River tug down to Lake Erie. The minute they were cut loose they always raced one another over the 240-mile course to Buffalo Harbor. The excitement eased the monotony of the voyage. And as the winning schooner hove to in the basin, the victorious crew broke out with the favorite chanty of the Blue Bottom fleet:

> Watch 'em, catch 'em, jump up in the Jupu Ju,
> Give her sheets and let her rip;
> We're the boys to crowd her through.
> Oh you should have heard 'em holler,
> As the wind went howling free;
> For we beat the fleet from Buffalo—
> Buffalo to Milwaukee.[6]

---

[6] Walter Waitt, Lorain *Journal*, July 26, 1939.

There were other, more singular, diversions. The handsome 132-ton topsail schooner *Michigan,* closely resembling in design and rig the Atlantic schooners of the mid-century, had a successful career, chiefly on Lake Erie, for eleven years. She went out of service in a blaze of notoriety which throws some light on the social history of a century ago. This is Captain Walker's account of her passing:

"... the *Michigan* was bought by parties as a speculation, and under the direction of Capt. Rough, was fitted out with a variety of living animals on board and sent over the Falls of Niagara. Among the number of animals was a full-grown Arabian camel, one elk, a variety of dogs, one bear and a number of swan, geese, hawks, who were left to roam about on deck, until the gallant craft made her last and fearful plunge over the precipice into the abyss below. The scene attracted a large concourse of spectators, estimated from 50,000 to 100,000 persons, who gathered from far and near. Capt. Levi Allen of this city Buffalo was one of the ship's crew who assisted in this novel enterprise, and had it not been for him and others of the crew, old Capt. Rough, in his zeal to have everything rightly adjusted before leaving his favorite ship, would have been drawn, with all hands, over the falls. The crew, with the utmost exertion, rowed the yawl on shore, some distance below the mouth of Chippewa Creek on the Canada side, just above the cataract, to the great relief of the multitude who witnessed this almost miraculous escape."[7]

The books on the sailing ships have almost nothing to say about the thousands of vessels that sailed Lake Erie in the golden age of the schooners in the mid and late nineteenth century. The fresh-water sails beating up from Buffalo to Detroit, running for shelter in the lee of Long Point or the Erie Islands, do seem unromantic beside the stirring adventures of the *Golden Hind,* the speed records of the Yankee clipper *Flying Cloud,* or the Scotch-built tea clipper *Cutty Sark.* But they did write a significant chapter in American shipping history. The centerboard schooners with their tall main-masts, their lower foremasts and mizzenmasts, and their billowing raffe sails achieved a grace and a rakish line unchallenged by any of the Atlantic clippers, and the two-masted *Challenge* skimmed over the lakes at thirteen knots. Some of these ships passed down the

---

[7] *Pub. Buf. Hist. Soc.,* V, 293.

canals and sailed the seven seas. Many of them went down in storms because the narrow lakes gave them no room to run indefinitely before the wind.

They served their glorious day, however, and disappeared under the competition of the age of steam and stupendous movement of ore and coal and grain. As the big carriers came to the lakes, the white sails were stripped away, the tall masts came down and the trim hulls became lowly and prosaic barges dragged along with cargoes of lumber and coal.

On April 26, 1926, a somewhat battered and service-scarred old barge sank in the dredged channel of the River Rouge. She was cleared out of the river a month later and discarded as a total wreck. For years she had been towed up and down the lakes loaded with coal for the big industries of Detroit and the lake ports. Few took any notice of the wreckage or bothered to mourn the passing of a decayed tow barge. But that barge was once the proud schooner *Thomas Gawn*. She was built and launched at Lorain by her owner, Mr. H. Wallace, in 1872, and she had served on the lake for fifty-four years. Through the heyday of the sailing-ship era, and on into the 1880's and 1890's when the big steel ships began to take possession of the lake traffic, the three trim masts of the *Thomas Gawn* were hung with sails, and she was a pretty sight getting under way on Lake Erie as the winds caught her canvas. But as the decline of the sails set in, and she became obsolete, her canvas was stripped off, her masts were brought down and, like her sister ships, she became a humble tow behind the ships of steam and steel. Her loss was more than the passing of a coal barge; for she was the last of the schooners on the lake.[8]

---

[8] Lake Carriers' Association *Report* (1926).

Chapter 14

Beacons

SAILING the Great Lakes looks deceptively easy. Actually it demands a high order of skill. The first ship on Lake Erie demonstrated most of the dangers constantly confronting mariners on these waters. The mist and the fog over the lake on that famous night of August 7, 1679; the long arm of sand bar upon which La Salle almost went aground; the adverse wind on the Detroit and St. Clair Rivers; the storm that struck the *Griffin* on Lake Huron; the mysterious loss of the ship on her homeward passage, presumably in a northwester roaring down Lake Superior and across the Straits of Mackinac; these were only samples of the hazards of lake navigation.

For almost a hundred years after La Salle, no captain attempted to brave the dangers on Lake Erie. By 1763 His Majesty's sloop *Michigan* and schooner *Huron* were launched in the Niagara River above the Falls, and from that day to this men have been mapping, charting and marking these lakes to make them safe for navigation. For another half-century after these launchings, however, there were no real aids for mariners on Lake Erie except the natural landmarks visible along the shores and the word passed from master to master about channels, rocks and shoals. The lake floor was uncharted, of course, and these dangers could be located only by diligent use of the leads to take soundings. It was unsafe to sail at night, and ships generally cast anchor at dusk in some sheltered harbor. The storms were (and are) sudden and fierce, and there was little room to run before them. Ships that could find no safe harbor from the storms in those early days usually faced disaster. Hundreds of them have gone down on Lake Erie alone.

Just how personal, even temperamental, navigation of the lake was in the early decades of the nineteenth century is recorded by Captain James Sloan of Buffalo who wrote his recollections not long before he died in 1868, aged eighty. In the summer of 1815 he made three trips across Lake Erie carrying Lieutenant Armstrong's company from Buffalo to Detroit. His mode of navigating, he says, "was to keep close in shore, noting the mouths of the creeks and rivers so as to make a harbor in case of necessity. There were no harbors in those days, and the rivers were sometimes barred over. Such superfluities as an anchor or compass I never carried, but once; and this was the cause of my losing my cargo." Unfortunately, the captain never explained just how this remarkable misfortune befell him, or how his anchor and compass caused it.

The number of ships increased phenomenally on Lake Erie, as we have seen, during and immediately following the War of 1812. Aids to navigation became more imperative. Until 1818 there were no lights on the lake—nothing to mark Buffalo Harbor, nothing to guide ships around the treacherous bar of Presque Isle at Erie, nothing to indicate the entrance to the channel of the Detroit River where boats often lost their way among the islands. Something would have to be done. Who should do it?

Congress was at first uncertain of its responsibility for navigation on the Great Lakes and unconvinced of the importance of lake shipping. The uncertainty was dissipated by the rapid growth of Ohio and the Northwest Territory in the first years of the nineteenth century, and by the increased volume of lake commerce which made safety and regularity of schedule a matter of money and lives. Congress assumed the burden, and a bill authorizing two lights on Lake Erie was passed in 1810. The War of 1812 interfered with the plans. They were not built until 1818, when permanent peace had come at last to the Great Lakes. In that year the first lighthouses at the mouth of Buffalo Creek began to guide ships into the unimproved harbor.

It should be remembered that these Lake Erie harbors are all in the mouths of the oxbowing rivers that flow languidly into the lake. They are all very much alike in contour. Buffalo Creek is a contortion of S curves which finally cuts into Lake Erie at a sharp angle. Only a narrow wedge of land separates the creek from the lake for a quarter of a mile or more. Ships must enter the channel carefully to avoid grounding on this spit of land. Buffalo Light and the Coast Guard Station are on this prominent but low-lying point. The first light was a stone tower about sixty feet tall. Its oil-burning lantern had good visibility for a distance of about five miles. In the same year the Presque Isle Light flashed its first signals across the entrance to the bay at Erie, Pennsylvania. It was probably a near duplicate of the Buffalo Lighthouse.

Other lighthouses were soon erected at various ports and danger points along the south shore, which was for years a graveyard of ships. Sturgeon Point, twenty miles west of Buffalo, was an important zone because the lake widens here and the point catches the full force of the wind and the storms blowing out of the West. They kick up high seas and pile up the water at the east end of the lake until the overflow raises the level of the Niagara River. Here the sailing ships and the early steamers leaving Buffalo in fair weather felt the harsh brush of the winds. Often they worked or fought their way forward, trying to make the safety of Dunkirk, where twelve feet of water lay over the sand bar at the entrance. Many ships did not reach this refuge harbor halfway between Buffalo and Erie. The *Walk-in-the-Water* was wrecked at Buffalo Creek; the *Washington* and the *Erie* were lost off Silver Creek; and they were but the beginning and more celebrated of the scores of sails, steamers and propellers, large and small, that ran aground or went down in this vicinity in storms and collisions. A lighthouse and beacon were set up near the Dunkirk Harbor to guide ships into this haven. Early in the century a breakwater was built to give added protection. These navigation aids alone could not make an end of accidents and disasters, many of which were the result of carelessness aboard, but they did markedly lower the rate of the losses.

Just fifteen miles farther west on a lake-shore point was the Barcelona Light, erected in 1821. The coast line in this region is generally sheer and rises several feet above the lake. Early in the pioneering period escaping gas had been discovered between Dunkirk and Barcelona. Fredonia, three miles west of Dunkirk, was famous for its "inflammable spring" which gave off enough natural gas to light a village of almost 2,500 inhabitants. Barcelona was favored with the same phenomenon. When the lighthouse was erected, it seemed perfectly feasible to use this gas for fuel. It was channeled through wood pipes from a creek bed half a mile away to the lighthouse on the shore, and its beacon was visible for several miles out on the lake.

Other lights were erected at Conneaut, 117 miles from Buffalo (also a danger point for ships), at Ashtabula, twenty-five miles farther west, and at Fairport, thirty miles to the east of Cleveland. These lights provided landmarks and kept mariners warned along the entire 185 miles of the voyage between the Buffalo and Cleveland Lighthouses.

The first light at the shallow, three-foot harbor at Cleveland on the mouth of the Cuyahoga River was erected in 1820. The Marblehead Light, whose ninety-foot tower, still standing, is one of the most graceful on the lake, was built in the following year to mark the tricky entrance to Sandusky Bay.

The light at Otter Creek Point at the west end of Lake Erie, about halfway between the mouth of the Maumee and the entrance to the Detroit River, was built in 1829. Another one was set up at Gibraltar, at the mouth of the Detroit River, in 1838 to guide the increasing number of sails and steamers into that somewhat treacherous channel. The first light at Windmill Point, outlet from Lake St. Clair into the Detroit River, had been erected the year before.

By the time the first immigrant tide began to flow into the Western Reserve and onto the wharves of Detroit there was a fair number of primitive lights at the more important ports of call on the south shore of the lake.

They were, of course, only a beginning. As the seasons came and went, each new year outdistancing the records of the last, still more aids became urgent. Constant improvements have been made, and are continuing to be made all round the lakes: deepening the harbors, dredging the channels, building breakwaters, laying buoys, installing fog horns, submarine bells, radio signals, and charting the lake floor. It has been hard even for men with vision and imagination to foresee over a period of years the tremendous growth of commerce and ships on the lakes. Only a few years ago a twelve-foot channel seemed deep enough to float any ship that man could use on these waters. But before improvements to this depth could be completed at Buffalo, Cleveland and in the Detroit River, the shipbuilders were turning out designs for carriers of fifteen, eighteen, twenty, twenty-two-feet draft. A vast activity goes on every year to keep pace with this expansion, and no season on the lakes ever closes without seeing some improvement in the channels and in the lighting service.

The Navigation Committee of the Lake Carriers' Association presents its recommendations for improvements in harbors and channels at each of its annual meetings; and the Association's *Annual Report* records the progress made year by year. The activity for 1943 on Lake Erie, for example, included placing a lighted buoy above the sunken *Cleveco* barge near Cleveland; white reflectors on Cleveland Harbor Channel Buoys 2 and 4; a new buoy to mark a shoal above Fighting Island; improved buoys at Belle Isle, Scott Middle Ground and Peach Island; and raising the Belle Isle Light thirty-three feet and relocating it atop the brick lookout tower at the Lake St. Clair Coast Guard Station.

The roads and harbors are now so well marked and charted that they are not unlike the traffic system on modern highways with their curve warnings, speed signs and intersection lights. A chain of buoys guides ships straight through shallow Maumee Bay into the river at Toledo; another chain marks the passage into Monroe, Michigan; and still another guides ships through the South Passage around the Lake Erie Islands to Sandusky, Huron and Lorain. There are now two score important lighthouses and range and pier lights marking the shores and harbor entrances on the south shore between Buffalo and the Detroit River Light.

The new lighthouses at Buffalo, Cleveland, Lorain and Huron are in sharp contrast to the tapering stone column—solid, thick, medieval—of the Marblehead Light. They are crisp, angular and modernistic concrete structures standing guard at the entrances to their harbors, flashing powerful beams for ten or fifteen miles out over the lake. The lights are generally of incandescent oil vapor; the oil is forced under air pressure into a vaporizer where it is heated and mixed with air, and burned under a mantle. The lenses are an intricate revolving mechanism. The important lighthouses are also equipped with fog signals, for on the Great Lakes fog is one of the most tenacious enemies to safety. The average of 116 stations on the lakes showed 332 hours of fog per year. When the fog gathers over the lake, the fog bells ring on the end of the breakwaters, and the big diaphones, operated by reciprocating pistons, send forth their disturbing and uncomfortable cry, rising to a fierce bawl like a distressed animal and ending abruptly in a grunt.

The north shore of Lake Erie in the early days was not so well marked, though the need for lighthouses was less urgent along the Canadian coast since most of the traffic was between the south shore points.

Long Point and Point Pelee were the only serious danger zones because they jut far out into the lake toward the ship road between Buffalo and Detroit. The Ontario port towns, never very flourishing, declined in importance in the mid-nineteenth century when the railroads were built across the arrowhead of Old Ontario. They have never revived, and in more recent years the big new highways and the development of the giant lake freighters have left these ports with their early memories in relatively peaceful isolation.

The lights and buoys remain in service, of course, and are frequently improved. Several of the harbors on the Canadian shore have been deepened in recent years, or are now being dredged to accommodate heavy-draft freighters carrying coal to the Ontario cities. They too have the most up-to-date buoys, cans and lighthouses. They are primarily for the vessels putting in at these ports, rather than for general service to ships passing across the lake.

There are sixteen important lights along the Canadian shore line. Ships bound east for Buffalo or the Port Colborne entrance to the Welland Canal steam out of the Livingstone Channel to Detroit River Light where they make their turn (ESE 7/8 E) and head for Pelee Passage. This part of the route is entirely in Canadian waters. The master or the mate checks on the white light at Colchester Reef, about twelve miles from Detroit River Light, which the ship passes close to port. The lights at Kingsville and Leamington are visible to the north across Pigeon Bay. Off to the south among the islands is Middle Sister Light, and to the southeast are the Pelee Island lights. They are well to starboard of the ship's course. Straight ahead is the powerful white flash of Pelee Passage Light guarding the narrow channel between the shoal of Pelee Island and Grubb Reef.

Just off Grubb Reef the wheelsman turns the ship fourteen degrees more to the southeast to clear the Southeast Shoal Light which stands on the reef formed by Point Pelee as it slopes down into the lake. Once safely round this point, the ship sails out into the open lake, and heads northeast (the course is ENE 1/8 E) straight across the middle of the lake for Long Point, 133 miles away. The lights on Pointe aux Pins and on the tall Rondeau Harbor Range (Round O, as the lake sailors call it) are seventeen miles north on the curving Ontario shore, and are seldom visible to the ships that pass them by. Port Stanley, on the top of the arc of the lake shore, is far off to the north from the charted course. Its fixed white light gleams over its own neat harbor set snugly in a protecting half circle of hills. It used to be much frequented by both British and American ships when it served as an outlet for St. Thomas, London and other Old Ontario towns. Around the middle of the century the *Mohawk* ran on regular schedule from Buffalo to Port Stanley. There it made connections with the London & Port Stanley Railroad which in turn connected with the Great Western.

A few miles to the east is Port Burwell. Like Port Stanley, its lighthouse gives off a steady light over its fine small harbor cut back into the sand-hill shore line. One of the first lights along the Ontario coast was built here in the early nineteenth century to guide the schooners that called at the port for lumber and farm produce for the eastern markets.

Those days are not even a memory to the men on the big freighters who take no thought of these ports. They do not even see their lights as they steam past on a straight course another thirty-five miles toward Long Point Light. The Point (like Manhattan, really an island) is only one to three miles wide, but it is about twenty miles long, and it juts its marshy arm halfway across Lake Erie toward Dunkirk. From the wheelhouse of a vessel crossing the middle of the lake from Cleveland to Buffalo you can often see both shores on a clear day. The lighthouse on this dangerous point is equipped with storm signals, foghorn and radio beacon, in addition to its revolving white light. Vessels pass a mile or two offshore.

At the north edge of Long Point Bay is the Port Dover Light to guide ships into the mouth of the Lynn River. Dover has a fine harbor which still serves as the port for the Ontario towns back of Long Point. The "Lake Erie Cross" uplifted on the promontory at the mouth of the river to commemorate brave Galinée and Dollier is more arresting than the harbor light. The light is not visible to vessels passing east and west over the main seaway.

Vessels bound for the Welland Canal forty-four miles east of the Point change course slightly to the northeast as they pass Long Point

Light. They can barely see the other two Canadian lights on the north shore, the one at Port Maitland on the Grand River in the Ontario tobacco country, and the other on Mohawk Island about three miles farther east. As the ships near Port Colborne they pick up the breakwater and Port Colborne Light and head into the canal.

Ships bound for Buffalo do not alter course at the Point, but continue their straight line sixty-six miles to the narrowing corner of the lake. Off to port they see Point Abino Light where the *Walk-in-the-Water* ran into the fatal storm. Here the lake narrows rapidly into the funnel of the Niagara River. The master takes over the ship and guides it into Buffalo Harbor where the Main Light flashes white each five seconds, where the light on the south side of the entrance winks alternately red and white, and those on the long breakwater burn a constant red.

The lights and buoys are given vigilant attention by the Lighthouse Service. For Lake Erie, as far as the mouth of the Detroit River, the service is administered by the Tenth District with headquarters at Buffalo. The intricate channels in the Detroit River are serviced by the Eleventh District at Detroit. The Lighthouse Tenders are trim little craft, the smaller ones being only sixty feet long with a draft of four feet. They gaily fly the national ensign and their own distinctive Lighthouse Service pennant, adopted in 1869. It is triangular in shape, with a red border and a blue lighthouse on a white field. The vessels are named for flowers, plants and trees: *Crocus, Iris, Heliotrope, Cactus, Maple, Mangrove.* They supply lightships and isolated stations, and place and tend buoys. They are equipped with machinery to hoist the heavy buoys from the lake to the deck when they are gathered in at the close of each navigation season to be repainted and overhauled. Often you may see them making port in late November or in early December, braving winter winds and riding high seas with their masts, sides, decks, pilot-houses and hoisting gear heavily coated with ice.

This end-of-the-season work always comes with a rush. Many of the 698 lights on the American side of the Great Lakes are closed during the winter when the ice grips the lakes and the ships are massed and tied up at the ports like sheep folded in a sheepcote. The lightkeepers are taken off at the last minute by the Lighthouse Tenders. They leave enough fuel in the light to keep it going for

another fortnight after the men have gone, to guide the last straggling ships trying to beat the inexorable winter with one final pay
trip. This more hazardous service, of course, is for the big isolated
stations like Rock of Ages and Stannard Rock lights on Lake Superior, Spectacle Reef Light on upper Lake Huron, and St. Helena
Light in the Straits of Mackinac, rather than for the lighthouses on
smaller and more intimate Lake Erie where they may usually be
reached from the shore.

The chain of islands between Marblehead Light and Point Pelee,
however, have their epic of danger and heroism. They are well
spotted with lights. The South Bass Island Light, built in 1892, is
one of the newer structures; most of the others date from the mid-
century. There is a beacon on Green Island, and one on West Sister
Island. Pelee Island is marked with lights, the Middle Ground Light
being romantically visible across the channels from Kelleys Island
to the south and Point Pelee to the north.

When winter closes in on Lake Erie, these islands are most effectively isolated. The keepers who tend these lights are often cut off
from the rest of the world for weeks at a time. Sometimes their
food and supplies run short while they are frozen in or battered by
Lake Erie storms. A generation or two ago there was always danger of fire. The islanders still tell of the burning of Green Island
Lighthouse on the night of December 31, 1863, and of the rescue of
the lightkeeper and his family. A winter gale swept over Lake Erie
on New Year's Eve, following heavy rains and mild weather. The
thermometer made a record drop from 60° above to 25° below zero
in a single hour, so polar was the front that moved down on the lake.
The Green Island Lighthouse was tended by Colonel Drake. One of
his sons had crossed over to Put-in-Bay to attend a New Year's party.
Drake and the other six members of his family were in their house
adjoining the light tower listening to the wind and to the raging
sea beating against the shore of the island. Almost simultaneously
the party at Put-in-Bay and the family on Green Island saw flames
shooting up into the wind from the lighthouse. Colonel Drake and
his family braved the freezing wind and threw buckets of water on
the flames, but the building burned fiercely in the wind. Drake
then rushed back into the house through smoke and fire and rescued
a feather bed and a straw tick to protect his homeless family. They

huddled under the mattress in a sheltered spot during the rest of the night while the storm raged and passed.

Drake's son and the men of Put-in-Bay tried to reach Green Island during the night, but the waves were too high. The following morning, when the three-mile strip of water had frozen lightly, they managed to cross the ice by using cutters and planks. They laid one board on the ice, walked to the end of it, placed another one down and took up the one they had just crossed. In this laborious and dangerous manner they reached the lightkeeper and his family, and took them back to shelter on Put-in-Bay. A new lighthouse was built on the island, but no winter ever goes by without many retellings of the story of the night the Green Island Lighthouse burned to the ground.

Emergencies also arise at the more accessible lights when the sudden weather changes hit the lake. A heavy storm struck so quickly in January 1928 that two keepers were caught in the Ashtabula Lighthouse. At the end of two days the tower was caked over with ice from two to five feet thick, and mountains of ice were piled up on the crib and around the base. The keepers managed to thaw open the door; then with pick and crowbar they dug a trench for forty feet to reach the side of the crib and escape. The keepers and the Lighthouse Service have, indeed, established a brave and quiet record for themselves in caring for the lights and ministering to the needs of the men in the service.

The Lighthouse Service and the United States Coast Guard are always on the alert. They have to be, and it is all in the day's work. No one knows at what minute a disaster may occur. In late April 1944 the new shipping season was well under way, with every available ship hurrying over the shipping lanes with materials for the war. In the early morning of April 29 a soupy fog blanketed Lake Erie. All the foghorns were throating their three blasts at one-minute intervals, signal bells were ringing, and all the modern apparatus for safety under these hazards was in operation. Forty-two miles off Long Point the 448-foot *James H. Reed,* built in 1903 and owned by the Interlake Steamship Company, was feeling her way toward Buffalo with 7,500 tons of ore from Escanaba, Michigan. At 5:30 on that morning the *Ashcroft* of the Canada Steamship Lines, proceeding from Buffalo to Toledo to take on a cargo of coal, reached the same spot under the blanket of fog. The ships crashed. The *James H. Reed* was fatally rammed and sank within a few minutes. The bodies of ten of her crew were recovered; two were missing. They had drowned or died of exposure in the 42° water. The *Ashcroft* brought twenty-three survivors and five bodies to Ashtabula. The body of Second Cook Camille Losey, of Toledo, wife of the steward, was recovered by the *Sherwin,* and taken aboard the Coast Guard tender *Crocus.* The *Clarence B. Randall* picked up two bodies and brought them in to Conneaut. The *Sinaloa* picked up two more and took them to Port Colborne.

The next day the United States Coast Guard notified all shipping that the *James H. Reed* was lying in sixty-six feet of water, 42 miles and 247 degrees from Long Point Light Station, with spars showing above water, and that she was marked with lighted buoys showing uninterrupted quick-flashing white lights, and that a buoy had been set 500 feet bearing 68 degrees from the wreck.

A few minutes later on that same foggy morning, the 412-foot *Frank E. Vigor* of the Columbia Transportation Company, carrying two cranes, was easing along through Pelee Passage, Buffalo-bound with 6,000 tons of sulphur. At that same moment the *Phillip Minch* of the Kinsman Transit Company was proceeding through the passage upbound light. She rammed her bow into the starboard side of the *Frank E. Vigor* with such force that the two ships stuck fast for several minutes. Some of the *Frank E. Vigor's* crew climbed directly aboard the *Phillip Minch* before the ships separated. The *Frank E. Vigor* then came loose, keeled over and sank. Captain Donald Acton of Lakewood and all his thirty-one men were rescued, and taken to Lorain aboard the *Phillip Minch,* which stayed afloat despite a huge hole in her port bow. And the next day, likewise, the Coast Guard announced to all shipping that the *Frank E. Vigor* was sunk in seventy-five feet of water, 28.5 miles, 77 degrees, from Southeast Shoal Light, and that a Coast Guard vessel was anchored 1,800 feet due west to mark the location until lighted buoys could be placed.

Part of the blame for these disasters was unofficially charged to green and inexperienced crews who were trying to stop the gaps made by the drain of man power from the Great Lakes shipping into World War II.

ICE BOATING ON MAUMEE BAY

SUMMER ON THE SANDS AT PRESQUE ISLE

In spite of all the care taken to chart the lake floor and mark the hazards, a ship occasionally damages her hull on unmarked wrecks which may have shifted their position on the restless floor of the lake. In 1923 the *Seeandbee,* Hugh McAlpine, Master, was making a regular routine trip from Cleveland to Buffalo over the route sailed in safety by a thousand ships. The course lies six miles off Fairport, ten miles off Dunkirk, passes north of the Buffalo Can, then turns southward past Waverly Shoal buoy and into the harbor entrance. The captain himself, a man of great experience on Lake Erie, was in charge of the *Seeandbee* when she approached the harbor. As she cleared Waverly Shoal buoy at a good distance, the ship struck some submerged object and scraped her hull. The damage was so severe that the ship had to go into dry dock at Lorain for repairs.

Yes, sailing on the Great Lakes is dangerous business. Many men get drowned or killed every year despite all the safety precautions. But the danger tends to decrease, and the chance of survival gets better all the time. The weather reports, the radio, the Coast Guard, the number of ships on the lakes all lessen the dangers. The services extend to casual fishermen on the lake for pleasure.

What has been done on the Great Lakes in this regard is nicely shown by two episodes that occurred on Lake Erie. In September 1817, Solomon Sweatland of Conneaut went deer hunting along the lake. When the deer ran into the water to escape the hunter and his hounds, Sweatland jumped into his fourteen-foot dugout canoe and pursued them. Well out from the shore he encountered adverse wind and heavy seas. He headed his canoe toward land, but he made no headway. The wind drove him steadily out into the open lake. A neighbor saw him far out, his canoe plunging in the high seas, drifting outward. He sounded alarm, and the neighbors took to a small boat to attempt a rescue. They worked out into the lake about five miles, but the seas were running so high that they gave up and returned to shore, as the deer had done, certain that no boat could live in such seas. Sweatland was given up as dead in the waves. His wife went into widow's weeds and his funeral was preached in the village.

But Sweatland was not dead. He put his hollow log boat before the wind and let it drift. Two schooners passed by without sighting him. He trimmed the canoe to the waves by standing erect and moving cautiously from bow to stern. He bailed out the water with his shoes. By a miracle his craft remained afloat and was driven across the lake, over fifty miles, to the Canadian shore, where it was beached near Long Point, forty miles from any habitation. Like Ulysses cast ashore from the wine-dark sea, he rested; then he started his long journey on foot back around the lake. On his way he found a quantity of goods cast ashore from a wrecked vessel. He finally reached a settlement where he was well received and cared for. When he had recovered his strength, he went back in a boat with some men from the settlement and recovered the goods he had found on the beach. Then he went by land on around the foot of the lake to Buffalo. There he sold his treasure, bought some handsome clothes and took passage on the *Traveller* for Conneaut. Captain Brown of the *Traveller* ordered the deck gun fired, and the crew shouted cheers as the packet put in at the harbor and returned the dead husband to the living widow.

In late August 1944, Edward Miller and Arthur Bensel of Willoughby sailed out from Chagrin River in a twelve-foot flat-bottomed rowboat with an outboard motor to fish in Lake Erie. They had not returned at midnight. This was reported at 1:00 A.M. to the Coast Guard Station at Fairport Harbor. A lifeboat went out to search for them, but at 10:00 A.M. it had found no trace of the missing fishermen. The Coast Guard then called Major Kent H. Smith, executive officer of the Ohio Wing of the Civil Air Patrol, to fly the region in his seaplane. Starting at Willoughby, he flew twenty-mile-long courses north over Lake Erie. On the fourth course Major Smith sighted the fishermen in their crippled craft; they were waving their oars wildly to attract attention. He then radioed the Coast Guard via the Department of Commerce radio stations at the Perry Emergency Field and the Cleveland Airport. He began to circle over the boat first at 1,400 feet and then, because low scud was flying and high seas were running, at only 600 feet. The Canadian freighter *James B. Eads* was at that moment steaming westward toward the spot where the seaplane was circling. The Coast Guard radioed the freighter, and the ship's officers sighted Major Smith's plane. They turned the freighter off course, rescued the fishermen, and took them on to the Detroit River where a Coast Guard unit "received them in good condition."

Chapter 15

Storms and Hazards

THE men of the lake fleet have a robust scorn for the attitude of condescension on the part of their salt-water brethren. They return the compliment with a certain arrogance of their own. They assert that ocean sailors are grossly ignorant of the dangers and responsibilities of sailing on the lakes. It is really a sore point with them; and they mention it often. They remind you that their ships carry each season a tonnage which makes the transoceanic fleets look like a small coastal trade by comparison; and that their captains put a 640-footer, loaded with 18,000 tons of ore, through narrow channels, into small rivers, and lay her alongside a wharf without the aid of special pilots or tugs, and do it as a matter of course, all in the day's work. Taking an oceangoing ship out of New York Harbor, across the wide-open ship roads of the north Atlantic, and dropping anchor at Plymouth is easy, monotonous routine in comparison with the skill required to bring a freighter across the lakes and through all the intricate channels from Duluth to Buffalo in the rain, the fog and the sleet of early November. The ocean liner has a margin for error and a big sea to play about in, but a miscalculation of only a few inches along more than a hundred miles of the lake channels, crowded with ships like trucks on a highway, would bring disaster.

The lake men take a grim satisfaction in recalling the fate of two ocean steamers, the *Wexford* and the *Leafield,* when they left the safety of the sea for the risks of lake navigation. These ships had sailed the seven seas, and for thirty years had ridden out all the ocean storms. They came into the lakes in 1913—those quiet, fresh-water ponds where you could always see land, where a port awaited you every few miles, and where sailing was as serene as an afternoon of yachting. The storm of November 9 hit them suddenly with devastating fury, and they went down in the lakes with all hands.

The facts compel respect. In the mid-nineteenth century each season saw wrecks and disaster overtake from 300 to 500 ships. In

161

the score of years between 1878 and 1898 a total of 5,999 ships were wrecked on the Great Lakes. Nearly a thousand were wrecked or stranded between 1903 and 1922, and more than 400 in the last twenty years. Each *Annual Report* of the Lake Carriers' Association contains a section on Vessel Losses during the year. The report for 1943 is a sample. It records the loss of the *George M. Humphrey,* owned by the Kinsman Transit Company of Cleveland:

"The most serious single vessel loss in lake history occurred at 2:50 a.m. on June 15 when the 600-foot steamers George M. Humphrey and D. M. Clemson collided in the Straits of Mackinac, 1⅞ miles, 79° off Old Point Mackinac Light. The Humphrey loaded with 13,992 gross tons of iron ore for delivery at South Chicago sank almost immediately in 74 feet of water, but all aboard were promptly rescued, 31 persons having been picked up from lifeboats and the water by the steamer Lagonda while eight others were saved by the D. M. Clemson. In characterizing this as the most serious vessel loss ever to occur on the Great Lakes, the fact is taken into consideration that prior to 1943 a total of 87 steamers 600-feet, or more, in length had been constructed without one of them having been totally lost in collision, or other disasters."

The wrecks which litter the lake floor and which during nearly two centuries have strewn almost every mile of the Lake Erie shore line with bodies and ship fragments are combinations of acts of God, the geography of the lakes and shortcomings of mariners. The acts of God have been chiefly in the form of storms, ice and fog. The storms are formidable in the swift fury of their descent. The lakes, great though they are, impose rigid limits upon the navigator. In western Lake Erie he cannot run a dozen miles off a fixed course without running aground, and even in the open center of the lake he has no chance to ride out a storm by running with it. He is caught in a tank, along with several score other ships against which he may be tossed at any minute. The fog is only a more quiet danger. Warm, moist air slides over the colder surface of the lakes without notice, and within a few minutes blankets these tight and swarming ship channels with fog so heavy that the wheelsman cannot see the lookout.

Even if there were no human or mechanical failures in the operation of the ships, the casualties would still be relatively heavy. Yet it is only in recent years that marked progress has been made in overcoming these natural dangers. A century ago the losses were heavy. The vessels were wooden shells, coated with inflammable paints and varnishes. They were powered by engines that exploded all too easily and they burned wood which was stowed on deck, ready to burst into flame when the sparks fell among the logs. They were firetraps with no fire-fighting equipment. No season went by during which people on the shore were not awed by the sight of flames lighting up a dark spot on the lake as they devoured another ship and drove screaming passengers to plunge into the waters.

In the summer of 1838 the fine new steamer *Washington,* on a voyage from Buffalo to Cleveland, was destroyed off Silver Creek. At two o'clock in the morning fire broke out near the boiler. In a few minutes the entire ship was ablaze. It was impossible to control the flames once the fire was under way. Captain Brown headed his ship toward shore, but the wheel ropes burned off and the vessel was adrift. Many of the panic-stricken passengers died in the flames. A honeymoon couple jumped overboard together and drowned in each other's arms. An Englishman threw his two children overboard, then jumped with his wife. He and the children drowned, the wife was saved. These scenes were repeated over and over again. The *North America* steamed to the rescue, piloted by the flames of the *Washington.* At least forty of the passengers were lost. The surface of the lake was covered with hats, bonnets, baggage and blackened fragments of the wreck.

One of the worst disasters of the era occurred aboard the *Erie* in the summer of 1841. She sailed from Buffalo, bound for Chicago, at four o'clock in the afternoon with 200 passengers and a crew of thirty. One hundred forty of them were steerage, many of them Swiss and German immigrants, with all their worldly fortune aboard. There were also six painters aboard on their way to Erie to paint the S.S. *Madison.* With incredible stupidity, these painters placed their demijohns of turpentine and varnish on the boiler deck directly over the boilers. At eight o'clock in the evening, when the *Erie* was eight miles off Silver Creek, a mild explosion was heard through the ship as the first demijohn overheated and blew up. Instantly the others burst, scattering flaming turpentine and varnish over the wooden vessel. The entire ship roared into flame as the dry timbers, furnishings and freshly varnished interior caught fire. The strong wind whipped the ship into a raging inferno. Burning, screaming passengers leaped into Lake Erie and were drowned. Others were burned to death on board. Captain Titus ordered the small boats lowered, but the high sea swamped two of them. Flames enveloped the stored life preservers. All passengers perished except twenty-nine. Only one woman was saved; she caught an oar tossed to her by Captain Titus and drifted with it until the rescue-ship *Clinton* picked her up.

The *Clinton* had left Buffalo the same day, but she had put in at Dunkirk when the wind increased. She had got under way again and as night fell she saw the flames of the *Erie* shooting up some miles astern. She promptly turned back and reached the burned ship at ten o'clock. The upper works were all gone, the engine was standing and the hull was smoldering. The *Clinton* picked up the few survivors and took them back to Buffalo. She tried to tow the hull of the *Erie,* but it sank about four miles offshore. It was later salvaged and the hard money, nearly $200,000 worth, it was said, was recovered.

The *G. P. Griffiths* was a popular Lake Erie steamer of the 1840's. She was steaming along a few miles east of Cleveland at three o'clock in the morning on June 17, 1850, when fire broke out near the engine room. Day was just beginning to break, the Ohio shore was in sight and no one was greatly alarmed. The captain headed for land as the passengers dressed and came on deck. But a mile from the shore the ship ran aground on a sand bar. Panic then struck the passengers. They screamed and jumped overboard and were drowned. One hundred and fifty-four bodies were recovered and strewn on the sand. They were interred there on the Erie shore, most of them unshrouded, uncoffined and unknown.

The *Atlantic* was another of the fine side-wheelers in the immigrant trade of the 1840's and 1850's. She was making her regular trip from Detroit to Buffalo in August 1852. She stopped at Erie to pick up about 200 Norwegians who were going to Quebec. The ship was so crowded, however, that she had to leave seventy-five of the Norwegian company on the Erie wharf. She was running in the after-midnight darkness and fog a few miles off Long Point and nearing her destination when the propeller-driven *Ogdensburg,* going west, hit her on the port side just forward of the wheel. There was no apparent damage, since the *Ogdensburg* had reversed her engines before the collision, and both ships went on in the fog and darkness, thinking all was well. The *Atlantic* steamed on two miles and suddenly began to sink. Her passengers were awakened and told to prepare to abandon ship. They threw overboard settees, chairs and mattresses for life preservers. The fires in the boilers went out with a hiss of steam. The process of abandoning ship was proceeding in calm order when the Norwegians suddenly went mad. They could not understand a word of English when the captain tried to direct them and explain what was happening. They started leaping overboard in the darkness in spite of all efforts to restrain them. The ship went down at two-thirty in the morning. The *Ogdensburg* had stopped for repairs after the collision. She heard the terrified shrieks of the drowning Norwegians two miles away. She rushed back to the scene in time to pick up 250 of the passengers. More than 300, most of them Norwegians, were drowned. The *Atlantic* sank four miles offshore in 160 feet of water. The Adams Express Company had $60,000 aboard, and many attempts by divers were made to recover it. They failed, and the treasure still lies with much other wealth on the floor of Lake Erie.

The famous mid-century luxury ship *Chesapeake* had a slightly preferable fate. She was a favorite among the well-to-do for summer cruises. She boasted of an exceptional cuisine and kept aboard a merry band of musicians. The *Chesapeake* steamed out of Buffalo on June 9, 1847, side by side with the *Constellation*. Off Conneaut at midnight the schooner *Porter,* Buffalo-bound, turned to starboard to pass the *Constellation,* but her helmsman got confused and mistook the running lights of the *Chesapeake* for shore lights on the point. The schooner struck the port bow of the *Chesapeake.*

A strange confusion then resulted. The watch on the *Constellation* apparently did not see or hear the collision and steamed on. The crew of the *Porter,* thinking their schooner was wrecked, jumped aboard the *Chesapeake,* which also immediately continued on her way. But when her captain discovered that the crew of the *Porter* was aboard his ship, he put about and came up alongside the *Porter.* The schooner was sinking and in a few minutes went down. Just then one of the engine-room watch ran topside to tell Captain

Waine that the *Chesapeake* was sinking. He immediately headed for the shore, ordering all hands to man the pumps. By this time the passengers were aroused. They fell to bailing, but the ship continued to settle. The engine-room fires were quenched by the inrushing water. It was still midnight-dark, and a high wind was blowing offshore. The captain dropped anchors to hold his position. The ship sank in half an hour; but as she went down, the upper deck separated from the hull, and floated like Noah's Ark. The steamer *Harrison* had meantime passed by without seeing the *Chesapeake*. When she put in at Conneaut, one or two of the first survivors had staggered in with the news of the disaster. The *Harrison* went back and picked up the passengers who were still clinging to their odd life raft. Only seven were lost.

Half of the eighty passengers aboard the packet steamer *Anthony Wayne* were saved by the same kind of mechanical accident. She was making her regular run from Buffalo to Sandusky on Saturday night, April 27, 1850. As she was passing the mouth of the Vermilion River, eight miles out on the lake at one-thirty on Sunday morning, the ship blew up. Many of the passengers asleep in the staterooms never knew what happened. The ship sank in twenty minutes, carrying forty to their death. As the vessel went down the hurricane deck parted from the hull and floated above the wreckage. Screaming men and women clutched the floating superstructure and held on until the schooner *Elmyra* arrived and picked up the survivors. There were about forty of them.

Besides the loss in lives, the value of the treasure that lies on the floor of Lake Erie is enormous. The steamer *Clarion* went down off Bar Point near the widening mouth of the Detroit River, carrying with her a cargo of locomotives. The *Lexington* sank in the same vicinity with a cargo of whisky. The *New Brunswick* sank off Point Pelee with a rich load of walnut and oak lumber. The *Cleveco* went down with her cargo of oil. Automobiles have been washed off the spar decks of transport ships, and uncounted tons of coal, iron, sulphur, corn and wheat, newsprint, pitch and salt have been deposited at the bottom of the lake, as mishaps of one kind or another have through the years taken their annual toll.

Fortunately not all the potential accidents actually happened. A curious little book, published anonymously in 1843, entitled, *Steam-*

boat Disasters and Railroad Accidents, records in glowing superlatives the escape of the S.S. *Constitution* during a Lake Erie storm in
October 1837. The circumstances were almost identical with those in
which the *Walk-in-the-Water* was lost. The *Constitution* was caught
in a gale of hurricane proportions. The engineer had up steam to the
full safety capacity of his boilers, and just about every ounce his
wood-burning fire could produce. The fierce gale, however, was
driving the ship toward a reef in spite of the frantic churning of
her paddle wheels. Captain Appleby went below to ask for more
steam. The engineer told him that if he increased the pressure the
boilers would blow up. The captain returned to the wheelhouse without giving an order. The ship continued to lose way and fall back
nearer and nearer to the reef. Again he went below to explain to
the engineer what the alternatives were: take the risk of blowing
up, or accept the certainty of breaking up on the reef. Then the
engineer broke in the heads of two barrels of oil, dipped firewood
in them and stoked the furnace. The crew threw oil into the furnace
with ladles. The engineer pulled down the lever on the safety valve
and sat on it. The steam pressure climbed, the paddle wheels spun
faster, and the ship picked up speed in the teeth of the gale. She
finally made headway against the storm and plowed past the reef.
The boilers failed to explode and the *Constitution* was saved. The
anonymous author commended the engineer for his surpassing
bravery in the accident that did not happen.

There is often only a shadow line between safety and tragedy on
the lakes. The excursion steamer *Eastland* overturned at the Clark
Street Bridge dock in Chicago on July 24, 1915, drowning 812
people. It was seemingly an act of capricious fate. Twenty years
later the big pleasure steamer *Tashmoo* was returning from a cruise
down the Detroit River to Lake Erie with 1,500 holiday passengers
aboard. She struck a rock in the channel and stove a large hole in
the bottom of the hull. She began to ship water at an alarming rate.
It flooded into the engine room and rose toward the fireboxes. The
stokers remained at their stations to keep the vessel moving. The
master made a quick decision. He did not alarm the carefree passengers who were dancing in the ballroom and promenading on
deck. He crowded all speed and put in at the Amherstburg dock a
few minutes before the ship began to sink. She went down in twenty

feet of water and the passengers were safe before they knew of the danger that had so narrowly passed them by.

The record of such disasters is a long one. In Disturnell's list of ships down to 1857 are regular entries like these for Lake Erie ships:

> *Robert Fulton,* built in 1835, wrecked in 1842
> *Saratoga,* built in 1846, wrecked in 1854
> *Adelaide,* built in 1830, wrecked in 1840
> *Little Western,* built in 1834, burnt in 1842
> *Thames,* built in 1835, burnt in 1838
> *Ohio,* built in 1830, sunk in 1837
> *Sandusky,* built in 1833, burnt in 1843
> *Northern,* built in 1851, sunk in 1856.

An enthusiastic admirer of the lakes and an indefatigable traveler, Disturnell made this observation on the necrology of lake vessels: "Were it not for the almost criminal carelessness or recklessness of many of the owners and masters of steamers navigating these lakes, whereby hundreds of valuable lives have been lost and millions of property destroyed, no more safe, instructive, or grand excursion could be found on the face of the globe."

Amazing improvements in ship construction have eliminated accidents like these almost entirely. But some losses still occur even in the best years. Citizens of interior towns, whose newspapers seldom mention the Great Lakes, are quite unaware of the unconscious anxiety from which people on the lake are never free.

One of the first newspaper reports published on the lakes told of the loss of the *Young Phoenix* off Long Point in 1818, with a list of Irish immigrants bound for the free lands of Ontario on the north shore of Lake Erie. They escaped with their lives, but all their worldly goods were lost and they began life on Lake Erie barehanded and destitute. From that day to this the press of the lake towns has featured news of the fatal happenings on the lakes. And each year a given number of men and ships are lost.

The season of 1925 was, according to the report of the Lake Carriers' Association, "probably the cleanest year's record that can be found in lake history." The steel freighters and the larger wooden vessels weathered heavy storms, gales and severe cold without loss.

But tragedy stalked Lake Erie none the less. On May 2 the steel sand sucker *Kelley Island* was loaded off Point Pelee, and about ready to get under way. Without orders from the master, some hands manning the sand-pumping gear disconnected the sixteen-inch suction pipe and removed the shell plates around the hole admitting the flanges of the suction pipe through the side of the vessel. The lake poured into the ship with terrific force. The *Kelley Island* capsized and sank, drowning the captain, mate, two engineers and five of the crew. On the night of September 2 the *Colonial,* a wooden passenger steamer, caught fire and burned off Barcelona, New York. Four members of her crew were drowned.

And in 1941, a season which surpassed the record of 1925, the big 10,000-ton *B. F. Jones,* of the Cleveland-owned Interstate Steamship Company, swerved slightly from the channel and ran aground a few yards east of Livingstone Light on Belle Isle. Three tugs bent lines to pull the vessel free. The tug *America* lunged against her line at full speed ahead. She broke loose, sped suddenly forward and capsized, drowning six of her crew. The following year the tug *Admiral* turned over while hauling the tanker *Cleveco* on Lake Erie near the close of the season in early December. A capsized tug is a trap from which there is small chance of escape. Fourteen men were drowned in the *Admiral.*

Tragic as these accidents are, they are a grim part of the routine of lake navigation, like the yearly toll of lives and motorcars on the highways of the nation. They are entered in the record not as exceptional occurrences but as occupational hazards. The historic storms, however, are in a separate category. The geographical position of the Great Lakes places them in one of the wildest storm regions on the North American continent. The vast polar air mass, which builds up terrific pressure in northwestern Canada, slides down over the unobstructed plains of Saskatchewan and Manitoba. Sometimes it rushes into the bowl of the Great Lakes on a gradient so steep that the winds reach a speed of seventy-five to eighty miles an hour. The moist, warmer, subtropical air mass from the Caribbean region moves northward into the bowl and the two fronts meet in furious war. The polar mass thrusts its cold shoulder under this warmer air, forces it up, cools, condenses and precipitates its moisture, and produces the deluge of rain, sleet, snow and hurricane wind velocities which descend upon the lakes and play havoc with cities on the shore. When this happens on an extreme scale during the shipping season, the toll of vessels, lives and property is catastrophic.

It happens often enough, usually in November, just when the lake fleet is rushing to complete the shipping season before the ice closes in for the winter. A storm of first magnitude roared over the lakes in November 1842, sweeping up vessels before it, and leaving nearly a score of them strewn in wreckage on the Ontario shore of Lake Erie alone. Another one scourged the waters in November 1869. It raged for four days, sweeping from Duluth to the Thousand Islands and out to the North Atlantic. Wrecked in its wake lay the remains of ninety-seven lake vessels; the bodies of an uncounted number of lake sailors were washed up on the shores.

At least once a generation this intense fury is unleashed. Vivid in the memories of all men around Lake Erie are the last two visitations of these November storms in 1913 and 1940. Old lake captains sitting round a table in the Hotel Cleveland in reminiscent mood argue over the relative intensity of these two storms. Some declare that 1913 was the worst in all history, others hold out for the merits of 1940. The elaborate newspaper accounts which covered those harrowing days would indicate that they were twin giants born of the same mother of destruction, and that there was even a terrible suggestion of demonic purpose behind them both.

On Saturday, November 8, 1913, the Weather Bureau reported that a polar air mass was moving down; there would be snow or rain with some drop in temperature with winds west to southwest. On Sunday the storm, increasing in strength, had reached the lakes, but the Detroit papers announced that "ample" warning had been given and that shipping was seeking harbor. The *W. G. Pollock* of Cleveland, upbound, was forced aground on the bank of the St. Clair Flats Canal, but her condition was not dangerous. The *Mary Elphicke* had been blown ashore off Bar Point, but she had been released. Another unidentified vessel was reported on the rocks off Point Pelee. Before the day was over the wind was blowing across Lake Erie at a velocity of forty-six to forty-eight miles, driving before it a blinding snowstorm that made navigation almost impossible.

On Monday the storm had grown more furious. Detroit, Toledo, Cleveland, Buffalo and the towns between were being lashed with a seventy-five-miles-per-hour wind and buried under snow. Cleveland was hardest hit. Five inches of snow fell on the city that day. By Tuesday it had increased to twenty-one inches, with heavy drifts piled up to vast depths by the driving wind. Telephone and telegraph lines went down and for two days the city was cut off from the rest of the world. The electric lights went out; except for the center of the city, Cleveland was in darkness. Streetcars could not run. Three hundred passengers were marooned in four interurban cars at Gates Mills and relief parties had to fight their way through deep drifts to rescue them. Three trains were stalled in a row twelve miles east of Cleveland. The conductor of the last train got off, lost himself in the drift and was killed by another train. Cleveland's water, drawn from the lake, turned "coffee color." Damage to the city reached $2,000,000. Buffalo was hit only a little less severely.

Despite the warnings, many ships were caught on the lake. The *G. J. Grammar* was driven aground off Lorain. The Coast Guard placed a breeches buoy in position ready to take off Captain John Burns of Buffalo and his crew of twenty-two if the vessel should break up. (She held firm.) The *Santa Maria,* a reproduction of Columbus' caravel, was on Lake Erie bound out for San Francisco. She had aboard "what is cherished as" the original anchor with which Columbus set sail to America. By a lucky chance, the little craft was blown ashore into a mudbank at Erie. Lightship No. 82 was caught and sent down with all hands off Point Abino, fifteen miles from Buffalo, near the spot where the storm struck the *Walk-in-the-Water.* The vessel was later washed into Buffalo Harbor. The *Henry B. Smith* of Cleveland disappeared with all hands. Loaded with 11,000 tons of ore, she left Marquette for Cleveland on Sunday evening. The seas were already washing over the breakwater as she left the Marquette bins. She was not seen again.

As the terrible week passed, news from the lakes poured in. Nine other ships and two barges were added to the list of sinkings, twenty-six vessels were grounded and severely damaged, and 235 lives were known to be lost. Among these tragedies was the mysterious story of the *Regina* and the big Cleveland freighter *Charles S. Price.* The *Price* left Cleveland on Sunday, crossed Lake Erie, passed up the Detroit and St. Clair Rivers and reached the foot of Lake Huron, determined to fight the storm and finish out her trip. On Monday an overturned steel vessel coated with ice was sighted, floating bow up on the main ship road about eight miles north of Port Huron. It could not be identified, but Captain Tom Reid of Sarnia, who went to the scene in a tug, was certain that it was a 600-footer, and that its crew of forty were dead. The tug stood by to warn other ships. Toward the end of the fatal week, reports came in from various points on the shore of sailors' bodies washing in. Among them were men in life preservers from the *Regina* and the *Charles S. Price*. They were carried to morgues in the lake villages. Anxious wives, sweethearts and friends came in to identify them and search for their loved ones. After the custom on the lakes, Mrs. Howard Mackley had waved to her husband, second mate on the *Charles S. Price,* as the vessel steamed up the St. Clair River. She came to view the bodies, but her husband was not among them. She did recognize the body of Herbert Jones, the ship's steward, with his apron frozen on him.

Then the strange story of Milton Smith was reported on the front pages of the nation's press. He was assistant engineer on the *Charles S. Price*. As the vessel was getting ready at Cleveland for its last up-bound trip, Smith had a premonition, he said, that something was about to happen. He decided to pay off and quit the vessel for the season. The vessel sailed without him the day before the storm struck. She departed against high winds. When he heard the news of the unidentified vessel above Port Huron, and of the *Price* life preservers, Smith journeyed to Port Huron and over to Thedford, Ontario, to look at the victims. The first body he viewed was that of his friend and chief engineer, John Groundwater of Cleveland. There could be no doubt that the capsized vessel was the big *Charles S. Price*. But the mystery deepened when the coroner informed him that Groundwater of the *Price* was wrapped in a life preserver from the missing *Regina*. The mystery was never solved. But as the storm blew over and the lakes again grew quiet, a Detroit diver went down to look at the name on the still floating overturned vessel. It was the *Charles S. Price*. There were no survivors. A few days later the air in the tight hold of the vessel bubbled out and the ship sank.

Exactly twenty-seven years afterward, on November 10, 1940, the same series of phenomena occurred and another furious war of the weather fronts was joined over the lakes. It was described in the press as one of the worst on record for "magnitude, intensity, and diversity." Warm air moved in counterclockwise from the south, cold air rushed in from the north, cut under it with hurricane force and battered the region with seventy-eight-miles-per-hour winds. In some places it even reached the ferocious force of a hundred miles per hour. It struck suddenly. As it tore through Chicago it blew over the world's largest sign advertising a distillery product. It raged through Detroit, lashing the city and blowing down WJR's 733-foot steel antenna tower. It caught the Automotive Trades Steamship Company's 480-foot *George H. Ingalls* as she was getting under way for Cleveland with a cargo of automobiles, and drove her half a mile up the river north of Belle Isle. It swept across Lake Erie, driving the water toward Buffalo and lowering the Maumee River ten feet below normal. Boats and yachts were left stranded at the Bay View Yacht Club. It blew the lights off the Anthony Wayne Bridge in Toledo. The temperature dropped from 63° to 25° in four hours, then slid on down to 15°. Birds and wild life were frozen. Duck hunters out in motorboats were marooned in the Maumee flats. The Coast Guard Lighthouse Tender rescued many. Several perished in the storm and the cold. Two men capsized off Little Cedar Point. They clung to an open duck blind while the waves washed over them. They were rescued. Airplanes were wrecked in the gales. Plate-glass windows were blown in and chimneys pulled down in all the Lake Erie cities. Telegraph and telephone lines were toppled over, and cities were isolated. Lightships were driven out of position. Ships scurried into Sandusky Bay for shelter. Pickands, Mather & Company's 7,200-ton *Davock* was lost with thirty-three of her crew. And as the storm moved east of Buffalo and dissipated itself over the Atlantic, the people on the lake gathered up their dead and began once more to repair the damage.

The loss in men and ships was much lighter in 1940 than in 1913. On that basis some lake men argue that 1913 was the worst on record. But others point out that the 1940 storm was actually more violent, and that if the 1913 vessels had been caught in the 1940 blow the wreckage would have been even greater. The difference is in the improvement of the ships, the communication system, the weather-observation-and-information service, channels and navigation aids. The vessels now have ship-to-shore telephones, they have weather reports every few hours by radio, and the ships are sturdy. These advantages were not enjoyed in 1913. In that year, moreover, there were still many wooden ships. The high mortality rate in those days was due in large part to the breakup of these outmoded vessels. As they have disappeared, to be replaced by the fine modern steel vessels, the accident rate, even in the storm years, has been notably lowered. The forewarned vessels are now better able to keep out of the way of the storms, and to withstand them if they do get caught. The general improvement was proudly noted by the Lake Carriers' Association in 1941 when they recorded that during the entire season no losses occurred to any of their members.

Part II

Chapter 16

Mid-Century Cities

DETROIT

IF CADILLAC had visited his city on the straits a hundred years after
he founded it, he would in all likelihood have been disappointed
with the progress it had made. It had not lived up to the promise
of its location facing the sun and the south on the bend of the arterial
river connecting the lakes. It had grown slowly, and it was more of
a way station, a fur-trading post and a bastion than a land of homes,
until three decades after Captain Moses Porter hoisted the American
flag over it in 1796. The population was French and British, not
American. Porter found only 300 dwellings there at the end of a
century of settlement, and they were not very prosperous. So long
as the wars and the threat of war continued, the fort and not the
farms held the center of attention.

With characteristic optimism, the Congress nonetheless created
Michigan Territory in 1805 with Detroit as its capital. But before
the new government could meet, the town was wiped off the map
by fire. On the morning of June 11, John Harvey, the village baker,
knocked live ashes from his pipe before entering the door to his
barn. A high wind was blowing. It caught the burning tobacco,
blew it through the door into the haymow and fanned it into a
roaring blaze. Lashed by the winds, the fire spread through the
town, licking up everything in its path. Within a few hours Detroit
lay in ashes among its blackened chimneys.

The fire with its harsh purge of the village was ultimately a
blessing, just as the Chicago fire was later to be. For Judge Augustus
B. Woodward, one of the great American pioneering citizens of
Detroit, devised a new city plan inspired by L'Enfant's Washington

175

model. With all barriers burned away, he proposed wider streets stemming from Grand Circus Park and the Campus Martius center, with radiating avenues (present-day Gratiot, Woodward, Grand River and Michigan) to serve the future expansion of the city. The plan displayed foresight and imagination, and modern Detroit has good reason for honoring the memory of Judge Woodward.

The War of 1812 retarded the recovery and growth. In fact it spread ruin everywhere, reduced the town to misery and threatened it with actual starvation. Many loyal Britishers left with Procter after the soldiers had partially burned and sacked Detroit. The war cut off food and supplies, and when the remnants of Harrison's army took up garrison duty there in the winter of 1813-1814, they were practically without rations and quarters. Filth diseases ravaged the community. Seven hundred soldiers and many civilians died. Judge Woodward, in a letter to Secretary of State James Monroe, described the desperate plight of the capital in these graphic words:

"The desolation of this territory is beyond imagination. No kind of meal or flour is to be procured and nothing for the subsistence of the cattle. More than half the population is destitute of animals for domestic or agricultural purposes. The fencing of their farms is entirely destroyed by the incursions of the enemy and has been used as fuel for the military. Their houses are left without glass and in many cases the flooring has been burned. Their clothing has been plundered from them by the Indians. It is a literal fact that the inhabitants of the River Raisin have been obliged to resort to chopped hay, boiled, for their subsistence. . . ."

His appeal brought some relief; Governor Cass was authorized to distribute $1,500 worth of flour among the starving.

Resilient Detroit, with an energy which she was to display again and again, pressed forward against all discouragement. In 1813 Lewis Cass was made governor of Michigan Territory, and he took up his residence in Detroit in 1815. Among the ruins of war he held a Pacification Ball at the Woodworth Hotel to commemorate the coming of peace at last to the western frontier. But Detroit had one more blow to absorb. Just as it seemed on the brink of great prosperity, Surveyor General Edward Tiffin made his discouraging report to prospective settlers for the western lands. The region around

Detroit, he declared, was swampy and sandy, and there was "not one acre in a hundred, if there should be a thousand, that would in any case admit of cultivation." And he reinforced the slander by adding that "subsequent accounts confirm the statements and make the country out worse, if possible, than I had represented it to be."

The report was, of course, unscientific and based on insufficient evidence, though it was true that the till plain clay near the river was heavy and spotted with quagmires. The first highway and railroad builders discovered this to their sorrow when their roads slowly sank and disappeared in certain regions, and they had to fill in the soft spots with logs and stones to provide a solid roadbed. But only a few miles inland the character of the land changed for the better and was suited for farming. The pioneers had no way of knowing this, or of checking Tiffin's error in declaring that Michigan was "unfit for cultivation, an irreclaimable marsh and wilderness, which was not worth the expense of a survey." Naturally they did not rush immediately to the Detroit region to starve in the swamps and sand when they could float down the Ohio River and take up land in Indiana and Illinois that was fabulous for its fertility. By-passed Detroit continued dormant for another decade. In 1816 it had but 850 inhabitants. Only about 400 people came to Detroit during the first twenty years of American possession. In 1820 the entire territory had a population of only 8,096.

Around Detroit two-wheeled French carts still bore the town and near-by country traffic over the worst of roads. Cows grazed on the town common, and hogs with rings in their noses foraged about the streets. Oil lamps at the street corners cast a pale light over the dirt streets where the mud was ankle-deep in wet weather. The good houses were on Piety Hill below Cadillac Square, overlooking the little Savoyard River (now an underground sewer; the hill was later razed and carted to the river front). Our pioneer forefathers took little thought for the water front of their towns on the rivers and lakes; their interests were utilitarian and, in too large a measure, their views prevailed into our own time. The riverbank, which drew from Cadillac a prose poem of admiration for its beauty, was a dumping place for refuse and dead and rotting animals.

This was the ground-level view of the town when President James Monroe visited it for five days in August 1817. But this great gentleman, growing rapidly old-fashioned in his knee breeches and silver-buckled slippers and oiled hair, had the courtesy to take notice only of the fine citizens who, under the leadership of Governor Cass, entertained him handsomely, provided him with a carriage, and rode on horseback in a procession of honor to the town. As a climax they gave him a magnificent ball at the Woodworth and welcomed him as "Our Nation's Chief," and "the Pilot who weathered the storm."

The President, like so many other travelers of that era, was only making a flying visit to these western domains. Other men, shrewd and businesslike, or kindly and humane, looking beyond the poor estate of the Detroit of the moment to the city of the future, came to stay and live and work. The beloved Father Gabriel Richard had arrived in 1798 to take charge of the parish of Ste. Anne and to labor among the Indian missions. He spent the rest of his life at Detroit and became one of its most venerated citizens. He helped it through every crisis and labored for its advancement. When the fire of 1805 left the entire population huddled among the burned ruins, homeless and without food, Father Richard went up and down the river collecting canoeloads of provisions from the habitants for their relief. Seeing the Detroit children growing up without schools, he gathered them in and taught them; and he was one of the leaders in bringing a public-school system to the town. He brought in the first printing press to print elementary school texts for his charges, and to issue pamphlets and a newspaper. This first newspaper, the four-page Michigan *Essay and Impartial Observer,* published on August 31, 1809, contained a column and a half in the French language for the French citizens. The good father sometimes preached in accented English interspersed with French words to his Protestant friends. His parishioners and admirers elected him as their territorial representative to Congress in 1823. He was a strange and striking figure in Washington in his knee breeches, silk stockings and long black coat; but he represented his region well, and got for it an appropriation to begin the construction of a road out Michigan Avenue toward Chicago.

Judge Woodward was a coworker with him in giving shape to Detroit. This tall, raw-boned, Virginia lawyer had arrived in Detroit in 1805. As a judge of Michigan Territory he assumed active leadership in all civic affairs. Besides planning the town, he drew up the act of 1817 for founding the University of Michigania, or, as it was in danger of being called, the Catholepistemiad. With driving and confident energy he pushed forward his program for the city, never for a moment believing that any of the setbacks which Detroit experienced in its early years could be anything but temporary.

Lewis Cass came, and with Detroit as his capital, governed Michigan Territory from 1813 to 1831. He bought a farm on the edge of town, his house was a social center on the frontier, and he labored to bring good government and peaceful development to the city and the Territory. His efforts and his confidence were rewarded, for in due course the expanding town flanked his farm and skyrocketed its value, and during the land boom of the 1830's he sold a portion of it "as far back as Larned Street" for $100,000. He was a tower of strength in negotiating with the Indians to open up Michigan to peaceful settlement. He issued the first proclamation for the observance of Thanksgiving Day in Detroit on November 25, 1824, a direct result of the first wave of migration which came out of New England. When surveyors discovered the excellent prospect and good lands at Pontiac, Cass went out with other Detroit citizens to found the village in 1819, thus linking that center of future manufacturing to the mother city. He helped lay the foundation of Detroit's cultural activity by organizing and acting as the first president of the Detroit Athenaeum, with its library and reading room—a forerunner of the celebrated Detroit libraries and art center of the modern city.

Lewis Cass was also responsible for bringing Douglass Houghton, Henry Schoolcraft, and other young men to Detroit. Americans everywhere were manifesting their zeal for lectures and their interest in science. Eastern cities, including Buffalo, had regularly organized lecture courses featuring distinguished British and American literary and scientific figures. Detroit sought similar advantages. Cass, Major Biddle and others searched for a person qualified to lecture on chemistry and geology. Douglass Houghton was recommended to them. They invited him out. He arrived in 1830 with ten cents in his pocket. His patrons were astonished and disappointed to discover that he was a mere stripling, twenty years old and small of stature. He soon excited their unbounded enthusiasm and admiration with his charming ways and his brilliant lectures. He was promptly made physician and botanist to the Schoolcraft expedition for discovering the source of the Mississippi River in 1832. When he returned, he set up practice as physician, surgeon and dentist in Detroit. He became mayor of the city. In 1837 he organized the State Geological Survey. The Legislature passed a bill authorizing it, Governor Mason signed it, and appointed Houghton to direct it. His new duties took him to the Upper Peninsula where he discovered the ore beds which were to transform the whole economy of the lake region and revolutionize life on Lake Erie.

Cass did a monumental work for Detroit. His memory is perpetuated by Cass Avenue, by a marble bust in the Public Library, by the park which he donated to the city, and by the great Cass Technical School, with thousands of students and a faculty of about 1,000 members. But the good citizens of present-day Detroit seem to pass by these memorials without associating them with the portly and vigorous old gentleman who was once such a statesmanlike figure in their city and in the nation.

There were also some shrewd businessmen in Detroit. Oliver Newberry, for example. This picturesque figure, whose ships we have already admired, arrived three years after Monroe's visit to Cass's capital. After serving in the War of 1812 and making a start in business in Buffalo, he decided to move farther west. Walking with a pack on his back over the shorter route through Ontario from Buffalo to Detroit, he arrived at the bank of the river in 1820. He was impressed with the panorama that greeted him. There above the trees shone the spires of Ste. Anne's. Along the river were the orchards and neat white houses of the old French families, the strips of poor lands indicating poverty and wretchedness, and the marshes where muskrats were abundant and birds sang in the marsh grass. At the wharf was Ed Baldwin's ferry to carry passengers across the river for $3\frac{1}{2}$ *d.* each. And there were young men from the Thames River with barrels of cider to smuggle across by night to avoid the duty—just as they did a century later in the prohibition era.

Newberry crossed over and settled, and for the next two score years he was one of the business leaders and interesting personalities of Detroit. His bachelor life, his enterprise, and his eccentric habits became a byword in the city, and indeed all round the lakes. His dress was as careless as his business habits. Reverend W. Fitch, who knew him well, recalled how he used to keep his accounts on loose pieces of paper which he carried around in his tall beaver, or silk, hat. The miscellaneous stock in his store at Jefferson and Cass Avenues was shelved in the same individual fashion. Fitch tells of a lady who came into his store one day to ask for a certain kind of valuable ribbon which she supposed she would be unable to find this side of New York. Newberry was sitting on the counter wearing his hat and swinging his boots with his trousers tucked inside of them. Without getting up, he reached over behind the counter and brought out a handful of loose ribbons from a basket half-full of cut nails. Among them was just the piece his customer wanted.

Newberry's business procedures were singular, but he prospered richly. He had timed his arrival in Detroit exactly right, for by the time he got his retail store well established, the Erie Canal was opened and the population began to move westward in earnest. This canal, more than any other single influence, brought the surge of pulsating life to Detroit and the Lake Erie towns. The seeds of future greatness, though planted, lay dormant until the waters of the canal era flowed to Lake Erie to nourish them with people and commerce. Journeys that formerly meant months of hardship and expense were now accomplished over the canals and Lake Erie with ease at low cost in weeks or even days. New Englanders left their rock-filled hills and meadows to seek land and opportunity in southern Michigan and the West. Immigrants arrived at Detroit by the thousands in 1820's, and their number steadily mounted. New York quickly became an outlet port for settlers' produce, and supplanted Montreal as the supply depot for needed goods. New York merchants sent representatives to Detroit. Commerce flowed both east and west over the canal to and from the lakes. And it grew in volume each year. Detroit, as both a way station and an embarkation point for the lands farther west, felt the tremendous stirrings of the continent.

Newberry aided the movement and took advantage of it. He branched out from his general store to engage in the commission business and forwarding trade for these immigrants. He secured contracts from the government to furnish supplies to the military posts on the Upper Lakes and at Chicago. To circumvent the high shipping charges on the lakes he started his own merchant fleet which in time grew to be the largest operating west out of Detroit.

He bought the old government arsenal lands fronting the river at Wayne and Cass Streets, and established his own shipyards. He leased dock and warehouse space at various points on the lakes and sent out agents to look after his business. In partnership with George W. Dole he established a warehouse and the first crude elevator at Chicago to receive grain for shipment to the East. He made frequent trips aboard his own vessels, much to the annoyance of his captains.[1] During the land boom of the 1830's he lent huge sums of money to Detroit to keep it solvent. And when the railroad era arrived, Newberry was one of the large promoters, investors and directors. As much as any one man, he helped make Detroit the gateway port to the West to supply its needs for clothing and machinery and food, and to bring back in return its beef, hides and grain.

Uncle Ben Woodworth came to preside over the Steamboat Hotel and to operate the new stagecoach lines that began to reach out from Detroit to the frontier towns like Monroe, Pontiac and Ypsilanti. He built the wharf at the foot of Randolph Street where the *Walk-in-the-Water* made her landing in 1818, and he was standing there in the front of the crowd to welcome the steamer and to conduct the passengers to his hotel. He operated a ferry to Windsor. He was the friendliest and best-known businessman and civic promoter of his day. He was firm for law and order, and when the sheriff of Wayne County refused to do his duty by hanging a wife murderer in the jailyard,[2] Uncle Ben accepted the painful appointment as acting sheriff and pulled the trap on the scaffold with his own hands. His son and aid, who might have carried on his father's hotel and transportation business, was blown up with his own little steamboat *General Vance* when her boiler exploded while he was standing on the deck immediately above it at the Windsor dock.

Captain Sam Ward also came out to Detroit. He too was a vigorous, imaginative Yankee, born in Wells, Vermont. He had built the little schooner *Salem* at Conneaut in 1818, and had made a success by trading along the lake. And now, like Newberry, he saw the coming importance of Detroit. In 1820 he moved into a rough log house at Yankee Point (now Belle River) and went to work. He made brick from the local clay, created Cottrellville Township, got a

---

[1] See M. M. Quaife, *Lake Michigan* (Indianapolis, 1944).
[2] Now the site of the Downtown Public Library.

post office for it, and began building ships for the lake trade. He was the enterprising man who sailed the first ship out of Lake Erie by unshipping her masts at Buffalo and taking her down the Erie Canal to the Hudson River and New York City. With his capable nephew, Eber Brock Ward, he built and operated passenger ships from Detroit to Buffalo and Chicago in the hectic days of the mass migration across the lakes. When the railroads cut too heavily into the passenger trade on the lakes, Eber Brock Ward shifted his interest to iron. He was active in promoting the building of the Sault Canal, and it was his schooner *Columbia* that brought down the first ore from Lake Superior. He was one of the pioneer captains of industry who converted Detroit and Lake Erie into their present industrial pattern, as we shall see.

Dr. Zina Pitcher, another of the great mid-century figures in Detroit, arrived in 1836 to make his contribution. Born in 1797 in New York, he entered the office of a private physician at the age of twenty-one to study medicine. The death of his father when Zina was only five years old had deprived him of any opportunity for formal education. He hired a fellow student to tutor him in the classical languages to repair the deficiencies. He became assistant surgeon in the Army under Monroe, and surgeon under Lewis Cass when Cass was Jackson's Secretary of War. Dr. Pitcher was stationed at various posts around the lakes where he studied natural science during his leisure hours. He left the service in 1836 to settle in Detroit. He became its leading physician and surgeon and one of its finest citizens. He was three times mayor: in 1840, 1841 and 1843. As mayor he persuaded the common council to unite with him to petition the state legislature, then holding session in Detroit, for a law authorizing public schools in the city. The law was passed, Father Richard's dream was realized, and Dr. Pitcher became president of the board of education. He is still known in Detroit as the father of its public-school system, and he wished for no better monument. He was so prominent in the city that when ex-President Van Buren visited Detroit in 1842, it was natural that the reception for him should be held at Dr. Pitcher's house.

By an odd circumstance Dr. Pitcher's professional reputation is kept green in the memory by the service he performed for an obscure boy who was later to become one of the great iron men of the

Upper Lakes—the Honorable Peter White. Peter had shipped aboard the schooner *Bela Hubbard* which sailed between Detroit and the Sault. The schooner capsized off Thunder Bay Island. Peter and the rest of the crew engaged to work their way back to Detroit aboard the *Chicago,* sister ship to the *Vandalia,* the first propeller on the lakes. At Bay City Peter and his friends went ashore to see the lumber town. It was dark when they got back to the wharf. They climbed over lumber stacks on the dock and jumped to the deck of the *Chicago* several feet below. Peter landed in the hold and broke his arm.

By the time the *Chicago* reached Detroit, Peter's arm was swollen to three times its normal size. He was hurried ashore to a Detroit doctor who, after the tradition of the day, not knowing what else to do, determined to amputate the arm. Other surgeons came to witness the operation. They raised no question about the diagnosis. Fortunately for Peter White, Dr. Zina Pitcher came to see the case. He found Peter strapped tight in a reclining chair. While the operating surgeon got ready, Dr. Pitcher examined the swollen arm and asked some questions. Had any effort been made to reduce the agonizing swelling? None had. Dr. Pitcher, ignoring the strict ethics of his profession, ordered the operation postponed while the swelling was reduced by applications of hot water and whisky every fifteen minutes. After two days of this treatment Peter's arm was down to its natural size. Dr. Pitcher then fastened Peter in a chair once more, but instead of sawing off his arm, he pulled the broken bone quickly into place, set it and bound it in splints. At the end of four months Peter was well again. He stayed in Detroit for a year, working in a store on Jefferson Avenue.

Peter White formed a lifetime devotion to Dr. Zina Pitcher and always kept near him a photograph of his benefactor. When the great doctor died, the Detroit newspapers eulogized his labors and called for subscriptions to erect a monument to his memory. Peter White in Marquette read the notice. He sent a handsome subscription and an eloquent letter. His money was used to plant flowers each year on Dr. Pitcher's grave. We shall have more to say about Peter White in Chapter 27.

Scores of men like these assumed leadership and built the city of Detroit into the commanding place of importance which it was reaching in the mid-century. The slanderous fallacy of Tiffin's report was exposed by the thousands of eager people who sailed to Detroit. Many of them fanned out into the countryside around Detroit to cut timber, clear farms and gardens, and plant fruit trees, instead of hurrying on across the thumb of Michigan or up the lakes to Illinois or Wisconsin. By the 1830's the number of ship arrivals and the volume of immigrant travel was something to marvel at and to write about on the front page of the Detroit newspapers.

All through the 1830's land values rose. The upswing began when the government sold the old military post in the center of town in 1827. This area proved to be a harvest for speculators who bought and resold at a fat increment. With thousands of people floating about in the city looking for an opportunity to make their fortunes, it was inevitable that a speculative boom should result. The Detroit boom reached fantastic proportions. The land office was a scene of wild excitement as people crowded in and elbowed each other for the opportunity to buy lands which they had never seen. The hotels could not accommodate them. They milled about in the streets talking about the wonders of Michigan, buying and selling, and gathering around the auction blocks that had been hastily set up by the speculators. New towns were laid out overnight on paper without a survey, complete with fine streets, a public square, and the promise that it would be the future metropolis of the West. And, smitten by the get-rich-quick fever of the decade, men bought lots at prices a thousandfold above their value. Wildcat banks sprang up to issue notes and reap a harvest from this whirlwind. The speculative balloon swelled out to its full dimensions in 1837. Then the buyers discovered that the future metropolis in which they had invested was a desolate swamp, that the river which was to carry commerce to its doors was a dried-up ditch, and that the bank which held their fortune had faded away like the morning cloud. The balloon exploded. Yesterday's rich men, unable to buy today's bread or pay their hotel bills, were left with nothing but a lesson in economics and such memorable axioms as "Don't take any wooden nickels."

Detroit floundered for three years in the backwash of this misguided enthusiasm. But the improvements in the city which the boom had stimulated remained after the crash. Hotels had been erected, shops opened, new streets laid out with houses of wood and houses of brick fronting on them, the bogs in the streets were filled up, and new churches and public buildings graced the town in transition from military post to metropolis.

Visitors, and there were hundreds of distinguished ones, came to see the city. Their reports were generally excited and filled with praise. The best way to get the feel of the expanding town on the river is to see it through the critical eyes of one or two of these travelers who had the gift of language. Here is the first impression which the city made on Mrs. Jameson in 1837, as she emerged from the wilderness of Old Ontario after her visit with Talbot.

"The day had been most intolerably hot; even on the lake there was not a breath of air. But as the sun went down in his glory, the breeze freshened, and the spires and towers of the city of Detroit were seen against the western sky. The schooners at anchor, or dropping into the river—the little canoes flitting across from side to side—the lofty buildings—the enormous steamers—the noisy port and busy streets, all bathed in the light of a sunset such as I had never seen, not even in Italy—almost turned me giddy with excitement."

She turned in happily at the American Hotel, but the "nervous flutter" of life in the midst of this "crowded civilized town" banished sleep and rest for the English lady.

Heat, fatigue and "some deleterious properties" in the water at Detroit made Mrs. Jameson so ill that she had to remain at her hotel for several days to recuperate. She just missed Daniel Webster, to whom she had letters of introduction, and she deeply regretted not hearing the "display of that wonderful eloquence which they say takes captive all ears, hearts, and souls." But even in her illness and disappointment she still found Detroit the most interesting of all the places she had yet seen "in these far western regions." She was impressed by its French ancestry, by the five times its flag had changed, and by its "warlike and tragic experience." She lamented that her own country had yielded it to the Americans and recorded that the British commissioner, when he realized the foolish bargain that he had made, "covered his eyes with his clenched hands and burst into tears." She marveled at its position on the strait—"one of the finest imaginable"—and at its importance as a frontier town and a place of trade which increased every day. She strolled in the cool of the evening along Jefferson Avenue, admiring the rows of large and handsome brick houses, and the white painted wooden dwellings with their bright green doors and windows.

She mingled with the crowd of immigrants pouring daily into the city from the steamers and windjammers at the wharves, and swarming on its plank "footways" before going into the backlands. She admired the excellent shops and the theater, she noted the large number of taverns and gaming houses, and she was greatly impressed by the free library and the booksellers' shops where she "read in the papers long lists of books, newly arrived and unpacked, which the public are invited to inspect." She rode idly back and forth on the ferry, studying the passengers—English, American, French-Canadian; the "trim girls with black eyes and short petticoats, speaking a Norman *patois,* and bringing baskets of fruit to the Detroit market; over-dressed, long-waisted damsels of the city, attended by their beaux, going to make merry on the opposite shore." And she commented caustically that, although the passage required only about ten minutes, yet there was a tavern bar on the lower deck, "and a constant demand for cigars, liquors, and mint julep—by the *men* only, I pray you observe, and the American chiefly; I never saw the French peasants ask for a drink."

On Sunday morning she made the round of the Detroit churches. At the Roman Catholic church she found that "the music and singing were not good." Only a small congregation "of the lower classes" was gathered at the Methodist chapel. The Baptist church, the largest in town, was plain on the outside, but its interior was "handsome and in good taste." The congregation was respectable, serious and well dressed, and the minister's prayer, after an incoherent sermon, was "eloquently fervent." She still had time for the Episcopal service, "the *fashionable* church of the place." Her observations are feminine: "the women were well dressed—but, as in New York, too much dressed, too fine for good taste and real fashion"; the bishop, instead of being an old gentleman with a wig and lawn sleeves, as would have been true in England, was "a young man of very elegant appearance, wearing his own fine hair, and in a plain black silk gown." And with this experience fresh in her memory and notebook, having now recovered from fatigue and Detroit's drinking water, she boarded the steamer *Thomas Jefferson* and sailed up Lake St. Clair, bound for Mackinac.

Harriet Martineau had crossed Lake Erie and stopped at the American Hotel in June 1836. Her brief account of the city is in a slightly different tone. Her boat arrived early in the morning. She had breakfast at a long common table where she "had the pleasure of seeing the healthiest set of faces that I had beheld since I left England." The hotel situation was an exact duplicate of that in World War II: "the place was so full, and the accommodations of Detroit are so insufficient for the influx of people who are betaking themselves thither, that strangers must patiently put up with much delay and inconvenience—We had to wait till near one o'clock before any of us could have a room in which to dress."

Miss Martineau found the streets "wide and airy," and the houses, churches and stores "poor for the capital city of a Territory or a State." But she added that "this is a defect which is presently cured, in the stirring northern regions of the United States." She, too, noted the thousands of Irish, Dutch and German settlers pouring into Detroit, and stopping there to earn money "to carry them further." She was particularly charmed by Detroit society; it was "very choice." "It was wholly unexpected to find ourselves in accomplished society on the far side of Lake Erie."[3]

As this "accomplished society" got under way again in the 1840's, it again transformed the physical appearance of the city and laid the pattern for the next phase of its commercial development. Until the dawn of the automotive-industry era, which centered in Detroit and stamped it with its mold, the city was forced to remain resilient, even opportunistic, in its enterprises. It kept a sharp eye on the interests and needs of the changing nation and adapted its energies accordingly. It became a financial and investment center for developing the interior and Upper Michigan. As the demand for wagons and carriages rose, Detroit turned to the profitable industry of manufacturing them. When copper was discovered in the early 1840's in the Upper Peninsula and along the northern shore of Lake Huron, Detroit set up smelters for processing the ore. The demand for lumber brought sawmills to the city—twenty-eight of them in the year 1840. Detroit flour mills and tanneries processed grain and hides and

---

[3] Harriet Martineau, *Society in America*, I, 232ff.

shipped them back to the farms and down Lake Erie. The call for seeds led young D. M. Ferry, a bookstore clerk, to go into the seed business, and build it into the greatest house of its kind in the world.

The necessity for overland transportation forced Detroit to become a railroad center as well as a lake port. The city turned out in mass on July 4, 1843, to celebrate the completion of the crude strap railroad from Detroit to Pontiac. The straps of iron nailed to wooden tracks would break loose, curl up in "snake heads" and sometimes pierce the wooden stagecoach cars and injure passengers; passengers in winter would get out, gather up sticks, break them into lengths and help stoke the boiler of the engine to get up enough steam to continue their journey; and jokesters would tell of drummers delayed because the farmers along the road set their dogs on the train to seize the wheels of the locomotive and bring it to a stop. But by 1852 Detroit was connected to Toledo and Chicago by a genuine railroad; in 1854 the Great Western across Ontario reached Windsor and the car ferries to Detroit;[4] and in 1855 Buffalo was linked to Cleveland by rail.

These activities brought more people and more wealth to Detroit. Its population was about 10,000 when Mrs. Jameson visited it. By 1850 it had reached 21,019, and by 1860 it had more than doubled again. It lifted itself out of the mud by paving its streets and placing horse-drawn coaches on them. It buried the Savoyard River sewer, cleaned up the river front and constructed new wharves, docks and warehouses. It built more churches and schools. Its 10,000 foreign-born, mostly German and Irish in mid-century, gathered in their own communities—the Germans choosing the section along Gratiot and Mack Avenues, the Irish monopolizing the western edge of town. The business center below the Campus Martius added new and finer and taller stores and offices to witness its flourishing state. And the well-to-do began building mansions on the better streets. The Palms mansion, erected on East Jefferson in 1848, attracted attention to this favored spot on the river where the houses could face south toward Belle Isle and have their lawns run down to the quiet strip of water between the island and the shore. The McGraws, the John Newberrys, the Palmers and other wealthy business families

---

[4] The Michigan Central tubes under the river were not completed until 1910. Cost: $8,500,000.

moved out there. James F. Joy, General Alger, and the political circle consisting of Governor Baldwin, Senator Chandler and their friends, turned West Fort Street into a fashionable residence section. The Buhls and their industrial friends and associates chose Lafayette Street. Woodward Avenue between the Campus and Grand Circus did not achieve fashionable status until after the Civil War, but there were several impressive homes among its trees at the mid-century.

So Detroit moved through its formative period, lived the good life as best it could, adapted itself to the age of progress, and got itself ready to take a prominent part in the era that was to give Lake Erie its dominant place in the economy of the nation.

TOLEDO

Visitors entering Toledo see the broad yellow Maumee River with the bridges arched over it. From their hotel windows and from the crowded streets in the heart of the city they glimpse the long freighters moving carefully up and down the channel or taking on coal at the docks along the riverbank. Almost without exception they exclaim, "But where is the lake!" And they discover with surprise that this great Lake Erie port city is not on the lake at all, but on the Maumee River, a half-dozen miles up from Maumee Bay, which in turn is in the southwest corner of the lake.

If they press their inquiry further, they also learn that Toledo, now one of the greatest transshipping ports in the whole wide world, is among the youngest of the Lake Erie cities. Beautiful Sandusky on its land-locked bay a few miles to the east was a thriving town while the site of Toledo was still a riverbank, a forest and a collection of ponds and swamps. Sandusky in fact was nineteen years old when Toledo was unauspiciously born in 1836. Even in 1850 Sandusky had about 1,500 more inhabitants than its younger rival. It was the canal that made the difference. Sandusky worked hard for it and lost; Toledo got it and began advancing to her present high position of power and influence.

The growth of Toledo is an epic in American enterprise. Off to the southwest of the site of the city lay the Black Swamp. It stretched a

Photo by Herbert Rebman. Used by courtesy of The American Shipbuilding Company

THE "CHAMPLAIN," HEAVILY LOADED, DOWN-BOUND IN OPEN LAKE

JAY COOKE'S MANSION, GIBRALTAR ISLAND, NOW A PART OF THE OHIO STATE UNIVERSITY

Flagpole marks "Perry's Lookout."

miasmic barrier about forty miles wide and a hundred miles long in places between the Maumee, or Miamis of the Lake, as it used to be called, and the Sandusky River. It was almost as much as a man's life was worth to try to cross that barrier in the early decades of the nineteenth century. In dry seasons it was a swamp; in the spring it was generally covered with water up to a foot or more deep. It was overgrown with forest and littered with the trunks of fallen and decaying trees. The sound of horses' hoofs miring into and pulling out of this muck mile after mile all day long in the forest gloom was enough to drive crazy the few hardy souls who traveled through it in wet weather. There was no road across it until 1827, and even at the middle of the century it was so infested with mosquitoes, so toxic with fevers and ague that few ventured to travel through it or to live near it. Settlers naturally avoided it and chose either to remain in the Western Reserve or to go on west into Indiana or Michigan to find homesteads.

Moreover, the Maumee Valley was the last stronghold of the Indians as they were driven gradually north and west out of the Lake Erie region. Anthony Wayne's decisive victory was fought just a few miles south of present Toledo. But for many years after the Battle of Fallen Timbers the remembrance of the Indian wars and massacres lingered over the valley to discourage settlement. And just as that memory was fading, the region was ravaged by the War of 1812 and the attempted invasions by the British and Indians. The victories of Perry and Harrison, however, secured the region from further danger, and the return of peace opened up this desirable river valley with its wide and deep waterway into Lake Erie. In the rapidly expanding America of the 1820's the hazards of the past were soon forgotten, and a few adventurous people moved to the banks of the Maumee River.

The first settlers selected the beautiful region ten miles up the river near the head of navigation at Maumee and laid out their town in 1817. At one time this village and its neighbor Perrysburg had a fair chance of becoming the great city of northwestern Ohio. The river widens here into a lake that is about two miles long and a mile wide. The two villages stand on high curving bluffs above the river. During the first third of the century the Maumee River was crowded with sails and steamers which passed by the few log houses at what is now Toledo without even putting in to call, and ran on up to Maumee with passengers and produce. But the upper river was shallow, and as the size of ships increased to drafts of more than seven feet, these towns were cut off from the big lake trade. A few men down the river foresaw that day coming.

The leading citizens of Perrysburg and Maumee had looked down with patronizing scorn upon the attempts to found a village at Toledo. There were two sites for the settlement. One was known in the early days as Port Lawrence. At the close of the War of 1812 it consisted of a log warehouse at the foot of Monroe Street up near the mouth of Swan Creek. John T. Baldwin with his wife, four sons and a daughter came out to live in the warehouse. It took them ten days to sail from Cleveland by way of Detroit to this spot. Above their rude shelter at the mouth of Swan Creek were the decaying remnants of Fort Industry, a stockade fort which Anthony Wayne had caused to be erected in 1794 after the Battle of Fallen Timbers. On down the river toward Maumee Bay was the beginning of another village known as Vistula, or the Lower Town. Among the few log houses erected there around 1816 was the brick residence of the most notable of the early settlers, Major Benjamin Stickney, negotiator with the Indians and optimistic promoter of the Toledo region. He had made the brick himself at Swan Creek. His fine house stood near the present location of the Libbey Glass Company Plant down on Ash Street. Stickney Street perpetuates his name.

Between these two villages, right in the heart of the city now, was a large pond where boys paddled canoes and caught frogs. The frogs were so abundant here and in the lesser ponds and marshes that for years Toledo was referred to as "Frogtown." The villages were connected by Summit Street over a ridge that was known as the Hog's Back. Even as late as 1850, the two settlements were separated by this Hog's Back. Summit Street was graded through the ridge, making it look like the bed of an empty canal. A plank walk was laid through the cut to prevent foot passengers from sinking in the mud. It was a treacherous passage subject to landslides in wet weather. A local poet attempted to describe the feeling of the citizens in a long effusion published in the Toledo *Blade* in 1852:

O'er Summit street wher'er I cast my eyes,
What curious thoughts along my senses creep.
Napoleon crossed the Alps; his high emprise
Won him a deathless name, but not a step
Of all the peaks he crossed, so hard to rise
As Summit street, beneath whose lowest deep
There is a depth no mortal ever scanned,
A gloomy deep of mud devoid of sand.

And so on for many lines. It reminds us of the attitude of present-day Toledo citizens toward their outmoded railroad depot. A huge signboard requests visitors not to judge the city by this dingy union station.

The two villages determined to consolidate in 1832 and to take the name Toledo for the very good reasons suggested, it is said, by merchant Willard T. Daniels: "It is easy to pronounce, is pleasant in sound, and there is no other city of that name on the American continent." The name indicated the confidence of its citizens in its future greatness. Its newspaper took the symbolic name Toledo *Blade,* and, under the pen of its various capable editors, especially Jessup Wakeman Scott, proclaimed the promise of "the Great City of the Future." It was still mostly promise, for the total population was about 100. But the Ohio-Erie Canal had already reached Cleveland, and the talk was growing excited about the Miami-Erie which would soon be lengthening up to Lake Erie from Cincinnati. Toledo was certain that it was the natural terminus for it. The broad Maumee estuary led by deep waterway into the corner of the lake with Detroit only about sixty sailing miles away, and with all the produce of the rich Maumee-Miami valleys and eastern Indiana ready to flow through. So the land companies sold lots, various companies built docks and warehouses, shipbuilders built steamers and schooners, and everybody clamored for the canal.

By this time both Ohio and Michigan woke up to the fact that Toledo might be worth possessing. It was a compliment to the hardy citizens who had held onto their hopes in season and out that these two great states staged the "Toledo War" of 1835-1836 over the boundary line at the mouth of the Maumee. Ohio's constitution, framed at Chillicothe under the terms of the Ordinance of 1787, provided explicitly that its northern boundary should be a line drawn from the southerly extreme of Lake Michigan due east to its intersection with Lake Erie, "and thence with the same through Lake Erie to the Pennsylvania line." This provision was based on the assumption that the map used by the Congressional Committee in framing the Ordinance of 1787 was correct in showing that such a line would intersect Lake Erie north of the Maumee River. But the maps of that day were geographically uncertain. A hunter who had roamed through the region and had been a prisoner of the Indians at the southern lobe of Lake Michigan appeared at the Ohio convention and warned the delegates that the old maps were grossly inaccurate, that Lake Michigan reached farther to the south than the cartographers suspected, and that they should guard against losing valuable territory on their northern boundary. The delegates took heed. They inserted into the constitution (and here was the catch) these pregnant words of reservation:

"Provided always and it is fully understood and declared by this convention that if the southerly bend or extreme of Lake Michigan should extend so far south that a line drawn due east from it should not intersect Lake Erie, or if it should intersect said Lake Erie east of the mouth of the Miami river of the Lake, then and in that case with the assent of the Congress of The United States the northerly boundary of this state shall be established by and extended to a direct line running from the southern extremity of Lake Michigan to the most northerly cape of Miami bay...."

The Congress did not trouble itself with the boundary line when it ratified the Ohio constitution and admitted the state into the Union. When the line was run in 1817, William Harris, the surveyor, was guided by the Ohio document. Known as the Harris Line, it ran to "the most northerly cape of Miami bay," and gave the site of Toledo to Ohio. Governor Cass of Michigan Territory promptly protested, and President Monroe sent John Fulton to survey the boundary in accord with the exact wording of the Ordinance of 1787. Known as the Fulton Line, it intersected the Maumee River about eight miles south of Lake Erie. The strip included, of course, the site of Toledo and its fine harbor, as well as 468 square miles of Ohio-claimed territory.

So long as the dispute was over a wild forest, neither side pressed its claim. The Black Swamp isolated the Toledo region from settled Ohio, and Michigan actually governed it by default. But when the Maumee took on importance as the potential outlet for the canal in 1835-1836, both states revived interest. Both claimed the wedge, particularly at the Maumee, and that was the occasion for the "War." The citizens of the villages at Toledo in November 1834 formally asked Ohio to claim them. Governor Lucas recommended their request to the Legislature, and that body created Ohio townships in the disputed territory. It also named commissioners to reset the northern border. In the meantime Governor Cass had gone to Washington as President Jackson's Secretary of War, and twenty-one-year-old Stevens T. Mason became acting governor of Michigan. This young hothead countered Ohio's claims with a "Pains and Penalty Act" providing stiff punishment for anyone who assumed authority in this region not derived from the Territory of Michigan. He called out the Michigan militia to enforce the act; they came into Toledo about 1,000 strong, and terrorized the neighborhood. Governor Lucas with his military staff and the Ohio boundary commissioners reached Perrysburg about the same time—March 31, 1835. They recruited about 600 volunteers to defend Ohio. It looked as though the shooting might start at any time over a purely judicial question.

At that point President Jackson dispatched posthaste two emissaries to arbitrate the dispute. By traveling day and night they arrived before the troops started firing. Governor Lucas accepted their mediation, dismissed his army and directed that the boundary survey proceed. But Governor Mason refused to submit the case to a congressional decision. He called the proposal "dishonorable and disreputable." The emissaries returned to Washington where their report placed Mason in an unfavorable position with the President and the Congress. In the meantime the Ohio surveying party was molested by Governor Mason's men. Nine members were actually seized, taken to the village of Tecumseh and held for a time before they were released on bail. Wild reports of this incident spread through Ohio, whipping up feeling as they passed from mouth to mouth. Governor Lucas called a special session of the Legislature in June 1835; it created Lucas County, covering the disputed strip, and ordered properly designated judges to hold court in the name of Ohio at Toledo on the first Monday in September. Ohio also sent delegates to Washington to apprise President Jackson of the situation and to point out that Indiana's northern border would also be involved. Jackson took Ohio's side, and promised not to let Michigan enter the Union until she yielded. Then he removed Governor Mason from his office.

Mason resisted and brought on the final act in the little frontier drama. He again assembled his militia near Monroe and held them ready to prevent the Ohio judges from holding court in Toledo on the announced date of September 7, 1835. But the judges arranged a *coup d'état* of their own. Protected by a band of twenty Ohio guardsmen, the three Lucas County judges rode into Toledo from Perrysburg in the dead of night, held their brief but formal court in the schoolhouse on Erie Street at three o'clock in the morning, appointed county commissioners, and then rode quickly back to Perrysburg before day dawned and the Michigan militia arrived.

The record of this remarkable first session of the court read:

"The State of Ohio, Lucas County, 55: At a court of Common Pleas, began and held at the court house in Toledo in said county, on Monday the 7th day of September, Anno Domini, Eighteen hundred and Thirty-five. Present the Honorable Jonathan H. Jerome Senior Associate Judge of said county, their Honors Baxter Bowman and William Wilson Associate Judges. The court being opened in due form by the sheriff of said county, Horatio Conant being appointed clerk of said court, exhibited his bond, with sureties, accepted by the court agreeably to the statute in such case made and provided. The court appointed John Baldwin, Robert Gower and Cyrus Holloway, commissioners for said county. No further business appearing before the court, the court adjourned without delay.

"J. H. Jerome, Associate Judge."

This document was stowed in clerk Conant's tall hat after the session. The story persisted that the gentlemen of the court stopped for a drink at Munson Daniels' tavern before clearing out of Toledo. While they were refilling their glasses some prankster rushed in with news that the Michigan men were invading the town. The members of the court fled up the Hog's Back, so the story goes, only to discover that Conant had knocked off his hat against a tree and lost the record of the court. Conant and two guards bravely went back, hunted for and found the document, and bore it safely up to Perrysburg.

Ohio had exercised legal jurisdiction over the region, and Mason could not undo it. His troops withdrew to Detroit to engage in the more noble action of celebrating the anniversary of Perry's victory. Only a few drops of blood were shed during the hostilities. They were drawn by Major Stickney's second son, called Two Stickney because his father did not name but numbered his boys. James Wood of Monroe, Mason's rival appointee as justice of the peace, tried to arrest Two Stickney. When, after warning, he insisted on taking Stickney, young Two stabbed him with a knife.

Congress, and not inflamed farm boys armed with rifles, settled the Toledo War. Michigan wanted to be admitted into the Union. Congress, supported by Jackson, agreed to admit her on condition that she accept Ohio's Harris Line to the mouth of the Maumee. Michigan acquiesced, and gave up her claim to Lucas County in return for statehood and the gift of the wilderness of the Upper Peninsula. So Toledo became an Ohio city, Michigan got the untold mineral wealth of the Lake Superior ore beds and, in another generation at least, everybody was happy.

With the Toledo War settled, the new Ohio city was incorporated in January 1837. It already had the first railroad in Ohio—the Erie and Kalamazoo, opened to Adrian, Michigan, in 1836. It was still a crude frontier town. Joshua R. Giddings from the Western Reserve town of Jefferson stopped there on business in 1836. Perhaps he was a bit lonely when he wrote to his wife from his room in the Toledo House, but he told her that on this Sabbath day at meeting time Toledo "appears little like home. No meeting house, no preaching, steam-boats coming and going. Railroad cars moving, a bustle of business about the bar room immediately below me, in short there is none of that sweet retired silence that throws around the Sabbath a loveliness and sanctity so grateful to the Christian feelings."[5]

In 1843 the first canal barge came down over the Wabash and Erie. In 1845 the Miami and Erie canal reached the Maumee, with most of the traffic coming into Toledo at Swan Creek. By that time

---

[5] Quoted from Giddings' MSS. in Francis Weisenburger, *History of Ohio* (Columbus, 1942), III, 9.

there were nearly 2,000 people in the town. Their number grew to 3,800 in 1850 and by 1860 it had swelled to over 13,000 as the railroads expanded their networks toward this port city. Settlers began to drain the Black Swamp to recover its rich land. Brick plants, sawmills, foundries, gristmills, wagon factories, grain elevators, warehouses, shipyards were established in the town. Ferries plied back and forth across the river. Ships sailing out to Detroit, Cleveland and Buffalo crowded the Maumee estuary.

Visitors and businessmen arrived daily. Hotels sprang up to accommodate them: the Eagle Tavern, Mansion House, National Hotel, the American, Toledo House, the Exchange, the Oliver. Runners for these hotels had to be restrained by a city ordinance in 1841. When we remember that laws always follow and never anticipate an offense, the ordinance becomes a vivid social document. It provided that no person should act as a runner for any hotel, tavern, stage, steam or canalboat within the limits of Toledo unless he was licensed to do so. A licensed runner was required to be an orderly, white male, to wear a band to indicate his hostelry, to wait quietly in plain sight until a customer asked for his service, and he was forbidden to "run down or discredit any Hotel, Tavern, Stage, Steam, or Canal Boat; nor use any disorderly, obscene or boisterous language, nor engage in any quarrels, broils, wrestling or fisticuffs with other Runners of whatever description."

The best homes in 1850 in the Upper Town were along Monroe Street, in the Lower Town along Lagrange Street. Soon they were retreating before the spread of business out to Cherry and Elm, along Summit Street facing the river, then out Jefferson and Madison to new suburbs—as they are still doing. An old picture of Toledo in 1852 looks very much like an Iowa farm village by Grant Wood. At the left is the square tower of Trinity Episcopal Church, in the center is the graceful belfry of Old First Church, and off to the right is the tall thin spire of Old St. Paul's Methodist Episcopal church. Cattle, hogs and geese are ranging about over the path-crossed common. This pastoral idyl could not long endure. It was quickly swept away during the 1850's by the upsurge of activity along the lake. The 417 canalboats were bringing vast quantities of goods into the town at Swan Creek—over 3,000,000 bushels of foodstuffs alone came in

during 1846, the first full year of operation of the joint Wabash and
Miami-Erie canals. The busy boats made nearly 4,000 clearances in
1850, and most of their cargo was sent on by ship across Lake Erie.
The tonnage continued to mount through the 1850's. More warehouses and elevators sprang up and more stores and banks were
founded to handle the prospering business that came in the wake of
this activity. A foundry, several sawmills, the Toledo Car Works,
the Bronson Tobacco works, and such industries were set up in the
growing city. Horse-drawn streetcar service was placed on Summit
Street. A bridge was built over the Maumee at Cherry Street where
the ferries scurried back and forth day and night.

Men of high character and superior minds came to make Toledo
their home. Morrison R. Waite, Yale '37, a young lawyer from Connecticut, came out and took an active part in local, state and national
affairs. When President Grant visited Toledo, Waite made a notable
speech of welcome to the distinguished guest. Grant was so impressed
with Waite and his record in public service that he appointed him
Chief Justice of the Supreme Court. Jessup W. Scott, also a lawyer
from Connecticut, chose Toledo as a city of opportunity and moved
there in 1844. As editor of the Toledo *Blade,* he encouraged civic
pride in the young community. He labored with his fellow citizens
to improve the cultural opportunities of this commercial center. He
founded the Toledo University of Arts and Trades in 1872 and donated to it a large tract of land just outside the city limits of that
day. He helped to establish the first public library, an institution
which has become one of the best in the country among cities of comparable size. His memory is perpetuated by the Scott High School.
The work of these men and others like them has been steadily advanced through the years by Edward Drummond Libbey, glass manufacturer, founder of the great Toledo Museum of Art, and other
benefactors.

Around the mid-century the railroads came in with a rush. Rival
Sandusky was already ahead of Toledo in railroad service. It was
connected with Dayton by the Mad River & Lake Erie line (the first
chartered in Ohio) in 1844. The road was immediately extended to
Cincinnati, and by 1850 it was bringing in double trains of passengers to and from the Buffalo steamboats. But Toledo had already

made a modest start with a railroad to Adrian, Michigan, opened in 1836, the first actually constructed in Ohio. The first cars were drawn by horses, but shortly afterward a small and primitive engine, the "Adrian No. 1," began to chug over this forty-mile strip of the projected Erie and Kalamazoo road. The Toledo *Blade* carried in its issue of May 16, 1837, a picture of this remarkable engine and its four-wheeled trailer car, with this announcement from the commissioners of the company:

"TO IMIGRANTS AND TRAVELERS.—The Erie and Kalamazoo railroad is now in full operation between Toledo and Adrian. During the ensuing season trains of cars will run daily to Adrian, there connecting with a line of stages for the west, Michigan City, Chicago and Wisconsin territory. Emigrants and others destined for Indiana, Illinois and Western Michigan will save two days and the corresponding expense by taking this route in preference to the more lengthened, tedious and expensive route heretofore traveled. Baggage at the risk of the owners."

From that tentative beginning the railroads developed the intricate network which now centers at Toledo and spreads out like a spiderweb in all directions except northeast. The story of the railroad companies through their myriad transitions and reorganizations is too complicated to be told here with any profit. The Toledo, Norwalk and Cleveland road was opened on December 30, 1852, when the first train arrived from the east. A line through Sandusky was launched at about the same time. They were consolidated under one management and later became a part of the New York Central System. Other lines radiated north to Detroit, west to Chicago, southwest to Indiana, south to Cincinnati and Columbus and the Hocking Valley coal fields, and southeast to Wheeling and Pittsburgh. These roads gradually superseded the canals. They brought in coal and farm products and laid them alongside the estuary of the Maumee for transshipment over Lake Erie. And it was that combination of rails meeting ships on the Maumee which laid the basic pattern for the rise of Toledo as one of the most important of the Lake Erie cities.

CLEVELAND

Cleveland, wrote Henry Howe after visiting it a century ago, "is one of the most beautiful towns in the Union, and much taste is displayed in the private dwellings and disposition of shrubbery. . . . The natural advantages of this place are unsurpassed in the West, to which it has a large access by the lakes and the Ohio canal. But the Erie canal constitutes the principal source of its vast advantages; without that great work, it would have remained in its former insignificance."[6]

By "former insignificance," Howe must have meant to remind his readers that Cleveland had but three inhabitants in 1796; sixteen in 1798; 152 in 1813; not yet 200 in 1820; only 500 in 1825 (the year the first earth was turned for the Ohio-Erie canal); and about 1,000 in 1830. The canal reached from Cleveland to Portsmouth in 1833; and in 1835 Cleveland had 5,080 people; in 1840, 6,071; and in 1846, when Howe made his visit, 10,135—a flourishing city indeed.

Until Cleveland finally won her struggle to become the Lake Erie outlet for the canal, she was confronted with serious rivalry from the other lake-shore towns in the Western Reserve. For many years it was indeed a tossup among Sandusky, Huron, Vermilion, Lorain (then called Black River), Cleveland and Ashtabula for the position of the "town-with-the-greatest-promise" on Lake Erie. Even the founding father himself, after his first survey of the shore, expressed his despondency and momentary doubt when he sat down before a crude table in this towering forest and wrote to the Connecticut Land Company, "Those who are meanly envying the compensation and sitting at their ease, and see their prosperity increasing at the loss of health, ease and comfort of others, I wish might experience the hardships for one month; if not then satisfied, their grumblings would give me no pain. It is impossible to determine upon a place for the capital." But that high bank overlooking the Cuyahoga River, right in the center of the Reserve, finally appealed to him as the most likely spot, and there he laid out the street pattern and public square of his town, as it stands today, and gave it his name.

Other men were not so sure about this location. John Melish, an

---

[6] *Historical Collections of Ohio* (Cincinnati, 1900), I, 498.

early traveler who is remembered because he kept a lively journal, visited it around 1810. He struggled over the almost impassable road from Canton to Cleveland, hearing the wind make a noise "like distant thunder" on the woods, stopping at crude inns where the landlords had no bread, nothing to make it with, no beef, no sugar, only "bad tea, bad potatoes, and pork." Sustained by "a little whisky and water" given him by a fellow traveler, which he found "a real cordial," he rode into *"the city."* From a distance he glimpsed the "beautiful, blue, placid surface" of the lake through the trees, and he was so entranced that he hastened to the bank to behold "the lake in all its glory." "To the northward," he recorded, "no land was to be seen; and to the east and west, the banks were high, and the scenery very picturesque; the view was really sublime. I was delighted with it; and, full of the pleasing sensations which such a view was calculated to incite, I pursued my way to the tavern. But O! what a contrast was there! the people looked pale, sickly, and dejected."

Melish had his own theory as to the origin of their malady. He looked down from the Cuyahoga bank to the river below. It was a sorry contrast with the clean open beauty of the lake. "The mouth of the river is choaked up by a sand-bar," he wrote, "which dams up the water, and prevents it from having a free passage. It stands in a deep pool, two or three miles long; and the water being stagnant, and contaminated by decaying vegetables, afflicts the inhabitants on its margin with fever and ague. . . . The smell was almost insufferable." He noted a brig just built in the river; it was trapped there because it "could not get into the lake by reason of the sand-bar." He concluded that the two most discouraging features of the location were "the want of a harbor, and the sickness at the mouth of the river." He recommended that both could be overcome by clearing a channel, removing the brush in the river and building a breakwater to the west. (He was right.) Pending these improvements, Cleveland "though dignified with the name of a CITY" would remain "a paltry village" with little hope, according to Melish, of adding to its present "16 dwellings, 2 taverns, 2 stores, and 1 school," with whisky selling at fifty cents a gallon and the taverns charging three dollars per week for board.

Melish was not seeking a home or a place to establish a business; he was just traveling. But his view of the prospects of Cleveland was shared by men looking for a permanent location in the lake region. They too examined carefully the Cuyahoga Flats, the acres of sand at the river's mouth, and the unhealthy prospect of the village. They saw that ships could not get into the river from the lake, and that in dry weather people could cross on foot from one bank to the other. Convinced that this would be a handicap of long duration, they went round the shore to the west, seeking a deeper harbor. They found one at Black River (Lorain). In its natural state it was one of the best harbors on the lake. The river was over 200 feet wide for a distance of three miles and it was about fifteen feet deep. It could accommodate the largest-draft vessels on the lake during the first half of the century. They found another a little farther west at Vermilion, and some of the lake men even preferred it to Black River. The Vermilion River was not so deep at the lake entrance, but it was easily dredged, and it became, as we have seen, a thriving shipbuilding center in the early days. Captain Alva Bradley, one of the greatest shipowners on the lakes in his day, chose it for his shipyards in preference to Cleveland or Black River. Huron also had possibilities, but they were overshadowed by her near neighbor Sandusky on her handsome bay. Howe recorded without qualification, as late as 1846, that "Sandusky has the largest and best harbor on the great chain of lakes, having the advantage of a large and land-locked bay, while the other lake ports are mostly the mouths of rivers. The bay is eighteen miles in length, furnishing ample room for all the water craft that ever could be required." Words that seem strange indeed a hundred years later.

I have talked with many Cleveland people whose families settled in these port towns farther west, but later moved into the metropolis. Their ancestral homes in several instances still stand near the lake or river fronts in Lorain, Vermilion or Huron, some even in Milan. Their story is always the same in its pattern. The grandfather of the generation now in its sixties (the Bradleys are a good example) came west over Lake Erie. He stopped briefly at Cleveland but moved on to a better prospect at Black River (or Vermilion, or Huron) and engaged in the shipping business. When the canal came down the Cuyahoga, followed by the railroads, Black Rock (Vermilion, Huron) lost its business, and the family decided to move to Cleveland, where it has lived and prospered with the city ever since.

Cleveland did not attain its eminence without sacrifice and bitter trials that tested the hardihood of its first settlers. The pictures of these pioneers convey the assumption that they were patriarchal, for the men are bearded and the women look old in their high-necked dresses and bonnet-style hats. Actually they were young men and women in their twenties or early thirties. They had small children and babies in the wagons, carts and boats that brought them west from New Hampshire, Vermont and Connecticut. They were a long time on the way. Children were born to some of them along the road through the wilderness. Lorenzo Carter came with his wife and five children in May 1797 to join the three brave souls who had remained on the Cuyahoga through the winter after Moses Cleaveland and the surveying party left for the East on the rainy afternoon of October 18, 1796: Mr. and Mrs. Job Stiles and Joseph Landon.[7] The fifth of these Carter children was born on the road near Buffalo on the Niagara, and the mother was attended by a young Canadian girl pleasantly named Chloe Inches. Chloe came on with the Carters to Cleveland where she married William Clement at the Fourth of July celebration of 1802. James Kingsbury brought his wife, aged twenty-seven, and three small children out from New Hampshire. They left on June 9, 1796, and arrived at Conneaut on August 16. After barely surviving the harsh winter of 1796-1797 they moved to Cleveland and founded the village of Newburgh up the Cuyahoga, now a part of Cleveland. Nathaniel Doan and his family came in 1798; they were ninety-two days on the road from Connecticut. They had traveled down the Connecticut River, west along Long Island Sound, up the Hudson and the Mohawk, across to Lake Ontario and along the Lake Erie shore to Cleveland. Doan was the colony's first blacksmith, and later the host at Doan's Tavern on the Euclid Road. Abram Hickox brought his wife and five children from Connecticut in an ox-drawn wagon. Abram walked every step of the way. Others who attempted the journey never reached Cleveland; they died on the road, or were caught in Lake Erie storms and drowned, or they perished from exposure on the desolate

---

[7] Landon did not stay. He overtook the rest of the surveying party at Buffalo. But Edward Paine came in to take his place.

shore after being washed in from the lake. The entire Hunter family died on the rocky shore after the boat in which they were moving to Cleveland was wrecked in a terrific storm almost within sight of the haven on the Cuyahoga. Of the first eighteen deaths in Cleveland during the first decade, eleven were drownings.

But in spite of all hardships brave men and women kept coming on, and they drove back the wilderness on the bluff above the Cuyahoga River in those early days. Their cabins stood on the east bank facing the river in the section of the city now grown dingy, except for the lyric arches of the bridges that lift their spans high above the threadbare streets and the Flats below. With one backward sweep of the imagination we blot out the bridges, the Terminal Tower, the Rockefeller Building, the broad avenues with their big stores, hotels and public buildings, and draw over the face of the city its primeval curtain of forest. There were eagles on the lake shore and wolves where the Statler Hotel stands. On March 2, 1815, Horace Perry, Justice of the Peace in Cleveland, recorded that Alonzo Carter appeared in person before him with the scalp of a full-grown wolf, and, after being duly sworn, received according to law the sum of $4.00 bounty from the state. At that sum per head, wolves were a cash crop for early Clevelanders. We watch these few hardy settlers as they kill wolves and hack their way back into the forest along Euclid Avenue and Ontario Street to clear living room for their houses, shops, gardens and farms. And we write firmly into our memories the insistent fact of isolation and loneliness and hardship in this wilderness nearly 200 miles from Buffalo. For when the winter pressed in and the ice closed the lake to navigation in early December, Cleveland was as effectively cut off from the world as old Quebec on its rock above the St. Lawrence. The sailing of the last ship from the Cuyahoga at the end of the navigation season was a ceremony as melancholy as the sight of the last sail disappearing toward France around the bend at the Isle d'Orléans. It meant that the people of Cleveland would see few or no new faces until late April, that no flour, no cotton and no wool would come in, and that they must live through the winter on their own resources.

The resources were, in those early years, slender indeed. There was no gristmill handy until Wheeler Williams set one up by the falls at Newburgh near the close of the century. Each family operated its own hand mill when the imported supply of meal and flour dwindled. Some of the heroic exploits of these men consisted simply in fighting their way to a mill and fighting their way back with supplies. For food they depended heavily on game from the wilderness up the Cuyahoga River and at Shaker Heights. Some of them learned the truth of a statement made by Amzi Atwater, one of the original surveyors, that "the flesh of rattlesnakes, if it can be eaten without prejudice, is extraordinary good food. It is white and tender like fish." Housewives bought their wash water from one-legged Benhu Johnson at 12½ cents a barrel. The men and boys got their hats from Mr. Walworth, and their drinking liquor, in small quantities, from the still at the spring near the Cuyahoga. Jabez Kelley furnished candles for special occasions, and soft soap to the citizens as a by-product of his chandlery on Superior Lane. Mr. Williamson cured their furs and oak-tanned the leather for their boots. Their lamps by night were rags wrapped through buttons and set in saucers of lard. It was mid-century before the streets were lighted with sperm-oil lamps. Illness was a desperate experience at best, but in those first bleak winters the nearest physician was twenty-four miles away at Hudson, which was settled in 1799, just three years after Cleveland. Almost everybody in the settlement suffered acutely through the first years from ague and intermittent fever.

Yet these young citizens in a new world managed withal to live a good life. They were perhaps less conscious than we of the grueling severity of their lives. They indulged in no self-pity. They celebrated Independence Day with hilarity and rejoiced in their freedom. They built churches and attended the services; they paid their ministers, they established schools for their children, they greased and powdered their hair and went to balls and dances, they held elections, and they performed their civic duties. They also formed a reading-circle library as early as 1811, as good New Englanders should be expected to do. It had the largest number of members in proportion to the population on record, for there were sixteen and that was twenty-five percent of all Cleveland. They read, among other titles, a history of Rome, Johnson's *Lives of the English Poets,* Goldsmith's *Greece,* and *Don Quixote*—respectable fare for a village in the wilderness on a riverbank. They published their first newspaper in 1818, under the imposing masthead of *The Cleaveland Ga-*

zette and Commercial Register and with the heartening slogan
"Where Liberty Dwells, there is My Country." It did not have the
high tone of Cincinnati's first paper, which preceded it by more than
two decades; for that paper printed on the first page of its first issue
the Monk-Calais passage from Sterne's *Sentimental Journey,* whereas
this first issue in Cleveland featured a "Shocking Murder," a piece
about "The Sea-Serpent Again," and, instead of poems by Byron
and Gray, it included a joke about an Irishman and his sixth wife:
"I was trying to—to get a good one." But later issues supplied
Cleveland with news about Napoleon in exile and other great events
of the outside world.

We have already noted that the first Cleveland ship, the *Zephyr,*
was launched in 1808. She was built by the indefatigable Lorenzo
Carter; she brought in salt, flour, grindstones, hardware and household goods, and she took out furs and grain. This clumsy little
schooner was, therefore, Cleveland's first effort at communication
and transport. Other ships followed regularly through the years
down the ways to Lake Erie. But Cleveland's future depended upon
her ability to become the outlet as well as the intake port for the
region being opened to the south of Lake Erie. The position of
Buffalo and Detroit was assured because their very location made
them unavoidable to visitors and to the thousands of immigrants
who funneled through them into the West. Cleveland, on the other
hand, was just off the natural route, well down toward the southwest
corner of the lake, and just another port like Painesville and Conneaut. It was the leadership and vision and drive of her early citizens that overcame her disadvantages.

By 1810 there were enough people in the vicinity to form Cuyahoga
County, with Cleveland as the county seat. Five years later Cleveland was granted a village charter by the Ohio Legislature. And
before another five years had passed, stagecoach lines were established which before long linked Cleveland (after a fashion) with
Norwalk to the west, Columbus to the south, Pittsburgh to the southeast and Painesville, Erie and Buffalo to the east. In the 1830's a
stage left the office of Otis & Curtis at 23 Superior Street daily at
two in the afternoon for Buffalo, and another started for Detroit.
Caravans of Conestoga wagons hauled goods over these same routes
—they could hardly be called roads because they were a desert of

dust in drought and a sea of mud without bottom in spring and autumn. Dickens' description of such a road to the lake as he found it in 1842 is one of the best things in his *American Notes*.

"At one time we were all flung together in a heap at the bottom of the coach, and at another we were crushing our heads against the roof. Now one side was down deep in the mire, and we were holding on to the other. Now the coach was lying on the tails of the two wheelers; and now it was rearing up in the air, in a frantic state, with all four horses standing on the top of an insurmountable eminence, looking coolly back at it, as though they would say, 'Unharness us. It can't be done.' . . . A great portion of the way was over what is called a corduroy road, which is made by throwing trunks of trees into a marsh, and leaving them to settle there. The very slightest of the jolts with which the ponderous carriage fell from log to log was enough, it seemed, to have dislocated all the bones in the human body. . . . Never, never once, that day, was the coach in any position, attitude, or kind of motion to which we are accustomed in coaches."

Coach and wagon transport would not make Cleveland a metropolis. It would be a lake port or it would be nothing. Kelley, after convincing Ohio that it must have canals to pull itself out of stagnation, also convinced his colleagues in the legislature that Cleveland was the best outlet for a canal to Lake Erie. Though the village had only 500 inhabitants when the construction was begun, it was squarely in the middle of the Western Reserve, and the Akron route would serve the east central section of the state. There were fewer barriers up the Scioto through Columbus and Marion to Lorain or Sandusky; but the proposed Miami-Erie was not far to the west, and the Akron summit was not formidable enough to offset the advantages, as Kelley saw them, that were offered by Cleveland. The canal went to Cleveland.

The effect was all that Kelley had predicted. If canalboats were to bring the produce from the interior to the wharves of Cleveland, then, obviously, ships must have a channel from the lake into the Cuyahoga. The Congress appropriated $5,000 as an initial sum for river clearance and harbor improvement. With this small sum, and the help of citizen volunteers, a channel was cleared through the sand bar a little to the east of the oxbowing river bed. Breakwater piers were built and a lighthouse was erected. The channel and the canal basin were the gates that joined the interior to the lake. The result is dramatically suggested by the influx of people which sky-rocketed the village of 500 into a bustling young city of 6,000 in a single pioneering decade. By the mid-1830's lake vessels were making nearly 2,000 calls each year at this port. They deposited thousands of immigrants and they exchanged an enormous tonnage of goods annually.

Cleveland began to spread out on both sides of the Cuyahoga above the Flats. But the river separated the communities. Moses Cleaveland's town on the east bank received a village charter in 1815. On the west was a rival village known as Ohio City. Lorenzo Carter operated a ferry on the river below his tavern of rafted logs which floated on the water and could be drawn aside to allow boats to pass through the river. Our forefathers, however, had a sharp sense of rivalry, and they fought for the aggrandizement of their respective villages. The merchants of Ohio City did not want a bridge over the Cuyahoga because they feared that their trade would migrate to Cleveland. When the first wooden bridge was built to span the little river, the Ohio City tradesmen had it declared a public nuisance, and they actually attacked it with axes, crowbars and blasting powder. They blew up the west abutment, and began ripping out the floor. The Cleveland men marched down in force to prevent the destruction of their bridge. The rival bands were in full conflict, cudgeling each other with sticks and throwing stones, when the sheriff arrived and restored order. The bridge was saved. In due course the merchants saw that free trade over a bridge was good for all concerned. Instead of tearing them down they built more— and now one of the attractive features of Cleveland is the score of bridges flung across the low gash of the Cuyahoga. By mid-century (1854) the two towns were united into one municipality, making a flourishing city of nearly 40,000 people on the lake.

We have already noted how water transport on the lake and into the Western Reserve brought immigrants by the thousands, produce by the thousands of tons and general prosperity to the whole region. But the whole country was moving forward at such speed that slow canalboats could not cope with the traffic demands. The canals were scarcely completed and improved before the railroads outmoded them. Just twenty years after the first spade of earth was lifted at Newark for the Ohio-Erie canal, Cleveland was buzzing with plans and projects for a network of rails to link the city with other lake-shore points and the interior. One road would extend from Cleveland to Pittsburgh, one to Columbus and Cincinnati, one east along the lake shore to Ashtabula and Erie, and another west to Toledo. The line to Columbus was first to be undertaken. As usual the promoters' plans and enthusiasm outran the stern realities of finance and construction. The enterprise was headed for bankruptcy and abandonment before it was really well started. It needed a man of organizing skill. To whom should they turn? To Alfred Kelley, of course, then living in Columbus in his beautiful new Greek-revival mansion (still standing, but now a garage) on East Broad Street. Richard Hilliard called upon him and spent much of the night urging him to take over the project. Kelley, now nearing sixty, was reluctant to take up more burdens. But his public spirit was undimmed, despite his twoscore years of herculean labors for the improvement of his state, and he saw clearly enough that the railroads would be as necessary to Cleveland and Ohio in the 1850's as the canals were to the 1830's. He accepted the responsibility.

Under his superior leadership which overcame all obstacles, the railroad was completed and opened to traffic early in 1851. For the third time in three decades the citizens on the Cuyahoga gathered to celebrate another epic in the growth of their city: first to welcome the first steamship *Walk-in-the-Water,* then the first caravan of canalboats, and now the first steam-railroad train. On February 21 the train came up from Columbus loaded with over 400 officials and distinguished guests. Among them were Governor Reuben Wood of Cuyahoga County, Cyrus Prentiss, president of the road under construction to Pittsburgh, and Alfred Kelley. As the train came in, thousands of Clevelanders cheered and cannon boomed a welcome. The passengers and receiving citizens marched to the Public Square for the speeches and ceremonies. Ministers preached sermons on the new era. And after a week end of celebrating such a tremendous accomplishment, the guests rode back to the south on the same steam marvel. Within a few more months, Cleveland was connected with the coal fields and furnaces of the Mahoning-Pittsburgh area, and the farming communities east, south and west.

The railroads threw a panic into the lake fleets. Steamcars quickly superseded canalboats. Would they not also wreck the lake-shipping business? The 1850's were a dark hour for the marine industry. But once again the breath-taking speed of American development saved the day. The vast iron and copper deposits along Lake Superior were uncovered, cities rose on the Great Lakes shores, agriculture spread to the western prairies, the Civil War came on. Ships were still the cheapest and most available, if not the swiftest, form of transportation across the long northern miles. And the Lake Erie shore was the inevitable meeting place of the coal brought in by cars from the Pennsylvania, Ohio, Virginia and Kentucky mines, and the ores brought down by ship from the lonely ranges on Lake Superior. Shipping weathered the brief crisis, and then expanded more rapidly than even the most optimistic could predict. From that day to this, almost a full century, the lake has held a steadily increasing place in the vital transport of the nation's business.

The effect of all this activity upon Cleveland is known to all. Men no longer questioned the location of the most important city between Buffalo and Detroit. They came, settled, worked and prospered. Enterprising men, seeing the inevitable pattern of development with Cleveland as its center, moved in from by-passed ports and towns. Woolen mills were set up in the 1840's, using the skilled foreign workers for making blankets, cloth and garments. That was the beginning of an industry which is still one of the big businesses of modern Cleveland. W. J. Gordon arrived and became president of the Cleveland Iron Mining Company, the firm that received on the Crawford & Price docks the first iron ore to come through the Sault in 1855. William A. Otis came and established the Otis Foundry Company. J. D. Bothwell came, acquired with Ferris the Nypano docks, and developed the steam-engine unloader. Robert Wallace came and, with Parkhurst and Company, built engines— including Bothwell's hoist. John Ballard came and opened a small foundry in 1828. In 1834, following the opening of the canal, the iron men formed the Cuyahoga Steam Furnace Company, which built the first locomotive to operate along Lake Erie, and cast cannon for the United States Army. Alva Bradley, shipbuilder and lake captain of Vermilion, moved to Cleveland, built up the largest fleet of carriers on the Great Lakes, and became the most powerful figure of his day in the lake-shipping business. Samuel Livingston Mather came out from Connecticut, developed his vast iron and steel business and founded a family dynasty which still carries on the business and its tradition. Fayette Brown came up from Pittsburgh, went into banking, then into the Jackson Iron Mining Company, and helped make Cleveland an iron and steel city. Jephtha H. Wade, formerly a portrait painter at Adrian, Michigan, became absorbed in Morse's telegraph, improved it, moved to Cleveland, spread his lines across the continent from coast to coast, organized the Western Union Telegraph Company and became its first president. Charles Brush came, built dynamos, invented the carbon-arc lamp to light the darkness of the city streets, and eventually merged with Thompson and Edison to form the General Electric Company. Henry Sherwin came and, with E. P. Williams, began to make paint to cover the world. Marcus Alonzo Hanna came and likewise founded the Hanna dynasty in iron and steel. John D. Rockefeller came and founded the Standard Oil Company. Henry M. Flagler, S. Andrews, O. H. Payne, Stephen V. Harkness joined him, made Cleveland for a time the oil capital of the world, and amassed huge fortunes. Henry and William Chisholm came, manufactured iron, and built up the great firm which became the Cleveland Rolling Mill Company. Leonard Case came, helped build the canal and the railroads, and, like his son who came after him, gave much of his wealth to the Cleveland that had produced it. Amasa Stone came, built bridges, operated railroads and banks, and spread his benefactions over Cleveland, notably at Western Reserve University. Men of learning, like Jared Potter Kirtland, came, and founded the Cleveland Academy of Natural Science. . . .

The list is a long one, including scores of men of lesser genius and prominence who came to lay the foundation of the great post-Civil War city on the lake. It was a remarkable combination of men and opportunity, time and place—one of those unique moments in the history of the race when a new city and a new world are to be developed. Considering the limitations of human beings, their baffling contradictions of selfishness and generosity, of public spirit and private business ferocity, it must be said that, on the whole, they did very well by their responsibilities. They flaunted their early and sudden prosperity along Euclid Avenue. At the mid-century the region east of Halle Brothers and the Statler was farm land, and Euclid Avenue was a country road. Rockefeller, Bradley, Harkness, Hanna—most of the names we have just mentioned and several more—moved out to these farms and created the lavish mile or two of mansions which made the name of Euclid Avenue to this day synonymous with the raucous millionaire splendor of those early years of exploitation, now somewhat better known as the era of the Robber Barons. That street, now so tarnished, also stimulated the laboring groups to form protective unions; it is significant that one of the first and most powerful of the unions—the Brotherhood of Locomotive Engineers—set up its headquarters in Cleveland.

Perhaps we have said enough to indicate the difficult struggle through which the city passed between the year of its founding and the Civil War, and how it emerged at the end of its first sixty years ready to make a dramatic leap from a frontier lake village into its present position as the sixth largest city in the nation. How it made that transition will be the subject of a later chapter or two.

BUFFALO

The town which Joseph Ellicott laid out at the foot of Lake Erie, which the British burned in 1812, which Pickering, the Prince of Wied and almost every traveler to America visited as a matter of course, began to expand at a fantastic rate after 1825. One of the old harbor views of Buffalo, published in 1815, shows the landing of Harrison's army at Buffalo Creek October 24, 1813, following his defeat of General Procter.[8] We assume its general accuracy. The sailing fleet is at anchor outside the peninsula. Small boats are lightering the 1,500 victorious troops into the harbor. There are the neat fences on the terrace and riverbank in the background, but the harbor, the peninsula and the winding creek are as primitive and unimproved as they were when La Salle anchored the *Griffin* off shore in 1679.

A dozen years pass by, and the canal comes to Buffalo, bearing its

[8] *The Picture Book of Early Buffalo* (*Pub. Buf. Hist. Soc.*, Vol. XVI).

vast tonnage of goods and thousands of passengers to be shipped to the West. We look at another view of the harbor taken from the New York Canal *Memoir* of 1825. Well-dressed gentlemen and their ladies are promenading along a formal walk on the peninsula, gazing and pointing toward the harbor. The river is crowded with sailing ships and steamers, two and three-story warehouses line the bank, and a cluster of prosperous stores, hotels and houses, dominated by a tall church spire, have spread along the high terrace overlooking the lake and harbor. We turn to still another view—the city as it appeared from Lake Erie in 1833. It seems incredible that this could be the same spot at which Harrison landed a score of years earlier. The new lighthouse on the tip of the peninsula dominates the foreground. Craft of every style and description, from a small pleasure rowboat with a white awning stretched over its stern to the latest-model steamer, fill the river to capacity. And across the dim background spreads a city of metropolitan dimensions.

These pictures help us to recapture some of the excitement of those epic-making years when hundreds of thousands of people were on the move to the lake region, when new cities sprang up almost overnight where only a wilderness had been before. The temper of the time and the exuberance of the people were expressed by one of the early boosters of this Lake Erie gateway city after the Erie Canal was opened: "Buffalo has no rival—it can have none. Cities west of us may arise to wealth and importance, but they will be our tributaries; . . . thus rendering Buffalo what it may ever claim to be—the Great National Exchange."

Behind this growth of Buffalo were several remarkable men who were outstanding in a generation of giants. First among them was Samuel Wilkeson, honored in Buffalo by too few citizens as the father of the city. For a quarter of a century following the War of 1812 this civic-spirited Scotch-Irishman labored to found Buffalo as the great port city on Lake Erie. He was the man who successfully fought the village of Black Rock and made his village the terminus of the canal. He organized the citizens of Buffalo to improve the harbor, and he carried through his herculean task in time to persuade the authorities of the superior advantages of Buffalo as the outlet port. While he was struggling against almost insuperable odds to deepen the channel and build a breakwater and a pier, an ice bank jammed the outlet of Buffalo Creek, an eddy formed alongside the pier, and the newly dredged four-and-a-half-foot channel filled with sand for a distance of more than 300 feet, leaving a draft of only three feet. This misfortune alarmed the canal authorities. A judgment bond was executed against the real estate in the village of Buffalo for $150 a day for each day after May 1 until the channel was cleared for the entrance of vessels. Wilkeson and his fellow citizens subscribed the money to carry on the work. Each gave according to his purse. Young Oliver Newberry put up $20. The work went forward and the channel was cleared on time, ready for the grand opening of the canal.[9] We pause to wonder what the history of America would have been without such men as Judge Wilkeson. His modest tombstone out in Forest Lawn Cemetery, difficult to find, bears the words "URBEM CONDIDIT"—"He Built the City." It is overshadowed by the impressive monument to Seneca Chief Red Jacket near the entrance. Perhaps it is quite as well. For those who can see it, Wilkeson's memorial is the city itself.

Frances Trollope, mother of the novelist Anthony, and a onetime resident of Cincinnati, stopped at Buffalo in 1828. She observed that "all the buildings have the appearance of having been run up in a hurry, though everything has an air of great pretensions; there are porticos, columns, domes and colonnades, but all of wood." Mrs. Jameson arrived by train from Niagara Falls in 1837. She praised the city and the hotels, and recorded that "long rows of magnificent houses—not of painted wood, but of brick and stone—are rising on every side."

The difference is arresting.

The man responsible for it was Benjamin Rathbun, one of the notable, and notorious, characters of Buffalo in the mid-1830's. He was a Connecticut man, born in 1790, who went West to make his fortune. According to his own account, he was a passenger from Albany to New York "on the first vessel ever moved by steam in the world, when Robert Fulton the inventor was his own In dianeer [sic]." He was in Toledo for a time in 1818, when, as he said, "There was not a dwelling house in the place."[10] He chose the

---

[9] *Pub. Buf. Hist. Soc.,* Vol. V.

[10] *Pub. Buf. Hist. Soc.,* Vol. XVII; this volume is particularly rich for a study of early Buffalo.

rising village of Buffalo as the spot offering the widest opportunities in the opening West. In 1833 the settled population and the importance of Buffalo had increased to the point where it could be incorporated as a city. A thousand travelers were arriving and leaving at this transfer point every day. The citizens and their business were overflowing the limited facilities of the city. They needed more houses, more churches and hotels, more shops and stores, more warehouses, docks and banks. Rathbun built them. In the single year 1835 he erected ninety-nine buildings of all kinds at a cost of half a million dollars. They included fifty-two first-class stores, thirty-two dwellings, a theater and the American Hotel. Most of the three and four-story brick stores that line lower Main Street in the old photographs of Buffalo were Rathbun-built. The Webster block was filled with twenty-two of his buildings. He was called in the public press the "Girard of the West." A traveler observing the scope of his work wrote in 1836, "Rathbun is the same to Buffalo that Astor is to New York. He has erected a hotel that for size and beauty will compete with Astor's mammoth; and he has commenced clearing the ground for one still larger, so that the prospect of this city becoming the second in the State is very flattering."

This unusual man who was transforming Buffalo was, according to one who knew him well, "retiring in manner and seldom seen by the men in his employ." "A gentleman in appearance," he "dressed with taste and wore black, cut in the latest fashion with a white cravat, appearing more like a clergyman than a business man." His office from which he directed his vast enterprises was only a room in his pleasant house at Eagle and Main Streets. But he employed between 2,000 and 3,000 workmen, many of them immigrants who had come to Buffalo with the canal, or who had stopped there to earn money to make their way farther west. They swarmed in the Buffalo streets which were filled with his teams and building materials.

Rathbun became the largest merchant in the West in the 1830's. "His stores shops and warehouses were full of dry goods, groceries, hardware, building material of all sorts, grain and provisions." An inventory of his stock in 1836 included "upwards of a million feet of pine and whitewood boards and plank; hundreds of cords of stone, nearly two million brick, and a great store of tools for his workmen of all sorts, including everything for building wagons, coaches and railroad cars. . . . He had a thousand barrels of salt, great store of corn, coal and other commodities." He ran his own stage routes over the half-dozen roads leading into Buffalo, bringing passengers to his palatial hotel. He had "between 30 and 40 splendid Stage Coaches" and "about 200 of the finest Horses in any stage establishment in America." "He had 50 wagons, and sleighs, two canal boats, two large omnibuses, and pleasure carriages, barouches, light wagons, etc., enough to equip the greatest metropolitan liveries." All this, be it noted, in a frontier city of only 16,000 population where scores of other capable and successful men were also doing business.

With such a man as Rathbun working miracles in Buffalo, it is no wonder that the city became famous for its growth and provoked astonished comment from all visitors. Rathbun became known and respected throughout the country; bankers in Boston, New York, Philadelphia and Cincinnati, as well as in Buffalo, were happy to honor his signature and finance his enterprises. At the height of Rathbun's career, while his buildings were rising all over Buffalo, Ebenezer Johnson, a banker of the city, presented a Rathbun check to Thomas Farnham, another banker, for payment. The check bore Farnham's endorsement, but Farnham said he had never seen it before. He went over to his safe, got a Rathbun check likewise endorsed by Johnson, and presented it for payment. Johnson likewise had never before seen the check. The word spread quickly to other bankers holding Rathbun's paper. Charles M. Reed of Erie was in conference with Nicholas Biddle at the United States Bank in Philadelphia. Biddle presented him with a $50,000 note that was almost due; it was made by Rathbun and carried the endorsements of Reed and a half-dozen prominent Buffalo men. Reed hurried back to Buffalo and called a conference. The bankers collected their holdings of Rathbun's notes and checks. The endorsements were all forged. Rathbun had always paid or renewed his notes before they were due, his word was as good as his bond, and no one had had any reason to suspect his paper. Following the exposure, the empire valued at $1,500,000 collapsed overnight. Rathbun, with his aides, was arrested on August 3, 1836, and thrown into the jail which he himself had built.

Rathbun professed ignorance of the forgeries. He said that he had entrusted the financial responsibility of his business to his brother Lyman Rathbun and his nephew Rathbun Allen. Both of these men escaped, never returned to Buffalo and were never brought to trial. But Benjamin was convicted and sent to prison at hard labor for five years. Among the assignees appointed to liquidate the bankrupt estate was Millard Fillmore. In his account of the affair Fillmore wrote that Rathbun, at the time of his failure, employed "some 2,500 workmen of all nations and tongues, and they were among the preferred creditors, but fearing they were to be cheated out of their pay, they threatened to plunder Rathbun's stores." The assignees paid them off at once to prevent a riot. The other preferred creditors got about fifty cents on the dollar.

Buffalo was sorely shaken by the bombshell of Rathbun's failure. We forego speculation on the economic principles which it illustrates, but we observe with reassurance that the city did not collapse. The financial house of cards fell, and Rathbun went to jail, but his fine rows of brick houses were still there for Mrs. Jameson to admire. Moreover the tremendous wave of immigration was funneling into Buffalo, bearing with it a rising tide of commerce. The city briefly licked its wounds, wrote off its losses and swept forward with the boom in true nineteenth-century spirit.

Everything favored its prosperity—even the winds and the weather. We have already noted how the winds pile up the ice in vast fields in the narrowing eastern point of Lake Erie at Buffalo. This one phenomenon often delayed for weeks the entrance and departure of vessels at the harbor. In the meantime travelers and immigrants by the thousands were arriving in the city each day to take passage for the West. They were forced to stop over in Buffalo until the lake was open. The hotels filled and overflowed. There were a dozen good hostels and several exceptional ones like the American, the Western, the Mansion House, the Commercial, the Eagle and the Ohio House. In fact the hotels, with their ornate domes, dominated the skyline in Buffalo a century ago as the elevators do in our time. The first object visible in the city from out on the lake on a clear day was the metal dome on the Ohio House. Lake captains sailing down to Buffalo watched for it as a landmark. Sometimes they could see it "glistening like a huge diamond, 20 miles away."

Merchants likewise profited by these enforced delays. Ladies visited the clothing and millinery shops, "the best and gayest in appearance." Commission merchants with advance information on the weather laid in supplies of food to be sold at a fat profit to feed the visitors during their enforced stay. A good living was to be had by anybody with enterprise. One of the most successful of the drifting entrepreneurs was a character who lent color and interest even to mid-century Buffalo by his marginal business deals. He was familiarly known as "Old Beals." He landed in Buffalo in the early 1840's as a captain-owner of a condemned laker which he had bought at Aurora and was to pay for within thirty days after the delivery of its cargo. Beals disposed of his grain, but the boat sank mysteriously at Black Rock.

Beals was in business.

When an ice jam was predicted, Old Beals would go downstate, buy apples, poultry and other farm produce for a song, fetch it into overcrowded Buffalo, and sell it out in job lots to the regular dealers. He bought a cargo of coffee from a sunken canalboat, roasted it, packaged it as "Buffalo Pure Ground Coffee," and sold it in Cleveland. Steamers down-bound for Buffalo on their last voyage, loaded with fresh-dressed Ohio hogs, were sometimes delayed by storms for several days. The pork spoiled. When the steamer docked, Old Beals was on hand to buy the lot for a few cents on the dollar. He promptly resold to a lard-oil refiner for a handsome profit. He bought spoiled full-cream Hamburg cheese from the captains who were delayed during the summer months, added "rectified corn whiskey" and turned out "a prime article of old brandy cheese, commanding good prices in the New York Market."

He also bought a fleet of condemned canalboats, hauled them ashore near the foot of Court Street, and converted them into a village for poor workers which became known as Bealsville. It was a convenience for the laborers, but an eyesore to the community. Lake Erie itself finally cleared the slum. During the October storms of 1844 a southeast wind blew a gale for a solid week, piling up the waters in the western end of the lake, and laying bare much of Buffalo Harbor. Suddenly and without warning the wind shifted to the northwest. It blew down on the city with hurricane force, and carried with it an immense tidal wave as the waters rushed back down the lake. The tide swept over the peninsula, up the harbor, and mauled the river front and the terrace. It hurled ships up into the town, smashed others, ripped through the canal, demolished vessels and strewed the flats and the city streets with lumber from the yards and schooners, and with craft of all kinds from the harbor. The 600-ton steamer *Columbus* was lifted out of the river and deposited up on Ohio Street. Bealsville was completely washed away. Many of its inhabitants were drowned. Their bodies were carried to the courthouse. The homeless were sheltered in the basement of the Market. Old Beals himself, by coincidence no doubt, went into a decline, closed up his affairs, sickened, and died in 1850.

At the other extreme in Buffalo's speculative days was Colonel Alanson Palmer, better known to all citizens as "Lance" Palmer. He at one time owned the American Hotel. He dressed at the height of fashion, and beyond, and went about town in his gilded coach, flashing on his ruffled shirt a portrait of Andrew Jackson set in diamonds. He became a millionaire and built himself a castellated mansion on Tupper Street near Main. He was into everything from a windmill at Point Abino to a patent for the first cracker machine. His reckless manner of doing business is illustrated by a story of one of his transactions. One day while he was drinking with a friend he blurted out: "I'll give you $150,000 for everything you own, except your wife and babies and household effects." And the transaction was done on the spot. Out of pure vanity, he built a full-rigged ship, the *Julia Palmer*. She was finished in mahogany and shining brass, and she carried proudly on her bow a bust of his wife Julia set in elaborate scrolls and cornucopia work. The whole town turned out for the launching to see Lance Palmer break the bottle of champagne over her bow, and hear him announce, "Ladies and Gentlemen, I propose to call the gallant craft after my beloved wife, Julia Palmer." The cannon was fired and the vessels in the harbor rang their bells in salute. The ship was placed in the lake trade, but she lost so much money that she was later converted into a steamer. Palmer was a leading citizen for a decade. His dash and style and his generosity were a byword in Buffalo. But he was caught and pulled down in the Rathbun collapse. He lost his paper fortune, ended in the poorhouse and was buried at public expense.

Among the wide variety of occupations which flourished in mid-century Buffalo were those attached to the shipbuilding trades, and of these the "steamboat artists" were especially interesting.

Across the second story of one of the buildings in the Webster block in the 1840's was a gigantic oil painting of the steamer *Buffalo* rounding the lighthouse pier, and entering the harbor with her colors flying. People gathered in the street to marvel at the huge painting of the wonderful ship on which they would voyage to Detroit. The canvas advertised the studio of the Miller brothers, who specialized in stained glass and "house, sign, ornamental and steamboat painting." Their steamboat plates and woodcuts were in great demand. No vessel was complete until it was properly decorated with the Miller brothers' art. They adapted their subjects to the name of the vessel. The *Buffalo* flaunted scenes of burning prairies; the *Oregon* was decorated with landscapes of the Rocky Mountains and Pacific coast; the *Hendrick Hudson* with Hudson Valley scenes; the *Niagara* with views of the Falls; the *Albany* with Indian and Dutch themes. The Millers made the mid-century steamer fleets into floating art galleries.

Elsewhere in Buffalo the best people were thriving and making this city a place of culture and social interest. Testimony to its gaiety and variety is almost universal. The Eagle Street Theater was active. Mrs. Jameson left a charming account of a performance of *Romeo and Juliet* starring a New York actress in 1837. She was surprised to find the theater so neat and prettily decorated, and that she was to sit in a private box, a luxury she had not expected in this young and democratic city. The performance seemed to her rather ludicrous because Juliet, who was excessively handsome and tall, looked over the head of her diminutive Romeo, who was dressed in the costume of Othello, turban and all. The rail of the balcony did not reach up to Juliet's knees, and Mrs. Jameson sat "in perpetual horror lest she should topple down headlong." Mercutio "was an enormously corpulent man with a red nose, who swaggered about and filled up every hiatus of memory with a good round oath." The pit amused her as much as the performers; it was filled by "artisans of the lowest grade," and lake mariners sitting in their straw hats and shirt sleeves. "They were most devoutly attentive to the story in their own way, eating cakes and drinking whiskey between the acts, and whenever any thing especially pleased them, they uttered a loud whoop and halloo, which reverberated through the theatre, at the same time slapping their thighs and snapping their fingers. In their eyes, Peter and the nurse were evidently the hero and heroine of the piece, and never appeared without calling forth the most boisterous applause."

This company could not have been exactly representative of Buffalo drama, for Forrest, Macready and Booth all performed there. So also did the incomparable Lola Montez, Countess of Landsfeld. This temperamental actress, however, did not like the Buffalo audience, and considered herself insulted by it. She ordered her wardrobe removed from the house. The theater burned early the following morning. The rumor that Lola started the fire by dropping her cigarette into a pile of rubbish went the rounds of Buffalo society and refused to die.

All the great lecturers and literary figures came to Buffalo to appear on the weekly series that ran from November to April— Emerson, Agassiz, Holmes, Bayard Taylor, Dickens, Thackeray, Fanny Kemble. They were entertained by the best families on old Franklin Street. People read books in those days and the bookstores flourished. Mrs. Jameson's eagle eye noted and was pleased to see several bookshops all loaded with American editions of English publications. She was not pleased that Toronto booksellers were principally supplied from Buffalo. Her respect for American literacy was further enhanced one rainy day when she was forced to remain indoors wandering dejectedly up and down the "ladies' parlor" in the "vast inn." A young girl, well dressed, was sitting in the parlor reading the poems of Felicia Hemans; she rose without a word, disappeared, and returned with a handful of books and several issues of "The Knickerbocker, of New York" which she courteously gave to the bored English guest. "A cup of water in a desert could hardly have been more welcome, or excited warmer thanks and gratitude."

Steele's bookstore was a favorite gathering place for gentlemen of the town where they could read and talk. These booklovers laid the foundation for the present excellent Buffalo Public Library, which has extensive traveling collections that reach the entire community and the classrooms in the schools. They supported their favorite newspaper, the *Commercial Advertiser,* founded by Hezekiah Salisbury and Bradford Manchester, as an educational institu-

By courtesy of T. H. Langlois

PERRY'S MONUMENT, LOOKING ACROSS PUT-IN-BAY FROM
PEACH POINT, GIBRALTAR ISLAND IN MIDDLE GROUND

By courtesy of The Jack Miner Migratory Bird Foundation

THE LATE JACK MINER LIBERATING A BANDED CANADA GOOSE
AT THE SANCTUARY NEAR KINGSVILLE, ONT.

By courtesy of the Pittsburgh Steamship Company

UNLOADING THE "LEON FRASER" AT CONNEAUT

tion. Wrote Mrs. Julia F. Snow, this paper "was and is the best daily I know of, in its unvarying quality day after day, year after year, for many decades." The same civic spirit led to the founding of the University of Buffalo in 1846, though it confined its work to the medical school until the 1880's. And to perpetuate the history of the city and preserve its records and documents, ex-President Millard Fillmore, with other leading men, founded the Buffalo Historical Society and he became its first president. Grover Cleveland, who came to Buffalo in 1854, aged seventeen, and became mayor of the city, was a member of this distinguished society.[11]

The Buffalo citizens loved parades and outdoor entertainments. They celebrated Old Home Week. They attended balloon ascensions. They gathered in the park on the Fourth of July to listen to the bands play "Yankee Doodle," "Hail Columbia" and "The Star-Spangled Banner." The great statesmen came to address them: Van Buren and John Quincy Adams, Henry Clay and Daniel Webster. Barnum brought his circus, parading the streets with elephants and camels and cages of lions and tigers. General Tom Thumb, the publicized dwarf, drew throngs to McArthur's outdoor pavilion. Everybody gardened and went to the annual exhibition of the Horticulture Society. The residential streets with their mansions and gardens were exhibits of art. New and interesting exiles from France, Poland, Russia and Germany arrived after each European revolution to grace Buffalo society and stimulate interest in music, dancing, painting, wines and foreign languages.

The heavy volume of commerce brought riches to mid-century Buffalo. Doctors, lawyers, bankers, grain merchants, meat packers, brewers, iron men and railroad operators accumulated wealth. They used some of it to build fine houses and castles around Niagara Square, along Main, North, Delaware, Pearl and Swan Streets. Some of them were at one time among the show places of the nation, like Millionaires' Row on Cleveland's Euclid Avenue. Judge Philander Bennett, who came to Buffalo in 1817, practiced law, and became president of a bank and vice-president of a railroad, and built in 1831 the most notable house in early Buffalo—a square stone man-

---

11 Buffalo is in a sense a presidential city. Besides sending these two citizens to the White House, Buffalo was the scene of the tragic murder of President McKinley, and Theodore Roosevelt took the oath of office at the Wilcox House at 641 Delaware Avenue.

sion crowned with a square dome surrounded by a balustraded observation platform. The Henry Huntington Sizer homestead at 98 Delaware, built for the grain merchant in 1836, a gracious square structure with Greek-revival portico, now housing offices of Spencer Kellogg & Sons, was the first residence in Buffalo to use gas for lighting.

The Pierre A. Baker mansion on Hudson Street was one of the Rathbun-built houses. From 1844 to 1890, when it was the home of the Jonathan Sidway family, it was celebrated for its interior decorations and furniture. The three downstairs drawing rooms had carved rosewood furniture, upholstered in satin damask, made by Cutler. There were elaborately carved marble mantels, ornamental plasterwork on the walls and ceilings, wallpaper with blue cornflowers on a dark-red ground, heavy dark-red velvet carpets, heavy cornices gilded with gold leaf, and enormous chandeliers hanging from the high ceilings.

William G. Fargo, a messenger boy, and agent for an Albany-to-Buffalo express firm, moved to Buffalo in 1841, helped organize the Wells, Fargo express company, became a leading citizen in the city, and built a huge three-story mansion with a five-story cupola looking out over Fargo's extensive grounds and across the thriving streets of Buffalo.

The Bronson C. Rumsey mansion and park was perhaps the most notable of them. This rich merchant built his great house on Delaware Avenue in 1862. He employed two English architects to design his park. They created an extensive lake, fed by a spring on the grounds, and ornamented it with a Swiss chalet boathouse and a Greek temple. They arranged romantic vistas through the native forest trees to direct the eye across the water to the Calvary Church spire, to a sylvan cascade, to the wooded island in the lake, and across the ample greensward to the fountain in the formal garden. They surrounded it all on three sides with a high, tight, board fence, but it was the social center for summer garden parties and winter sports for the select among the Buffalo families. Elmwood Avenue, with its heavy, routine traffic, now flows through the scene of these festivities.

The houses were filled with statuary, knights in armor and both originals and copies of masterpieces by European artists. The well-to-do also patronized Buffalo's first artist of repute, Lars Gustaf Sellstedt. After a life of wandering hardships, this self-taught Swedish painter landed in Buffalo in 1845 and made it his home for the rest of his life. He was a warm friend and boon companion of William G. Fargo. He organized art exhibits which were attended by Buffalonians as social events. And he painted portraits of most of the prosperous merchants of the mid-century: of Fillmore and Cleveland, E. G. Spaulding and General Peter A. Porter, of the Tracys, Austins, Scotts, Warrens, Spragues, Verplancks, and the rest of the notables.

Buffalo was a pleasant city in those days. The old residents remembered it nostalgically, and wrote of it in after years with sentimental longing. But this intimate, villagey air could not survive the terrific influx of new people with new enterprises. The downtown homes were pressed in the mid-century by the expanding business houses, the elevators and the manufactures. Those interests had been growing steadily in importance ever since the canal was opened. Edward Root built a foundry in 1826 to make plow irons and castings. Three years later John Hibbard manufactured the first steam engine in Buffalo. These pioneering ventures were followed by various other foundries, iron and steam-engine works, breweries, lumber mills, nail factories, soap factories and chandleries, and such industries which rose to supply the demands of the lake region. Skilled workers in brass and silver and expert bell casters came in. Buffalo bells rang by the score through the city and in all the lake towns. Buffalo mirrors, picture frames and porcelain bathtubs decorated the better residences around Lake Erie. The Buffalo stock market and flour mills received cattle and grain to be processed and shipped on to the East.

The coming of the railroad era frightened the lake men and shipowners. So long as these roads merely converged on Buffalo to transship goods by schooner and steamer up the lake to Cleveland and Detroit or out to Chicago they were welcome. But when they were extended westward, paralleling the lake shore to Cleveland, then to Toledo and beyond, the threat to shipping appeared dangerous. For they seemed to be a direct challenge to the strategic position of Buffalo as "the Great National Exchange." But the Civil War intervened, the demand for foods and for iron increased, and the need for lake shipping was greater than before. Buffalo's position was not damaged by the railroads. The city maintained its place as the beachhead between West and East where cheap long-distance water transportation met the network of railroads with their fast trains and short hauls to the great population centers of the seaboard. At the close of the Civil War it had established the foundation for its share of the iron and steel industry which would soon transform the cities on the shores of Lake Erie. But of more importance, it became a stockyard second only to Chicago, and it had already concentrated on the handling, storing and milling of grain as its outstanding specialty. The man of vision who was chiefly responsible for making Buffalo into the city of elevators was Joseph Dart. He deserves a modest monument in the form of a special chapter.

Chapter 17

Dart's Buckets

THE farmers on the fat lands back of these cities provided the first mass tonnage of commerce to flow east across Lake Erie. Most of it was grain, and it was bound for Buffalo. In the late 1830's the grain ships were jamming at the Buffalo wharves, waiting to get rid of their cargoes. The problem of unloading grain became acute in the year 1841 when an overwhelming volume of almost 2,000,000 bushels glutted the little harbor at Buffalo. This volume had risen at a rate beyond the imagination of the most visionary. No grain in quantity had come to Buffalo before 1830. Then the rapid influx of farmers to the virgin lands of the Western Reserve, and the opening of the canals across Ohio, placed that state first among the grain-producing regions of the nation. In 1835 Ohio sent 112,000 bushels down to Buffalo. The next year she shipped 500,000 bushels, and that quantity was increased 400 percent in the next five years.

Much of it was coming out of the new farm lands at the west end of the Western Reserve. Long lines of wagons, loaded with rich harvests of corn and wheat, came into Sandusky and Milan—285 loads in a single day at Sandusky as early as 1828. Over 350 lake vessels arrived in Sandusky Bay that year. Milan, eight miles back from the lake on Huron River, rivaled and soon surpassed Sandusky in shipments. That Reserve town was surrounded by virgin land covered with forests. The forests were cleared to get lumber to build ships and cities, or burned to make way for corn and wheat. The grain had to be got to a market, however, and in 1833 a group of citizens organized to improve navigation for five miles up the river and to build a three-mile-long canal to the village of Milan. They spent $75,000 on the project. It was opened on July 4, 1838, when the 150-ton schooner *Kervance* came up the river amid the most joyful celebration. Farm produce from eighteen fertile counties rolled in on wagons to this new Lake Erie port: 365 loads a day with 30,000 to 40,000 bushels of grain. Boys were employed as "runners" by the grain dealers to meet the wagons on their way to Milan, to quote prices and urge the farmers to come to their particular wharf to sell their grain. (Wade's first telegraph was established between Milan and Oberlin Heights to quote prices on grain.) Milan became one of the greatest grain-shipping towns in the West in the middle decades of the last century.[1] And most of the ships sailed down to Buffalo to sell or transship their grain.

Joseph Dart watched this phenomenon from the small wharves in Buffalo. He observed steamers, propellers and topsail schooners leaving the port every day crowded to capacity with immigrants for the West—Ohio, Indiana, Michigan, Illinois, Wisconsin. He saw them return with cargoes of grain from these western farms. He was sure that even the 2,000,000 bushels of grain of 1841 were only a beginning. These hardy men and women and growing children would soon be raising grain on more new land. And where would that grain find its market? Obviously it would come to or flow through this strategic port at the foot of Lake Erie.

Dart also studied with concern the congestion of ships in the harbor waiting to unload. There was the bottleneck and the costly delay. Each ship had to wait its turn at the docks. Every single grain of the bushels of cargo had to be lifted out of the hold by the most primitive, slow and laborious methods. It was raised in barrels by tackle and block, and weighed with hopper and scales swung over the hatchway. It was carried into the warehouses in bags or baskets on the backs of an army of men.[2] Only ten to fifteen bushels could be weighed at a draft, and the maximum unit unloaded in a day by a full set of hands was from 1,800 to 2,000 bushels. At that rate, as Dart easily calculated, Buffalo would never be able to receive the harvests of the West.

The process was still further complicated: ships could unload only in fair weather. If the winds were high, as they often were, or if it were raining, unloading was suspended and activity in the harbor was at a standstill—except for the cursing of the delayed captains.

---

[1] This was the birthplace town of Thomas Alva Edison, whose father came here from Canada in the boom days. It lost its position when its river and canal filled up with good Ohio soil, and when the Lake Shore and Michigan Southern Railroad by-passed Milan in favor of Norwalk.

[2] Even as late as 1865 this method was still in use at New York, Philadelphia, Baltimore and Boston.

Buffalo Harbor in the late 1830's and early 1840's was frequently crowded with vessels waiting for a change of weather.

Joseph Dart determined to remedy this sickness. He got his idea from the work of Oliver Evans. That pioneer American inventor developed and patented the elevator and conveyor for milling grain. He placed buckets on a leather belt revolving on pulleys. This contraption brought the meal from the millstones, or flour from the bolts, to an apparatus called "the hopper-boy," which in turn spread it over the floor, stirred, fanned and gathered it, without the help of a single hand anywhere in the process. That was at the close of the Revolutionary War, down on the Delaware at Brandywine. Millers could not believe it would actually work. One of them simply said, "It will not do, it cannot do, it is impossible that it should do." And a visiting delegation, after seeing it, reported, "The whole contrivance was a set of rattle traps not worth the notice of men of common sense." But the Ellicott mills near Baltimore tried out Evans' elevator and conveyor system. They saved $5,000 in labor costs and gained fifty cents a barrel in increased yield of superfine flour. The mills made a clear saving of $37,000 in one year. That was something worthy of notice of "men of common sense." Evans' invention went into use.

In after years Joseph Dart liked to reflect on the fact that during this epoch-making period the site of Buffalo was a lonely forest on the edge of a shallow creek, without a single white inhabitant. No one foresaw that a great city would rise there, and that Evans' invention would play a central role in the economy of that lake port. In 1841, then, with ships jammed in the harbor, with men carrying a little basket of grain from the deck into the warehouse, Joseph Dart thought of Evans and asked the question: Couldn't Evans' elevator and conveyor, powered by steam, be adapted to the unloading and transfer of grain? He was certain that it could be done. He set to work. He erected a building on Buffalo Creek at the junction with Evans' ship canal. People thought he was crazy. His friend Mahlon Kingsman, Esq., came to warn him against losing his money in this contraption. He tapped him on the shoulder and said, "Dart, I am sorry for you; I have been through that mill; it won't do; remember what I say; Irishmen's backs are the cheapest Elevators ever built."

Dart continued to believe otherwise. He completed a big ware-house, with large capacity for storage, and an adjustable elevator and conveyor, powered by steam to transfer grain from lake vessels to canalboats or directly to the bins.

But would it work?

It was an instantaneous success. The schooner *John S. Skinner* came in from Milan, Ohio, with 4,000 bushels of wheat. It docked in the early afternoon. Dart's contraption was put to work. Grain flowed from ship to bin, in Dart's words, "with cheapness and des-patch." The schooner was unloaded, took on ballast of salt and made sail out of the harbor for Milan before night fell. Lake men were astounded at the record set by the *John S. Skinner*. This ship sailed back to Milan with her salt, exchanged it for another cargo of wheat, sailed back to Dart's elevator at Buffalo and was again unloaded by Dart's contraption. She then sailed out of Buffalo in company with vessels which had come in with her on her first trip down. They had just got rid of their cargo on Irishmen's backs. Joseph Dart had made the *John S. Skinner* do the work of two ships. The future of Buffalo as a grain port was assured.

Kingsman came over to the wharf. "Dart," he said, "I find I did not know it all."

On that first elevator the buckets held only two quarts and they were spaced twenty-eight inches apart on the belt. They could raise about 1,000 bushels per hour. Improvements were immediately in-troduced. The buckets were placed twenty-two inches apart, then only sixteen, and their hoisting capacity was almost doubled. By the close of the Civil War, buckets holding eight quarts spaced a foot apart were raising nearly 7,000 bushels an hour and weighing the load correctly. By that time there were twenty-seven elevators and two floating elevators in Buffalo, capable of storing 6,000,000 bushels. They could move more grain in one day than was handled during the full year in which Dart's elevator was built.

There are now twenty-one electrically operated elevators for mov-ing grain from the lake carriers to storage, or to barges and cars for transshipment. Their immense circular towers, set in batteries along oxbowing Buffalo River, dominate the skyline of the harbor. They are the first objects to be lifted on the horizon of Lake Erie as a grain freighter steams down from Long Point toward Buffalo

Lighthouse. They look like the battlements of some immense forti
fied castle controlling the foot of the lake. From an American Air‹
lines plane speeding in from Cleveland along the rim of the lake,
they look like a child's complicated mechanical toy set up on the
dark S curve of the river, with hundreds of acres of railroad track
fanning gracefully out into the yards around them. The fourscore
of vast columns of the Concrete Central Elevator loom up at the
foot of the S. It alone has a storage capacity of 4,500,000 bushels.
It has 1,500 feet of berthing space at its pier on the twenty-two-foot
channel. It has four marine legs for unloading vessels, and it can
unload them at the rate of 85,000 bushels per hour.

A few rods around the S, opposite Farmers Point, is the angular
pile of the great Superior Elevator. It has a storage capacity of
3,700,000 bushels. It rises sheer above the river, which is twenty-three
feet deep at this point, and dwarfs the two 500-foot freighters which
can dock in front of it at the same time. Just around the next bend
is the Dellwood Elevator with a capacity of 1,700,000 bushels; and
at the point and around still another bend are congested into an
almost continuous structure the Marine Elevator "A" with a 2,200,000
capacity; the Lake & Rail Elevator, largest of them all, with storage
for 4,909,000 bushels; the American Elevator with storage for
3,500,000 bushels; the Electric Elevator holding 2,000,000; and the
Nesbit Elevator holding 3,000,000. On down toward the Erie Basin,
on the tongue of land between Buffalo River and the City Ship
Canal, is another mighty concentration of elevators: the huge Frontier Elevator, owned by General Mills, Inc., the second largest of
the Buffalo elevators, with a capacity of 4,750,000 bushels; General
Mills' Dakota Elevator; the 2,200,000-bushel Great Eastern Elevator;
Marine Elevator "B"; and the 1,200,000-bushel Kellogg Elevator.
Down at the south end of the outer harbor is the big 2,000,000-bushel
Canadian Pool Terminal Elevator. And at the extreme end of the
harbor the massive cylinders of the Great Lakes Portland Cement
Company's plant, which look like grain elevators, complete the
panoramic sweep of the elevator-dominated skyline of Buffalo.

All together Buffalo's elevators have a total storage capacity of
44,718,500 bushels. They are supplemented in winter by the vast
storage space in the holds of the freighters that winter at Buffalo.
This is a neat development in the economy of lake shipping. At the

end of the season many of the ore freighters are washed clean with a steam hose and loaded with a cargo of grain for their last voyage of the year down the lakes. They tie up at Buffalo with their load held in storage in the ship for the winter. Instead of paying rent for the privilege of letting their ships huddle in the ice-packed port, the owners are paid for their supplementary storage. In the spring the vessels are unloaded and they begin again their new season's activity of carrying coal and ore.

Dart's bucket contraption has a vast electrically operated suction-and-lifting system that handles these immense cargoes of grain with the ease and dispatch of a Hoover sweeper picking up cigarette ashes from the living-room rug. One of the beautiful sights on Lake Erie is these elevators, balanced by the tall buildings in the center of the city, in the late afternoon, seen from the deck of a westbound ship, with the sun on them.

Chapter 18

Underderground to Ontario

Tourists in Old Ontario often journey out to a cemetery near Chatham on the Thames. They stand by a wooden marker and read with surprise the words: "The grave of Rev. Josiah Henson, the original Uncle Tom of Uncle Tom's Cabin by Harriet Beecher Stowe." The famous Negro, after years of labor for his master, escaped from his slavery, endured starvation, fought off wolves in the Indiana and Ohio wilderness, and passed with his wife and child through friendly hands across the border into Canada to become the most notable of the fugitives. He aided 600 Negroes to reach Ontario, he visited Queen Victoria and fanned the flames of war to attain immortality through the pen of Harriet Beecher Stowe. He died at last in peace, and his abused and honored bones lie at the foot of this painted marker.

The grave reminds us of the almost forgotten years of the Underground Railroad which wrote a strife-torn and dramatic chapter at every port on the American and Canadian shores of Lake Erie.

Canada was a free land, hospitable to Negroes who fled to her protection from slavery in the South. She admitted them to citizenship on equal terms with the Dutch from Pennsylvania and the Irish from Dundalk. Negro refugees escaped to Canada by the thousands. They began to arrive there before 1800. The Indians of Chief Brant's refugee tribe, who were settled by the British government along the Grand River after the Revolutionary War, were among the first to receive the Negroes and give them succor. Escaped slaves were crossing the Western Reserve in growing numbers by 1815. Joseph Pickering saw several of them during his journeys about the north shore of Lake Erie in 1825-1826. Being somewhat scornful of American protestations of their love for liberty, he enjoyed telling about a slave who had escaped from her French master and had taken advantage of England's "just laws, which admit no slavery—

'They touch our country and their shackles fall!
That's noble!' "

233

The Frenchman "hired a number of 'the sons of liberty' to cross the river and kidnap her back again. . . . Having got her near the water, they carried her by force into a boat, and before the inhabitants could arrive to her rescue, she was wafted in triumph across 'to the land of the free and the home of the brave,' with the hearty execrations of the indignant Canadians."[1]

Pickering also recorded, with his countryman's interest in details of the land, that "black slaves, who have run away from their masters in Kentucky, arrive in Canada almost weekly (where they are free) and work at raising tobacco; I believe they introduced the practice. One person will attend, and manage the whole process of four acres, planting, hoeing, budding, etc. during the summer." On his tramp through the wilderness toward the Detroit River he overtook "a 'nigger' and his boy, just come from Kentucky, where he took French leave of his master, and brought a horse, which he sold near Detroit. There are some hundreds of these people settled at Sandwich and Amherstburgh, who are formed into a volunteer militia corps, and trained to arms."

At the outbreak of the Civil War there were between 60,000 and 75,000 of these Negroes who had found homes in Canada. Those who escaped became abductors for those who remained in slavery. About 500 of them annually made their way back into the States to rescue friends and members of their family.

These abductors, of whom Josiah Henson and Harriet Tubman were most celebrated, spread the news through the South that Canada was indeed the land of the free. Militiamen returning from the Ontario raids of the War of 1812 talked openly of the Canadian policy. Dr. Alexander M. Ross of Canada toured the South, encouraging fugitives, telling them of Canada, how far away it was and how to get there. And over the mysterious grapevine of slave communication in the South went the message: Escape to Ontario!

The quickest and friendliest route into Canada led across Lake Erie from its many port cities. And the route from the South to the Lake Erie shore was the Underground Railroad. Many stories survive to explain the origin of the name. They all agree on the central point of the mysterious disappearance of the fugitives once they crossed the Ohio River. The Rush R. Sloane version has greatest

---

[1] *Emigrant's Guide to Canada* (London, 1832), p. 142.

currency. A Kentucky slave named Tice Davids (Davis in some accounts) was whipped by his master and threatened with being sold down the river in 1831. He fled across the Ohio River. His master went over to bring him back, but Tice had simply disappeared. The Kentucky master gave up the pursuit, saying that his slave "must have gone off on an underground road."

The name stuck like a badge. Ardent antislavery men like Levi Coffin of Cincinnati and the Reverend John Rankin of Ripley operated two of the most famous terminals of the road to freedom on the Ohio River. Rankin aided Eliza and her child after they had crossed the floating ice. Levi Coffin, "president" of the Underground, sent hundreds of slaves out of Cincinnati with instructions which guided them from friendly house to house up to Lake Erie and across to Ontario. He got back regular reports of their ultimate safety in Canada. The Prince of Wales in 1860 visited the settlements in Canada which were main terminals of the Road. When he came to Cincinnati, he took off his hat and made a graceful bow as he drove by Coffin's house in an open carriage. People said he was paying respect to this end of the route "so that he could make a correct report to the Queen."[2]

Coffin often raised money and bought tickets to send fugitives up to Lake Erie by rail at night. And once they reached the lake ports they were seldom retaken.

Their destination might be any of the towns on the shore between Buffalo and Detroit. Those two cities were especially favored because they were separated only by the Niagara and the Detroit Rivers from Canadian soil. But Westfield and Fredonia, Dunkirk and Erie were often their embarkation points in the East, and friendly captains would touch at Fort Erie to let the fugitives go ashore before the vessels anchored at Buffalo.

Thousands crossed at Detroit.

Every port on the Ohio shore of the lake was a terminus of the Underground. There were eight important stations. Conneaut was the end of one route that led through eastern Ohio and the Western Reserve. Ashtabula was the terminus of four routes, Painesville of three, Cleveland of four or five, Lorain and Huron of one each, Sandusky of four and Toledo of four or five. These routes across

---

[2] Levi Coffin, *Reminiscences* (Cincinnati, 1898), pp. 595-596.

Ohio were the shortest distance between the slavery states and Canada, and the Quakers and the New Englanders in the Western Reserve were particularly friendly and helpful to the fugitives.

These abolitionists went to almost any length to aid them. They built houses with secret attic or cellar rooms and closets for concealing the fleeing slaves. Some of these are still standing. One near Marion has a garret constructed like a labyrinth and a cellar with two secret rooms big enough to hold a dozen fugitives. They are hidden by large cupboards fastened to the doors. The rooms are connected by two tunnels, one leading to the barn and the other to the corncrib, and slaves escaped in some instances through these passages while their owners were guarding the house.[3]

Oberlin was one of the busiest junction stations on the Underground, with five routes centering there and a militant group of abolitionists to receive and protect the fugitives. Eck Humphries reported that in his rooming house there he was shown by his landlady a windowless garret which was entered by a door only two feet high and concealed by a bed or almost any piece of furniture. Inside were the remains of the old cord bed with its frayed ropes still hanging to the pegs. The landlady remembered as a girl seeing the slaves being rested and fed there for their final journey down to the lake.[4] Other such rooms are exhibited at various places along the lake. For, though Ohio was not all abolitionist, there were many zealous men who would do almost anything to aid fugitives and thwart the searches of an irate owner. Judge Jabez Wright was the first to receive them in the Firelands. David Hudson, founder of the lake port of Huron, was an ardent worker in their behalf. John Brown's father helped them and passed his ardor on to his famous son, who made trips to Canada to see how the refugees were faring in their new homes.

Those who were friendly to the fugitives came to understand one another and to know which houses were open day or night, which families would feed or clothe the Negroes and which would give them money or speed their passage to Lake Erie. Some of the worthy and conscientious hosts were often hard put to it to protect a slave

---

[3] Wilbur H. Siebert, *A Quaker Section of the Underground in Northern Ohio* (Columbus, 1930), p. 11.

[4] Eck Humphries, *The Underground Railroad* (McConnelsville, Ohio, 1931), p. 7.

from a persistent pursuer and at the same time to keep their souls free of outright lies. They became shrewd, however, in guarding the truth. A deacon of Wellington was asked by a slave hunter if he had seen a fugitive go past his house that morning. The good deacon had seen him and, therefore, had to say "Yes."

"Which way was he going?"

"North," the deacon also had to answer, because the slave was headed toward Oberlin.

The man hunter inquired no further, and the good deacon was not obliged by his conscience to add that he had also seen the Negro go into a cornfield and turn south to elude his pursuer.[5]

When the fleeing slaves could not escape their pursuers, and were finally caught, these abolitionists on the Underground would form in a body, intercept the pursuer and demand to see his identification papers. Then they would make him go to the courthouse to prove that he owned the slave and had the right to return him to his plantation. Sometimes they required him to post bond, and to fetch witnesses to prove his statements. This procedure used up time and put the master to great expense. If he chose to go to all the trouble necessary to establish his ownership, he often found that in the meantime his slave had disappeared from protective custody in the jail.

The resourceful Yankees and Quakers were endlessly ingenious in finding ways to speed the slaves on to the lake. The late Professor Edward Orton of Ohio State University recalled seeing two sleigh-loads of them brought in from the Western Reserve to his father's house in Buffalo in 1838 to be passed on into Canada. Certain ships on Lake Erie became known as friendly to fugitives. The *Arrow,* operating from Sandusky, was known as an abolitionist vessel. The *United States,* the *Bay City,* the *Mayflower,* all sailing between Sandusky and Detroit, the *Forest Queen,* the *May Queen* and the *Morning Star,* all out of Cleveland, and the *Phoebus* out of Toledo, regularly took on fugitives. They would stop at Malden on their way up the Detroit River and set the slaves free. William Wells Brown, himself a fugitive, was employed on one of these ships; he became well known for his activity in taking Negroes aboard and delivering them from Cleveland to Canada without charge. His ship seldom sailed without first taking on a group of these frightened men and

---

[5] James Harris Fairchild, *The Underground Railroad* (Cleveland, 1895), p. 96.

women who huddled together on the wharf in the Cuyahoga. He gave passage to sixty-nine of them in the year 1842.[6] Hubbard & Company, forwarding and commission merchants of Ashtabula, would hide them in their warehouses and send them across to Port Burwell at night. L. S. Stow, on the Milan-Huron Canal, used to see them venturing out of hiding to get exercise while waiting for passage on a friendly ship.

Some captains made special voyages for running them across Lake Erie. Captain George Sweigels got $35 for sailing a group of them in a small boat by night from Sandusky to Point Pelee in 1853.[7]

Once aboard a ship bound for Buffalo or Detroit the slaves were safe, unless a storm drove them back to the American shore. There were a score of refugee ports on the Ontario shore of Lake Erie from Windsor to Port Colborne and Fort Erie. Sandwich and Amherstburg, being handy ports of call for all vessels going up the Detroit River, became favored gateways into Canada. Anthony Bingey of Amherstburg said that when he went to that village to live in 1845, fugitives were arriving in companies of fifteen or more and that these mounted in numbers in the years following until it was not uncommon to see thirty of them getting off the lake vessels and ferries at this point. Colchester, Kingsville, Point Pelee, Port Stanley, Port Burwell and Long Point all received a goodly share. Many went up the Thames and filtered into the unsettled lands of Ontario West.

Some of the refugees gathered near these Ontario towns and raised garden produce to sell in their markets. Others took up land and cleared farms for themselves. Some of them, of course, were lazy, dirty and shiftless, but the overwhelming majority were industrious and made good progress. They advanced rapidly from a crude cabin on a patch of cleared ground to comfortable homes and well-stocked farms. Dr. Howe, who visited their settlements, reported that they were better clothed and housed than the foreign immigrants. The settlements at Amherstburg were particularly progressive. They organized the first "True Band," with 600 members, to improve their schools, help the needy, settle disputes between whites and colored, and to promote good relations between the races.[8]

---

6 Wilbur H. Siebert, *The Underground Railroad* (New York, 1898), p. 83.
7 *Ibid.*, p. 146.
8 *Ibid.*, p. 230.

The climate was hard on the Negroes, and many died of respiratory diseases. They endured all the trials and hardships of any frontier, pioneering people making a new beginning in an undeveloped wilderness. But they worked hard as free men and justified the confidence of the Canadians who received them. Perhaps the spirit of those days is best recaptured by the story told by one of the lake captains who took on two fugitives at Cleveland in 1860. The captain was bound for Buffalo. Before he put in at that port he ran in close to the Canadian shore, manned a boat and landed the Negroes on the Lake Erie beach. He had, he said, given little thought to the emotions of these fugitives, but the scene of this landing touched him deeply.

"They said, 'Is this Canada?' I said, 'Yes, there are no slaves in this country'; then I witnessed a scene I shall never forget. They seemed to be transformed; a new light shone in their eyes, their tongues were loosed, they laughed and cried, prayed and sang praises, fell upon the ground and kissed it, hugged and kissed each other, crying, 'Bress de Lord! Oh! I'se free before I die!' "[9]

---

[9] *Ibid.*, p. 197. Quoted from E. M. Pettit, *Sketches in the History of the Underground Railroad.*

Chapter 19

Johnson's Island

THE fighting fronts of the Civil War ran far to the south of Lake Erie, but some of the excitement and upheaval reached these quiet shores. Canada, and especially Old Ontario, was in an anomalous position during the war. On the issue of slavery Canada, by all her heritage and traditions, was militant for freedom. She offered safety and protection and ready entrance to the fugitive slaves, as we have seen. But when war actually flamed between the States, Great Britain gave aid and comfort to the cotton-growing South, and Confederate agents, as well as fugitive slaves, found harbor in Canada. Southern prisoners of war who contrived to escape from Union prison camps were often passed through Canada and given passage to Southern ports via Cuba and the Bahamas. Relations between the United States and Canada were sometimes strained by these incidents. Fortunately, under the terms of President Monroe's agreement with Great Britain back in 1817, the naval force on Lake Erie was limited to two vessels "not exceeding 100 tons burden, and armed with one 18 lb. cannon." Though the two neighbors did build in excess of this limitation, their vessels never engaged in hostile action. But there was one now half-forgotten episode that brought the war close to Lake Erie.

Johnson's Island lies in Sandusky Bay about three miles from the city of Sandusky, and just off the peninsula facing Cedar Point. The island and the point form the entrance to the bay from Lake Erie. This low, tree-covered island was the scene of a grandiose plot during the Civil War to free the Confederate prisoners and raid the lake towns of northern Ohio.

The island contains only about 275 acres. In the old days it was known as Bull's Island, but its name was changed in honor of its proprietor when L. B. Johnson bought it in 1852. In the autumn of 1861 the Federal government leased a forty-acre tract on the southern shore and turned it into a prison camp for Confederate officers. Rows of barracks were erected to shelter the prisoners and house the 128th

Ohio Volunteer Infantry which served as the guard. There were also a hospital, an arsenal, a quartermaster's depot and cottages for the officers of the guard. This grim and barren village was enclosed by a wall of two-inch boards fourteen feet high. A parapet ran around the top of the wall, giving the sentry patrol a clear view of the prison inside and out. Cannon were mounted at strategic points to sweep the yard and command the approaches. As a final safeguard there was a twenty-foot dead line or neutral zone just inside the wall. This area was forbidden to the prisoners, and the guard had instructions to shoot on sight any man who crossed the line toward the wall. Just offshore lay the United States gunboat *Michigan* with her guns trained on the prison camp.

Some of the prisoners did, of course, attempt to escape. They grew desperate with monotony, having nothing to do but carve wood into figures, chip lake shells into pins and novelties, and see the national ensign hoisted and lowered morning and evening on the 100-foot flagpole in the yard while the band played "The Star-Spangled Banner." The sight of the famous "Gray Beard Brigade," a Federal unit of the guard which got its name from the fact that some of its members were octogenarians (one had fifteen sons in the Union Army) and all wore long gray beards, probably inspired less fear than plans for escape. A group of the Southern officers made an abortive attempt on the winter night of January 11, 1864. It was bitterly cold in the barracks. Many men were sick with pneumonia, many were dying. Ice was piled up on the shore of the island. The bay was frozen over. The temperature went down to 26° below zero. The coal oil would no longer vaporize and the lamps went out. The moment for escape seemed opportune. Five men got across the dead line and scaled the wall. Once over that barrier, they scurried across the ice to the mainland. But the cold was deadly and the men were ill-clad. Two of them gave up the effort and returned around the bay to Sandusky. Nearly frozen, they were taken into a Sandusky home and then sent back to the island. The other three made their way westward around Lake Erie. They endured sixty hours with no rest and with little food, but they eluded capture and crossed over into Canada at Fort Malden. Later they went on down to the St. Lawrence, obtained passage to Cuba and eventually got back to Wilmington.

Perhaps this attempt encouraged the big-scale plot that threw the whole region into a panic in September 1864. Captured officers, chiefly from Tennessee, Georgia, Alabama and the Carolinas, "the Flower of the Army," as they were called, had arrived by the carload and were ferried across to the island. Ten thousand of them were in the prison at one time or another, though 3,000 was the capacity at any one period. Other prisoners were held at Camp Douglas, Chicago, at Camp Morton, Indianapolis, and at Camp Chase, Columbus, making a total of about 26,000 men. It was estimated that there were enough officers in these camps to command an army of 80,000. If they could be freed, they could become a menace that would daunt the guarding forces in the North.

The plan was elaborate. The master mind was Captain Charles H. Cole, a resourceful and courageous officer who had once served under General Forrest's command. He wrote with invisible starch ink to Major Trimble, prisoner on the island, outlining the plot. Major Trimble smeared a bit of iodine over the starch and read his instructions.[1] He organized a cell of the "Southern Cross" among his fellow prisoners, who were bound to secrecy and pledged to rise on signal. Cole himself came to Sandusky to carry out the scheme. He was to seize the gunboat *Michigan* and give the signal for the uprising. He made many friends. He cultivated the officers on the *Michigan*. He was aided by Annie Davis, a personable spy who lived in West House, Sandusky. The officers found her company extremely agreeable, and she was successful in getting information about the gunboat and the routine in the prison camp. She and Cole managed to arrange a champagne dinner aboard the *Michigan* for the night of the uprising. The officers would be plied with wine and finished off with glasses drugged with a sleeping potion.

While this scheme was taking shape at Sandusky, a supporting operation was under way in Canada and on Lake Erie. John Yates Beall, a twenty-nine-year-old Virginian, was in charge. On the morning of September 19, Captain Atwood took the *Philo Parsons* out of Detroit on her regular run to the Lake Erie islands and San-

---

[1] There are many variations in the accounts of this episode. This is the version stoutly held by Sandusky and Erie islands folk, as told in Lydia J. Ryall's *Sketches and Stories of the Lake Erie Islands* (Norwalk, Ohio, 1913). For a documentary account see Frederick J. Shepard's "The Johnson Island Plot," *Pub. Buf. Hist. Soc.*, VIII, 1-51.

dusky. It was a day of unusual beauty; many people remarked the clear atmosphere, the sun and the winey smell of the vineyards ripening on the Bass Islands. The *Philo Parsons* stopped at Sandwich to take on about a dozen passengers with their baggage for Sandusky. She put in again at Amherstburg where she was boarded by a dozen more men with baggage, including a large, heavy, leather-covered trunk. Captain Atwood saw nothing amiss. He sailed his ship on schedule to Put-in-Bay. There he placed his son-in-law in command and left the boat. She went on to Kelleys Island, and then sailed for Cedar Point.

When the *Philo Parsons* was midway between this island and the point, the passengers from Canada became Confederate conspirators. They opened the big leather trunk, which was filled with guns and knives. Armed with these weapons they seized the vessel and ran her up within sight of Johnson's Island to reconnoiter. They then returned to Put-in-Bay. At that moment the little *Island Queen,* George W. Orr, captain, steamed in on her regular run from Sandusky to Toledo via Put-in-Bay. She had aboard some islanders, and forty to fifty soldiers who had served their 100-days enlistment and were being taken back to Toledo to be mustered out. As she came alongside the *Philo Parsons,* she too was seized by the Confederates. They jumped aboard, waving pistols and knives, and forced the crew and male passengers into the hold of the *Philo Parsons.* They shot Harry Haines in the face when he refused to come out of the engine room. They crowded the women and children into the cabins and then sent them ashore when they promised to say nothing of the conspiracy for the next twenty-four hours.

Beall lashed the *Island Queen* to the *Philo Parsons* and got under way again. About half a mile off Ballast Island he ordered the yawl transferred from the *Island Queen* and scuttled that vessel by opening her feed pipe and setting her adrift. She grounded on Chicanola Reef in shallow water.

By this time night had fallen over the lake, and the dinner party aboard the *Michigan* was growing merry. Beall steamed back toward Johnson's Island, and hove to about a mile offshore. His part of the scheme had been carried out with precision and he was all ready for the break of the prisoners. It was ten o'clock. Beall could see the outline of the gunboat lying in the bay. He waited for Cole to signal from the bridge. The prisoners on the island also waited. Minutes passed. The signal did not flash.

The wine flowed in the officers' mess on the *Michigan*. Cole was watching for his opportunity. Just as it seemed to be approaching, the commanding officer stepped into the wardroom, seized Cole, and said, "You damned rebel spy! You are my prisoner!"

Beall on the *Philo Parsons* waited for the signal. It never came. Captain Orr said he could hear the conspirators in counsel. "I have a notion to make the attempt anyway," Beall said. But he didn't. He waited another half-hour and gave up. Using old coal-oil barrels, he forced steam and crowded the vessel back up Lake Erie. Several of his men were sent ashore in the yawl above Amherstburg. He put Captain Orr and two of his men off in the uninhabited marshes of Fighting Island, where they were rescued by passing fishermen. The Confederates removed a piano and other valuables from the *Philo Parsons* at Sandwich and set the vessel adrift. Then Beall and his raiders scattered through Old Ontario.

During that evening and night wild excitement had spread through the islands. The usual crowds of people had come down to the wharf at Put-in-Bay to meet the vessels. But the vessels did not come in. Then darkness fell and most of the people went home. As the evening wore on, rumor began to spread. It grew rife with the passing hours. Paul Reveres began to scurry from house to house, and cross from island to island, knocking on doors, shouting, "Get up! Get up! The *Island Queen* and the *Philo Parsons* are in the hands of the rebels!" Most of the able-bodied men were away in the Union Army; only the old men, women and children were left on the islands to defend them. They grabbed up their valuables and hid them in caves or buried them in the orchards and vineyards. They gathered at the bay. A military company was hastily formed by Captain John Brown, Jr., son of the immortal John Brown. When he came to the island to find isolation and safety, he brought with him, it was said, some of the arsenal assembled for use at Harper's Ferry. He issued arms to this citizen militia to ward off the rebel attack.

The proportions of the impending blow grew with the passing hours. The citizens remembered the Perry's victory cannon; they wheeled it round to a commanding position, and loaded it with powder, iron and gravel for the defense of the island. Panic-stricken women hid in the limestone caverns along the shore. A couple of their neighbors returning under cover of night were mistaken for a Confederate fleet.

Good news and relief came with the morning. The women and children put ashore by Beall got safely home. A tug came in with the news that the plot had failed. The drifting *Philo Parsons* had been picked up by a tug in the Detroit River. Captain Orr and his men returned by train from Monroe, Michigan, to Sandusky with their story. They rowed out to the reef where the *Island Queen* was aground. The captain plugged up the feed pipe, pumped out the vessel and refloated her. Cole was taken as a prisoner to Johnson's Island under heavy guard. He was court-martialed and sentenced to death, but influential friends secured his pardon. He was to have received $20,000 for the successful execution of the plot. Beall was less fortunate. He was captured at Niagara Falls and hanged as a spy at Governor's Island, New York.[2]

The grim barracks of the prison camp are gone without trace. Only the Confederate cemetery remains to remind the visitor to the island of the sad days of the Civil War. The bones of 206 Southern officers lie there. Most of the exiles had died of pneumonia in the cold Northern winters. White wooden crosses were stuck in their graves. The years passed, the prison years were forgotten, and the cemetery fell into decay. Trees grew up in the plot to soften the harsh decay of the markers and their fading inscriptions. A generation passed and the hatreds of war cooled. The citizens of Sandusky became interested in paying respect to the enemy dead. In 1890 the graves were re-marked with rows of Georgia-marble headstones bearing the name, age, regiment and company in which the captive had served. The snows drift high around them in winter; the Lake Erie sun filters through the trees to warm them in summer. High above them is a statue of a Southern soldier pointing a Confederate flag toward the homeland.

A legend broods over this melancholy plot. When the age of steel reached the lake, Italian laborers were sent to Johnson's Island to

---

[2] Captain Atwood of the *Philo Parsons* told his story to Captain Orr of the *Island Queen*. He furnished the account to Lydia J. Ryall, who recorded it in *Sketches and Stories of the Lake Erie Islands*.

quarry limestone for the mills. A large colony lived in rough shacks not far from the tree-covered cemetery. One winter in March a terrific storm struck the lake and roared over the island and the bay. It raged with full force for three days and nights. The island was cut off from the mainland, for no man could risk the gales and the high seas. The wind raged so furiously that it threatened to blow the entire colony into the bay. Many of the terrified Italians sought refuge among the trees in the cemetery, and huddled under the Confederate monument. One of them was Nichola Rocci. While he crouched there with the storm roaring over him and the shores of the island awash with the waves, he heard the sound of a bugle. He looked up at the statue of the Southern soldier. It was moving. It turned around, and pointed the flag over the graves. Nichola faced with the flag. Then he saw a sight that made him afraid, for the graves were yielding up their dead. Hollow-eyed men in gray uniforms silently arose into the storm with muskets on their shoulders. Old and young, formed in ranks, marched solemnly through the cemetery and disappeared into the spray driven over the lake by the wind.

The Italian quarrymen fled back to their shacks, and as soon as the storm was stilled, they fled on to Sandusky and refused to return to the haunted island.

A lone farmer now tills a portion of the 275-acre island girded with trees and washed by the quiet waters of Sandusky Bay.

Chapter 20

Round Many Western Islands

T HE western fourth of Lake Erie is studded with twenty islands all large enough to have names of their own. They are called, in early frontier fashion: Mouse, Starve, Ballast, Green, Rattlesnake, Sugar, Gull, Hen and Chickens, East, Middle and West Sister, Kelleys, Pelee, and the Bass Islands. No such formation exists in any of the other Great Lakes. Kelleys, the three Bass Islands and Pelee lie in an archipelago squarely across the lake between the spearhead of Canada's Point Pelee and the Catawba-Marblehead peninsula. They rise up out of the water like huge green steppingstones for some legendary Indian god to stride over from one hunting and fishing ground to another. Seen from the air, the clusters of islands are neat and inviting, spread out with careless art like so many jewels dropped into the shimmering lake.

It is not easy to exaggerate their beauty under the timeless procession of the seasons. They are fresh as the morning itself in spring when the peach trees are in bloom. They are cool and inviting in summer when the grapes are ripening and the white sails fill the bays and harbors. They are almost dreamlike in late summer when the grapes have ripened in the sun and fill the air with their spicy odor, when the nights are crisp with approaching frost and the season is hurrying into autumn. Then the storms break, the last ships run through Pelee Passage, the waves whip against Perry's Lookout on Gibraltar, dash spray over Starve Island where it freezes into huge icebergs, the lake finally freezes over and the islanders settle in for the long winter.

This island area is so attractive and is now so accessible that it has become known as Vacationland to the thousands who come here each season for rest and recreation. But to the several hundred people who live here all the year round it is home: a fertile region, tempered by the lake, where there are grapevines to be dressed and harvested, wines to be pressed and bottled, fields to be tilled, quarries to be worked, fruit trees to be pruned and tended, fish to be caught, storms

247

to be weathered and visitors to be entertained or endured. The islands lend color to the lake over which passes on monotonous, routine schedule so much of the world's ore and coal and grain.

Not so many years ago the archipelago was an isolated wilderness. For a generation or so after Mad Anthony Wayne had forced the Indians to retire from Ohio nobody but a few adventurers, some fur traders and a few recluses bothered about the islands; there was plenty of good land to be had on the rim of the lake and on the uplands to the south. Why cross over to these rocks and timberlands so far removed from markets to live alone off the beaten trail of a westward-moving people?

Most travelers were like our friend James Flint, who merely looked at the islands from a distance. Safe aboard the "elegant" steamer *Walk-in-the-Water,* Flint viewed them from the deck as he left Sandusky (then Portland) and wrote in his journal: "There are numerous islands in the lake, which are all covered with a growth of timber, and were then [autumn 1820] beautifully variegated with the tints of the season. These are the islands in which rattle-snakes and other reptiles are said to be so numerous that it is dangerous to land on them."

But the more adventurous Tilly Buttrick, Jr., who spent some time at Sandusky in 1819-1820, decided to cross over and see for himself. He chose Kelleys Island, the one nearest Sandusky, about twelve miles to the north. It was then known as Cunningham's Island for a trader who lived there just prior to the War of 1812. Buttrick does not explain why, of all times, he selected the month of March to make his venture, for he was apparently in the vicinity throughout the summer. We have only the bare fact that he did. The bay was frozen over. Buttrick and a companion, with the aid of three men from the village, tied a rope to their canoe and dragged it across the ice-covered bay. When they were halfway over, the ice broke and Buttrick and his companion, each holding one side of the canoe, crashed through. They kept their heads above the water and balanced the canoe while the others pulled them and the canoe out onto thicker ice.

The three men left Buttrick and his companion on Cedar Point and crossed back over the two miles of ice. Buttrick's description of the adventure from that point on has its own flavor:

"The beach here was clear of snow and ice. We turned our boat up on one side so that it might make a partial shelter for us during the night, and built a fire in front. We then walked across the neck of land to the other side, saw the lake clear of ice except a few floating pieces. Our object in crosing the bay that afternoon was, that we might be ready to start on the lake early in the morning, when there is generally but little wind, it being then easier and safer, the water being smooth. We then returned back to our boat, rekindled our fire, took our supper, dried my clothes as well as I could, and camped for the night. But soon the wind began to blow, and the snow fell very fast; within two hours it blew a heavy gale; our fire was blown away, the boat fell over, and our only course was to run back and forth upon the beach to prevent our perishing in the storm, which sometimes appeared impossible for me to do. At length, to our great joy, the morning came, the wind ceased, and the snow abated. The ice, which we crossed in the afternoon, was broken up and driven into heaps, with the addition of what had driven from the lake, and all up and down the lake shore presented the same dreary appearance. We were now hemmed in on all sides, and it was impossible to cross either with a boat or on foot, and our only resource was, to prepare a camp in the woods, which we did by cutting down trees and bushes, sticking the ends into the ground which was not frozen, and forming the tops together over our heads. We thus made us a comfortable cabin, built a large fire, ate our breakfast, and dried our clothes. We here remained seven days, when all our provisions had become exhausted, except some dry beans. . . .

"We were now in sight of the village, and kept a large fire burning in the night to satisfy the people that we were alive. During the day we were constantly watching for the separation of the ice, so that we might pass; and on the seventh day, in the afternoon, we thought we might accomplish our retreat. Accordingly we put our boat in to the water, and our things on board, and with a pole pushing the ice from the boat, we made our way along for some distance, when we saw a boat coming in the same manner to meet us. Coming up with her, found it to be the same men who crossed the bay with us on the ice, and who had come to relieve us. They turned their boat about, and we all arrived safely home the same evening without accomplishing our visit to Cunningham's Island."[1]

The islands were beautiful enough to the eye as they lay under the

[1] R. G. Thwaites, *Early Western Travels* (Cleveland, 1904), III, 85-87.

bright noonday sun or under a gray mist off there in the midst of the lake, but as Buttrick's experience proved, they were so difficult of access during many months of the year that the pioneers were quite willing to leave them to their isolated solitude, to the rattlesnakes and the wild hogs.

Another race of men had been there, had perished and had been forgotten. They left a few records for men of our time to read and ponder. The most notable of them are the Inscription Rocks on Kelleys Island. The one on the north shore represents pipe-smoking figures carved in the rock. The one on the south shore is world-famous. The rock, beaten against by lake action for so many years, is separated from the mainland strata and juts out over the water. Charles Olmstead of Connecticut was on the island in 1833 studying the equally famous glacial grooves which are so prominently exposed here. He came upon this smooth-surfaced rock, thirty-two feet long and twenty-one feet wide, which rises about eleven feet above the normal lake level. His eye was immediately caught by the strange inscriptions crudely carved into the flat stone. There were more than a hundred of them. They represented an Indian chief, his pipe, his various instruments of magic, a journey on snowshoes, a road, serpents, feathers and articles of leather worn by chieftains, war clubs and other details from Indian life.

Olmstead's discovery excited wide attention. The United States Government sent Colonel Eastman to the island to investigate it in 1851. He made detailed drawings of the carvings which were submitted to archaeological experts. A learned Indian, Shingvauk, who understood pictography, interpreted them to be the rather complex story of the Erie Indians: their occupation of the islands, the coming of the Wyandot tribe, the invasion of the Iroquois, and the evacuation in travail of spirit of the Erie from their temporary home in Lake Erie early in the seventeenth century. The carving presumably dates from about 1625. The natural process of erosion and the scuffing of the shoes of thousands of visitors climbing over the rock have obliterated or damaged many of the characters. The rock and the glacial grooves near by were acquired by the state of Ohio and taken over with appropriate ceremony by the Ohio State Archaeological and Historical Society in the summer of 1932.

The Lake Erie islands, Kelleys Island in particular, have through the years yielded all sorts of relics of the vanished Indian life that once flourished there. Tomahawks, hatchets, clubs, rude grindstones, arrowheads, pipes, pottery of all kinds, stone pestles, needles and fish-hooks, and like instruments and artifacts have been found scattered in abundance over the islands, mute evidence of a vanished life and civilization. Extensive earthworks may still be traced on the islands and some of the mounds are still conspicuous. These have yielded Indian skeletons from their burial places. One mound, discovered on South Bass Island more than fifty years ago, was formed into a mausoleum by an enclosure of black stone slabs foreign to the region. The stump of a tree four feet in diameter was implanted in the mound. When the tomb was opened, eight skeletons were bared, one of which had been a warrior who had walked the earth at the height of a little over seven feet. Other bone frames have been found in the extensive caves along the shore of this island. One of them was wedged between rocks, as though the victim had been trapped there and had died in agony. These relics are all that remain of the Indians who had lived there and had departed long before the white men came.

Permanent settlement of the islands was delayed until near the mid-nineteenth century. The international boundary line had been drawn through the center of the lake, dividing the archipelago almost exactly in half. Pelee, Middle, Hen and Chickens, East and Middle Sister Islands all fell to Ontario; the rest were allotted to the United States, or, more specifically, to Connecticut's Firelands section of the Western Reserve. No one paid much attention to them. Speculators bought up the most desirable island lands and held them while the mainland around Sandusky, Huron and Port Clinton was being settled. That settlement went on at a rapid rate from about 1820 down to the Civil War. Sandusky in particular, with its protected bay and harbor and its rich hinterland, became one of the most important ports and shipyards on Lake Erie. Thousands of immigrants flowed through it to take up lands along the Sandusky River, to clear the Marblehead peninsula, and to drain the eastern end of the Black Swamp. By 1838 there were over 10,000 people in the vicinity, enough to create Erie County with Sandusky as its seat. In 1840 Ottawa County was organized with Port Clinton as the county seat.

The islands lying just beyond the entrance to Sandusky Bay had, meantime, aroused but little interest. But with these thriving towns on the mainland to nourish them, and with lake traffic increasing each year and sailing past them or dropping anchor in their harbors or just offshore, their long slumber was interrupted. The speculators opened them for exploitation and settlers moved over to cut the forests and make homes. The islands have always been geared to Sandusky and Port Clinton and largely dependent upon them to round out their economy. Several small vessels make regular trips between the islands and the mainland during the open season between the breakup and the closing in of the ice.

Kelleys Island, with its 2,800 acres of land (four square miles) is by far the largest of the American group of the Lake Erie Islands. Its greatest width is seven miles. A road traverses most of its eighteen miles of varying shore line. Though it is well cultivated, it is luxuriant with trees and shrubs. Its year-round population is about 600.

In the early days when it was known as Cunningham's Island, and when Tilly Buttrick, Jr., tried to visit it, it was covered with fine virgin red cedar which would now be worth a lumber baron's fortune. Much of that stand of cedar was burned in the engines of the first steamers on the lake. The *Walk-in-the-Water* made steam for her first run to Detroit in 1818 with cordwood of red cedar from Kelleys Island. Mr. Killam had rowed over to the island early that year with his family and one or two workmen. He had chopped a clearing in the cedar forest, and when the *Walk-in-the-Water* hove to off the island and called for fuel to keep her engine running, Killam towed out his cordwood and sold it to Captain Job Fish.

Fifteen years later Datus Kelley and his brother Irad bought the island, which is a part of Erie County. They found three or four squatter families living there on six acres of cleared land. The rest of the island was still covered with forest. The Kelleys ejected the squatters, settled on the island and built homes for their families. They cut and marketed timber, and then sold off their land in small farms to carefully selected settlers. They would permit no one to come to the island who seemed to them to be lacking in character or thrift. Within seven years they had built up a colony of sixty-eight substantial, hard-working folk, many of them from New England, who tilled the land and, between seasons, quarried limestone from the immense deposits on the island. Vessels put in at the island docks to take on timber and stone for the growing cities round the lake. (Many of the better houses in prosperous Buffalo were built of Kelleys Island stone and lumber.)

The lumber was exhausted just as the interest in grape culture reached the Sandusky region. One of the settlers had planted an acre of vineyard in 1846. The vines throve in this environment. In 1851 the first wine cellar on western Lake Erie was built on Kelleys Island. By the outbreak of the Civil War, German immigrants in considerable number had come in for the express purpose of growing grapes and making wines. By the end of the century the island was covered with vineyards and the wine cellars were stored with excellent vintages. Visitors discovered the charm of the island, built cottages and made it a favored summer-vacation resort.

The rich limestone quarries, however, soon surpassed the vineyards and the tourist trade in profits if not in romance. Datus Kelley left an interesting note on the stone business in the early 1830's when he wrote, "Our teams are now busy in hauling stone . . . [Esquire Bill] has quarried about 7 or 800 feet of stone at 6c per foot. Says he will quarry all we want." The demand mounted year by year, first for building houses, canal locks, piers and breakwaters, then for the inexhaustible maws of the iron and steel mills of Cleveland and Pittsburgh. Immigrant workers from South and Central Europe were brought in to work the stone. The island was scarred and pitted with quarries to a depth of forty feet. The Kelley Island Lime & Transport Company (familiarly known to the islanders as "KILT"), bought up quarries in 1891 and extended them until they covered a thousand acres. It opened kilns at North Bay for burning lime, had its own railroads and cars, docking and loading facilities, and employed over 400 men. It still operates its own limestone fleet of three freighters.

This industry dominated the island as the vineyards declined and the steel mills grew. But evil days fell also upon the limestone business. It was a sad time for the colonies of Italians, Slavs, Greeks, Hungarians, Portuguese, Poles, Macedonians, Bulgarians and Germans when, as the long weary depression dragged on through the 1930's, KILT announced that the quarries were to be closed, that the company would concentrate its interests at Marblehead, and that the workers would have to move elsewhere to seek employment. Their departure robbed the island of much of the Old World color which these people had given it with their peasant ways and their native tongues. Few of them spoke English and their isolation left them unassimilated. It was common a few years ago to see barefoot peasant women in native costumes with handkerchiefs or flowers on their heads gossiping together in the quarry villages.

The islanders themselves, i.e., the old German and a few New England families who came with the Kelleys, kept to their own ways with remarkable tenacity. One old islander gave an insight into the folk quality of these "native" residents when, several decades ago now, he summarized the history of Kelleys Island in these words: "In the beginning Kelley Island was eaten up by rattlesnakes. . . . Then came old Ben Napier, the pioneer of the archipelago. Old Ben turned loose a drove of hogs on the island, and the hogs ate up the rattlesnakes. Next, the Kelley family alighted on the spot, and the Kelleys ate up the hogs. Then came the Dutch, and the Dutch ate up the Kelleys." Accepting the kernel of truth in this observation, we may add that time and a changing economy has all but eaten up the "Dutch." But the fishing industry, the revival of grape growing, the renewed interest in the islands as a summer resort, and the coming of air service to the mainland have brought to the islanders hope for more prosperous days. The last solution the older generation would think of would be migration, but the young folk are breaking away in ever-increasing numbers to find employment on the mainland.

Eight miles north of Kelleys Island, across the boundary line, lies Canada's Pelee Island, largest (10,000 acres) in the archipelago. Together with tiny Middle Island, it is the most southerly fragment of Ontario. The nine-mile strip of water separating it from the tip of Point Pelee is shallow and obstructed by reefs and shoals. It is a dangerous region for ships. They must navigate carefully through the deep but narrow "North" or Pelee Passage around Southeast Shoal and between Grubb Reef and Pelee Passage Light off the northeast corner of the islands. Having this heavily traveled ship-road at its front door, however, has not relieved the isolation of the island except for the solace which the constant sight of ships may bring to

HULETTS AT WORK ON THE "FRED G. HARTWELL"
AT CLEVELAND

DECK VIEW OF A BATTERY OF HULETT UNLOADERS

THE "HENRY P. WERNER" OUT-BOUND LIGHT FROM BUFFALO HARBOR

its inhabitants. They never put in at its small wharves. It is dependent upon the infrequent calls of the shallow-draft interisland vessels, one of which stops on its car-ferry service trips across the lake between Sandusky and Leamington.

Like Kelleys Island, Pelee was once the home of Indians. Remains of ancient mounds and burial vaults in the limestone caves are still to be seen. Farmers still turn up stone hatchets, pipes and arrowheads as they till their fields and vineyards. Ottawa and Chippewa were living on the island when the white men came to the lake. They continued to camp there to hunt and fish until 1788, when the island was acquired by Thomas McKee, a half-breed, son of Alexander McKee, who became deputy agent for Indian Affairs in West Canada in 1778. The long-term lease, executed in Detroit on the first of May by seven chiefs and sachems, called for a payment of "3 bushels of Indian corn or the value thereof, if demanded annually." McKee moved to the island and built himself a "mansion." Local tradition says that he became wealthy, that he kept a pack of hounds for hunting elk, deer and other game, that he entertained lavishly and was for years a famous, almost legendary, personality in early lake history.

Time and fortune swept away this frontier splendor and in 1823 William McCormick of Colchester was able to purchase Pelee for $500. He was the son of Alexander McCormick, the Scotch fur trader, and a white girl whom he had found living among the Indians on Lake Erie. They had stolen her from Pittsburgh and held her for three years. McCormick, after buying her freedom, had to steal her away from her captors. William moved to the island with his wife and eleven children in 1834. It was a wild, lonely and malarial spot. Mosquitoes and flies swarmed over the snake-infested swamps. In stormy weather the lake invaded it, cutting the island in two. Over 4,000 acres of the island were marshlands. Wild ducks and geese, mallards and loons fed on the wild rice which grew in abundance in the marshes. Muskrats were so thick that McCormick took 6,000 skins a year for the fur trade. He built log houses on the bluff overlooking North Bay and the ship channel, constructed a dock and induced tenant families to come to the island. He constructed a sawmill to rip the red-cedar trees into railroad ties. He rafted oak logs, floated them out to vessels in the channel and shipped them to Europe where they fetched high prices. He had brought a fair portion of his island into production when he died and left his estate to his children.

After a long period of litigation which retarded development until the vineyard era, Thaddeus Smith of Kentucky, Lemuel Brown of Cleveland and John M. Scudder of Cincinnati bought up large sections, including the Big Marsh, drained and "Hollandized" it, and converted it into a healthy and beautiful spot for orchards, vineyards and gardens. That pattern of life, established sixty years ago, is still maintained. About a thousand people make a living on Pelee now. They raise potatoes and fine tobacco, grapes, apples and peaches, they fish over the shoals, and they quarry building stone for the Canadian market. A few tourists visit the island in summer.[2]

The smaller islands, American and Canadian, are little more than name-bearing green dots in the lake. Lying just off Catawba Point, like a piece chipped from the mainland, is little Mouse Island. It contains only three acres. That great nineteenth-century traveler, Henry Howe of Ohio, called it "a very small affair, so small one might some day take a fancy to pick it up, slip it in his vest pocket as he would a watch, and walk off with it." It used to belong to President Rutherford B. Hayes, one of the notable fishermen of those parts, who built a summer home there for his children. It is still owned and occasionally used by members of his family.

Green Island, with its twenty acres, is primarily a foundation for the Green Island Lighthouse and a home for its keeper. Ballast Island is a rugged ten acres of limestone cliffs and headlands. Perry got the ballast stones for his Lake Erie fleet from this handy quarry and thereby gave the island its name. At various times through the years it has been the home of canoe and fishing clubs, and is still used for summer camps.

Starve Island is a two-acre mass of rock off the southeast shore of South Bass. It took its name, as one might guess, from a skeleton found on the island, which legend built into the story of a sailor who got stranded there and died of starvation. If he stayed on the island he would certainly have starved, but legend does not state

---

[2] A charming account of life on the island was written by Oliver Warner, a young Englishman who recently visited his uncle on Pelee. It is called *Uncle Lawrence* (New York, 1939).

why he was stranded a half-mile from South Bass. No one lives on Starve Island.

Far off and due east from Put-in-Bay is Gull Island, which was named for the great flocks of gulls that used to settle over this green refuge and lay their eggs in the sand.

Rattlesnake Island, a commercially useless thirty-acre plot two miles northwest of Put-in-Bay, has a twofold right to its sinister name. In the days of James Flint it was said to be full of rattle-snakes. According to local rumor, the island was so thick with these reptiles that if a man should venture ashore, he would tread on three or four rattlers with every step he took. Under the influence of this rumor, it was natural that men looking across the water to the strip of limestone covered with red cedar should see it in the shape of a rattlesnake with head slightly raised to strike and the frag-ments of rock at the western tip as the monster's rattles. But if a visitor could see it from Perry's Memorial on South Bass Island with-out suggested prejudice, he would think of it as one of the attractive islands of the archipelago, and a suitable spot for a Wordsworthian soul to live in peace and receive elevating impulses from what is left of the vernal woods.

Hen and Chickens Islands, where a few fishermen still have their clubs, North Harbor Island, and the three Sister Islands are but pleasant landmarks on the route to the Detroit River.

In the center of the archipelago is the Bass Island group: North, Middle and South. South Bass, often referred to as Put-in-Bay, is the largest (1,450 acres) and in many respects the most interesting of them, partly because of the beautiful and famous harbor where Perry rendezvoused his fleet. It is thirty-five miles east of Toledo, sixty miles west of Cleveland and about the same distance southeast of Detroit. But it is only a few minutes' journey from the mainland by air, or a half-hour by the *Erie Isle* auto ferry which plies back and forth over the seven miles of water between the bay and the Catawba peninsula.[3] The ferry, like the summer-excursion steam-ers from the lake cities, rounds the north tip of Gibraltar Island,

---

[3] This peninsula is usually called Catawba Island. It is not really an island, except in the isolation of its jutting arm, and in the fact that it lies between the lake and the old Portage River bed.

which forms a breakwater between the arms of the bay, and puts in at the wharf by the park under the shadow of the towering Perry Memorial. It is a handsome memorial set on the thin neck of land that holds the two lobes of South Bass into one island. This spot was formerly a sand bar and marsh over which the waves of storm-tossed Lake Erie washed and broke without hindrance. It has been protected by sea walls, filled in to a safe height, and made into a neat fourteen-acre park with the gleaming Milford granite monument in the center. The memorial was dedicated on the centennial of Perry's victory, with the resurrected *Niagara,* attended by the *Wolverine* and surrounded by a thousand craft, looking on from the bay.

We have been on the top of the monument before, but it is worth a second trip. The elevator quickly whisks you up to the observation platform. The view is unsurpassed. From this vantage point 352 feet above the lake the striking loveliness of the five-mile-long island, its bay and its neighbors in the archipelago is laid out before you. The bay is even more attractive as you look down upon it. Boats are tied up to the wharves, fishermen are busy at the docks, and white sails dip with the wind and skim silently out to the open lake. If it is the week of the annual regatta which the Inter-Lake Yachting Association has held here since 1884, the bay will be jammed with over 200 competing craft and more than a thousand boats of all designs; and several thousand visitors will crowd beyond capacity the park and Put-in-Bay village and all but spill over into the lake. There in the park is the pyramid of cannon balls honoring the American and British officers who died in the battle. The village around the park, so frowsy and vulgar with its cheap entertainment joints for excursionists and its dilapidated hotels, from this distance looks clean and pleasant under the softening canopy of its trees. Gibraltar Island, set between the East Point and Peach Point arms of the bay, with the gray stone tower of Jay Cooke's mansion jutting above the trees, is a dream world re-created from the page of old romance. Its spell is not broken by the harsh, businesslike laboratory on the south terrace fronting the bay.

We look off to the southwest over the larger lobe of the island. The vineyards cut across the land in neat green rows. The country roads are hedged with yellow willow trees from which each year the vinedressers cut the tender shoots, and use them to tie the grape-vines to their wire supports. The island homes and the summer cottages are almost hidden under the trees around the irregular shore. Hersberger's airport is a flat open meadow down toward the tip of the island, and his plane taking off for Port Clinton looks like a grasshopper leaping over the green field along the edge of the blue lake, and soaring above the square tower of the South Bass Island Lighthouse. And on across the lake are Catawba, Lakeside, Marblehead and Sandusky on the low-lying mainland shore.

We turn to the east to view the green mass of Kelleys Island and to the northeast to look at Pelee. They are somnolent under a soft haze, as though they had never been touched by quarrymen or gar-deners. The lake freighters steam past on the horizon under their plumes of smoke. To the north, barely separated from South Bass and from each other, are Middle and North Bass, covered with trees and vineyards. North Bass looks like a huge poplar leaf floating on Lake Erie, with its roadway running like a stem through its center. The incongruous tower of the Lonz Winery rising up on the shore of Middle Bass stares across at the monument. Rattlesnake, Ballast, Sugar, Big Chicken, Little Chicken and Hen Islands surround the islands like emerald mountings for a particularly handsome group of jewels. And at the foot of the monument on this northeast side lies the upper, and smaller, lobe of South Bass, a fairyland of vine-yards and orchards and flat patches of green.

These islands were thrown in with the Western Reserve for good measure, as it were, like Michigan's Upper Peninsula, or Minnesota's iron range below the Pigeon River. No one paid much attention to them at the time. If Tilly Buttrick, Jr., had paddled over in 1819 he might have found, besides the rattlesnakes and wild hogs, only one or two solitary squatters. The Bass Islands belonged by law to Judge Ogden Edwards of Connecticut, but the judge found little profit in his ownership. He did send in an agent with some laborers to clear about 100 acres for wheat. The virgin land yielded abun-dantly. Some 2,000 bushels were shipped over to the mainland when the war clouds gathered over the lake in 1812, but the British and their Indian allies swooped down on the storage pen and destroyed it, and brought an abrupt end to this first attempt at husbandry.

The islands passed to Judge Edwards' brother. When he came

over a decade later to see the island which he had inherited, he found one lone French-Canadian squatter living like Crusoe among the red-cedar timber. Edwards ejected his squatter, built a nice house for himself and planted a small private colony made up chiefly of his workers. He brought over 500 sheep. He cut the cedar into cordwood and sold it to passing steamers or shipped it to Detroit and Cleveland. He took out limestone and shipped it off to the same growing cities. Because of its superior harbor, Put-in-Bay became a convenient port of call for the lake vessels. In the early days of the nineteenth century, when even the small sailing ships could not go into Buffalo, Cleveland, Sandusky or other harbors on the lake because of the sand bars at the mouths of the creeks and rivers, Put-in-Bay afforded a safe anchorage, and ships ran in there from all parts of the lake to escape the storms. A few vessels were partially built in this sheltered bay. The brig *Union* was launched here in 1813 and towed east to Grand River for fitting. Her decks were made of South Bass red cedar.

Except for these small enterprises, the Bass Islands lay undeveloped in their isolation until the middle of the century. In 1854 a wealthy Spanish merchant of New York, Rivera de San Jargo (Americanized as Mr. J. D. Rivera), got interested in the region and bought for $44,000 the three Bass Islands, Gibraltar and the fourteen-acre Sugar Island just off the northwest corner of Middle Bass. Rivera planned to turn the islands into a sheep ranch for which, as Edwards' experiment had shown, they seemed admirably suited. His flock increased until he had 2,000 sheep grazing on the cut-over lands. But the interest in grapes and wine was then intense, and the islands soon demonstrated that their thin but fertile soil was uniquely adapted to viticulture. Rivera decided to open the islands to settlement. He divided much of South Bass into small five to ten-acre plots and sold them for a few dollars an acre to individual gardeners and grape growers. Many New Englanders migrated to the Bass Islands, but they were soon outnumbered by the Germans who came to work in the vineyards and to buy plots of their own. Their descendants are still on the islands where the tombstones of their fathers and grandfathers bear the names of Vroman, Heineman, Doller, Fuchs, Burgraff, Ingold. A permanent population was thus assured, and in the post-Civil War years of optimism over the future of vineyards, it rose to about 800 people. The islands experienced a boom, and the best land sold at $1,500 an acre.

At the same time Put-in-Bay was discovered as a summer resort. Interest in Perry's victory remained fresh in the minds of his countrymen. As lake travel increased, people came in droves to celebrate the Fourth of July at Put-in-Bay, and to lay plans for collecting money to build a fitting memorial to Perry. Fifteen hundred people came to the celebration in 1852, 8,000 in 1858, and in 1859 it was estimated that 15,000 people from all around the lake gathered at the bay. They, of course, spread the word throughout the land about the attractions of the islands. Rivera encouraged visitors. A tourist boom resulted.

J. W. Gray, editor of the Cleveland *Plain Dealer,* visited Put-in-Bay and succumbed to its charm—and to its business opportunities. He bought the old Edwards house, the only frame house on the island, and remodeled and enlarged it into a summer hotel.

More and more visitors, tourists and excursionists came for holiday pleasure. Gray's hotel could not accommodate them. Within the next few years several of those huge Victorian summer-resort hotels, after the Saratoga Springs models, were erected around the bay: the three-storied Put-in-Bay House (burned in 1878), with a veranda extending 450 feet along the water front; the Beebe House; and as a climax, the Hotel Victory, erected in 1892 and advertised as the largest and most luxuriously appointed summer hotel in the United States. It stood on a twenty-one-acre plot of high landscaped ground near the southwest shore overlooking Stone Cove, once known as Victory Bay. An electric railway connected it with the boat landing at Put-in-Bay. It could accommodate 1,500 guests at one time. People came from all over the country, especially from the Southern states, and, as a contemporary wrote, "in contemplation of this architectural marvel—its size, design, and magnificence—are they lost in wonder."[4] It was 600 feet long, and the central portion surrounded a courtyard garden 300 feet square. It had three elevators, electric lights, steam heat, eighty private baths, an ornate dining hall that could accommodate 1,200 at one sitting; a vast lobby, a ballroom for dancing, a grand piazza along the full length of the main structure, a

---

[4] Theresa Thorndale, *Sketches and Stories of the Lake Erie Islands* (Sandusky, 1898), p. 94.

rustic bridge over the ravine, an electric fountain, and a boardwalk to the lake shore.

The Hotel Victory was a favorite for all kinds of big conventions until the end of the 1800's. Men of wealth came to the resort. They ferried over horses and fine carriages which lent a touch of elegance to Sight Road, and their yachts and fishing boats graced Squaw Harbor. Only the "better-class" people could afford to live in such luxury. The hotels which attracted them were doubly welcome as countermeasures "to prevent the lawless elements from monopolizing this, Nature's outing place, for the people of Ohio." For, beginning in the 1870's, the resort threatened to become a rowdy place because of "the influx of unwholesome characters on excursions from the cities of Cleveland, Toledo, and Sandusky, who are encouraged to come here and patronize the numerous saloons that have sprung up."[5] These Sunday excursionists gave grave concern to high-minded and conservative folk. The controversy over them is one of the lively chapters in the history of the islands.

The conservative residents and visitors were well represented by Jay Cooke, who owned and maintained Gibraltar Island, lying across the entrance to Put-in-Bay. This famous financier was born in 1821 at Sandusky where his father Eleutheros (*Greek*: to set free), was a prominent lawyer and public figure. The famous Christian Ottawa chief Ogontz, who lived with his adopted tribe at Sandusky, was a friend of the family. He used to carry little Jay on his shoulders about the streets of Sandusky. Years later, when Jay Cooke was a millionaire, financier to the government and railroad baron, he named his Philadelphia estate, with its fifty-two-room mansion in the Chelton Hills, "Ogontz" for his Indian friend at Sandusky.

Jay Cooke bought Gibraltar Island in 1864 and built his fifteen-room Victorian house on its highest point among the trees. He came here for the summer almost every year for the rest of his life. He loved the place. An octagonal four-story stone tower was appended to the house like a campanile. From its crenelated top Cooke and his guests could view the lake—and, if they cared to do so, which they didn't, they could look down on the Sabbath-breaking excursionists across the bay who gave them so much pain. Mr. Cooke was as zealous in his love for religion as for his island

<hr>

[5] Henry Howe, *Historical Collections of Ohio*, II, 368.

paradise. He kept a staff of servants on the island, he stocked his larder with the finest foods obtainable, and each year, in gratitude to the Lord for His Goodness unto His servant, he invited His ministers of different denominations to come there for relaxation from their duties. He paid their way from their homes to Gibraltar and entertained them bountifully. They fished and read and talked and played croquet on the lawn during the week, but the Sabbath was sacred and inactive. Jay Cooke even refused to allow the national ensign to be raised when General W. T. Sherman, at the height of his fame, visited the island on a Sunday in 1866. In fact he stayed in his room until the general was actually at the door and the host had to forego his convictions long enough to greet him. And when Sherman had gone away, Jay Cooke wrote in his record book for June 17:

"There was no sort of excuse for Genl Shermans [sic] journeying on the Sabbath—He should have remained in Detroit & permitted his officers & men to rest & attend Church & have attended himself that he might set a good example. Had he arrived on Monday we would have felt a *thousand fold more honored*. I would have had all flags flying & his welcome would have been more *sincere*—Tonight at Prayers we prayed for our rulers & Chief men——"[6]

Small wonder then that there should be a clash of culture and mores between the strict American churchmen of that day, and the gay and imbibing German folk who had come to the lake towns in such large numbers so recently. They made up large parties, chartered a steamer, stocked up with beer and came almost into Jay Cooke's front yard to enjoy their day of rest. Cooke's *Gibraltar Records* cast a white light of illumination and disapproval on these pagan goings-on. Time and again he enters sharp reproof. The Toledo Saengerbund came over on June 23, 1866. They had chartered the *Reindeer* of Detroit and hired the Union Silver Band. Cooke wrote, "The only interruption to our quiet enjoyment of this day has been a 'German' excursion, with band of music from Toledo. When shall these things cease." A few weeks later, while he was entertaining ministerial guests, the *Forester* brought over "a German pic nic party from Toledo," and for an hour Gibraltar's Sabbath quiet

---

[6] James E. Pollard, *The Journal of Jay Cooke or The Gibraltar Records, 1865-1905* (Columbus, 1935).

was broken by their actual invasion of Cooke's own private island.

"It was voted among us that Mr. Cooke and Mrs. McMeens [the housekeeper] should be a committee to consider a remedy. . . . It is said that the old settled convictions in regard to the American Sabbath are thus slaughed [sic]. . . . The gregarious profanation comes largely from our foreign German population. An American Sabbath ought not thus to be infringed on. It is the cornerstone of our free nationality."

Cooke's committees and the fulminations of the millionaire and his guests in the record book could hardly be expected to restrain the convivial spirit of their German and Irish neighbors on the lake. It is only a matter of record and not of moral controversy that conviviality and Sunday holidays prevailed over Jay Cooke's solemn Sabbath observance. St. Paul's Church, Put-in-Bay, which Jay Cooke helped to establish, and once legally owned, was forced to share the island with the Sabbathbreakers.

The "unwholesome characters" also prevailed in time over the patrons of the Hotel Victory. The hotel was already losing its elegance and its popularity before the outbreak of World War I. Its complete destruction by fire in 1919 was symbolic of the passing of an era. It was not rebuilt, and its site is now difficult to locate. The dingy little hotels of the present day, with only 200 rooms among them, fail to suggest even remotely any of the splendor of that gala era. Jay Cooke died, his mansion was closed and the famous guests no longer came to Gibraltar. Prohibition came, then the depression, and the vineyards fell into near ruin, the permanent population dwindled to less than 500, and sumac and hackberry invaded abandoned plots. But the annual regatta continues to bring its thousands of visitors, and the holiday steamers each year dump 150,000 excursionists into the park for their day or week end of recreation. They ascend the monument, visit the wineries and the limestone caves, ride rented bicycles over the country roads, patronize the noisy joints in the village, take motorboat rides over to Middle Bass, and scramble aboard the steamer in the evening for the return trip to Detroit, Toledo, Sandusky or Cleveland. The islanders immediately clean up the muss and return the park to its neat, well-kept appearance.

These holiday and week-end visitors concentrate around the park and the village of Put-in-Bay. They seldom molest the summer residents who have their cottages on the shore, especially those on the wooded west shore between Peach Point and Stone Cove. There are 125 cottages on South Bass, most of them owned and neatly cared for by people who, finding the island an ideal summer home, go there year after year with as much enthusiasm as Jay Cooke ever did. Among them is a considerable colony from the faculty of the Ohio State University. They ferry their cars to the island, drive to the village to market, make friends with the islanders and live in peace and quiet for a few months each year.

The director of the Franz Theodore Stone Laboratory and his staff, assistants and their students, also form a small year-round colony at Peach Point opposite Gibraltar Island. Julius F. Stone of Columbus bought this seven-acre island from the Jay Cooke heirs in 1925 and presented it to the Ohio State University as a laboratory for biological research. It is now a part of the university campus. In addition to the laboratory there are dormitories and a dining hall, and summer students live in the mansion where the generous millionaire formerly entertained his guests. Most of the research, however, is carried on in the laboratories on Peach Point, next door to the State Fish Hatchery. These research men and their families are accepted with cordiality by the natives and are on the friendliest terms with them, but they are foreigners, nonetheless, because they were not born on the island.

It is an important distinction. The islanders are a tightly knit group. They have lived in relative isolation for several generations, they have intermarried until almost everybody is somehow related to everybody else, and they have clung tenaciously to their ways and their separateness. They have remained rigidly aloof from both the summer residents and the week-end visitors. Some of them steadfastly refused to permit their daughters to work in the cottages or in the hotels until the depression laid its heavy hand upon them. A few were even reluctant to sell fish to them. They are happiest when the last "outsider" has departed, for the island then seems like a big house in the country when the summer guests have gone and the family is alone by its fireside.

Interesting characters have lived on the islands. The older residents tell of Captain John Brown, Jr., who after toil rests in the peaceful cemetery on South Bass. He was the oldest of John Brown's sons and shared with him the illusion that the slaves could be freed without bloodshed. After John Brown was executed in body in 1859 to become a marching soul through the 1860's, his son John fought on for the cause of freedom. He was disabled after a year of service with the Union Army. He wanted retirement as far as possible from the public eye. He found the isolation he craved at Put-in-Bay in 1862. He built a comfortable home with a big open porch around it among the trees on the south shore. He lived there quietly for thirty-three years. Presidents, statesmen and industrial barons visited the modest hero and recluse. His unaffected simplicity and dignity when confronted with this marked attention is a part of his permanent legend on the island. They say he seldom spoke of those flaming and portentous days when his father gathered his twenty-one men at the United States Arsenal at Harper's Ferry in the hope of setting the slaves of Virginia free; of the death of his brothers, the narrowest possible escape of a third, and the death by hanging of his zealous father. Negroes whom he had helped to free often called at Put-in-Bay to pay their respects to him.

Brown tilled his farm, cared for his vines and fruit trees, read widely in geology and phrenology, and taught science to the growing number of young people on the island. The remains of his brother Watson, who was killed at Harper's Ferry, were preserved by a medical college. They were recovered by a friend of John Brown, Jr., and sent to Put-in-Bay where for a time they were a grim scientific exhibit for the citizens and visitors.

Another of the brothers, Owen, also lived on the islands for two decades. He was even more picturesque than John, Jr. He had helped his father on the Underground Railroad, and had gone with him on the Harper's Ferry adventure. He escaped with a few followers at the height of the fighting in which his father was taken. His escape led to an impressive man hunt that was dramatized by a reward of $25,000 offered for his capture. His description was broadcast through all the surrounding country. Yet Owen picked his way out of Harper's Ferry, across Maryland and into the Pennsylvania mountains. He hid in the brush by day, traveled by night and lived on corn and potatoes foraged in the fields. His pursuers were at times so hot upon his trail that he could hear the bloodhounds yelping and panting. One of his companions was taken near Chambersburg when, desperate for food, he went to a farmhouse door to ask for bread. Owen said he could hear the band playing as they marched him to the train to be carried to Charlestown for hanging. Owen escaped the intensified man hunt and found safety on Put-in-Bay. He lived as a bachelor recluse on the islands. For several winters he was caretaker for Jay Cooke on Gibraltar. The tall, bearded hero of the North became, like his brother, a legend on the islands, where some of the oldest residents still remember the twinkle in his eyes and his charity to needy islanders.

The islanders also tell of Uncle Jimmy of Ballast, one of the strange collection of men without family who came to the islands and spent their lives in Thoreauesque seclusion and simplicity. For years ageless Uncle Jimmy lived in a weather-beaten cabin, the sole inhabitant of Ballast's ten acres, except for his dog and cat, his horse and cow, the eagles that nested on his island and the flocks of gulls that dipped over the cedars to the rim of sand on the shore line. From time to time he would row across to Put-in-Bay to sell his fish and to buy sugar and meal and coffee. He watched the big steamers going back and forth from Detroit to Cleveland and Buffalo, and the little steamers from the islands to Sandusky and Port Clinton.

As he tended his fishing lines through the day or sat by his cabin door with his cat in the evening, he thought about these steamers. Sometime he would go aboard and make a trip to Sandusky. One day, after long brooding, he reached his great decision. He left his dog and cat, his horse and cow, rowed over to Put-in-Bay, and took passage to Sandusky. People came to the wharf to see him off. He stood at the railing looking at the strange sight of the familiar islands and the lake from a steamboat deck. In the afternoon he boarded the vessel again at Sandusky. As she was approaching Kelleys Island her boiler blew up. The islanders heard the explosion, but they thought it was a blast in the quarry. A few hours later a telegraph message reached Put-in-Bay telling of the disaster. "Nearly all on board are injured or killed outright." The vessel was towed back to Sandusky. The dead were carried ashore. Among the burned and scalded victims was Uncle Jimmy. He died soon afterward. His friends brought him back to South Bass Island and buried him in the little cemetery at Put-in-Bay in sight of the island where he had spent most of his life. And there is a stone slab set up to his memory. It reads simply: "To the Memory of Uncle Jimmy of Ballast Island, Erected by His Friend, George W. Gardner."

Until very recent years the isolation of the islands during the winter was almost complete. The natives stored their necessary provisions before the ferry made its last trip of the season. After that the mainland could be reached only by crossing the miles of treacherous ice. Horses and cars have crashed through and been lost while attempting passage. The islanders developed a skiff mounted on steel runners, which they called an "ironclad," as the best means of negotiating the ice. They pushed or pulled these boats over the frozen surfaces, walked over the cracks on a plank, and rowed across the wider fissures to get to Port Clinton.

Many of the tales which still while away a winter's evening on the islands tell of the heroism of the crossings from Kelleys or the Bass Islands to Sandusky or Port Clinton to bring in provisions, to carry the mail or to fetch a doctor and medicine. They tell of Henry Enfers who carried the mail under contract to Kelleys Island for forty years: how he once sailed his ironclad across the ice in the record time of twenty minutes, and how he once spent eight hazardous hours fighting his way over the same passage when the ice was too thin to support his weight.

They tell of the bravery and skill of the Hitchcock brothers, mail carriers, who made the trip through running ice in the severe winter of 1897-1898. They were caught in one of Lake Erie's storms which broke up the ice and drove them down the lake before the wind. Watchers on the mainland saw them struggling and wired to the anxious friends on Kelleys Island: "Look out for the carriers; they are fast in the ice and drifting that way." But after hours of climbing from one block of ice to another, the brothers managed to cross the storm-tossed floe and stumble exhausted on the shore. They were covered with ice stiff as a knight's armor. The waiting friends and neighbors had to break and cut away their frozen clothes to free them. One wonders what messages were in the mailbags that made such foolhardy crossings so imperative regardless of weather.

The necessity, whatever it was, has disappeared before the age of air transport, which has made these islands as accessible in winter as in spring or summer. Milton Hersberger, mechanic and veteran barn-storming pilot, wrought the transformation. He came to the islands in 1930, and leased and cleared small landing fields on South Bass, Middle Bass, North Bass and Kelleys. In these cramped quarters the longest runway is 1,600 feet and the shortest is only 1,000 feet. But Hersberger, who won the dead-stick landing contest at the National Air Races in 1930, doesn't need even that much space to take off and land his plane. With his hangar and main operating base on South Bass, he established a regular year-round schedule of service flights to the other three islands and to the mainland. The government gave him a contract to fly the daily mail. His service operates like a combination interurban bus and delivery truck that flies through the air. The islanders, skeptical at first, became air-minded, and now they board his planes at their pleasure, winter or summer, to fly over to Port Clinton, as casually as the residents of Lakewood take a trolley for Cleveland. They no longer stock up for the winter; they order goods from Montgomery Ward or Sears, Roe-buck, and Hersberger flies them across the piled-up windrows of ice on the lake. Kindly and accommodating Mrs. Hersberger, who keeps her car at the Port Clinton field, makes frequent trips with her husband and does shopping for her neighbors in the mainland town.

Hersberger flies in hardware, beer and tons of groceries: meat, oranges, canned goods, bread; he flies out fish and wine; and he stows passengers among his piles of cargo. He flits back and forth, day in and day out, morning till night, in all kinds of weather, from South Bass to Middle Bass, on to North Bass, back to South Bass and across to Port Clinton. He unloads and reloads, and then skims across to Kelleys with mail and freight and passengers. Again he trades cargo and flies back to Port Clinton to pick up the incoming mail for the Bass Islands. Back he goes with the mail to the waiting islanders at his postage-stamp airfields on South, Middle and North Bass. Then he flies to his home base once more, to prepare for the next schedule of flights which fill up a long and arduous day. And the mere sight of his *Trimotor* sailing through the sky and binding the islands together has altered the psychology of the islanders. For they know that if "island fever" hits them and they are threatened with claustrophobia, they can board Hersberger's plane, go to the mainland towns for a day and see a moving picture.

Chapter 21

Grape Juice and Lake Erie Wines

THE southern rim of Lake Erie is vineyard country: grape juice along the New York and Pennsylvania shore, celebrated wines around Sandusky Bay and on the western islands. Fredonia, the beautiful city that grape juice built in the heart of the eastern vineyard belt, erected in its Lafayette Park a statue of Mrs. Esther McNeil. She was one of the pioneer organizers of the Women's Christian Temperance Union back in the 1870's. It is said that her zealous crusade against wine and its corruptions turned this favored strip into a world center of unfermented grape juice instead of a region for vintage wines. In the western vineyards M. Hommel should be honored with a monument. While Mrs. McNeil was crusading in Fredonia, M. Hommel from France was carving out his cool, deep, limestone cellars in Sandusky and laying down his first vintage of champagne from Ohio grapes. The result was a nice balance of the produce of the Lake Erie vineyards. Dr. Welch of Westfield supplied one portion of the democracy with juice from the Concord grape; Dorn, Engels & Krudwig, Meier, and M. Hommel of Sandusky, Lonz of Middle Bass Island, and Heineman of Put-in-Bay gratified another portion with a rich variety of wines, champagnes and sparkling Burgundies that won praise and prizes from the expert vintners of Italy and old France.

The eastern grape belt, five to seven miles wide, begins a few miles southwest of Buffalo near the edge of the Cattaraugus Indian Reservation, and runs with the shore line fifty-five miles to Harbor Creek, Pennsylvania. The clay soil and the climate are ideal for vineyards. The water of the lake, circling far to the south, tempers the strip of land between the shore and the parallel rim of hills. It holds the temperature a few degrees higher in winter, modifies it a degree or two in summer, and lengthens the growing season at each end by several days. It is severe on the respiratory tracts of the citizens, and medical specialists flourish throughout the region; but it is quite perfect for grapes.

Deacon Elijah Fay, an immigrant from Massachusetts, discovered in 1824 just how well suited it was. He had the purple thumb of the true vinegrower. He experimented with different varieties, including the Catawba that is still so favored around Sandusky; but he found the large, rich, aromatic, purple-skinned Concord to be the best of them all. To this day, while other varieties are grown there, the whole region specializes in the Concord. Its sweet bouquet floods U. S. Highway 20 and State Highway 5 in September, and drifts out over the vineyards to Lake Erie in the evening on the gentle offshore breeze.

The number of vineyards increased steadily with the advance of the century. Six hundred acres were yielding grapes a few years after the end of the Civil War. In the 1880's the growers were shipping fresh grapes in baskets to market in carload lots. By the 1890's the planting of vineyards had reached the proportions of a boom. An extensive basketmaking industry grew up in the vicinity to supply containers for the crop. Migrant Italians came in to work in the vineyards and gather the ripened grapes; many of them remained to plant and tend vineyards of their own. A goodly portion of the viticulturists are now Italians; they are scattered throughout the region, and their children populate the schools of Silver Creek, Dunkirk, Brocton and Westfield.

Serious overproduction and speculation in the 1890's brought on a temporary collapse of the industry. It was rescued and revived, however, by the enterprise of Thomas Branwell Welch, D.D.S., and his son Charles Edgar Welch, also D.D.S. The older doctor had carried on experiments in his kitchen in his off hours to find a method of preserving grape juice in unfermented form. His ultimate success is brilliantly attested by the world renown of his product. His formula was perfected in the 1890's and by 1900 his plant at Westfield was shipping Welch's Grape Juice in bottles to markets throughout the country. The big plant that now turns out some 3,000,000 gallons each year was built in 1910. Armour & Company have a plant near by. About 5,000 carloads of basket grapes are also sent out from the vineyard belt each season. The clusters are expertly cut with grape shears and carried to the packing house in thirty-five to forty-pound boxes. There they are sorted and packed in five to ten-pound baskets ready for fast freight or express shipment to the metropolitan centers.

Dr. Flagg, an early Ohio vintner, said in 1846, "I am confident that the introduction of pure light wine as a common beverage, will produce a great national and moral reform. . . . The temperance cause is rapidly preparing public sentiment for the introduction of pure American wine."[1] Whether that happy thought affected the purpose of the Ohio vinedressers is problematical, but the fact remains that they looked upon *wine,* not unfermented juice, as the life-blood of the grape. The vineyards extend from Ashtabula to the Maumee. From Ohio Highway 254, which follows the rim of one of the old shores of Lake Erie from Rocky River west toward Lorain, you may look down upon miles of neat vineyards flourishing on the ancient lake floor. The greatest concentration is around Sandusky Bay and on the chain of islands across Lake Erie to Canada. This lake belt in Ohio has about 10,000 acres in vineyards, and it produces approximately 30,000 tons of grapes each year. This is small compared to New York's 86,000, and California's nearly 2,500,000 tons, but the difference is in acreage and not in quality, as any Lake Erie vinedresser will tell you and proceed to prove.

We have already noted that settlers first chose the Ohio River, and moved north to the lake in the canal era. Grape growing followed the same pattern. An enthusiastic group of viticulturists led by Nicholas Longworth, "the father of American grape culture," planted vineyards along the Ohio River in the vicinity of Cincinnati. They built wine cellars and imported French manufacturers to tend their wine presses. They held regular meetings to discuss their problems, and annual exhibits at which people could inspect and sample their wines. Longworth sent a gift of his best wine to Longfellow, and got in return an enthusiastic poem on "Catawba Wine." Longfellow, who had drunk the wines of Europe, decided that Catawba was a noble vintage.

> For richest and best
> Is the wine of the West;
> That grows by the Beautiful River;
> Whose sweet perfume
> Fills all the room
> With a benison on the giver.

---

[1] Robert Buchanan, *The Culture of the Grape, and Wine-Making* (Cincinnati, 1856), p. 38.

There grows no vine
By the haunted Rhine
By Danube or Guadalquivir,
Nor on island or cape
That bears such a grape
As grows by the Beautiful River.

While pure as a spring
Is the wine I sing,
And to praise it, one needs but name it;
For Catawba wine
Has need of no sign,
No tavern-bush to proclaim it.

When the Civil War broke out there were 1,200 acres in vineyards around Cincinnati. Longworth himself had three cellars and an investment of $200,000 in vineyards and equipment. His product was becoming famous when mildew and black rot killed the vines.

The Lake Erie belt, however, proved to be relatively free from these scourges. As the Cincinnati vineyards declined and disappeared, the northern ones flourished, and produced one of the pleasantest eras ever to grace the lake. There were disappointments, of course. Longworth used to tell his Cincinnati friends the sad story of Father Ammen, one of his best German vinedressers. Ammen's wife died. He told Longworth, with tears in his eyes, "that she was just so good in the vineyard as one man, and he might so well have lost his horse." He went north to plant a vineyard. All his vines were killed. He returned to Cincinnati and caught cholera. He refused to take any medicine.

"I take none," he said. "What I want to live for? My grapes all rotten."

"A few hours, and he was no more," Longworth added; "peace to his ashes."

The Lake Erie islands, though often visited, were settled relatively late. The discovery that they were uniquely adaptable to grape culture attracted settlers in numbers around the middle of the nineteenth century. An acre of vines was tried out on Kelleys Island in 1846. The vines throve on the limestone soil under the protection of the tempering lake waters. By 1850 they were bearing enough grapes to make wine, and the following year the first wine cellar was built. German and American settlers moved in on South Bass Island in 1850, and within a few years had transformed it into one vast vineyard. Other Germans, most of them immigrants and vinedressers direct from the fatherland, settled on Middle Bass's 750 acres and planted vineyards. It too became one great arbor, with many presses and wine cellars. The big Lonz Winery, the most famous of the island cellars, was erected by the docks on the south shore in 1884. Its stone turrets are a part of the island scenery, and its Silenium clubroom an object of pilgrimage. Within its cool walls, under the oak-beamed ceiling, on a flagged floor are tables for guests who come to drink the famous Lonz wines and admire the bacchic windows while they sip. Lonz's dry wines have won many prizes in Europe, among them the Gran Premio of Italy. This cellar makes about 50,000 gallons of dry, sweet and sparkling wines each year.

North Bass, about the same size as Middle Bass, was made into a vineyard in the 1850's. When the Fox brothers came over to the island from neighboring Pelee, they found it a wilderness of wild grapes—the kind Cadillac and other travelers discovered in abundance along the Detroit and St. Clair Rivers and in parts of Old Ontario, and from which the early settlers made a wine resembling port. If wild grapes could thrive untended, why not Concords, Delawares and Catawbas, under the hand of trained vinedressers? So North Bass likewise became a vineyard.

Grape culture also spread to Pelee Island, that 10,000-acre fragment of Old Ontario lying in plain sight of Ohio's North Bass. Thaddeus Smith of Kentucky and his associates bought forty acres there and planted the Vin Villa Vineyards. Other viticulturists followed. Lemuel S. Brown bought 625 acres in 1878 and planned to bring in German immigrants to raise stock and dress vines. He did not know that in wet seasons much of his land was swamp. The discovery failed to daunt his enterprise. He aroused the interest of wealthy Dr. John M. Scudder of the Cincinnati Eclectic Medical College. They bought and drained the 4,000 acres of the Big Marsh. They brought in steam dredges, dug canals and installed pumps to force the water out of a central pound. Malaria disappeared, the plague of mosquitoes and snakes abated, and the marsh became a vineyard and a garden with wine cellars and steamer service.

This district in Lake Erie became known as the Wine Islands. The dry soil gives to the grapes an exceptionally distinguished flavor, and the tempered climate lengthens the growing season on the islands two or three weeks beyond that of the mainland. The clusters may often hang on the vine for fullest ripening until as late as the middle of November.

The Ontario mainland is too far north for extensive arbors, though the soil itself is good, and wild grapes used to grow there in abundance. In the mid-century, when the vineyards were spreading over the islands and the Cincinnati wineries were flourishing, attempts were made to raise grapes along the north shore of Lake Erie. James Cousins imported cuttings from Cincinnati and planted a vineyard two miles from Amherstburg. But a severe winter followed, the temperature fell to 17° below zero, and all the cuttings were frozen and killed. Other plantings fared better. Catawba and Isabella grapes ripened well and, although the Canadian region never attained commercial importance, it did supply fine grapes for local consumption.

Eighty or more varieties of grapes were grown in these Lake Erie vineyards, but the Catawba was, and is, the general favorite. It covers more acres than all the others combined, and commands the highest prices. It makes a light or straw-colored wine with a fruity aroma. Some vintners press and manufacture it to retain its pinkish color and muscadine flavor which add to its value. No sugar is required for fermentation, though Nicholas Longworth used to add pure rock candy to make his champagne. It is the latest of the vines to ripen, and it is praised by the vinedressers as "a good keeper."

The Catawba, a native of North Carolina, was discovered on the Catawba River in 1802. Major John Adlum, an enthusiastic viticulturist, saw a vine growing in a garden at Georgetown, D. C. He was impressed by its quality and immediately began to propagate it. He sent some cuttings to Longworth in 1825. This grape became so popular that ninety-five percent of the Cincinnati vineyards were planted in Catawbas. They proved to be better suited to the Lake Erie Islands than to the Catawba River or the Ohio. Adlum was proud of his contribution to American civilization. Longworth wrote in the *Horticulturist,* "Major Adlum had a proper appreciation of the value of the Catawba grape. In a letter to me, he remarked:—'In bringing this grape into public notice, I have rendered my country a greater service than I would have done, had I paid off the National debt.' I concur in his opinion."

Adlum had at least done the Wine Islands a service; he gave them a picturesque economy, a tradition and a festival. The German and American viticulturists set the plants at intervals of from four to five feet in neat rows about eight feet apart. Vinedressing is a year-round occupation; each year is broken into its seasons, and each season is marked by its appropriate activity in the vineyards. Pruning is an art in itself. It may begin in late November, when the last bunch of Catawbas is snipped from the vine, and continue until April portends the coming of another spring. In the Lake Erie belt the grafted plants are cut back to three or four buds the first year. In the second year the vinedressers prune them back five or six buds, being careful to retain three of the most virile shoots to grow the cluster-bearing arms for the third and productive year. Thereafter the vines are always cut close and each new season's crop is grown on "scant wood." The fruit is larger, finer-flavored and ripens earlier.

It is a very pleasant experience to watch the expert vinedresser at work. With a quick eye he selects three or four of the strongest new canes and trains them fanwise along the trellis. Last season's wood produces the cane which bears the new season's clusters. Much of the old wood must be pruned away. It is a winter's job. By the end of April the brush is piled up in small heaps all over the vineyard, ready to be burned. Brush burning is one of the minor festivals. All over the islands and along the mainland shore bonfires light the sky. Whole families tend them and pile on new brush. The sharp, pleasant odor of burning grape wood drifts over Lake Erie where the freighters are passing, and over the fishing grounds where fishermen are tending their nets.

As the winter frost leaves the ground, repairing of the vineyards begins. The vinedresser goes down between the long rows in his horse-drawn cart, and drives in the cedar posts with a sledge hammer. Then he and his sons walk the rows to tighten the wire trellis. (In the Lake Erie belt there are generally three wires on the posts to support the vines.) By the time this work is done, the vines are ready for spraying and for the first tying. Shoots from the yellow willow tree are used for ties. These small trees, rounded by the yearly cutting of the shoots, grow like hedges along the roadsides on the islands.

It is a part of the winter routine to split the willow shoots and cut them into twelve-inch lengths ready for this part of the ritual. In late June, when the vineyard has put out its new shoots, entire families may be seen moving along the fresh green rows, making the second tying with twisted rye stems which are grown for the purpose.

The picking season starts in late August when the early varieties begin to ripen: Golden Pocklington, Massasoit, Niagara, Hartford, Salem, Warden, Champion. Before these are entirely gathered the next group has come on: Concord, Cape, Isabella, Ives Seedling, Delaware, Norton's Virginia Seedling. And last of all the Catawba.

The rush months are September and early October. It is a season of excitement. In the big days of the vineyards it was a gala occasion. Grapes must be ripened on the vine, for they do not mature after they are picked. Hundreds of pickers were needed to gather the crop. They came to the islands in droves from the mainland. The little steamers hurried back and forth from Sandusky to the island docks loaded to capacity with baskets, and with boys and girls, men and women, all in holiday spirit. For many it was vacation with pay for a few weeks. The warm sun fell on the lake and on the islands. The ripening grapes filled the air with a bouquet unlike that of any other harvest in the world. There was laughter and singing, and there was romance in the cool of the evening.

They snipped off the purple, green, yellow and ruby clusters with short-bladed grape-picker's nippers. Sorters plucked out the dry, rotten or imperfect berries from the table clusters, and packed the grapes neatly in baskets like a New England farmer stacking hay on a wagon. These were picked up at the docks and hurried off to market aboard the fruit-company steamers. The vintage grapes were likewise sorted and taken to the wine presses at the cellars to be fermented, kegged, bottled and nurtured into fine wines: dry Riesling, claret, Delaware, Catawba; sweet Tokay, sherry, port, muscatel, Haut Sauterne; sparkling Burgundy and champagne.

The gala days pass, the Concords are all picked and basketed, and Indian summer comes to the lake and the islands. The crowds of pickers leave the vineyards. Early November finds the nights growing cooler. Only the late Catawbas still hang ripening on the vines. The rains begin, the vineyards are muddy, the days cold. The vinedressers hurry to gather the last clusters as the lake captains crowd steam to make the last passage through the Sault. Winter comes, and another season has gone through its appointed cycle. Most of the grapes have gone to market or into the huge wine vats in the cellars. A few clusters have been stored in crates or trays in cool, ventilated cellars, where the temperature remains evenly in the upper 30's, to be kept and sold during the winter.

Prohibition days almost wrecked the economy of the islands and the Sandusky mainland. Acres of vineyards were pulled up or destroyed by rootworm. On South Bass Island alone at the height of its productivity there were 600 acres in grapes and the annual production was 1,500,000 pounds; in 1930 the acreage was only half that area and the yield had dropped to about two tons per acre. Thousands of the hardy roots, so resistant to Phylloxera, were sent across the Atlantic where they were grafted with the finest vines of France that were being killed off by this devastating parasite. Wine cellars all over the islands fell into decay, and only their foundation stones are now visible. Peach orchards increased in the favored region and the Catawba Fruit Company shipped thousands of baskets of Elbertas to the city markets. Rumrunners scurried across the narrow channel between Canada's Pelee Island and Ohio's North Bass. Some of the vineyards and old wineries held on and survived into the New Deal era and the age of repeal. Some made a modest living by shipping kegs of fresh grape juice to thousands of private American cellars, sending along with their product a grave warning that the juice would turn to wine under certain clearly specified conditions which the buyers should be at pains to avoid.

The end of the prohibition experiment brought new hope to both Sandusky and the Wine Islands. Vineyards which had gone untended were trimmed again; acres that had been given over to wild sumac were rescued and replanted. Though the market for good wines improved, the expected boom did not come immediately. It arrived in the wake of World War II. When the distilleries ceased making hard liquor, the demand for wine rose to an all-time high. The big wineries had weathered the arid years of prohibition, but they had no large reserve stock to meet the sudden call of the 1940's. A wine shortage, especially in dry sherry, developed and prices were high. The wineries were drained and their revenue soared. They turned to a new phase in Lake Erie economy by buying up and planting land in large tracts which had formerly been tended by small vinegrowers. In a general way, the four big Sandusky companies divided the Wine Islands among themselves: Meier has the dominant interest on North Bass, Lonz on Middle Bass, E & K (Engels & Krudwig) on South Bass, and Sweet Valley on Kelleys Island.

All these companies, and others operating chiefly on the mainland, have entered brightly into the new prosperity of vine growing. Their wineries are among the most interesting places to be found on the lake. The John G. Dorn Winery, founded in 1869 and still operated by the same family, has in its big cellars some of the old wine casks used by Nicholas Longworth. M. Hommel Wine Company has an enormous cellar full of aged casks of from 2,000 to 5,000 gallons, and thousands of bottles of the finest champagne and Burgundy. The taproom at Hommel's is a happy meeting place for people from all over the country and M. Hommel himself is a rare host and tireless talker about wines, wine making, and the superior qualities of Lake Erie vintages. He and his fellow vintners are Jeffersonian in praise of wine and say with the great President, "No nation is drunken where wine is cheap; and none sober where the dearness of wine substitutes ardent spirits as the common beverage."

Chapter 22

Fishing Grounds

THE trimotored Ford plane owned and piloted by Milton Hersberger flies from the Port Clinton airfield to the islands of Lake Erie. It takes off, a little bumpily, from the small green meadow on the mainland, rises easily over the lagoons, the orchards, vineyards and summer homes on Catawba Island, and soars northward toward the archipelago.

Lake Erie has nothing more beautiful to show than the view from this high-winged plane. The twenty islands, each under a different light, are spread out across the seascape in romantic serenity. The smoke plumes of the freighters heading for th? Detroit River Light or steaming down the North Passage toward Point Pelee are visible on the horizon off the Ontario shore. Then you look down through the landing gear and out through the whirling propeller at the lake itself. The brown streak of the Portage River runs out into the lake almost to Green Island. The blue-green surface of the lake to the east is gently restless with the flash of waves breaking into whitecaps. And dotting the full expanse of this western segment of the lake are the small fishermen's boats and the launches of the fishing fleets from Sandusky and Port Clinton, Vermilion and Lorain.

You are viewing the portion of Lake Erie which supports the largest fresh-water catch in the world.[1] It far exceeds any of the other Great Lakes in production of fish, though the bulk of the production is now "rough fish." Of the Canadian waters, however, Lake Erie, until very recent years, produced almost twice as many ciscoes (herring) as all the other Great Lakes combined.[2]

From the time of its discovery to the present day, this south shore of Lake Erie and the archipelago to Point Pelee have been celebrated for their fishing banks. The Indians discovered them long ago. They regularly crossed Ohio from the Ohio River to the lake over the

---

[1] Bert Hudgins, *The South Bass Island Community* (pamphlet), p. 31.
[2] *Publications Ontario Fisheries Research Laboratory*, No. 21.

paddle-and-portage routes up the Miami and down the Maumee or up the Scioto and down the Sandusky or Portage to these fishing grounds. When Wayne drove out the Indians, the white settlers took over. They were not long in making serious big business of the fishing industry.

The lake is a natural habitat for a wide variety of fish. Ninety-one different species of fish and two of lampreys have been identified in Lake Erie. Its waters around the islands are shallow; over large areas they are less than thirty feet deep, and in few places between the islands and the Michigan and Canadian shores do they exceed thirty-five feet. Numerous shoals lie only a few feet beneath the surface; Colchester Shoals and Southeast Shoals in Canadian waters on the south edge of the shipway to the East are marked with lights. They are dangerous for ships, but they are hospitable spawning grounds for fish.

Fishing in this region and in the Detroit River became important to both Americans and British during the War of 1812 when the food supplies of the soldiers around Detroit and Amherstburg were limited. And when the first high tide of immigration began to flow over the lake to Detroit, quickly outrunning the produce on the western farms, local fishermen brought in fish to feed them. Seines were in use in Maumee Bay in 1815, and the practice spread. Several fishhouses in Detroit did good business. Many of them had their own boats, employed fishermen to operate them and fished the Detroit River and western Lake Erie as well as the St. Clair and lower Lake Huron. In 1826 Detroit made its first shipment of whitefish and lake trout, salted and barreled, to the eastern market. The experiment was so successful that three years later seven vessels were busy on Lake Erie carrying this new trade. In these early years professional fishermen, using seines and lines, took an ever-increasing number of whitefish, herring, yellow pike, perch and lake trout from the Detroit River.

Sandusky, however, became the center of the fishing industry on western Lake Erie. The village passed through its pioneering stage in the years from its founding in 1816 to its elevation as the seat of Erie County in 1838 with a population of 1,500 and a flourishing business as an important port of call for the steamers and schooners between Detroit, Cleveland and Buffalo. By 1840 it had 4,000 citi-

zens: Yankees from Connecticut, Irish from New York or direct
from the home island, and Germans. This was the port from which
Dickens sailed on his unhappy voyage in 1842.

The Germans moved to Sandusky Bay in great numbers in the
late 1840's and during the 1850's and 1860's. They built breweries,
started wineries and intensified the fisheries. The catch in western
Lake Erie increased steadily until it reached approximately 25,000,-
000 pounds annually. It has held rather consistently to that figure
during the last half-century. Over 10,000,000 pounds of this catch
went through the Sandusky fishhouses. They almost monopolized
Railroad Street, and gave to this charming lake city the name "Fish-
town." Their launches fished east and west of the islands and north
to the Canadian shoals. Fishermen from Put-in-Bay brought their
catch to the Sandusky or Port Clinton markets for distribution by
water and rail to the cities of the West, South and East. Choice fish
were plentiful—yellow perch, northern pike, bass, pickerel, herring
and whitefish.

To this day Sandusky is the leading fishing port on the lake. Lay
Brothers, Bickley Fish Company and Post Fish Company maintain
their own extensive wharves, launches, and fishhouses on the bay
front near the foot of Wayne Street. Port Clinton has likewise
been a fishing center ever since the ship bearing Scotchmen across
the lake was wrecked here in 1827 and the immigrants decided to
found a village on Lake Erie instead of going on to Chicago. They
too were joined by Germans, and the fish sheds spread along the
sluggish Portage River estuary. Three fishhouses carry on the industry at the present time. There are other houses at Huron, Vermilion and Lorain. Each morning during the season the motor
launches from these ports regularly put out from the weather-beaten
docks for the fishing grounds in the western lake. In the late summer they fish north of Vermilion to the east of the islands. As the
waters cool, they move westward toward the archipelago in search
of whitefish and pickerel, but too often get nets full of sheepshead
and carp.

There is also considerable fishing at the east end of the lake, centering around Dunkirk, Irving and Barcelona on the New York
shore. New York prohibits the use of pound nets, but the gill-net

boats from these ports annually take an important catch of herring, blue pike, suckers, whitefish, saugers and trout.

Nearly all the towns on the Ontario shore engage in commercial fishing, though the more important houses are at Kingsville, Merlin, Ridgetown, Port Dover and Nanticoke. The commercial fisheries at Kingsville alone take about $250,000 worth of fish annually from Lake Erie. These houses have all co-operated with the University of Toronto staff in their studies of the habits, spawning periods and life cycles of ciscoes, yellow perch and other commercial fish in Canadian waters. You may see the stakes or buoys of their pound and gill nets anywhere between Point Pelee and Maitland, the pound nets about two miles offshore and the gills about five miles out. The best grounds are between Pelee and Rondeau, and just east of Long Point. Port Dover, with its ten steam tugs and fifteen motor launches engaged in the fishing industry, is the largest of the fishing centers. Many sportsmen come to Normandale, home of one of Canada's biggest fish hatcheries, to Turkey Point and the Inner Long Point Bay at St. Williams for the bass-fishing season which opens on July 1.

Whether the commercial fishing tugs and launches have put out from Port Dover, Merlin, Barcelona or Sandusky, the methods of fishing are about the same—except for New York's prohibition of the pound nets. These are impounding-type nets, anchored to the soft bottom at depths up to ninety feet, which trap the fish through a tunnel. They are popular among the fishermen at the western end of the lake. The gill nets are also common. The fishermen on Lake Erie haul them out in 250-foot lengths and drop them over the side about the fishing grounds. A weight on the bottom edge and a float on the top of these four or five-foot-wide nets hold them upright like a tennis net in the water at any desired depth. The fishermen "pay out the twine" (as they call the nets) in gangs over the fishing grounds, anchor them at the ends and mark them with flagpoles. Lake fish swim into the two-and-a-half to four-and-a-half-inch meshes; the little ones go on through, but the bigger ones ram their noses through the mesh, get fastened there, and the fishermen haul them out by the gills. They raise the big pound nets with windlasses from one boat while fishermen moving alongside in other boats scoop out the fish with dip nets and throw them into the lake boxes or wells where they flop and glisten in the sun. Then the nets are reset and the launches speed back with their morning catch, generally arriving at the wharves and fish sheds on the mainland in the early afternoon.

In the big, well-equipped fishhouses the processing of the fish is rapid and mechanized. Dollies are rolled out on the wharf to meet the fleet as it comes alongside. The launches are unloaded and the catch is hurried into the sheds. Rough hands grown expert through years of practice quickly separate the species and toss them into boxes. Some of them are passed on to the skinners, then into the freezers, and are stacked in the huge refrigerator rooms like rows of brick. Some are iced and immediately shipped off by express or by truck. Lay Brothers of Sandusky still saw their own ice in the lake during the winter and ship their fish appropriately packed in their own native frozen habitat. The rest of the catch goes to the electric scaler, then to the cleaner and into a special refrigerator for quick freezing for later marketing. Millions of pounds of Lake Erie fish are caught and handled in this manner by the commercial fisheries throughout the season.

The most spectacular fishing on Lake Erie gets under way in January when the ice covers the lake. It generally freezes a sheet from a foot to a foot and a half thick, though in severe winters, when the temperature may fall to 19° below zero, it has reached a depth of more than a yard. As soon as the ice is firm enough to support a man's weight, the fishermen haul out their ice-fishing shanties. The old-fashioned ones of the 1890's were heavy wooden affairs that had to be dragged by men or a horse out onto the ice above the fishing grounds. Nowadays, after decades of experience, the shanties have become standardized. They are framed of light wood, set on sled runners, covered with canvas and painted. They are just big enough for a man to sit in comfortably—four feet square, with a door and a small window or two, and a hole in the floor.

Throughout January, February and March, when the lake vessels are huddled in protected harbors frozen tight in the ice, and all shipping is dormant waiting for the spring thaws, you may see the fishermen setting out from port towns of the United States and Canada, and from the Erie islands, with these shanties. Women and children often join them in the daily adventure. If, as often happens, the water near the shore is not frozen, or the ice is mushy, they load the shanties on fishing boats—one, two or three to a boat—and row out to the firm ice sheet. They drag or push the shanties to the fishing bank, which may be two or three miles out on the lake, and anchor them firmly with lines to the ice. If the fishing is good, the shanty may stay in place for several days at a time. As the season nears its close, however, the shanties move in toward the shore. In a good fishing year a village of 250 shanties may spring up in this manner on the ice sheet.

The fisherman, with sharp-cleated ice creepers strapped to his boots, goes forth to his day's fishing pushing his sled with a box full of equipment: an ax to chop a hole through the ice, a compass to give him direction if a snowstorm strikes or fog settles thick over the lake, a small wood or charcoal stove with fuel for the shanty fire, his fishing tackle and minnow bait, his lunch, and coffee and tobacco for the day's comfort.

The best years are those when winter descends quickly and freezes firm ice over the shoals, but leaves open a strip of water along the mainland or the islands. Then the fish gather under the protective ice cover where they can be hooked through the shanty floor, and the catch can be taken to a mainland market by boat. Around Sandusky and the Bass Islands from 40,000 to 100,000 pounds of fish are caught and marketed in this way during the winter season. In recent years Milton Hersberger has been flying quantities of this catch from the Bass Islands to the mainland at a cent a pound and has broken the isolation that once settled over the region during the winter months. Herring used to be the main catch—fine specimens weighing, it is reported, up to nine or ten pounds—and in those days the clusters of shanties were called Herring Village. A man could catch enough before breakfast for his family and have a few to give to his neighbors. But the catch at present is largely pickerel, sauger and perch. "A day's catch may be worth fifty cents or several dollars. . . . A record day's catch in the winter of 1935-1936 netted the fisherman $31.00. Individual ice-fishermen make as much as $600.00 in a season."[3]

This ice fishing, though largely commercial, is also a sporting affair. Hundreds of sportsmen who love fishing go to the lake

---

[3] Hudgins, *op. cit.*, p. 32.

during the winter. They shove off from the mainland towns, or they fly with Hersberger over to the Bass Islands and rent a shanty from the liveries. It is a different sport from summer fishing in a boat or launch, but a man who enjoys sitting on a hard board under a blazing sun for hours on end to take a few bass or, more likely, a carp and a sheepshead, does not mind the hardship of being cooped up in a shanty on the cold ice of Lake Erie. And a fat pickerel on the end of a line through a hole in the ice notably reduces the chill.

Sportsmen fish the entire Lake Erie shore. Almost every port town and village has a boat livery with guides and equipment for rent to visiting fishermen. The favored region centers around the American and Canadian islands. A generation or two ago swank fishing clubs maintained wharves and quarters on the islands for their private seasonal use. The Middle Bass Club, the Pelee Island Fishing Club and others were made famous by the celebrities who came here for the summer sport. Presidents Cleveland, Arthur, Hayes and Harrison; Robert T. Lincoln, Phil Sheridan, Cassius M. Clay, Mark Hanna, George Pullman, Marshall Field—these are but a few of the men in the public eye who retired to these quiet waters and exclusive clubs for fishing. Jay Cooke made of his private Gibraltar Island a kind of fishing club to which he invited his friends and, for a few weeks each season, ministers without their wives.

These clubs have died out in more recent years. The only one that now maintains its buildings in good order is the Quinnebog Club on Canada's Hen Island. The Castalia Trout Club is back on Cold Creek a few miles west of Sandusky. The creek from its source at Blue Hole is stocked with a spectacular quantity and variety of brown, rainbow, speckled brook and steelhead trout which lie temptingly with heads upstream in the cold, crystal-clear brook. But the stream is controlled by the private club, and nonmembers will get arrested if they poach on the trout.

There is plenty of fishing elsewhere for everybody who cares for it—and thousands do. This whole region is getting to be known as Vacationland by the common citizens and they are taking advantage of its playgrounds and its fishing facilities. They sit in boats on the lagoons, the rivers and the bays. They hold poles over the bridges and breakwaters and from stones in quiet nooks. They troll the reefs

DETROIT WATER FRONT IN 1794

AS IT LOOKS TODAY

DOWNTOWN CLEVELAND AND BRIDGES OVER THE CUYAHOGA

The Main Avenue development is in the foreground.

from launches hired at the boat liveries. They rent cabins on the islands and along the mainland shore for a few days or a few weeks and daily try their luck at taking a smallmouthed bass. And few fishermen return from their vacation adventure without a string of fish—even if it is only a sheepshead, a gar pike and a few white crappies.

As early as the first decade following the Civil War the population of the most desired firm-meat fish showed indications of declining. The states and the Federal government began to experiment with hatcheries to restock the streams and the lake, and to regulate the fishing seasons. The Ohio State Fish Hatchery was founded at Toledo on the Maumee in the 1870's to propagate pickerel and whitefish to increase the stock. A few years later the Toledo Hatchery was closed and work was concentrated at Sandusky in a little two-room building on the bay. In the season 1887-1888, 65,000,000 pickerel and 100,000,000 whitefish were hatched. They were put up in cans and given to anyone who would place them in an inland stream or lake. The hatchery was at first unable to produce bass or perch because during the spawning season the males retired into deep water where they could not be taken. From that day to this, billions of fish have been hatched and placed in Lake Erie and its tributary streams. The New York Conservation Department hatched nearly 600,000,000 trout, whitefish, ciscoes, pike perch and smallmouthed bass in Lake Erie in the single decade between 1918 and 1927. This activity has been in response to the pressure of both the commercial fisheries and the organized sportsmen.

Yet this earnest and expensive program of hatching and restocking has failed to maintain these desirable species in Lake Erie. The scientists urged a more fundamental approach to the problem. As a result, intensive basic studies have been carried out during the last two decades on Lake Erie by the Ohio State University's Franz Theodore Stone Laboratory on Put-in-Bay, by the New York State Conservation Department, by the Ontario Fisheries Research Laboratory and other agencies. Chemists, hydrobiologists and limnologists have co-operated to make the study complete in all its complex associations. They have developed special equipment for sampling the water and the lake floor. The Franz Theodore Stone Laboratory developed a special research fish shanty with which Dr. Milton B.

Troutman has been able to make the first year-round studies. The labors of these scientists and their findings are as exciting as a ten-pound bass on the end of a line off Rattlesnake Island. And they give a direct challenge to the citizens who have made the Lake Erie shore one of the marvels of the industrial world.

We have already noted the short, northward-flowing rivers which empty into Lake Erie. In this western region they fan out sluggishly into the wide estuaries of Maumee Bay, the Portage River mouth, Sandusky Bay and the lagoons at Vermilion. Until a few decades ago these streams ran relatively clear and vast beds of aquatic vegetation grew abundantly in the bays. They provided feeding and nesting grounds for wild ducks and other migratory birds; they furnished nature's perfect habitat for the spawning of the delicate fish; and they nurtured insects, worms and snails upon which the young fish could feed and thrive. The lake bottom around the islands was hard and clean and favorable for the spawning of herring and whitefish. If this happy condition had not been disturbed, the chances are that the depletion of the fish would not now greatly concern us. They would have continued to reproduce in quantity.

But the condition was disturbed on a gigantic scale. The hospitable environment was destroyed—washed out, silted over and made into a biological desert by erosion, wave action and pollution. T. H. Langlois and other research men who began with an interest in the dwindling fish supply on Lake Erie soon discovered that the causes lay back along these short streams that flow into the flat-rimmed edge of the lake bowl. This region south of Toledo, and southwest of Sandusky and Port Clinton, is flat. In pioneering days it was covered with swamp forest. One large section of it was known as the Black Swamp.

The region was first ditched and drained by the Irish in the 1850's, and the work was continued by the Germans, who populate the area, between 1860 and 1880. It now presents a scene not unlike that in the Low Countries, with ditches and furrows cutting across it, and miles of drain tile lying under it. The German farmers, who raise corn, oats, wheat, soybeans and sugar beets, leave the soil without cover during the rainy season. Their cattle graze on the ditch slopes and their hogs wallow on the creek banks, churning them into muck which the rains carry down into the streams. Untold and irreplaceable wealth in the form of some of the world's best topsoil goes down the Sandusky, Portage, Maumee and Raisin Rivers in brown streams of silt over the bays at their mouths and spread out into Lake Erie. The Franz Theodore Stone Laboratory has made regular analyses of the nitrate content of Lake Erie; they show that nitrate is carried off the farms where it could grow rich crops of soybeans, and is spread out over the floor of Lake Erie where the whitefish should spawn. The aquatic vegetation perishes and the good fish flee this barren environment. The muddy water spreads out from the estuaries to Kelleys and the Bass Islands. Other experiments at the laboratory have shown that the turbidity of the lake water off South Bass varies directly with the amount of water coming in from these south-shore streams. And the mud flows in greatest quantity during the spring months—the very season that is so critical in the life of Lake Erie fish.

The process becomes a vicious circle. This aquatic vegetation was a partial defense against wave action from the lake and retarded erosion of the lake shore. Its death and disappearance gives free play to the attack of the waves which, as we have seen, cuts off more and more acres of the shore line and, at the same time, stirs up the muddy soil from the lake floor. This heavily turbid state of the waters shuts out the sunlight, and the small floating organisms—plankton—upon which the good fish feed, die in the roily waters.[4]

This pitiful process has an immediate effect on the commercial fishing and the sportsman's pleasure in Lake Erie. In a balanced aquatic life plankton should be at its peak crop during the spring when the fish eggs hatch and the young are feeding. But that happy state of balance has been destroyed. Unfortunately the very species that cannot live under these conditions are the ones most sought after by the commercial fisheries. The once thriving herring cannot tolerate the turbid water; they have almost disappeared as a commercial catch. The yellow pickerel thrives or perishes according to the weather. Their habit is to run to spawning areas up the rivers when the ice goes out in the spring. If the rainfall is light and the waters remain relatively clear, the pickerel will reproduce in quantity. This happened in 1926 and in 1941, and the fishermen were

---

[4] T. H. Langlois, "The Work of Water in Producing Fish," *The Ohio Conservation Bulletin* (April 1943).

happy to find their nets filled with these first-choice fish. But usually the spring rainfall is heavy, the snow melts and runs off in swollen muddy torrents, and few pickerel are spawned. Then the catch drops off and the cry of overfishing is raised against the commercial fleets.

The researches at the laboratory have also shown, however, that the total fish population is not seriously affected by these changes. If the fish which men prefer to eat die or fail to spawn because these same men have wrecked the spawning grounds, others, which they do not want, quickly take their place. The rough, soft-flesh fish like the carp, sauger and sheepshead, can thrive in turbid water. And they do. They have increased at a great rate and they fill the nets of the commercial fishermen. And there are many disappointed sportsmen who feel a tug on their line, but draw up a silly-looking sheepshead instead of a fine black bass.

The disastrous slump in the whitefish and herring industry in the last two decades was not limited to the archipelago. Both the New York and the Ontario regions were affected. Henry O'Malley, United States Fisheries Commissioner, called a conference on the subject at Cleveland. The Federal Bureau provided the government steamer *Shearwater* for the use of the New York State Conservation Department in 1927-1928 to survey northeastern Lake Erie over the seventy-mile stretch between Buffalo and the Pennsylvania state line. A representative from the province of Ontario joined the survey staff.

The survey, made by biologists and chemists, was designed first to discover "the normal physical, chemical, and biological condition in the lake and the natural requirements for successful production of fishes"; and secondly to find out to what extent these conditions have been altered by man, thus rendering the lake floor unfit for spawning. The findings were just what we would now expect them to be.

The lake water is rather turbid, its transparency low. The lake as a whole is "remarkably free from pollution." Much of the lake shore is rocky cliff, or beach that is exposed to the action of the waves. The fish naturally seek the sheltered bays, the lagoons and the weed beds at the mouth of the streams emptying into Lake Erie. Along the shore, however, at these favored points the concentration of industries has affected the water. The iron and steel mills on Rush Creek discharge their wastes into the lake, causing almost total destruction of plant and animal life. This condition is conspicuous as you look down on the lake from a plane flying along the shore line from Cleveland to Buffalo. The iron in the water is neutralized by the alkalinity of Lake Erie and, in solution, becomes reddish-brown in color. You may see these deep, reddish-brown areas near the shore, shading out in lighter hues until they merge imperceptibly with the clear blue-green lake water. The heavy growth of weed beds west of the government dock in the Dunkirk Harbor absorbs much of the pollution. Until the recent installation of the disposal plant, sewage from Dunkirk went into the lake east of the dock. The red wastes from the Lackawanna plant of the Bethlehem Steel Company at Buffalo Harbor pollute the American shore almost to Niagara Falls. And out of Buffalo Creek flows "the industrial effluents and the raw sewage of a great part of Buffalo."[5]

In view of these and other discoveries since this particular survey was made, the disappearance of herring and whitefish from northeastern Lake Erie is not mystifying, and it was not caused by the gill nets of the fishermen who curse roundly when the filthy sludge deposits get into their nets and cause them great annoyance.

The remedy, say the research men, is not so much in government regulation of the size of the mesh in the nets, or a limit on the catch of the sportsmen, or even in the expensive fish-hatchery program, but at the industrial plants, the city sewers and in the barn lots, hog wallows, ditches, farming methods and erosion control on a thousand farms around the Lake Erie bowl. Re-establish the environment which alone can produce the good fish, and these species will be their own hatcheries, for they reproduce at astronomical rates when conditions are favorable. And you will have firm, sweet pickerel, herring and whitefish on your table instead of flabby, game-flavored carp and sheepshead.

---

[5] *A Biological Survey of the Erie-Niagara System. Supplemental to Eighteenth Annual Report, 1928* (Albany, 1929), p. 23.

Part III

Chapter 23

Wedding of Coal and Iron

THE Lake Erie cities, with all their manifold activities, were not entirely sure of themselves or their direction until the latter half of the nineteenth century. They were drifting along with the national currents, opportunistically, as it were, not yet imposing their individual genius upon the pattern of American life and industry. Detroit in 1860 was making steam engines, wagons and buggies, and smelting copper. But there was nothing distinctive about that. Other cities on the lakes and in the interior were supported by the same industries. Buffalo was, of course, a grain port, but by no means exclusively; several hundred industries were flourishing there. Cleveland was showing an interest in iron, feeling its way into the new era, and casting about for direction. It was uncertain whether it would be dominantly an oil capital, a maker of engines and machinery, a garment center, or whether there might be a bright future in iron, steel and tools.

The uncertainty extended to transportation. The railroad boom of the 1850's and the panic of 1857 frightened many businessmen, especially those interested in lake shipping. It looked for a time to the fainthearted as though the ships were doomed, if not to extinction then at least to a minor role. And if the railroads supplanted the shipways, Buffalo and Cleveland, and perhaps Detroit also, would lose the advantages which their strategic position on the lake had given them. The Civil War allayed those doubts. With communication lines to the south cut or threatened at the critical moment when the nation needed the fullest possible production and movement of war goods, the lake cities lent their efforts, and traffic flowed in still greater volume over the accessible and unmolested lakes. Railroads could offer speed, but only at relatively heavy costs; and they could not carry the full burden. Ships still afforded efficient transportation in the cheapest form ever devised by man. As the crisis passed and the nation recovered, the ship-roads over Lake Erie took their unquestioned place of pre-eminence, even in the modern age of rails, for cheap carriage of heavy goods.

But what goods? And to which of the Lake Erie ports?

The miracle of the geology and geography of the Great Lakes was soon to provide the definitive answer to that question. The demands of the war and the Reconstruction and the westward movement of the population were emphatically for iron and steel. The urgent requirements quickly outran the resources and capacities of the old charcoal furnaces and the bog-iron deposits in Pennsylvania and southeastern Ohio. Attention shifted northward, first to Michigan's Upper Peninsula and then to the ranges back of Duluth. Detroit's Douglass Houghton, surveying along Lake Superior in 1840, found copper at Keweenaw and evidence of iron near Marquette. Surveyor William A. Burt confirmed Houghton's report by locating a whole mountain of iron in 1844. New discoveries followed in rapid succession: at Vermilion in the 1860's, and right on down the fabulous Minnesota range during the ensuing years until the colossal Mesabi pits were found and opened in the 1890's. Here almost on the wild shores of Lake Superior were Vulcan's own treasure house and stock pile of the precious ore.

The ore was of no use until it was smelted and processed. The small, mid-century furnaces had used charcoal for smelting. That was a slow and laborious method, and the forests were disappearing. Quantity production required coal—mountains of coal. The coal veins lay in equally fabulous quantities in the hills of Pennsylvania, West Virginia, Kentucky and southeastern Ohio. These two primary ingredients for making iron and steel were separated by a thousand miles, but they were joined by the free waterway of the Great Lakes system. That is one of the stupendous facts in American history, for it has given this country its supreme industrial advantage over other nations. It is the key to the development of Lake Erie.

Men debated for a time whether they should smelt the ore at its source or send it down the lakes to established furnaces. Both schemes were tried. The Pioneer Iron Company, engineered by a Detroit man, went into production in the forest at Negaunee, Michigan, in

1858. Nearly a dozen other furnaces were built in the Upper Peninsula during the 1860's. They all failed because production costs were too high. As coal was substituted for charcoal, the advantages of shipping the raw ore down the lakes were intensified. The proportion of coal to ore required to make iron and steel in those days was about four to one. Furnaces already in extensive operation near the coal fields were in close proximity to manufacturers and markets. The sensible procedure was to bring the ore to the coal. They met inevitably on Lake Erie, and their wedding had issue in the age of steel.

The port cities again considered their future. All of them had their small foundries and ironworks. Now they projected larger ventures. Detroit went into the iron industry. Eber Brock Ward, Captain Sam's nephew, saw that his lucrative passenger-steamer trade to Chicago would be permanently captured by the Michigan Central Railroad. He turned to manufacturing. With a group of eight Detroit associates he formed the Eureka Iron and Steel Company in 1853, and built a blast furnace and rolling mill on a 2,200-acre field along the Detroit River at present Wyandotte. At the close of the Civil War he installed the new Bessemer converter which was among the earliest if not the first to manufacture Bessemer steel. With admirable foresight he invested in the Lake Superior iron mines. He clearly foresaw the revolutionary developments impending in the steel business in the 1870's and urged his associates to convert and modernize their Wyandotte plant regardless of the expense. They did not have Ward's creative vision. The future seemed too risky and they hesitated. They procrastinated too long. Ward died of apoplexy on a Detroit street in 1875, the Wyandotte plant fell behind the competition, became obsolescent, was finally shut down, then burned, and in the 1890's, as Cleveland forged ahead, its machinery was junked and the enterprise completely abandoned. Detroit did not become the steel city of the nation.

It found many other things to do, enough to keep its health and vigor if not yet to advance it to the forefront among the rising cities of the nation.[1] James McMillan and John S. Newberry, with other Detroit men, had organized the Michigan Car Company in 1864. Various other works of this kind were established at this railroad-

---

[1] In 1890 it was still fourteenth, and in 1900 only thirteenth.

terminal city on the river, including the Peninsular Car Company of Frank J. Hecker and Charles L. Freer. They were brought together late in the century as the American Car & Foundry Company. This giant industry attracted several thousand workers, and brought the wealth which built the handsome mansions on Woodward Avenue and made possible the great Freer art collection that later went to Washington, D. C. George M. Pullman, having invented the sleeping car, chose Detroit as a manufacturing center in 1871. William Davis constructed a refrigerator car in 1868, and within a few years the firm known as George H. Hammond and Company was shipping fresh western beef in refrigerator cars to the markets in the East. Hazen S. Pingree, who became a notable reform mayor of Detroit from 1890 to 1897, was making a fortune as a manufacturer of shoes. Dr. Samuel P. Duffield, Hervey C. Parke and George S. Davis from 1867 on were laying the foundation for Detroit's preeminence in pharmaceutical laboratories and the manufacturing of drugs. And Detroit was also active in woodworking, rolling cigars, processing tobacco, and wholesale distribution of hardware, clothing and groceries.

The city improved its water supply, installed gas, electricity, telephones and street railways; it bought Belle Isle in 1879 and commenced the improvements that have made the island into a world-famous recreation ground; young James Edmund Scripps founded (in 1873) the Detroit *News* and built it up to a position of power and influence alongside the *Advertiser and Tribune.* . . . Yes, there was plenty of activity to keep the city interesting, resilient and prosperous, as though it were getting ready for the day when Henry Ford would come.

At the other end of the lake Buffalo was studying its future. Its position as a grain-receiving port and milling center was secure, but it needed a broader base for its industrial welfare. It had formed an Association for the Encouragement of Manufactures in 1860. Perhaps the association was unnecessary, for the Civil War and the era that followed brought diverse industries to the strategically placed city. But doubts were raised again as the age of iron came to the lakes. Buffalo, like the other ports, had its quota of foundries and ironworkers. In 1860 the first blast furnaces were erected, to become in

1862 the Union Iron Works. The first open-hearth furnace in Buffalo did not begin operation until 1888. Despite the near-by coal fields, however, and the expanding network of railroads connecting them with Buffalo, the city did not become a leading steel center until after 1903, when the Lackawanna Steel Company chose it as the location for a huge plant.

It was, however, a pioneer in the coal business on the lakes. The first coal came into the city in 1842, when Guilford R. Wilson moved his business from Elmira to Buffalo.[2] He handled only 2,500 tons during his first two years in Buffalo. The first shipments up the lake were carried as ballast free of charge by the grain fleet sailing empty back to Chicago. But that neat arrangement did not last long. Coal was soon an important upbound cargo for a two-way pay load, and the business has steadily increased. It is now by volume the largest item exported from the Buffalo wharves—well over 1,000,000 tons each season.

Buffalo exploited its position on the lake and its proximity to Niagara Falls to attract the diverse industries which have made it great. It manufactured iron and steel ships, marine boilers and engines, locomotives, Wagner palace cars, and steel barbettes for the United States fleet of new battleships and cruisers that defeated the Spaniards at Santiago and Manila. It made iron for bridges, cast iron for pipes, all sorts of farm and milling machinery, scales, soap and starch, linseed and lubricating oils, fertilizers, wallpaper and several hundred other products.

No city on the continent was more sure of its future, or more youthful in shouting its accomplishments and potentialities than Buffalo. It quoted with glowing pride the prediction made in the 1880's by a special representative of the New York *Times* who came up to make a study of the city's prospects.

"As I look forward to Buffalo's future, I am not at all certain that Chicago will be the largest city on the lakes. I strongly incline to the belief that the Erie Canal will eventually draw to Buffalo commerce of a region which living men will see inhabited by 25,000,000, the larger proportion of whom will be producers of bulky, primary products, and all of whom will be large consumers of coal and iron.

---

[2] This was three years before Daniel P. Rhodes and other Cleveland men opened the Brierhill Mine near Youngstown and commenced hauling coal by canal up to the lake.

If Buffalo secures this trade, and she can, then Buffalo and not Chicago will be the second American city."

The *Times* added, of course, that Buffalo "will inevitably become the greatest milling city on earth."

A few years later Buffalo, which had learned well how to deal in superlatives, announced itself as "one of the most rapidly growing cities in the universe." Its claims to supremacy could not be ignored, declared its *Manual of the Common Council* for 1897: "they shouldered their way to the front, in comparison with the claims of other cities to attention, like Titans striding through an army of pigmies, for they showed among other things that the lake tonnage of this city crowds closely that of Liverpool, and prove by actual figures that Buffalo is the fourth greatest port of entry and clearance on the globe." From a place far in the rear Buffalo had "swept to the front, in the procession of cities, with giant strides," and through its enterprise had been achieved "the greatest miracle of science—the subjection of the power of the Falls of Niagara to the uses of mankind."

Its previous *Manual* had told the story of the miracle of its achievements and its expectations for the future. And how had Buffalo's rivals responded to the story of "noble work accomplished"? Alas, says the *Manual,* "at the heels of the mastiff of progress snarl ever the yelping kennels of disappointed ambition and baffled hope. . . . From Rochester and Cleveland newspapers came vituperation, and from Detroit silence." But the cities "cast in more noble molds"— Philadelphia, New York, Baltimore, St. Louis and San Francisco— assured of their own greatness, paid generous tribute and "hailed the growth of the greatest inland lake city in the United States, next to Chicago, with acclamation and praise." The envious attitude of its Lake Erie neighbors was regrettable, but the *Manual* concluded that "Buffalo, having secured the approval of the great, can well afford to smilingly pursue the tenor of its way to that position of proud pre-eminence . . . which shall stamp it as the greatest inland city in the world."[3]

---

[3] The newspapers of the period are filled with items of rivalry; the Cleveland papers exulted when Buffalo's commerce in 1870 fell 166,954 tons behind the 4,258,168 of the previous year, while Cleveland gained 635,918 tons over its previous 2,803,691 tons: "the natural result of an advantageous position; sustained by the enterprise and activity of a community whose faith in the future of the Forest City has become a fixed and steadfast principle."

Buffalo moved forward in this confident spirit across the turn of the century and in 1901 celebrated its progress and dramatized its future by staging the magnificent Pan-American Exposition. The title was significant, for Buffalo was inviting the attention of the whole Western Hemisphere to this Buffalo-Niagara region. The assassination of President McKinley on September 6 in the Temple of Music on the Exposition Grounds, and Theodore Roosevelt's breathless overland dash to Buffalo to take the oath of office, intensified the international interest in the city with a note of high tragedy.

Young Toledo did not enter this late-nineteenth-century competition. The city on the Maumee went forward rather quietly, making itself a transshipping port, especially for coal. The railroad tracks extended mile by mile along the almost unlimited space beside the river, and the trains from the south pulled longer and longer strings of cars loaded with coal across Ohio, over the divide and down to the water front to meet the lake ships. By 1890 Toledo had eighteen miles of docks and was shipping 2,500,000 tons of coal each year. And Edward Libbey, Michael Owens and Edward Ford were making Toledo the glass center of America with their bottles, plate glass, drinking glasses and beautiful cut-glass pieces for the tables and sideboards of the nation's middle-class homes.

The Ontario towns did not challenge any of this growth on the south shore of Lake Erie. With their lumber cut off and marketed, and with the Great Western Railroad serving the interior countryside, they quietly went to sleep.

But Cleveland was no less concerned than Detroit and Buffalo over its prospects in the division of labor among the lake cities. In 1860 it was termed "a commercial city," receiving products from the Western Reserve and shipping them to the East. Its chief industrial interests in the order of importance were represented by twenty-one flour mills, twenty-seven clothing factories, seventeen shops for making machinery and engines, and nineteen boot and shoe factories. Its business leaders were talking in those years about the necessity of Cleveland becoming a "manufacturing city." Cleveland, they said, by the very nature of its position on the lake shore could not hope to compete with Detroit, Buffalo and Chicago, nor even with Toledo, as a distributing port. But it could have a great future as a manufacturing center. It made the transition during the Civil War, and by 1885 its interests, in the order of importance, were machinery, railroad equipment, iron and steel products and stoves, followed by clothing and boots and shoes, with crude-oil refining coming rapidly to the fore under John D. Rockefeller.

Behind that significant transition was the group of Cleveland men who thought they saw a future in iron and steel. The Cuyahoga Steam Furnace Company had started operation at Cleveland in 1835, and had built the first locomotive west of the Alleghenies in 1842. J. N. Ford and W. A. Otis had construced a forge on Whiskey Island in 1852. They added a rolling mill in 1859, and laid the foundation for the big Otis & Company mill which helped supply Grant's armies during the Civil War. Henry Chisholm, a Scotch orphan boy who worked himself up to master carpenter and had migrated to Montreal to practice his trade, came to Cleveland in 1850 to construct breakwaters for the railroads on the lake front. He liked the city so well that he settled there. He founded the Chisholm, Jones & Company rolling mill at Newburg in 1857. It became the Cleveland Rolling Mill, and by 1885 it was employing 5,000 men and producing 150,000 tons of finished products each year. Chisholm installed the Bessemer process to make steel rails. To avoid the hazards of a one-product plant, he branched out to make wire, screws and "agricultural and merchant shapes from steel." He was so successful that Clevelanders soon learned to refer to him as "the greatest of all the men who have had an honorable share in the development of these industries."[4] And these industries were giving Cleveland such rapid growth that by 1870 it had passed Detroit in the race for population: Detroit seventeenth in the country, Cleveland sixteenth.

The Cleveland men had a vision and an interest that went beyond that of their rival industrialists in the other lake cities. They saw that the ore for the steel age would come from Lake Superior, that it would have to be transported down the lakes and that it would meet the coal from the coal fields somewhere along Lake Erie. Was there any better investment than that offered by the basic raw materials for making steel? Or any center for controlling the shipping more favorable than Cleveland and vicinity? Here, evidently, lay Cleveland's unique opportunity. Cleveland moved in to take full advantage of it.

---

[4] *Magazine of Western History,* II (1885), 343.

Chapter 24

Cleveland Iron Men

TWELVE major carrying fleets operate on the Great Lakes. They have 384 freighters moving back and forth with almost clock-like regularity between the source harbors on Lake Superior and the manufacturing and outlet ports on Lake Erie. These vessels are actually floating freight trains, except that their voyages have more color and romance than the run of a train between Conneaut and Pittsburgh or between Bluefield, West Virginia, and Toledo. The main body of the ore fleet puts out from Duluth-Superior. Off the Apostle Islands it is joined by the ships from Two Harbors and from Ashland. The carriers from Marquette enter the growing procession above Whitefish Point. Together they march through the Sault and on down the St. Marys River into Lake Huron. A few of them turn west through the Straits of Mackinac and head for Chicago, Indiana Harbor and Gary at the head of Lake Michigan. But the main body sails down Lake Huron, splits up and scatters to the ten big ore-receiving docks from Detroit to Buffalo. In 1944 these vessels carried over 90,000,000 tons of ore. The load of each ship was equivalent to about 390 freight cars.

The movement of the coal fleet is the chart of the ore freighters in reverse, with Toledo, Conneaut and Buffalo playing the role of Duluth-Superior and Two Harbors. This form of transportation is so much cheaper than rail transport that a Toledo coal merchant, wishing to ship coal to Detroit, can save money by having it dumped from the cars into a lake carrier, sailed up to Detroit and unloaded there on the wharves. The economy of Lake Erie revolves around this relatively simple principle. Without it the United States would still be great, but its industry, dependent as it is upon steel, would not be so stupendous, and its character would be different.[1]

---

[1] The war production could not have been achieved without this gigantic, delicately balanced transportation system of the Great Lakes. If Hitler and Hirohito had bombed the locks at the Sault out of existence in April 1942, they would have paralyzed American industry and might easily have won their war for world conquest. Nearly 300,-000,000 tons of ore came through those locks in the three shipping seasons of 1942-1943-1944—to be turned into the ships and armor that beat the enemy back.

Most of the lake fleets are owned or controlled by companies whose officers are concentrated chiefly in the Union Commerce Building, the Union Trust Building, the Hanna Building and the Rockefeller Building in Cleveland. A Pittsburgh Steamship ore boat operating between Gary and Two Harbors may not voyage nearer to Cleveland than Mackinaw City, but as it steams through the Straits it will blow its identification signal to the telegraph station on shore to be reported to headquarters in Cleveland. It will signal again at the Sault to be reported again to Cleveland. The master of the vessel may not know his destination until he is nearing the Minnesota shore of Lake Superior; he will get final orders from Cleveland. And the mines will have received from Cleveland the order for the exact quantity and mixture of ore which the vessel is to load. For Cleveland is, and has been for nearly a century, the heart, or the controlling brain center, of both the ore fields and the shipping companies.

From the day when ore was discovered on the Lake Superior ranges, Cleveland men have been in the forefront in mining and shipping. It was John Hay of Cleveland who first hurried out to Keweenaw in 1843 to get control of all but about fifteen percent of Lake Superior's black oxide copper. He raised $108,000 capital in Cleveland, and in ten years took out of the Copper Country for Clevelanders something like $4,000,000. It was a Cleveland syndicate which bought up the Jackson mine, Cleveland Mountain and other ore deposits around Marquette shortly after Surveyor Burt and later prospectors had uncovered the fabulous deposits. This Cleveland group was headed by one of the great names on Lake Erie, Samuel Livingston Mather of the New England family of Mather which was made famous in a less mercantile age by the Puritan divines, Increase and Cotton Mather.

Born in Middletown, Connecticut, in 1817 and graduated from Wesleyan University, Samuel L. Mather came to Cleveland in 1843 to look after some land interests for his father, who was an executive in the Connecticut Land Company. He was immediately attracted to the city and to the prospects for developing the Lake Superior ore deposits. He determined to risk his future in this business. He helped organize the Cleveland Iron Mining Company in 1853, with J. W. Gordon as president, and he served as vice-president. Mather became its president in 1869. This was the company which sent the

Columbia down to Cleveland in August 1855 with the first cargo of ore to be shipped from Lake Superior. Mather's group bought a half-interest in the barquentine-rigged *George Sherman* in 1867 and got into the shipping business for themselves. That was the beginning of the Cleveland-Cliffs' present fleet of twenty-three carriers operated from the Union Commerce Building, and of the great Mather dynasty in Cleveland which we shall examine later.

William J. Gordon, a benefactor of Cleveland, came to the city in 1839 at the age of twenty-one. He went into the wholesale grocery business during the first boom years of the canal era, and made enough money to buy heavily into the Cleveland Iron Mining Company. He used a part of his great wealth to purchase several tracts of land on the lake shore east of the city. He engaged landscape gardeners to develop them into a magnificent park. He willed 120 acres to the city of Cleveland to be open to the public as Gordon Park.[2]

Up from Pittsburgh in 1851 came Fayette Brown to be, in the words of a contemporary, "one of the leading iron men of Cleveland," and one who "had as much to do with making this city the great iron centre that it is as any man now living."[3] He was born to a pioneering family at Bloomfield in Trumbull County, Ohio, in 1823. At the age of eighteen he was clerking in his brother's wholesale-dry-goods store in Pittsburgh. He determined to give up this safe job to seek his fortune in Cleveland. He formed a banking partnership with George Mygatt (Mygatt & Brown). The city was already buzzing with the excitement of the ore discoveries around Lake Superior. Brown made a voyage to Marquette in 1857 to examine the prospects for himself. He was convinced of their value, but the Civil War broke into his plans, and he had to delay them while he served the Union as paymaster in the Army. When the war was over, Brown went back to the Marquette country as manager and general agent for Cleveland's Jackson Iron Mining Company. He was a friend and co-worker of a remarkable group of entrepreneurs composed of Colonel Pickands,

---

[2] The Cleveland industrialists have always taken pride in their benefactions to the city. As James F. Rhodes wrote back in 1885, "The endowments made [to] the different charitable institutions, the Wade Park, the Adelbert College, the Case Scientific School, the Hurlbut Art Gallery, testify that many of our rich men have felt that there is something nobler in life than mere gain of money, and that something besides great wealth is needed to make the influence of a city enduring." "The Coal and Iron Industry of Cleveland," *Magazine of Western History*, II (1885), 337.

[3] *Ibid.*, p. 350.

Jay C. Morse and Samuel P. Ely of Cleveland, and Peter White of Marquette. He personally strode across the snow-covered Upper Peninsula to locate and build the Munising Railroad and the town of Munising to expedite the movement of ore from the mines to the Cleveland docks. With this end of the business in operation, Fayette Brown returned to his offices in Cleveland and the development of a fleet of carriers to transport ore down the lakes.

Fayette Brown turned his business over to two almost equally remarkable sons, Harvey H. and Alexander. Alexander developed the Brown unloader, as we shall see later. Harvey, whose first activities were as agent for the iron companies, got interested in shipbuilding and lake transportation. He bought into Captain E. M. Peck's Northern Transportation Company, which operated a fleet of wooden ships, about the time when shipbuilders were seriously thinking of changing over from wood to iron. Harvey was one of the advanced thinkers who insisted on the experiment. The shipbuilders, however, were convinced that, while iron would serve for the sides of a ship, it would be hazardous as a bottom because of the scant clearance over sharp rocks in the shallow passages along the Great Lakes lanes. If a hole were jabbed in the iron vessel, it would certainly leak like a sieve and go down. So they built a vessel with iron sides and a wooden bottom. It was the first of its kind on the lakes. Appropriately it was christened the *Fayette Brown*. The pioneer for whom it was named died in 1910.

Another of the men who helped concentrate the ore business in Cleveland was Captain Alva Bradley, born in Connecticut in 1814. He migrated to the Western Reserve with his parents when he was only nine years old. He grew up on a farm within sight of the waters of Lake Erie between Lorain and Vermilion. As a boy he got a job stamping charcoal in wooden-soled shoes at a few cents a day. At the age of nineteen, educated only in the simple art of the three R's, he left the farm to ship on the lakes. He found a berth as cook's helper on a Vermilion schooner. He was a natural sailor with more than a sailor's ambition. He rose through the ship to become master and then owner of the vessel. He had many of the shrewd, homespun qualities of Henry Ford, and in his later years looked like that great Detroit magnate. He was a warm friend of Samuel Edison and Nancy Elliot, father and mother of the inventor. When Samuel left Vienna,

Ontario, to set up a mill for making shingles at the once-thriving shipyard and shipping town of Milan, Ohio, Captain Alva carried letters and messages across Lake Erie for the young couple. Nancy shipped on his schooner when she came to Milan to join her husband in 1839. And when their son was born in 1847 in the little brick house, still standing on a side street above the river in Milan, he was named Thomas Alva Edison for the kindly Captain Bradley. The captain took a lifelong interest in young Thomas, and got him his job at Port Huron where he practised telegraphy and began to tinker with electricity.

Captain Bradley started building ships at Vermilion in 1841. His grandson, Alva Bradley, has the contract for his first ship, the 104-ton *South America,* to cost about $3,500. In 1844 the captain added the 135-ton *Birmingham,* which he sailed for three years over Lake Erie and up to Lime Kiln Crossing with wheat and lumber. Year by year he added new ships to his fleet. The old ledger in which he entered their names and receipts for the year, beginning with the *London* in 1858, is also preserved by his grandsons. He had married Ellen M. Burgess, daughter of Judge Burgess of Milan, in 1851 and settled near his shipyard in Vermilion. But the pull of Cleveland was too strong. The captain moved his office to that dominant city in the Reserve in 1859, and bought a small farm out in the country just beyond present 59th Street and Euclid. John D. Rockefeller's farm at 49th Street adjoined it. Harkness' place was near by, and these men, with Andrews, Sheridan and other cronies, gathered often around a base-burner in a kind of club at the southwest corner of Wilson and Euclid to trade yarns and talk business. Rockefeller was urging his friends to go into oil. Harkness and others joined him, but Captain Bradley bought Cleveland real estate and went on building up his lake fleet.

In 1868 he moved his shipyards to Cleveland. More and bigger ships were entered by name in the ledger, larger returns were listed opposite them. During 1873 Bradley added six new ones, including the *Alva Bradley* which brought him $17,860 during its first season of operation. By that time he could see that the age of schooners was ending and the era of steam and steel had come. He ordered two steamers for the season of 1874 and began the transition in his own fleet. As the ore rolled out of the mines on the Upper Peninsula in ever-rising volume, Bradley added ships to receive it and sail it down to the Lake Erie ports. He was the most powerful man on the lakes. His fleet was beyond all competition. He fixed the annual rates for the shipments. If he wanted to raise them, he did so. He once added a dollar to the rate on Rockefeller, and Rockefeller had to pay it. Other owners always came to Bradley with the question: "What will the rates be this season?" And as the captain set them, so they were. The shipping men made him president of the Cleveland Vessel Owners' Association, a forerunner of the powerful and efficient Lake Carriers' Association with headquarters in Cleveland.

By modern standards Captain Alva conducted his business in a singularly personal manner. He sat down near the lake front one day with Jim Wallace of the Globe Company to make a contract for building a new vessel for the Bradley fleet. When they had finished talking it over, Bradley wrote a few words on the back of an envelope. That was the contract, and all the captain had to say about it was, "If a contract is too long, any lawyer can break it."

When Captain Alva died in 1885 he left his vast fleet and his estate to be carried on by his son, Morris A. Bradley. The son had all the shrewdness and some of the sentiment of his father. He personally conducted the business in all of its details. The telephone at his bedside, East 131, rang several times each night, waking him from his sleep to give directions about vessels and passengers. One night the call was from Port Huron. The *John Martin* had been cut in two, and her captain drowned. He was a great friend of M. A. Bradley's. Bradley hung up the receiver and said, "It's not worth it!" He lost interest in the fleet, began to liquidate it and transferred his capital to Cleveland real estate, which his son Alva continues to manage from a spacious and pleasantly old-fashioned office in downtown Cleveland.

R. K. Winslow, a bearded, driving man who looked like General Grant, chose Cleveland as his headquarters in 1859, and built a fleet for the iron ore and grain trade which for a time threatened to rival that of Captain Bradley. George Ashley Tomlinson came to the lakes in the 1880's to enter the ore and shipping business. This interesting man of adventure had been a cowboy in Wyoming, a rider for Buffalo Bill's circus, a writer for the New York *Sun* and an editor in Detroit. He married the daughter of Captain James Davidson, the big shipbuilder at Saginaw in the days of the wooden schooners. He went out to Duluth as the Mesabi Range was opening up to secure cargoes for the Lower Lakes. His fame spread to the Lake Erie ports because he got the ore for the carriers. He purchased a vessel of his own and shipped ore down to Cleveland on contract. The venture paid. He established headquarters in Cleveland. He added to his fleet, modernizing year by year, until he had seventeen freighters carrying cargo by charter bidding. It became the largest, as it was the last, of the "one-man outfits."

Andrew Carnegie was strangely blind to the firm grip which these Cleveland men were getting on the ore ranges and the lake fleets. He was reluctant to invest in the ore mines or to acquire vessels to transport ore to his enormous mills. He thought it was better to buy on the open market and to contract with the lake men for the shipping. John D. Rockefeller thought otherwise. He had lent money for developing the Mesabi Range. During the panic of 1893 he called his loans, and inherited, as it were, an interest in the ore and shipping business. He formed a company and built a fleet. He cleared $79,000,000 in this business before he sold out. He could not understand, he said, why "the steelmakers had not seen the necessity of controlling their own ore supplies." Rockefeller's success, and the determined activity of Carnegie's partner, Henry Clay Frick, induced the magnate at the last possible moment to buy into Mesabi ore and to acquire the Pittsburgh, Shenango & Lake Erie railroad from the lake to his Pittsburgh plants. Then he filled in the gap between the mines and the receiving docks by buying six vessels for the Oliver Mining Company. That small fleet became the giant Pittsburgh Steamship Company of Cleveland, largest on the lakes, operating seventy[4] of the biggest freighters in 1945.

Marcus A. Hanna, millionaire friend of James A. Garfield and William McKinley, and United States Senator from Ohio, had come to Cleveland from his birthplace in Lisbon, Ohio, in 1852 to enter the wholesale grocery business. He, too, saw the bright prospect of a fortune in iron. He formed a company with other Cleveland men for dealing in coal and iron. His driving energy and business ability soon brought him into full control of the business which in 1885

---

[4] The recent commissioning of several new freighters retired some of the older, smaller ships. Though the number of ships is fewer, the tonnage has been increased.

became M. A. Hanna & Company. He acquired extensive interests in the Lake Superior ore mines and in the southern coal fields, in furnaces and steel mills, in street railroads and banks. Hanna wanted his own fleet of ships to carry his own ore to his own mills. He ordered them built, painted them black, and as the Black Line the steamers *Geneva* and *Vienna* and the schooners *Genoa* and *Verona* went into operation in record shipbuilding time. From that beginning rose the great Hanna line of fourteen carriers which now operates on the lakes, and serves the interests of the National Steel Corporation into which the M. A. Hanna Company was merged in 1929.

The oportunities for making fortunes in Cleveland seemed to be unlimited. It was, indeed, the Horatio Alger period in American industry when the brave and bold with do and dare were bound to rise. Penniless boys rose in a few years to be millionaires. Take the story of Henry Coulby, for example. He was a poor English boy. His widowed mother had lost her home, her old family furniture had been sold and dispersed, and she was living in poverty. Henry had heard of the Great Lakes and of Cleveland; he sailed to America to seek his fortune. He landed in Baltimore in the early 1880's, penniless. He worked on an oyster boat on Chesapeake Bay to earn enough money to get to New York. There he inquired about Cleveland and how one got to that city on Lake Erie. He was amazed to learn how far away the city was. He had no money for passage, so he walked the entire 600 miles to "the city of the future." There he fell in with the firm of Pickands, Mather & Company just as it was rising to its high position in the nation's steel industry. Within a few years he was a partner in the company and president of the Pittsburgh Steamship Company (1904-1924). And this man, who seemed so cold and hard to his business associates in Cleveland, who had in his early days borrowed money from Captain Alva Bradley to visit his mother, had the satisfaction of returning quietly to England, buying back his mother's house and collecting the old bureau, the settee, the vases and all the things she loved. Then he called for her at her squalid room, took her to church, walked with her down past the house and asked her to go in with him to see the room where he was born. And when they had entered, Henry Coulby said simply, "Mother, here's your house." The great cold-blooded business magnate, whose name is carried back and forth over the lakes on the biggest of the ships in Pickands, Mather & Company's Interlake Steamship fleet, wept in his old age as he told the story.[5]

The list of Cleveland iron men is extensive, but these are some of the more prominent ones, and they show the pattern of development which has concentrated the steel business so heavily in this city. The companies have maintained their control through almost endless changes, reorganizations and interlockings of directorates. It would be profitless to recite them or to attempt to untangle them. Take the great Mather interests as a single example. Samuel Livingston Mather, who died in 1890, was succeeded as head of the Cleveland Iron Mining Company by his distinguished son, William Gwinn Mather, who was born at Cleveland just two years after the *Columbia* docked in the Cuyahoga. This son had gone into his father's business immediately after graduating from Trinity College, Connecticut, in 1877. He became president of the company in 1890 and continued in that office until 1933. He then became chairman of the board of directors. He consolidated the Cleveland Iron Mining Company with Samuel Tilden's Iron-Cliffs Company. This company, however, is a subsidiary of the Cliffs Corporation formed in 1929 by William G. Mather, E. B. Green and Cyrus Eaton as a holding company with substantial interests in six important iron and steel companies.

William G. Mather's half brother Samuel, in the meantime, was having a parallel career. These sons of Samuel Livingston were no gentlemen of leisure or young men about town in Cleveland. They went to work in the tradition of their father and rose through merit and industry. Samuel had gone out to the Cleveland Mountain to work for his father. He was severely injured at Ishpeming, and was forced into a few years of inactivity. He then plunged into the business with energy and imagination. He made the acquaintance of Jay C. Morse of Painesville, who had gone to the Upper Peninsula for the Cleveland Iron Mining Company, and of Colonel James Pickands of Akron and Cleveland, who had served in the Civil War and then migrated to Marquette to become one of its most prosperous wholesale hardware and coal merchants. Samuel Mather approached

---

[5] I am indebted to Mr. Alva Bradley for this episode.

them with a proposal that they form a partnership to exploit the iron and coal business. They accepted. The powerful firm of Pickands, Mather & Company, with offices in Cleveland, was formed in 1883.

Samuel Mather's son, Samuel Livingston of Cleveland, began his career at Ishpeming in the iron-ore department of the Cleveland-Cliffs Iron Company in 1905, then returned to the home office in Cleveland, first as assistant secretary, then secretary and, since 1926, as vice-president. But he is also a vice-president of Cliffs Corporation. Mesaba-Cliffs Mining Company and Munising Paper Company. He is a director of Arctic Iron Company, Athens Iron Mining Company, Bessemer Limestone & Cement Company, Bunker Hill Mining Company, Cleveland-Cliffs Steamship Company, Cleveland City Forge Company, Great Lakes Towing Company, Lake Superior and Ishpeming Railway Company, Lakeside & Marblehead Railway Company, Lamson & Sessions Company, Michigan Mineral Land Company, Monarch Fire Insurance Company, Munising Wood Products Company, Negaunee Mine Company, Pettibone Mulliken Corporation, Presque Isle Transportation Company, Thompson Products, Inc., and Youngstown Sheet and Tube Company.

The Cleveland-Cliffs subsidiary of Cliffs Corporation, in addition to its own ore mines and docks and connecting railroads, has twenty-three freighters on the lakes to carry raw material for the steel mills on the Cuyahoga and Mahoning Rivers in which it holds heavy investments. It also owns the Cliffs Power & Light Company in the Upper Peninsula, and at least a third of a million acres of timber. It supplies wood to its own Munising Wood Products Company, which makes all kinds of wooden articles, and for the Cliffs-Dow Chemical Company of which it is part owner. It operates its own coal mines, steamers and docks at Port Huron, Escanaba and Green Bay. Its profits run about $3,000,000 a year.

That is only a part of the story, however. Oglebay, Norton & Company was also acquired as a subsidiary of Cliffs Corporation in 1930. Oglebay, Norton exchanged its control to Cliffs in return for $1,000,000 worth of Cliffs stock. Oglebay, Norton shar holders also became executives of Cliffs.[6] The president of Oglebay, Norton is Crispin Oglebay, Yale 1900, bachelor, sportsman and race-horse man,

---

[6] *Fortune Magazine* (July 1940) discusses these intricate and self-contained Cleveland organizations.

with his house and stables at beautiful Gates Mills outside of Cleveland. This Wheeling-born mining and shipping magnate came to Cleveland in 1903 as secretary of the Hoffman Hinge & Foundry Company. He is a director, president or vice-president of a score of important companies doing upward of $15,000,000 worth of business each year on or around the Great Lakes. Most of them have offices in the Hanna Building. They include Ferro Machine & Foundry Company of Cleveland; the Bristol, the Fortune Lake, the Castile, the Montreal, the St. James, and the Cleveland-Cliffs mining companies; the Columbia Transportation Company, which has a fleet of seventeen freighters on the lakes to carry ore and coal to and from Lake Erie; the Atwater, the Saginaw, and the Toledo, Lorain & Fairport Dock companies; the Pringle Barge Line and the Kelley Island Lime and Transport Company; and the Brule Smokeless Coal Company.

Through these tightly knit and interlocking organizations, big, powerful, paternal and enormously efficient, the Cleveland iron men took control and developed a large share of the nation's iron and steel industries. They have molded the character of Cleveland as individually as the grain merchants and millers have molded Buffalo, or the automobile manufacturers have formed the pattern of modern Detroit. The channels and shipways of the Great Lakes and the ports on Lake Erie are their life line, and they have united to improve them and to increase the tonnage capacity of the fleets which, in 1944, reached an all-time high for the seven-and-a-half-months' season of navigation: 184,155,384 net tons.[7]

And the story of that progress is also an exciting drama.

---

[7] This figure is two-and-one-half times greater than all the war cargoes carried by America's 1944 Atlantic-Pacific ocean-going merchant fleet, according to the statistician of the Lake Carriers' Association.

Chapter 25

Lake Erie and the Sault

THE control gauge of Lake Erie was far away at the Sault. The falls in the St. Marys River regulated the size and the movement of ships. So long as the rivers connecting Lake Superior with Lake Erie remained shallow, the shipbuilders could at least construct slight-draft ships with keel boards to sail through them; they were a handicap but not a barrier. But they couldn't sail a ship over the falls in the St. Marys River. In this important sense, the Sault was as vital a spot to Lake Erie shippers as if it had been in the Detroit River at Bar Point. The rise of Lake Erie to its supreme position as outlet to the chain of lakes is inseparably linked to the engineering at the Sault. Every shipbuilder on the lakes had to begin his designs with the dimensions of the locks at the Sault, just as a naval architect must start with the 110-foot-beam limitation imposed by the Panama Canal.

The Sault, therefore, becomes a sort of umbilical cord to Lake Erie, and we must at least cast a glance up the waterway to see what went on at this nineteen-foot cataract over the pre-Cambrian rim of Lake Superior.

The first canal which Charles T. Harvey built in 1855 had two locks, each 350 feet long, 70 feet wide and 9 feet deep. That seemed ample at the time, but it was antiquated within a few years. Here is the way the shipments of Lake Superior ores poured through the Sault to the Lake Erie ports:

Year	Gross Tons
1855	1,449
1856	36,343
1859	68,832
1860	114,401
1864	203,055
1865	243,127
1866	278,796
1867	473,567

Year	*Gross Tons*
1869	617,444
1870	830,940

Translate those cold symbols into mines and men, wharves and ships, port towns and furnaces, and they grow quick with the adventurous expansion of the American continent through one of its major crises. The raw material for steel had been found in the lonely wilderness of Lake Superior. Now it was floating down to energetic Lake Erie. For it was cheaper to bring ore to the center of coal and limestone and furnaces than to carry these up to the ore beds. But the largest of the ships could carry only about 1,800 tons, and they were jamming in the bottleneck at the Sault.

We must have bigger locks, the lake men said.

In 1881 the new $2,200,000 Weitzel Lock, designed by General O. M. Poe and built by Alfred Noble, was opened, just ten years after the first contracts were let. It was named for the distinguished Civil War general who had supervised its completion. It was 515 feet long, 80 feet wide and 16 feet deep, and it moved a ship over the falls in one operation. But the river channels were still only about twelve and a half feet deep. A sixteen-foot channel was immediately projected through the St. Marys, the St. Clair and the Detroit Rivers. The St. Marys had to be deepened in various places, a channel had to be dredged through the St. Clair Flats, and a cut had to be made through a rock reef at the mouth of the Detroit River. All this was completed in 1884. Again the cold figures of the flow of ore through the Sault tell the warm drama of this commerce:

1876	992,764
1878	1,111,110
1881	2,306,505
1882	2,965,412
1887	4,730,577
1888	5,063,693
1889	7,292,754
1890	9,012,379

The lake-port cities were booming. Again the drama of cold figures that stand for eager men and women converging in these cities:

Buffalo in 1850: 42,261; in 1870: 117,714; in 1890: 255,664
Cleveland in 1850: 17,034; in 1870: 92,829; in 1890: 261,353
Toledo in 1850: 3,829; in 1870: 31,584; in 1890: 81,434
Detroit in 1850: 21,019; in 1870: 79,577; in 1890: 205,876

People coming in, ore coming down, and once again the ships jamming at the Sault, wasting a day or more, waiting their turn, idle, losing money.

We must have bigger locks, the lake men said.

In 1896 the Poe Lock was completed. It too was designed by that great man of the lakes, General O. M. Poe, who spent the rest of his life after the Civil War in improving navigation at the Sault and through the channels. His headquarters were at Detroit. He built with imagination. The new lock was 800 feet long, 100 feet wide and 22 feet deep. It was designed to accommodate four vessels in a single lockage. And it did—for a few years. But so fast was industry on the Great Lakes moving at the end of the last century that by the time the Poe Lock was completed "there were a number of boats so large that two of them could not be locked through together."[1] And by 1899 there was at least twenty feet of water in all the channels between Duluth and the Lake Erie ports.

Again the drama of the cold figures:

1894	7,748,932
1895	10,438,268
1897	12,469,638
1898	14,024,673
1900	19,059,393
1902	27,571,121

More work on the river channels and the harbors at the lake ports to deepen them to eighteen, to twenty, to twenty-two feet.

1905	34,353,456
1906	38,522,239

We must have bigger locks at the Sault, the lake men said.

A new canal and lock was started in 1907; still another in 1911.

[1] George A. Marr, *Michigan Technic* (March 1924).

They were each 1,350 feet long, 80 feet wide and 24½ feet deep. The Davis Lock was opened in 1914, the Sabin in 1919.

        1915 46,318,804
        1916 64,734,198
        1920 58,527,226

And down in the Lake Erie cities men and women from all parts of the world continued to come in.

        Buffalo   in 1910: 423,715; in 1930:   573,076
        Cleveland   in 1910: 560,663; in 1930:   900,429
        Toledo   in 1910: 168,497; in 1930:   290,718
        Detroit   in 1910: 465,766; in 1930: 1,568,662

World War II came to the lakes.

        1939 45,072,724
        1940 63,712,982
        1941 80,116,360
        1942 92,076,781

We must have another and a deeper lock, the lake men said.

Congress authorized it in March 1942. It was opened on June 26, 1943, when the 615-foot self-unloader *Carl D. Bradley* passed up and the 614-foot ore freighter *Enders M. Voorhees* of the Pittsburgh Steamship Company of Cleveland passed down with 14,500 tons of ore. The lock is 800 feet long, 80 feet wide and 30 feet deep. It was named the MacArthur Lock.

As General Poe said not long before he died in October 1895:

"In thirty-five years I have watched the increase of the Great Lakes commerce, but neither I nor anyone else has been able to expand in ideas at the same rate. The wildest expectations of one year seem absurdly tame by the side of the actual facts of the next."

Chapter 26

Bothwell, Brown and Hulett

THE Sault was not the only bottleneck to swift movement of ore. The cargoes had first to be taken on at the Lake Superior docks and they had to be unloaded at the Lake Erie ports. The development of the ore beds and their outlets, and the invention of the unloading machines were almost as vital as enlarging the locks at the Sault.

When the locks were opened to traffic in June 1855, the *Columbia* was among the first of the sailing ships to pass through into Lake Superior. And just two months later—on August 17, to be exact—this graceful Lake Erie brig, Justice Wells, Master, locked through again, this time on her way down to Cleveland. It was a portentous moment in the history of the lakes and of the nation. For she was carrying 132 tons of ore to the Cuyahoga River port from the Cleveland Iron Mining Company on the newly discovered Marquette Range. That was the first shipment of Lake Superior ore—the crude, tentative beginning of one of the great industries of the modern world.

The greatest single problem now was that of unloading the cargoes at the docks on the Lake Erie harbors. It was a task of herculean proportions to get the ore out of the ship. Those first vessels were unloaded entirely by hand and muscle and back. Workmen built a platform in the hold of the vessel. Then they shoveled the heavy ore up to the platform. Another gang of sweating men shoveled it from the platform to the deck. From the deck it had to be handled a third time to move it from the ship to the dock. It took three or four days of unremitting toil to unload the 132 tons of ore from the *Columbia*. (Modern unloaders would need just eight minutes.) That was also an expensive process.

Naturally American ingenuity was provoked by such a challenge. Even if the cost had not made the operation well-nigh prohibitive, no good mechanically-minded American would long tolerate such a crudity. Why not rig up a block and tackle and let a horse hoist

315

the ore up from the hold? That was simple. The Cleveland men fastened a block to the ship's mast, lowered a tub on a rope, hitched a horse to the other end of the rope and let him walk down the dock drawing the tub up to the deck. There it was dumped into wheelbarrows and pushed over to the stock pile. This method cut the unloading time in half.

That was fifty percent better, but it was not good enough. One day in 1867 J. D. Bothwell, of the Cleveland firm of Bothwell & Ferris, operators of the Nypano Docks on the Cuyahoga River, stood on the riverbank watching a little steam engine at work lifting log piles to be driven into the river bed for harbor improvement. Then he looked over at his dock where his forty horses were busy unloading schooners. Why, he reasonably asked, couldn't such an engine do the work of the horses? If it could lift and drive piles, it could certainly pull a tub of ore out of the hold of a ship. He got Robert Wallace[1] to design an engine—a portable affair, six by twelve feet, attached to a boiler. It cost $1,200. Bothwell and Wallace had it all ready for operation when the *Massillon,* Smith Moore, Master, came alongside with 400 tons of ore. They still tell of Captain Moore's rage and profanity when he saw the dinkey engine on the dock instead of horses and how he protested. Bothwell proceeded with his experiment, however; Wallace's engine pulled up three tubs of ore at a time; and before the day was over the *Massillon* was unloaded and ready to sail back up the lakes. Another record had been set on Lake Erie. Orders for nine engines were placed immediately with Wallace by the Lake Erie docks, and the future and fortune of his company was assured.

From that day to this, new records have been set almost yearly; speed that seemed only a dream one season became a fact the next, and the following year was archaic.

Alexander E. Brown, a young engineer with a gift for invention, developed the machine that made Bothwell's unloader obsolete. He too was a Cleveland man, born there in 1852, the son of Fayette Brown. After he was graduated from the Brooklyn Polytechnic

---

[1] Robert's son, James C. Wallace, "Jim" of Cleveland, became president of American Ship Building Company. Robert used to say, "I had three boys. Two of 'em went to college, but Jim *he* wanted an education, so he didn't take much stock in books, but got a job out among men. That was what made Jim!" (Quoted in James Oliver Curwood, *The Great Lakes,* [New York, 1909], p. 16.)

Institute he was employed by a bridge-building company. He used to look down into the Cuyahoga Flats and watch the stevedores swarming like ants on the docks, shoveling and wheeling ore from ship to shore. He studied the engine-tub-wheelbarrow mechanism which had continued in operation, with some improvements, from 1867 to 1880. It was costing about fifty cents a ton to unload—it now costs only eighty cents to move it from Superior to Conneaut. It was also by that time much too slow, and was lagging far behind the loading facilities at Lake Superior and the increasing carrying capacity of the ore fleet. Vessels were delayed while men slowly pushed wheelbarrows up and down a gangplank. Why not transfer the tub or bucket directly from the ship's hold to the freight car or to the storage dumps? The young Mr. Brown saw a way to do it. He built the Brown unloader with cables running from the ship to the docks. His first machine was tried at the Erie Railroad dock at the foot of Pearl Street in 1880. It worked.

The wheelbarrows and the horses were now eliminated, but men were still down in the ship's hold shoveling the ore into the buckets by hand. Could this method also be improved?

The motto on the Great Lakes is that anything can be improved. Three firms went to work on a self-loading bucket: Hoover & Mason of Chicago, Wellman-Seaver-Morgan Company and the Brown Hoisting Machinery Company of Cleveland. They perfected an automatic grab bucket that would spread open its jaws and then close them on five tons of ore at a single bite. The buckets were soon in operation at Conneaut, Ashtabula, Fairport and Lorain. These Brownhoist unloaders are still used at several of the docks at the Lake Erie ports.

By the time the extraordinary decade of the 1890's got under way the now familiar cycle of development on the Great Lakes was fully established. The roaring furnaces called for more and more ore, and the iron ranges produced it. That called in turn for bigger docks with faster loading facilities for greater and still greater carriers. But the larger freighters had to have deeper channels through the rivers and deeper harbors at the Lake Erie ports. So the Sault Canal and the connecting channels were deepened, as we have seen, and the harbors were steadily improved and extended. Unloading had to keep pace.

One final step in speeding up the unloading time was taken by the ingenious invention of George H. Hulett in 1899. He devised a clamshell bucket operated by a hydraulic cylinder or electric motor which could close neatly on an enormous bite of ore in the big hopper-bottomed steel freighters. The machine, mounted on rails, had a tilting girder, and on the end of this girder was hung a vertical steel arm which lowered and lifted the bucket into the hold. An operator stood inside this vertical arm, making the journey down into the hold and back as the almost human arm and giant hand gouged out the ore and deposited it nimbly in the waiting freight cars or on the stock pile. This device, now famed on the Great Lakes as the Hulett unloader, was first set up and tried out on the docks at Conneaut by the Carnegie Steel Company. Its performance through the years has written the only comment necessary. In 1902 Mr. A. B. Wolvin's new *James H. Hoyt* was loaded with 5,250 tons of ore in just thirty minutes and thirty seconds. She came down to Lake Erie with this big cargo and docked under the Hulett unloader. In three hours and fifty-two minutes Hulett's machine had cleared her hold.

As the Hulett machines have been improved, the unloading time has been still further lowered. The present record is two hours and forty-five minutes for a cargo of 14,275 gross tons of ore, with a battery of the latest-type Hulett unloaders grabbing seventeen tons at a scoop at the rate of one bite every sixty seconds. The normal unloading time is four to five hours. The average stay of the freighters in a Lake Erie port is now only about seven hours, and the total turn-around time now averages only fifteen hours or less. And when we remember that each trip of one of these freighters adds from $6,000 to $8,000 in revenue to its owners, and about 15,000 tons of ore to the year's supply, we can understand why the name of Hulett is honored on the lakes.

These improvements in the unloaders have been largely the work of George Hulett's son Frank, who died in Cleveland in August 1944 at the age of sixty-eight. He had lived in Cleveland for sixty years. As a young man of twenty-three years, just out of Case School of Applied Science, he helped his father with the invention of the first Hulett stiff-legged ore-unloading machine. He then joined his father at the old Wellman-Seaver-Morgan Company of Cleveland,

CLEVELAND'S TERMINAL TOWER AS SEEN FROM
CUYAHOGA RIVER

SEVERANCE HALL, HOME OF THE CLEVELAND
SYMPHONY ORCHESTRA

AIR VIEW OF BUFFALO

The Niagara River is in the background.

working with him in developing labor-saving equipment to reduce the costly demurrage time of cargo vessels in the Lake Erie ports. In 1914 he organized and became president of the Hulett Engineering Company; and in 1926 he invented the Hulett unloading dock which made Cleveland the second largest ore-unloading port on all the Great Lakes and the first city in the manufacturing of unloading machinery.

The inventions of the Huletts revolutionized industry, changed the structure of the ore freighters, and altered the skyline of Lake Erie from Windmill Point to Buffalo Light. Certainly one of the most characteristic sights along the Detroit River and the Lake Erie shore is these giant steel structures, black and complicated-looking against the sky, lifting and lowering their stiff legs with elephantine grace as they bite ore from the long freighters moored under them, and deposit it in waiting cars or on the winter stock piles. Without these machines the country could never have shipped and handled the stupendous total of 92,000,000 tons of ore in a single year of war emergency. The arsenal of Democracy, and those dependent upon it, have reason to pay their respects to George and Frank Hulett.[2]

---

[2] Curiously, not one of the Great Lakes vessels is named for the Huletts. But the Maritime Commission did christen one of its Florida-built Liberty ships for Alexander E. Brown of the Brownhoist Company in 1944.

Chapter 27

Building the Ore Fleet

THE *Columbia,* which brought the first ore to Cleveland, had slid down the ways into the bay at Sandusky in the year 1842. She was only ninety-one feet long and twenty-four feet beam. She was rigged as a hermaphrodite brig; i.e., she had three jib sails, four square sails on her foremast, and a mainsail and gaff topsail on her mainmast. And, as we have noted, she carried 132 tons of ore—just eight bites for a Conneaut Hulett.

In 1942, exactly one century later, the *Irving S. Olds* was launched at Lorain by the American Ship Building Company for the Pittsburgh fleet. She was 639½ feet long, 67 feet beam and 35 feet deep. Instead of two masts and jib sails, she was driven by a solid bronze wheel propeller 17½ feet in diameter. She carried down to Conneaut in one voyage 18,161 tons of ore.

Between these two episodes was written the epic of ships on the Great Lakes—and most of the chapters were enacted along the shore of Lake Erie and on the banks of the Detroit River. The controls were the size of the locks at the Sault, the depth of the harbors and the unloaders on Lake Erie. The ships were transformed as these conditions changed. The *Columbia,* the *Massillon* and all that fleet in operation in the 1860's were not designed for carrying a bulk cargo of ore. Many steamers refused to take on the dirty stuff. They were built for passengers and package freight, there was no hold for ore, and it messed up their clean decks. Some of the schooners could carry it only on deck, like a flatcar. It was no slight achievement, in the circumstances, to bring down 200,000 tons a year in the 1860's.

Many new schooners were built for this trade in the late 1860's and through the 1870's. They were all wooden ships, of course, generally three-masters, and their largest carrying capacity was about 1,800 tons. These were the ships that massed in the harbor at Sarnia, waiting their turn to be towed through to Lake Erie. They came down Lake Erie under their own sails, they congested at

Point Pelee like a huge flock of white-winged migratory birds, and then broke formation to steer for the various Lake Erie ports. Their masts made the narrow rivers at Cleveland, Fairport, Ashtabula, Conneaut, Buffalo and Port Colborne look like a winter forest.

Many of the schooners were captain-owned and operated. The captain transported any cargo which he might pick up at a profit. If no better cargo offered, these captain-owners would buy a few tons of iron at $15 a ton and sail it down to Detroit or Cleveland on the chance of selling it at $20. One of the legendary figures on the Great Lakes laid the base of his fortune through deals of this kind. He was Peter White, a man whose active career covered the six decades from the discovery and opening of the Marquette range and the first shipment of ore through the Sault, to the revolution in construction of the ore fleet and the records piled up by the *Augustus B. Wolvin* and the Hulett unloaders at Conneaut. He was born at Rome, New York, in 1830, just five years after the Erie Canal was opened. Early in his career he went out to Marquette where he lived a most adventurous life doing odd jobs of all kinds: clearing brush from the ore range, driving oxen, building the Marquette dock, carrying mail by dog team through the snow-swept wilderness, making himself indispensable to the mine owners of Cleveland, becoming a representative in the Michigan House and collector of customs at Marquette, owning his own store, operating his own bank. Old-timers still speak of the ore region of the Upper Peninsula as Peter White's Country. The Civil War gave him his big opportunity, and he made the most of it.

Small furnaces, like those in Pennsylvania and southeastern Ohio, had been built near Marquette to make iron at the source of the ore. Peter White had been making money by selling this iron in small quantities to the captain-owners who wished to take a pay load back to Lake Erie. Often enough, however, they found no market and simply dumped their cargo on a convenient wharf. The war effort of the 1860's was making severe demands on the industrial capacity of the North. The furnaces could not get enough iron to make cannon and rifles and wagon tires for Grant's and Sherman's armies. Peter White suspected that their supply of pig iron was running short. He also surmised that some of his iron was lying on the docks at the Lower Lake ports.

He made a journey down to Lake Erie in 1863, following up the vessels which had been buying iron from him at Marquette. As he had suspected, this iron was gathering rust in small piles at the lake ports, much of it at Detroit. He bought back his own pig iron for six dollars a ton more than the masters had paid for it. That gave the ships a handsome profit. Then he went on to Cleveland. He walked into the office of Mr. Otis of the Otis Foundry Company and asked bluntly, "Want any pig iron?" The question was purely rhetorical. Of course Otis wanted iron. He wanted it so badly that he promptly offered $42 a ton for all Peter White could deliver. Peter White sold him 1,000 tons that day at a profit of $18,000. He cleared $35,000 on his profiteering deal in a single fortnight. He also made sales of charcoal iron from the Bancroft furnace on the Marquette range that same year at $95 a ton for the best grade, $90 for the second and $85 for the third. That was, and I believe still remains, the highest price ever paid for iron in the United States. The foundation of the fortune of the Honorable Peter White was laid and assured.

In 1905 the Cleveland-Cliffs Iron Company received a big new ship from the yards of the Great Lakes Engineering Works at Detroit. They christened it the *Peter White*.

The increased demand for ore after the Civil War encouraged shipbuilders to reconsider the designs of their vessels. In 1869, just two years after Bothwell's engine unloaded the *Massillon,* the Cleveland firm of Peck & Masters built the first steamer for the express purpose of carrying ore from the Jackson mine on Lake Superior to the Lake Erie ports. She was the *R. J. Hackett,* 211 feet long and 33 feet beam. Her machinery was aft, her navigation quarters were forward, her hold was unobstructed, and her hatches were spaced 24 feet center for easy loading and unloading. She could carry 1,200 tons of cargo. The next year she was joined by her consort, the *Forest City,* 213 feet long and 33 feet beam. This was the beginning of the steamer and consort tow system which was long popular on the lakes. In 1874 the *V. H. Ketchum* was launched; she was twenty-two feet longer and eight feet wider than the *Hackett,* and her draft was sixteen feet. She was, at the moment of her launching, therefore, too large for the dock facilities, but in after years, when the channels were cleared, she made huge profits for her owners. She had only one small cabin and pilothouse forward; her 'tween deck was open, and her engine was aft like the modern carriers. Her oak hull was braced strongly below deck. Her lines were trim because she could do away with the ludicrous arch above deck that had been used to give the ships enough strength to carry cargoes of iron. But even in 1874 a steamer carried sails as a matter of course. The *V. H. Ketchum* was a four-master with schooner rig.

The performance of the *R. J. Hackett* forecast the first major change in the lake fleet. She was the prototype of the modern bulk-freight carrier and the transition ship from sails to steam. These first ore steamers were not attractive ships. They were specifically built to fit the canal locks: first with nine feet and then fourteen feet draft, and from 200 up to 270 feet in length. And they were wooden ships.

But iron had already proved itself as material for ships on Lake Erie. In the same year in which the *Columbia* was launched contracts were let to Stackhouse and Tomlinson of Pittsburgh for building a 500-ton steam vessel of iron. They furnished the iron hull, engines, boilers and such equipment from their Pittsburgh works, transported them in sections to Erie, Pennsylvania, and put the vessels together there in the harbor where Sailing Master Daniel Dobbins and Noah Brown had built Perry's fleet in 1813. The ship, christened *Michigan,* was launched on December 5, 1843, before a large crowd who had come to see the "Iron Ship" sink, as everybody knew it must. She was the first iron warship, but she didn't sink. In fact, her hull is still tight, a century after her commissioning in 1844. She was the ship that guarded the prison camp on Johnson's Island during the Civil War. Officer Gridley, the man who fired the first shot at Manila Bay when Admiral Dewey said, "You may fire when you are ready, Gridley," was on the *Michigan* in 1870. Lieutenant Commander (Ret.) William L. Morrison, N. F. P.,[1] who raised Perry's brig *Niagara* from her burial place in the sands of Misery Bay, Presque Isle, commanded the *Michigan* (renamed *Wolverine* so the name Michigan could go to a battleship) when she escorted the *Niagara* on her centennial tour of the lakes in 1913. At that time the iron work of the *Wolverine* was still sound, and her original engines were reported to be "in as good condition as when built." This ship, now over a century old, has been lying unattended at Presque Isle for a score of years. When I last saw

---

[1] Naval Force of Pennsylvania.

her not long ago, she had through neglect fallen upon evil days; she had been defaced by those who knew nothing of her honor, and some were even suggesting that she be salvaged for her iron. There was no Holmes to write an "Old Ironsides" poem about her, but President Franklin D. Roosevelt urged that she be preserved and she probably will be.

The *Michigan* proved the case for iron, but it was not until almost two decades after her launching that the first iron commercial ship appeared on Lake Erie. She was the *Merchant,* built by the Evanses in Buffalo in 1862. She was followed from the same yards by the *Philadelphia* in 1868, the year before the wooden-hulled ore steamer *R. J. Hackett* began her career. And in the early 1870's came the first fleet of iron ships on the lakes: the *Japan,* the *China,* the *India* and the *Alaska,* built at a cost of about $180,000 each, to carry 150 passengers and 1,200 tons of cargo. The captain of the *Japan* was Alexander Mc-Dougall, who had had a part in her building, and of whom we shall speak in a moment. These were not ore ships; they were for three decades the most popular passenger vessels on the lakes and, despite their expense, they gave new impetus to the transition from wood to iron to steel. That transition began in the 1880's, immediately following the opening of the Weitzel Lock. The Globe Ship Building Company[2] in their yards on the Cuyahoga River at the foot of West 54th Street, Cleveland, built the first iron freighter in 1882. She was the *Onoko,* 287 feet long and 38 feet beam. For several years she was the largest dead-weight ore carrier on the Great Lakes. Four years later the Globe Iron Works built for the Wilson Transit Company a ship of steel. She was the *Spokane*—310 feet long, 38 feet beam and 24 feet deep. From then on, steel was the stuff for ships.

In 1888, just two years later, a new-type vessel made her appearance on the lakes. She was the product of the ingenuity and imagination, and also of the experience, of one of the great sailing captains. He was Alexander McDougall, and one of the big freighters of the Buckeye Steamship Company of Cleveland bears his name as she steams across the lakes towing the even larger barge *Marsala* at the end of a long hawser. This young Scotchman shipped on the lakes at the age

---

[2] Combined with the Globe Machine Shop and Foundry, and Globe Boiler Shop in 1886 to form the Globe Iron Works Company. Taken over in 1899, with other Great Lakes yards, by the American Ship Building Company of Cleveland.

of sixteen. He rose through the ranks to become, at the age of twenty-five, captain of the *Thomas A. Scott*. He was twenty-six when he helped design the *Japan*. His mind was, all this time, playing restlessly with the problem of design for Great Lakes ships.

"While captain of the *Hiawatha*, towing the *Minnehaha* and *Goshawk* through the difficult and dangerous channels of our river," McDougall wrote, "I thought out a plan to build an iron boat cheaper than wooden vessels. I first made plans and models for a boat with a flat bottom designed to carry the greatest cargo on the least water, with rounded top so that water could not stay on board; with a spoon-shaped bow to best follow the line of strain with the least use of the rudder and with turrets on deck for passage into the interior of the hull."

His distinctive design was called the "whaleback."

The first one, No. 101, appeared in 1888, and was towed from Two Harbors to Cleveland with a load of ore. McDougall got financial backing from Colgate Hoyt to continue construction. He built a new whaleback in 1889, and then followed it immediately with a third, which he named for Hoyt. Through his extraordinary genius in getting shipwrights and workers, finance and material, he managed to build forty-six McDougall whalebacks in the decade between 1888 and 1898. Ten of them were built at once in his yards at Superior in 1893 with a launching "every Saturday for eight Saturdays" and on the ninth Saturday he launched "two ships and a tug."

By the time the Poe Lock was opened in 1896, McDougall had ships ready for the increased traffic. They were efficient self-propelled shells filled with pay load and able to wallow through the lakes like great whales. They served their day, and one or two carried ore in the World War II emergency. But they were not the final standard type of ship for the Great Lakes.

The dimensions of the Poe Lock of 1896 freed shipbuilders from the handicap of the Sault in designing freighters for the ore trade. Up to that time there was not a single vessel with a net register of 2,000 tons, and the mean dimensions of the fleet were under 300 feet. More than half the tonnage built in 1896 exceeded 2,000 tons net register. The first 400-footers, the *Victory* and the *Zenith,* appeared in 1895. In the meantime John D. Rockefeller had acquired ore mines in the Lake Superior country. He saw, as Carnegie did not see, the importance of owning ore beds and ships to move the ore to Lake Erie. In 1897 he craftily ordered through the Bessemer Steamship Company ten ships, two from each of five shipbuilding companies on the lakes. Some of these were 475 feet long, and they towed barges that were 450 feet long. These were record dimensions, but they stood only three years. For changes were coming thick and fast to the lakes at the turn of the century.

William Livingstone, long-time president of the Lake Carriers' Association, and one of the most powerful of the lake men behind the deepening of the channels between the lakes, wrote in 1925 that "the thing which in my judgment most influenced the change in type and size of the bulk freighters on the lakes came about through the invention of the Hulett unloader, which was installed in 1899[3]. His judgment is borne out by the facts. With the barrier at the Sault over-come, with the channels deepened through the rivers, with the harbors cleared, and the iron ranges back of Duluth opened for exploitation, the future of the ore-carrying trade was not only beyond question but beyond the imagination of the day. Ships, more ships, bigger and better and faster ships were needed. The Chicago Ship Building Company on the Calumet River was building ships for ten companies, including American Steel and Wire, Bessemer and the Pittsburgh Steamship Company.

At West Superior, Wisconsin, the American Steel Barge Company, backed by the Rockefeller interests and Alexander McDougall, was building ships for the ore fleet and operating the only docks on Lake Superior for the repair of vessels.

The Milwaukee Dry Dock Company was operating two thriving shipyards at Milwaukee, building and repairing for most of the large transport companies. The Detroit Ship Building Company at Wyandotte, Michigan, just below Detroit, was building many of the finer lake and river steamers for the D. & C. Lines, the C. & B. Lines and others, as well as ore carriers for Bessemer. It also supplied engines, boilers, machinery, hardware and many other items to other ship-building companies on the lakes.

The Globe Iron Works, the Ship Owners Dry Dock Company and the Cleveland Ship Building Company at Cleveland were building and repairing ships for Hanna, Pickands, Mather & Company,

---

[3] Letter to Herman A. Kelley, January 10, 1925.

Bessemer and others, and also car ferries and passenger steamers. All these companies were organized under one efficient management in 1899 as the American Ship Building Company of Cleveland —the largest on the lakes and one of the big firms of its kind in the world.

The men behind this company recognized that the post-Civil War ships were antiquated. As the new mines were opened to feed the growing steel mills at Pittsburgh, they saw that the ore fleet must be completely redesigned, rebuilt and enormously expanded. They promptly turned out in their yards at Lorain a truly "modern" ore carrier. She was the *Superior City,* launched in 1899. She was built with the Hulett unloader in mind. Previous models had been braced with 'tween-deck stanchions to give strength to the long hull. These stanchions obstructed the arm and bucket of the unloader, but so far they were the only method devised by the builders to brace the hulls. Could a ship be constructed to give free access to the nimble arm of the unloader and at the same time remain strong enough to withstand the tremendous strain of a load of ore as the ship steamed across the 800-mile seaways of the lakes through storms and high seas?

The answer of the shipbuilders was the *Superior City.* Her designer got rid of the stanchions and substituted a side-arch construction. Her hatches were co-ordinated with the legs of the unloaders. She proved to have both freedom and strength, and she was maneuverable and seaworthy. The design became standard, and the hatches on all the later ore carriers have been spaced to accommodate the dock pockets at Superior-Duluth, and to receive a battery of these giant Hulett unloaders for quick handling of the cargo.

Since that time the ore fleet has been almost completely rebuilt. Of the Pittsburgh Steamship Company's fleet of seventy-three ships, the largest fleet on the lakes, only six of the vessels now in service antedate the year 1899. All the others were built between 1899 and 1942. They have grown steadily longer and bigger. In 1900 A. B. Wolvin ordered four new ships, each of 8,000 gross tons carrying capacity. They were 478 feet long at the keel, 52 feet beam and 30 feet hold; but their over-all length was only a few inches under 500 feet, and they are known on the lakes as 500-footers. All four of them—*William Edenborn, Isaac L. Ellwood, John W. Gates* and *James J. Hill*—at the age of forty-five years are still making regular voyages on the lakes carrying the 8,000 tons of cargo each trip for the Pittsburgh Steamship Company.

This same experimenter, A. B. Wolvin, took another radical step forward in 1904 by building a vessel sixty-two feet longer than any ship on the lakes up to that time. She was christened the *Augustus B. Wolvin,* and she still sails with the Pickands, Mather fleet of Cleveland. She is 560 feet over all, 56 feet beam and 32 feet deep, with her thirty-three hatches spaced on 12-feet centers to accommodate the loading pockets and the Hulett legs. Her sturdy side-arch construction frees her hold from all obstructions. Her sides slope inward toward the keel, making her belly one great cavernous hopper, 409 feet long, 43 feet wide at the top and 24 feet at the bottom. When you stand at the bow end of this ship and look aft through her unobstructed hold, gracefully arched over by its steel girders at the hatches, you feel as though you were in the Detroit-Windsor Tunnel, and that at any minute an automobile may come whirring out of the dunnage deck and race down the vast tube into the darkness at the engine-room bulkhead.

The *Augustus B. Wolvin* was the wonder of the lakes—for two or three years. Passengers on the steamships for a vacation voyage on the lakes used to watch for her as they sailed through the Detroit River and Lake St. Clair, and if they were lucky enough to sight her, they would shout to their friends: "There comes the *Wolvin!* The biggest ship on the lakes!"

Although there were 121 vessels of the *Wolvin* dimensions on the lakes by 1915, the class was quickly surpassed in size by the new ships for the fleet of the Pittsburgh Steamship Company. Harry Coulby, president and general manager of the company through the first decades of this century, immediately ordered through the American Ship Building Company four new ships, each nine feet longer than the *Wolvin.* They joined the steel fleet in 1905 bearing the celebrated names of *Elbert H. Gary, William E. Corey, Henry C. Frick* and *George W. Perkins,* and all four of them are still in active service, hauling their immense cargoes of ore to the Lake Erie ports, carrying back up the lakes from Toledo, Sandusky and Cleveland their equally huge cargoes of coal.

Before the masters of these big freighters had got the feel of their ships, learned how they rode the seas, how they sidled and squatted, how they steered and how their hatches squeaked, Coulby had ordered eight more vessels—still bigger ones. They were the new species called 600-footers because that was their over-all length; their official dimensions were 580 feet at the keel, 58 feet beam and 32 feet deep. Their carrying capacity was 11,300 tons on a 20-foot draft. They joined the expanding fleet in 1906 and 1907 with distinguished names like *J. Pierpont Morgan* (first of the class), *A. H. Rogers, P. A. B. Widener, George F. Baker, Norman B. Ream, Thomas Lynch, Thomas F. Cole* and *Henry Phipps.* When the United States entered World War I, thirty-eight of these 600-footers were ready to bring down the ore for the war plants along the Lake Erie shore and contiguous valleys. They too still make their weekly round trip through the season.

And listing their names reminds us of the custom of christening the lake ships. There are a few special names, like the Great Lakes Steamship Company's *Denmark, Finland, Norway* and *Sweden;* Hutchinson's *Mariposa* and *Maritana;* Pickands, Mather's *Arcturus, Canopus, Cetus, Cygnus, Pegasus, Perseus, Taurus* and *Vega;* Tomlinson's *Sierra, Sumatra* and *Sylvania;* and Wilson's *Kickapoo.* But these are the exceptions. By and large the fleet is a floating *Who's Who* or social register of the lake men who have wrought this mighty miracle of Great Lakes shipping and industry. It has its own private Great Lakes Red Book, listing over 1,500 vessels. Their names are a coded history of the lakes, chiefly of Lake Erie, too, and the big men of the lakes take a special pride of their own in being unobtrusive on land but conspicuous, in a modest way, on the shipping lanes.

So far as length was concerned, these 600-footers seemed to be near the limit of economical construction for the lake fleet. With them the revolution begun in 1898 was apparently complete. The fleet was modernized. The big ships had proved their worth. It cost only a little more to carry 12,000 to 15,000 tons of ore from Duluth to Cleveland in one of these big ships than it did to haul 7,000 to 10,000 tons in the slightly smaller vessels. The number of hands and the amount of fuel required to operate the *J. P. Morgan* and the *Superior City* were about the same. The big ships have steadily driven the smaller ones toward obsolescence; and it is always the smaller ships that are first laid up in a slack season and the last to go back into service in a boom period. Yet they disappear slowly. The average age of the carriers in the twelve major fleets is about thirty-three years, and that includes twenty-one new ships built in World War II. Old ships can be modernized; many of them have had their speed increased by seven-tenths of a mile per hour by streamlining their propellers and rudders. That single alteration permits them to make one more round trip each season, adding some $6,000 to $7,000 in yearly revenue, and keeping them in competition.

Additions were made annually to the fleet until the great depression of the 1930's. Then for the first time since the little shipyard at Black Rock began constructing vessels for Lake Erie at the beginning of the nineteenth century, not a ship was built on Lake Erie or in any of the Great Lakes yards. They remained idle until 1937, with the exception of 4,285 tons in 1934, and even in 1937 only 10,853 tons were added. Then the World War II demand laid its stress on the lakes and the shipyards suddenly became active to their fullest capacity. Most of the activity was centered on warships of various types and vessels for the Maritime Commission, as we shall see, but several new freighters were added to the ore fleets.

Five ships built to identical specifications were constructed for the Pittsburgh Steamship Company at Lake Erie yards—three at River Rouge by the Great Lakes Engineering Works, and two at Lorain by the American Ship Building Company. They joined the fleet in 1942 in time to help make that year the greatest in all history in the transport of ore: 92,000,000 tons. They also carried honored names: *Benjamin F. Fairless, Leon Fraser, A. H. Ferbert, Irving S. Olds* and *Enders M. Voorhees*. They were the biggest vessels ever built for the lakes: 614 feet long at the keel, 67 feet beam and 35 feet deep. Their over-all length is 639 feet 6 inches and they have been carrying from 15,000 to 18,000 tons of ore in a single voyage.

These same shipbuilding companies also built sixteen freighters for the Maritime Commission in these same yards and at Ashtabula and Cleveland. They were also as large as these five giants. Ten of them were 621-footers carrying 15,700 tons of ore and six were 620-footers carrying 15,600 tons, a load equal to that of 390 freight cars. The Maritime Commission turned these ships over to operators in the ore trade. They carried on the tradition of naming the ships for Great Lakes men: *Sewell Avery, Thomas Wilson, E. G. Grace, Champlain*.

These vessels cost money and they take time to build. One of these modern freighters represents an investment of approximately $2,000,-

000. The *Irving S. Olds* was built in a year and eighty-nine days; the *Benjamin F. Fairless,* constructed in the adjoining dock at Lorain, required a year and sixty-nine days; and the *Thomas Wilson,* which joined the fleet in 1943, was built in one year and four days.

This emergency building has expanded the fleet beyond normal needs, and creates a problem for postwar adjustment. It also raises again the ever-present question on the lakes. How much bigger will the ships grow? This story which we have outlined points to caution in predicting. Some say the limit has been reached. Conneaut is the only port that can now dock the biggest of the vessels. Others say that they will continue to get longer and wider and deeper, and that the channels and harbors will go still deeper to accommodate them.[4] In an article on "Shipping on the Great Lakes" the superintendent of Canadian Light Houses wrote, "Owners and agents are kept thoroughly posted on every little fluctuation in level and load down to the last inch that can be wriggled over the shoalest spot to be navigated, while they are ever demanding still deeper channels that they may build still bigger boats." That was written in 1898. It might have been last month. Perhaps General Poe's words are still wise with experience: "The wildest expectations of one year seem absurdly tame the next." In matters affecting size on the Great Lakes one learns not to predict.

---

[4] The newest and longest ships can no longer enter the narrow, winding Cuyahoga River. This is a matter of grave concern to the mill owners in the Flats and to the city of Cleveland. In 1945 they proposed a $35,000,000 postwar project to straighten and deepen the river in order to meet competition and keep Cleveland in its position of leadership.

Chapter 28

Aboard a Lake Freighter

THE long lake freighters are beautiful ships—after you have looked at them long enough to grow accustomed to their functional design. Landlubbers and salt-water men often say they are awkward and ungainly. The shipwrights who build them and the sailors who navigate them know better. They are a pretty sight as they march under their plumes of smoke across the dredged channel through Lake St. Clair at dawn on a summer morning, rocking the fishermen's boats with their wakes; as they swing round Detroit River Light, black against the sunset sky, and head east for Pelee; as you watch them through binoculars from the offices of the American Ship Building Company in the Terminal Tower at Cleveland while they steam through the breakwater protecting the narrow Cuyahoga River, pass the lighthouse and disappear in the mist toward Southeast Shoal Light; as you see them spaced on the blue horizon from an airplane high over Lake Erie; or as you stand on the bridge and feel the dynamic force of these living ships as they slide past each other in Fighting Island Channel with only a few yards between them and with the swish of the waters and the rhythmic hum of their engines sounding in your ears.

The design of the lake freighter is dictated solely by its function. And its function is to carry with safety the largest possible bulk cargo in the fastest possible time with the greatest possible economy. It is a floating freight train, a steel shell with an enginehouse aft and navigating instruments forward, with space between them for 15,000 to 18,000 tons of ore—or limestone, coal or grain.

The newer freighters are marvels of construction. An engineer can get excited over the blueprints from which they are built; even a layman finds them fascinating to inspect and contemplate as he watches the giant strokes of the pistons of the Lentz engines in the spotless engine room turning the sixteen-and-a-half-foot manganese bronze propeller eighty revolutions per minute and driving the ship across

Lake Erie at a speed of twelve miles an hour.[1] The longest run of a freighter in open water is only about thirty hours; the rest of the voyage is through narrow, winding and restricted channels. The lines of the vessel, the size and pitch of its propeller, the design of its rudder, bow and keel are all controlled by these operating conditions. Before the sixteen new Maritime Commission vessels were built in 1942-1943, model tests were made at the University of Michigan tank, the United States Experimental Model Basin and the David W. Taylor Model Basin. The engineers tried out various lines, rudders and propellers. They discovered that the cruiser stern increased propulsive efficiency and reduced "stern squat" in the shallow channels, that the streamline rudder had less drag and gave the ship greater maneuverability, and that the solid one-piece bronze propeller operated with minimum vibration. All these features were incorporated in the *Champlain* and her sister ships, which have been breaking all previous records on the lakes.

The engine room is a world in itself. Coal flows out of the bunker to the coal crusher and onto the conveying system which delivers it to the stoker to be spread under the vast boilers. Huge fans supply combustion air, and a special ash-conveying system casts the ashes overboard in the open lake. Motor-driven pumps keep enormous quantities of water flowing to the engine room, the lavatories, baths, laundries, and the galley and pantry. Sirocco-type fans ventilate the ship, and a refrigeration unit on the main-deck stringer cools the meat and vegetable rooms on the spar deck and drinking water for the crew.

The spacious pilothouse is no less interesting and equally mysterious to the uninitiated. It is divided into a chartroom aft and the wheel room forward. The charts, which the government has been making and improving for a hundred years, cover in detail all the open lakes, all the intricate channels and all the ports. The wheelroom has the latest devices for navigation and communication. There is a Sperry gyro compass with two repeaters, a Sperry course recorder and automatic pilot, a radio direction finder, three binnacles and compasses, and a Bendix transmitting-and-reply-docking-order telegraph—an array of safety devices that would have left Captain James Sloan gasping with astonishment and certain that the ship would meet sudden

---

[1] The propellers on the new Maritime Commission vessels are a foot smaller than on the five *Irving S. Olds*-class freighters.

disaster. All parts of the vessel are interconnected with the pilothouse by telephone, speaking tubes and signal systems. Indicators show how many revolutions per minute the shaft is making, the degree of list and the angle of the rudder. The engine dial signals to the engine room FULL, HALF, SLOW, STAND BY, STOP, FINISHED WITH ENGINES. A mate and a wheelsman stand in the pilothouse on duty to navigate the ship, each pair standing two four-hour watches. The captain himself takes over at all danger points and during fogs, and at night a lookout on the forecastle deck keeps vigilant watch for the running lights of other vessels: a headlight on the foremast, starboard green and port red side lights, and two lights on the mainmast. If he sees two headlights on the foremast he reports that the approaching steamer is towing a barge.

Perhaps the most useful of the modern innovations in the communication service aboard the lake vessels is the ship-to-shore radiotelephone. You may now pick up your own house phone and call any one of 318 ships belonging to thirty-nine companies operating on the Great Lakes. You will call the long-distance operator at Lorain and ask her to connect you with the marine operator. For a toll of seventy-five cents (plus tax) you may talk to any one of the ships for three minutes, and for ninety cents (plus tax) you may make a person-to-person call. All the vessels with telephones are listed in the Lorain directory, just like the houses on Erie Street.

This recently developed service has added enormously to the safety, efficiency and convenience of the crew of the lake fleet. The *William A. McGonagle,* let us say, is coming through Pelee Passage with a load of ore for Conneaut. The Conneaut docks, however, are full to capacity and will not be open for several hours, but the *J. P. Morgan, Jr.* is about ready to clear from Cleveland. The Pittsburgh Steamship Company calls the *McGonagle* and orders her into Cleveland, saving demurrage time. Tugs may be telephoned near the spot where they are needed. Vessels approaching a car ferry crossing during fog or low visibility may talk directly to the ferry's master to discover his position. And the men on the ships may talk to their families anywhere at any time.

We get some idea of what this service means when we consider what used to happen before it was invented. On her departure a ship would send a telegram to her port of destination, giving the time of sailing, the number of passengers on board, the tonnage of freight and the weather conditions. From that moment until she reached port the ship was out of communication. In stormy weather great anxiety was felt when ships were delayed. In 1896 the *State of Ohio* left Buffalo on her regular run. A terrific storm rose during the night. The steamer failed to arrive in Cleveland. A full day passed with no word of her. On the second day the *City of Buffalo* was sent out to search for her. She zigzagged over the course without sighting her or speaking any vessel that had seen her. Then the *City of Buffalo* ran up Long Point Bay. There at anchor among scores of freighters rode the lost *State of Ohio* under the protection of Long Point where all the ships in the eastern end of the lake had scurried to safety.

The lake vessels no longer get lost, thanks to the Lorain County Radio Corporation. After a period of experimentation and perfecting of its equipment, the corporation was granted a permit to operate its ship-to-shore system in 1933. Its first radiotelephone was installed on the *William C. Atwater,* flagship of the Wilson Transit Company, in April 1934. Only two vessels had sets in 1935. Then two emergencies occurred which dramatized the usefulness of the system. Captain Mason of the *Atwater* fell down a ladder and cut open his head. His ship was fifty miles from Marquette, the nearest port, and he was bleeding to death. First aid was not sufficient for treating him. One of his officers called a Lorain doctor over the ship-to-shore telephone. The doctor directed the treatment of the captain, and had an ambulance waiting at the dock in Marquette. Later in that same season a prominent Cleveland surgeon was a guest aboard a ship-to-shore-telephone-equipped vessel on the Upper Lakes. One of his patients, on whom he had operated, suffered a serious relapse. A call was put through to the surgeon on the ship. He prescribed the treatment for his patient, and the patient rallied and recovered. Incidents like that have meaning to lake men. They received wide publicity.

By the end of 1936, twenty-two vessels had installed the new equipment. In that same year the Lorain corporation was awarded a patent on a lockout system which assured privacy in telephone calls. Since that time the system has grown steadily until it is now almost universal on the lake vessels. It operates on eleven ship-to-shore frequencies and a special ship-to-ship frequency. More than 20,000 calls are made each shipping season, and H. E. Hageman, inventor and president of the company, is justly proud of his accomplishments at Lorain.

The pilothouse where we have been standing is, therefore, in communication with the rest of the world as well as with all parts of the ship. Below it in the texas house[2] is the captain's office and stateroom with private bath, and the luxurious owners' staterooms which are reserved for guests. You look aft from the navigating bridge over nearly 500 feet of cargo space. To pass on the older vessels from the spar deck forward to the dining room on the spar deck aft, the men had to walk down the open deck along the side of the ship. During storms or when the deck and the protecting cables are iced over, that journey is a hazardous venture and causes many accidents. In the new ships the deckhouses are connected by enclosed and unobstructed passages.

The long hull has two bottoms, the inner one being six feet above the keel. The watertight space between is for ballast. It is divided into ten tanks which extend up along both sides of the cargo hold from the forepeak bulkhead to the afterpeak. When the ship is running light, these tanks are filled with 9,573 long tons of fresh water for ballast. As the ore is discharged from the pockets of the ore dock through the loading chutes into the hold, huge ballast pumps discharge the water from the tanks. All the tanks are interconnected, and water may be pumped from one to another to trim the ship. They can be entirely emptied in three hours. The pumps and ballast tanks and the manipulation of the loading chutes now do the work that once was the profession of ore trimmers: men who went down into the hold of the ship with pick and shovel to level off and distribute evenly the ore as it poured through the hatches.

These newer ships are about fifty percent riveted and fifty percent arc-welded. The all-welded vessels were too rigid and did not stand

---

2 For many years I have been asking masters, mates, Coast Guard and naval officers, and lake men why this cabin on the forecastle deck between the pilothouse and the spar deck is called the "texas house" (with lower-case "t"). The only answer they ever give is a surprised look, accompanied by a lift of the eyebrows, indicating that they had never even thought about it. The texas house is the texas house, just as the spar deck is the spar deck. What more do you want? The term seems to have originated on the Mississippi River boats built by Henry Shreve. He was the first to name the passenger cabins after the states of the Union. In 1837, when the vast area of Texas was on everyone's tongue, the large cabin which Shreve built on the second deck of his boats was called "Texas," and the name has stuck and lost its capital T.

the vibration and the strain of voyage under heavy load. They cracked in two. You may see a few of these vessels on the lakes; they are recognizable by the longitudinal steel bands riveted to their sides. There is just enough, though infinitesimal, play in the riveted joints to give resiliency and to absorb the vibrations of the ship.

These vessels of any particular class are built to the same specifications from identical designs on common blueprints. Theoretically they are all alike. Actually they are just about as different as the children in a family. One will ride smoothly and silently and respond to the rudder with nervous sensitivity. Another will steer hard, it will creak and groan, and its hatches will rattle in any weather like a ghostship. You cannot predict what the ship's character will be until she is off the ways and is bringing down her first load of ore. Each year the Pittsburgh Steamship Company, in preparation for a new operating season, holds a convention in Cleveland for the officers of the fleet, including the masters and chief engineers. They exchange views on operating problems relating to particular ships and lake navigation. And one of the topics always most eagerly discussed by the younger officers who are about to assume command of a ship is: What are the characteristics and idiosyncrasies of the vessel? The master who commanded her last tells how she maneuvers and sidles and squats.

A few of the lake vessels are made conspicuous by a derrick frame that rises above the pilothouse aft of the deckhouse, and by a long arm stretched out horizontally in repose above the hatches. They are Great Lakes masterpieces of engineering efficiency—the self-unloaders. You will see them interspersed among the other vessels of the lake fleets in the Detroit River or up the St. Clair, carrying coal, limestone or sand. They are not useful for iron ore because it is compact and will not flow through the hopper; it has to be gouged out by the steel jaws of a Hulett. But the way they handle coal is something to marvel at. They are completely self-sufficient, independent of all docking machinery and equipment. A small dealer at Algonac orders 3,000 tons of coal from Toledo; another at Marine City wants 5,000 tons; and still another at St. Clair wants 2,500 tons of a different grade. The self-unloader takes on its cargo at the loading dock on the Maumee. It runs up the river, puts in near the bank, swings its arm out from ship to shore, starts up its machinery, spills out the 3,000 tons into the dealer's yard and then moves on. The bottom of the hold is a series of hoppers, and under the hoppers and above the keel is a conveyor belt. It carries the coal to the bucket-belt elevator, the buckets toss the coal on the conveyor belt of the arm, and this conveyor drops it ashore. And the process requires less time than it takes to put a truckload of coal into the basement of your house. These self-unloaders empty their holds of 10,000 tons of limestone on the stock pile at Ashtabula in four hours.

About 15,000 men operate the ore fleets. Each vessel carries a crew of from thirty to forty men. They range in rank from the master with his three mates and the chief engineer with his three assistants down to the deck hand and porter. Their wages have been going up: the chief cook on the larger vessels gets $261 a month, the wheelsmen $186, the watchmen, firemen and oilers $183, the A. B. deck watch $175, the ordinary deck watch $162, the deck hands and porters $148.50. Their subsistence is figured for purpose of tax-deduction schedule at $1.30 a day. That figure might be called modest, for good eating is traditional aboard the lake ships. In ordinary times the vast stainless-steel refrigerators and the vegetable rooms are stocked with the best the country affords: beefsteaks, poultry and fish, and fresh green vegetables. Guests who in normal times are invited to make a voyage on one of these freighters are generally surprised at the luxurious and spacious quarters provided for them in the owners' staterooms, and are pleasantly amazed at the quality of the cuisine served up from the galley.

There is, of course, a fairly heavy turnover each season among the personnel. It may reach as high as 5,000 men. Young fellows like to ship for a voyage or two in order to savor the romance of the freshwater seas and enjoy what they hope will be a vacation with pay. Migratory workers moving restlessly back and forth across the continent often try to ship down from Duluth or up from Buffalo. But the heart and soul of the fleets are the men who love the ships and the lakes and spend their lives on them. There is a quality of loyalty and devotion about them which borders on the sentimental. They live in a tight little world of their own into which outsiders gain only an occasional glimpse. It is practically self-contained. As soon as the shipping season starts with a rush in April the men go aboard the ships to which they have been assigned, and they seldom leave them again, except for an hour or two in port or for a few minutes while they take on bunker coal or lock through the Sault, until the ice closes over and they tie up for the winter in late November or early December. Their wives and families wave to them or shout a greeting as they pass through the narrow channels, or they write them letters to be delivered by the mail boat at Detroit as the ship steams by without slackening speed. Up at the Sault the library service puts aboard packets of books for the crew, and the Pittsburgh Supply Company's floating post office and store comes alongside to deliver mail and stores while the ship steams on.

Under the leadership of the Lake Carriers' Association, the men have their own welfare committees, banks, savings-and-benefits plans, and ship-safety committees "to minimize the element of personal injury aboard bulk freighters." The association has also carried on since 1916 an educational program for the men in the fleets. Located in Cleveland and staffed by experienced instructors, it offers courses to train men in engineering and navigation during the winter season. In twenty-six years of operation it has trained and issued licenses to 1,218 engineering students and to 923 students of navigation. Licensed officers attend the school to advance their ratings, and 1,082 of them have raised their grade. Other members of the crew go into the ship-yards to work during the winter, for that is the rush season for re-pairing and reconditioning and modernizing the ships and getting them ready for the opening of navigation the following spring.

There is always an electric wave of excitement in the ports when the word comes that the icebreakers have cleared a channel through the St. Marys River and Whitefish Bay, and the first ships head out from their winter berths for the ore docks at Duluth. A dozen of them leave port on the first day, and about the same number are placed in commission on each succeeding day until the entire fleet is under way. The stock piles which they had heaped mountain-high at Buffalo, Conneaut, Ashtabula, Cleveland and Toledo during the preceding season have dwindled low as the endless railroad cars have been loaded with ore and hauled off to the furnaces all winter long. Now the giant freighters, which have lain dormant in the ice for four months, come to life again and seem to share in the general excitement as they wallow through the spring seas and crunch the blocks of floating ice that wash against their high-riding bows. They are off in their native element once more to fill up their empty red bellies with ore on Lake Superior and disgorge it on Lake Erie to rebuild the stock piles.

Everybody aboard goes to work with quiet efficiency and feels through his legs the quality of the ship. There are no uniforms and no formalities, no shouting of orders and scarcely any visible evidence of authority. The master seems able to size up the most difficult situation with a casual glance out of the corner of his eye. Except during fogs and emergencies he may sit quietly in his office or stroll round the texas house as though he were merely a passenger on his own ship. Yet a dozen eyes are always vigilantly alert for the least sign of danger. The watches are four hours long, two each day. And when the duty hours are over, the crew may retire to quarters as well appointed as those on an ocean-going passenger liner. On the newer ships there are recreation rooms forward and aft. The three mates have staterooms with private baths on the starboard side of the spar deck below the captain's suite. The wheelsmen and watchmen share a suite only a little less elegant to port. The deck hands occupy rooms on the 'tween deck forward near the ship's laundry. The chief engineer has a large stateroom with bath on the spar deck aft, and his assistants, oilers, coal passers, steward and porter are bunked aft in descending order of rank, but all in very pleasant and acceptable quarters.

This is their home for the next seven and a half months.

Chapter 29

Down Lake St. Clair and the Detroit River

WHILE Harriet Martineau was visiting Detroit she had the "great pleasure" of "a drive along the quiet Lake St. Clair." The scenery of the lake, she says, was new to her. "I had seen nothing in the United States like its level green banks, with trees slanting over the water, festooned with the wild vine; the groups of cattle beneath them; the distant steam-boat, scarcely seeming to disturb the grey surface of the still waters. This was the first of many scenes in Michigan which made me think of Holland; though the day of the canals has not yet arrived."[1] Mrs. Jameson crossed it twice. Voluble though she ordinarily was, she only said, "This beautiful lake, though three times the size of the Lake of Geneva, is a mere pond compared with the enormous seas in its neighbourhood."

Her observations, though brief, are correct in both instances. All the travelers from those of the days of La Salle and Cadillac to the tourists of the present season who have crossed the lake or passed along its shores have testified, generally in superlatives, to its beauty. And as for its size, its greatest width is thirty miles, and the sailing course across it, almost due northeast-southwest, is eighteen miles. A body of water that covers 503 square miles is hardly to be called a pond, even though it is little more than a pond in depth. In most places around the lake it is only shoulder-deep a mile or more offshore. In just two small areas near the center of the lake does it reach a depth of nineteen or twenty feet. Most of its silted bottom is perfectly flat sixteen feet below the surface. It is really a heart-shaped bulge in the St. Clair and Detroit River system connecting Lake Huron and Lake Erie. As a matter of fact, a map of Lake St. Clair looks very much like a diagram of the human heart-and-blood-vessel system. For at Algonac the St. Clair River divides into an intricate network of arteries and veins and flows into the lake through seven

---

[1] *Society in America*, I, 235.

channels. The delta formed by these channels is known as the St. Clair Flats.

There is some confusion as to the origin of the lake's name. Hennepin said his party sailed the *Griffin* into these waters on Sainte Claire's day and named the lake in her honor. That seems both basic and satisfactory. But the fact seems to have been lost sight of in after years, at least by the natives. A fat *History of St. Clair County Michigan,* published in 1883, says that the river was named for Patrick Sinclair, a British officer in command of supply between the forts at Detroit and Mackinac in 1763. He built Fort Sinclair, and in 1765 purchased 3,759 acres of land on the river. The local citizens with a frontier English diction associated the name of the great man with that of the river and assumed that they were cause and effect. And the same source mentions that General Arthur St. Clair was thought to be the man for whom the lake was named. We prefer Hennepin's story.

The exploration of the lake was incidental to the discovery of the Great Lakes system. A few decades after the founding of Detroit, French families began moving from the fort to the lake shore to lay out their ribbon farms extending back among the maples and pines from a narrow frontage on the lake. Except for the interruptions occasioned by the wars, settlement spread rather steadily up Grosse Pointe and east from present Riverside to the mouth of the Thames. And there was considerable traffic down the Thames from Chatham and across the lake to Detroit. The eastern and northern shores are marshlands. The river has through the centuries carried down quantities of soil which it has deposited at its leisure on the floor of the lake. A navigation chart of Lake St. Clair looks precisely like a war map of the Russian advance across Poland into Germany. The seven channels in the mouth of the river are the spearheads of the drive; the Flats are the consolidated gains; and the tinted area of the lake floor, indicating depths of from one to three feet, and reaching a quarter of the way across the lake, is the fluid zone of the battle front.

The Flats are now a Detroit Vacationland and playground. In the early days settlers were attracted to this delta region by the depth of its fat soil. The web of the river divides the delta into triangular-shaped islands: marshy Ste. Anne far to the east; huge Walpole Island in the center, sloping down to Goose Lake and Johnston Bay;

stringy Squirrel Island east of South Channel—all belonging to Ontario; Harsen's Island west of the Channel; and Dickinson Island wedged between North and Middle Channel—a part of Michigan. Jacob Harsen settled with his large family on the island that bears his name sometime prior to 1800. It was good grazing land, and with a bit of draining it yielded rich crops. At Clay, a village on the delta, Albert Miller & Company bought up a tract of 1,400 acres of marshes and drained it in 1882 by dredging a ditch thirty-two feet wide and building a dike all the way round their holdings. It made wonderful farm land, but the inhabitants complained bitterly because they had been using these acres for pasture. They called Miller's project a "death blow to stock-raising." At the north end of the lake back of Anchor Bay lay the Capac Marsh of 2,200 acres. It was bought by G. C. Parks and others. They drained it with a five-mile ditch eight feet deep, and planted it in cranberries in the 1870's. French families found the land along the North Channel—a little more solid, but boggy enough to attract wild geese and ducks—particularly favorable to their way of life. They and their descendants have lived in and around Pearl Beach since the eighteenth century.

The whole region has been rather extensively developed in later years; it is now crisscrossed with canals and, in the more favored locations, built up with homes and summer cottages and duck hunters' blinds. The big lake freighters passing through the curving course of South Channel seem almost to brush the bright awnings of the cottages on the water front. Thousands of people come up from Detroit each season to Tashmoo Park on Harsen's Island, play golf at the Mid-Channel Club, fish through the ice in winter and gather for the duck shooting.

This is all very pleasant for the people on holiday, but for the men who sail the ships the delta was for years simply an inconvenient hazard to navigation, and occasionally a nightmare. It presented no rock escarpment like the Sault in the St. Marys or the cataract at Niagara for engineers to cope with. The river itself was a kind of canal which God had placed there by His own processes. But it was too shallow and tortuous to meet the needs of His commercial children. In places it was only four or five feet deep and the course of its most favored channel was serpentine in its winding. Senator Cass had got a canal dredged at the mouth of the river. It was 150 feet wide and nine feet deep, and it served its purposes for a time. But it was unprotected, and it filled up quickly. We have examined the cycle of expansion in which it was necessary to deepen the channels to accommodate bigger ships to carry more cargo to more and larger mills with increased speed and safety. The Flats and the shoals at the foot of the lake were the problem points on Lake St. Clair. A new canal was dredged and diked through the Flats to a depth of thirteen feet in 1871. It gave a straight passage through the shoal water where the natural channel was long and crooked. It was almost immediately deepened to sixteen feet, then to twenty, and now, after years of constant dredging and improvement, to twenty-five feet. Hardly a season ever goes by in which the Lake Carriers' Association does not report some further improvement in the channel or its buoy and lighting system. It took particular satisfaction in announcing the completion in 1920 of the five and a quarter miles of the Grosse Pointe Channel into the Detroit River. It was 800 feet wide and twenty-one feet deep. It too has been carried down four feet farther, and now the ship-road cuts like an arterial highway right across the playground lake from Big Muscamoot Bay to Windmill Point. Over $5,000,000 have been spent on its dredging and maintenance.

A heavy volume of traffic passes over the lake. The long freighters, after almost brushing the trees in the front yards of the cottages, move at reduced speed out of the South Channel into the St. Clair Flats Canal, leaving the boats at the cottage piers rocking gently in their wake. It is one of the most agreeable experiences on the shipping route to see the ships passing in the crowded watercourse; to hear the blasts of their deep, throaty whistles; to see the master and the mates, the engineer and the steward, waving to their families or shouting a greeting to their wives through a megaphone; to watch the small boys in bathing trunks gazing at the ships and dreaming of the day when they will grow up and sail on the lakes. The freighter steams slowly down the canal between the buoys to Lake St. Clair Light in the middle of the lake. There it turns southwest 1/4 west and heads straight for Front Light, a mile from the entrance to the Detroit River at Windmill Point.

Detroit's Gold Coast comes into view. Miss Martineau's description is still apt. The shores along Jefferson Avenue and Lake Shore Road from Windmill Point to Gaukler Point and Milk River are green and level, with trees slanting over the water. But instead of groups of cattle beneath them, the houses of the well-to-do and the mansions of the very rich repose in their private parks fronting the lake across a lush greensward. There among the trees, almost hidden from Lake Shore Road, but glimpsed somewhat romantically from the deck of the passing freighter, is the great sandstone mansion of Edsel Ford. Serene in the privacy of its eighty-five acres and its neat shore line, it reminds you of the country house of an eighteenth-century English milord with a fortune from the East India trade. Near by is the swank Grosse Pointe Yacht Club with its sleek white boats massed and moored in its trim and spacious basin. It is one of several yacht clubs on the lake and rivers.

Detroit men have been induced by the lure of their extensive waterways to invest heavily in yachts. Lake St. Clair is alive with flashing white sails on summer week ends, and its evening stillness is broken by the hum of motor-powered craft skimming like will-o'-the-wisps across the surface of the dark waters. Some of the bigger ones are ocean-going craft. The most famous of them was the *Mamie O.,* belonging to the late Robert Oakman, millionaire Detroit real-estate dealer. Powered by two submarine motors, lavishly fitted throughout, she was built in 1923 at a cost of $300,000. She had luxury accommodations for a dozen guests and a crew of eleven men. This palatial yacht was a select social center on the Great Lakes, and the paradise of sportsmen. They crowded aboard her for the Harmsworth Trophy Races on the speed course in the waters north of Belle Isle; she always occupied a prominent place among the boats gathered around the Detroit Yacht Club. The Detroit *Times* said that "she transported more celebrities than any craft ever to sail border or Canadian waters." From 1940 through 1943 the *Mamie O.,* moored at Riverside, could be seen from the deck of a freighter rounding Peach Island. Sailors wondered about her lying there idle, slowly depreciating. In late November 1943 they saw her cast her lines and sail gracefully up Lake St. Clair. Others sighted her moving swiftly through the Straits, sailing up Lake Michigan. Farmers saw her going past their cornfields on the Illinois River. She turned up at Miami. Workmen entered her, stripped her of all her finery and replaced it with huge transport racks. She sailed off to Central and South American ports as a banana bottom—a humble casualty of World War II. Reported purchase price: $15,000.

The Grosse Pointe Yacht Club is a landmark on lower St. Clair, for above its Venetian eaves and roof rises a 187-foot tower with an occulting green light visible for fifteen miles. Between it and the Municipal Pier and Crescent Sail Yacht Club at Grosse Pointe Farms are more of the Detroit mansions. They are the northward extension of the movement of wealthy families out Jefferson Avenue that was begun a century ago when Francis Palms built his mansion on the river. The houses on the shore seem to be coming out to meet the freighter as it moves down the channel into the converging funnel neck of the Detroit River. The ship turns nineteen degrees to west-southwest, passes the big Grosse Pointe Park suburb of Detroit, and enters the Detroit River at Windmill Point.

The trip down the Detroit River is routine and commonplace to the master, mates and crew of our ore carrier. They know every light and marker, every channel and slip along the river in the same way that a seasoned commuter knows all the stops and way stations into Grand Central or the Loop. It is June, the storms on the lakes are less frequent and severe, and the summer loading has gone into effect. The ship rides low in the water. Only the top Plimsoll mark on the vessel's side is visible above the water line—one of the three parallel dashes painted on the ship's side which always puzzle the landsman. The other two are drowned by the 16,000 tons we are carrying down on this summer voyage. These marks were named for Samuel Plimsoll, a member of the British Parliament who sponsored the legislation which limits the draft to which a ship may be loaded. They are located at a certain distance below the strength deck of the ship, known to shipbuilders as the freeboard. The lowest dash is the winter line; it represents the draft of the cargo to be hauled by this ship after November 1 and before April 15. The middle line shows the load limit for the intermediate seasons from April 16 to May 15, and from September 16 to October 31. The top line is the summer limit when less freeboard is required. American vessels have conformed to the rules formulated by the London

International Load Line Conference in 1930 since their ratification by the United States in February 1931. Each vessel is given a load-line certificate every five years by the American Bureau of Shipping or Lloyd's Register of Shipping. The Lake Carriers' Association has certain rules of its own for the Great Lakes.

Our vessel, on solid and even keel, passes quickly by the yellow brick acreage of the United States Marine Hospital, maintained primarily for American sailors, and the lighthouse on Windmill Point. The forty-two-foot octagonal steel tower is now reflecting the sun, but at night its 12,000-candle-power lantern will give out three flashes every ten seconds, each flash of one-second duration, as a warning to ships moving in and out of Lake St. Clair. We keep to starboard of Peach Island Light and head for Belle Isle. The river between Detroit and the island is narrow and generally shallow above the bridge, but it accommodates docks and piers for yachts and boats, the Fairview pumping station and the Naval Armory. The big ships use the wide Canadian channel to the south of Belle Isle. As we turn at Peach Island to enter the channel, the industrial east end of Detroit, dominated by the great pile of the Chrysler and Hudson plants, spreads out its impressive view. But we shift our gaze toward the sylvan playground island in the river, and the Livingstone Memorial Lighthouse on the tip of the south arm of the lagoon.

Even the voyage-jaded lake wheelsmen admire this light and the man whose memory it perpetuates. It is placed so that it looks straight up the channel toward Front Light. The bronze lantern on its fifty-eight-foot Georgia-marble shaft flashes every ten seconds at night a white light visible for fifteen miles, squarely abaft the beam from the pilothouses of freighters coming down the channel. It was erected by the Lake Carriers' Association and citizens of Detroit and dedicated in 1930. At its base in bronze is the portrait of the late William Livingstone (1844-1925), long-time president of the Association. He had lived in Detroit for seventy-five years, and was one of its most active and public-spirited citizens. No man of this golden age of the Great Lakes covered by his lifetime was more devoted to the development of the waterways than was William Livingstone. No one foresaw more clearly than he the future that lay before them. Throughout his life he was himself a shipowner with the lake man's point of view. He labored to keep the railroads from building bridges across the river. Railroad bridges would be unsightly and hazardous to shipping. At the same time he worked in season and out to get the Weitzel, Poe, Davis and Sabin Locks constructed at the Sault, and for the improvement of the river channels, particularly down at Lime Kiln Crossing. The great Livingstone Channel which our vessel will enter in a few minutes is a monument to his genius and influence.

Our ship slides along past the three miles of the southern shore of Belle Isle and enters the ten-mile strip of the river between Belle Isle Lighthouse and Fighting Island North Light. It is the most open section of the river, the one that charmed the eyes of La Salle and Hennepin and aroused the imagination of Cadillac. It is from 1,700 to 3,000 feet wide, with a minimum depth of about thirty feet. The current is flowing at about two knots. The two Coast Guard cutters based at Detroit, opposite the tip of the island, speed up and down the river to enforce the navigation regulations and to give assistance to any vessel or river craft in trouble. They exchange a salute with the master of the freighter or call a message to him through a megaphone as he goes by. The Post Office Department's mail boat, the *Oliver C. Mook,* runs alongside to deliver a pouch to the ship. It contains the latest lake memoranda and weather maps, and letters and telegrams for the men aboard.[2]

Two big freighters are tied up at the piers of the U. S. Rubber Products wharves, and another is edging in to the Detroit Coal and Dock Company wharf just below the Belle Isle bridge. The Grand Trunk Western Railway Company yards, wharf and car ferry fill up the four blocks of water front between Rivard and Beaubien Streets. The *City of Buffalo* and the *Put-in-Bay* are docked near the foot of Randolph Street, lending grace to the dingy and rotting wharves and sheds. Piercing the skyline to the northwest are the clean and singing towers of the mid-town skyscrapers. Over at the Windsor dock is the Canadian *Hamonic* getting ready for a voyage up to Duluth and the lake head. Farther along, the ferries are loading cars at the Pere Marquette yards and setting them across the river, above

---

[2] This floating post office, the only service of its kind in the world, meets all the lake vessels day and night. Any man on the ships may be reached by letter addressed to the Detroit River Station, Detroit, Michigan. The *Mook* delivers over a million pieces of mail each year, and receives from the men on the vessels over a third of a million pieces.

the Michigan Central Railroad Tunnel, to the Canadian Railways at Windsor. The high arch of the Ambassador Bridge casts a crescent shadow across the channel. It skips lightly aft over the 600-foot length of the freighter as she glides under the bridge.

Here comes a long ship up the river as though she were heading in for the Champion Fuel Company wharf or the Rail and Waterways Coal Company wharf just below the bridge. She is already unlimbering the arm of her self-unloader. She is to our starboard. Two sharp blasts from our deep whistle tell her that we, the downbound ship, will pass to port. She answers with two blasts, and the ships slide past each other a few yards apart, but each safely on course out of the other's path. On the Ontario side, largely monopolized by five big coal companies, freighters are docked under the elevators and unloaders.

We are now passing the vast concentration of industry around the mouth of River Rouge. Traffic on the river grows more congested. The stacks of the Detroit Edison Company and the flat domes of the oil companies' tanks glare in the sun. Gaseous gray smoke drifts from the Solvay Process Company down toward Zug Island. The ore freighter ahead of us puts in at the docks of the Great Lakes Steel Corporation at the mouth of the River Rouge where a self-unloader is pouring out a stream of sand onto the wharf. Smoke and steam rise from the enormous waste bed, and a yellowish-gray trickle of waste product oozes through the ugly, barren dike, leaving in its wake a solidified cataract repulsive to both nose and eyes. Signal blasts and answers come from the ships ahead and from those entering or leaving the River Rouge and the Short Cut Rouge Canal which lead to the Ford plants three miles up the river.

Like the other rivers around Lake Erie, the Rouge describes a huge S before it enters the Detroit. After flowing sluggishly down from the Ford plants to within half a mile of the Detroit, it almost turns on itself, bends back to the north for nearly a mile, then twists sharply again to the east to proceed another mile before reluctantly joining the Detroit River. This unscientific channel-making, for which the hand of Nature is notorious, was an annoyance and a challenge to modern engineering. When Henry Ford built his River Rouge plants, he proceeded at once to improve it. He had a deep canal dredged straight through to the Detroit River from the first turn at the base of the S. It made a delta of about 400 acres of land which is now known as Zug Island. It is exclusively industrial.

The old oxbow loop of the River Rouge is only about eighteen feet deep, but the canal and the river above it are twenty-one feet. The big freighters go up the three-mile channel to the turning basin, or to the two giant wharves on either side of the canal at Dearborn with coke, ore and limestone for the Ford plants. Here are the Ford blast furnaces, cement plant, soybean plant, glass plant, tire factory, coke ovens and by-products plant—all linked by the River Rouge channel and the Short Cut Canal with the Great Lakes waterways and the cheap shipping lanes of the world. Also up this channel go the tankers to the Standard Oil and the Texas Company wharves at the head of the Short Cut, and to the Shell Petroleum Company wharf halfway up the river. Other vessels carrying varied cargoes are bound up to the Peerless Cement Corporation, the Detroit Sulphite Pulp & Paper Company, the U. S. and the American Gypsum Companies, and other industries located for convenience on this waterway. The river is marked with spars and buoys, and the entrance to the canal is charted by an Outer and an Inner Light.

Our freighter moves at an even speed right on down past the busy Ecorse shipyards of the Great Lakes Engineering Works near the upper end of ten-mile-long Fighting Island—a useless marsh shaped like a map of Italy. We turn almost due south into Fighting Island Channel. The Michigan Alkali Company wharf juts out on the rounded bulge of the industrial city of Wyandotte, where Eber Brock Ward built his furnace, now a center for making soap, salt and soda. Halfway down the channel, the river splits again to form Grosse Isle. It is very narrow and shallow on the Michigan side— only twelve feet deep from the north end of the island to Trenton, and six feet from Trenton to Lake Erie. Someday the Federal project to deepen it to twenty-one feet in a channel 250 feet wide will be completed, and this shore will add its length to the twenty-two miles of slips, wharves and piers that now constitute the port of Detroit. Pending that day the lower reaches of the river remain undeveloped on the west, and ships must keep to the east of Grosse Isle.

The island is cool and inviting on a June day. It has lost none of the charm which caused Hennepin to describe it and Cadillac to covet it. George Croghan, who looked it over when he went out

DETROIT INSTITUTE OF ARTS

BUFFALO HISTORICAL SOCIETY

By courtesy of Buffalo Chamber of Commerce

NIAGARA FALLS IN WINTER

to Detroit shortly after its surrender by the French, said it was the finest island he had ever seen, but he could not take it for fear people would say he was neglecting his duty for "land jobbing." He recommended it to Sir William Johnson, and offered to get it for him if His Honor would care for a small estate in these parts. Sir William did not choose to have it. Alexander and William Macomb, merchants at Detroit, did; they got possession of it in 1776, and placed tenants on it. It was often molested during the wars, but its pastoral quietude has generally continued since the days when Perry's ships sailed up the river in pursuit of the fleeing forces of General Procter. We glimpse the fine homes of its present inhabitants as we sail by, and see the airplanes circling to land at the Grosse Isle Airport, maintained by the United States Government in connection with its naval base on the south end of the island.

The Fighting Island Channel through which we have been steaming among the islands was deepened to twenty-two feet, widened to 800 feet and opened to traffic in April 1915. Outside the channel the river is in many places only two to four feet deep. In fact the art of channel construction and of setting aids to navigation reaches its intricate perfection in this and the lower section of the Detroit River through which some 30,000 vessels of every type and description pass each navigation season. They are checked by the Westcott Marine Reporting Agency at the Livingstone Channel Lighthouse. We are now meeting a great many of them. Some of them have come up the St. Lawrence River Canals, Detroit-bound with sugar, rice, twine, cod-liver oil, chemicals and pickled fish. Others have come from the New York Barge Canal with gasoline and oil, sulphur and rubber, phosphates and coal tar, pineapples and wood pulp, automobile parts and tons of postal cards. We sight the *Dolomite IV*, a motor ship of revolutionary design, the first nickel-lined freighter for carrying gasoline, kerosene and caustic sodas. It is cause for wonder how so many vessels all bound on separate errands can move so effortlessly in such cramped space without running aground or jamming in collision. They rarely do either, for their movements are meticulously organized and co-ordinated.

As we have been coming down the river our freighter has had in her pilothouse the most complete and up-to-the-minute information about everything pertaining to navigation. The master could inspect the detailed charts furnished by the United States Lake Survey and the Hydrographic Office at Detroit if he did not already know them by heart. He knows with scarcely a glance at Mamajuda Light that he is opposite Point Hennepin and that just a mile and a half farther south he will turn into Ballard Reef. He has been getting radio weather service over the ship's receiver. The broadcasts of the United States Weather Bureau, giving weather information and warnings, have been coming in regularly. They have told the captain the present and the forecast velocity and direction of the winds. This information is especially important on the Detroit River. A high east wind will raise the level of western Lake Erie, a gale from the west will lower it, the draft in the Detroit River will be altered and the load limit affected. A change of level as high as six feet within eight hours has been recorded. During a heavy blizzard in January 1939 the river actually flowed backward for several hours. The depth of the water in these lower river channels determines for many ships the size of the load they can carry. On September 25, 1941, the water at the north end of the Livingstone Channel was seventeen feet, four inches, and an even seventeen feet at the Detroit River Light. Our freighter can get this information at any time by calling the Westcott office. A short-wave receiver was installed by this service in 1939 to aid navigation in this narrow bottleneck. This knowledge is very important to freighters moving through the channel with but a few inches to spare between their keels and the rocky channel floor; they are loaded with care and run at reduced speed because even moderate speed will cause these long narrow ships to squat in the water several inches at the stern.

Our freighter has been loaded, of course, with all these facts and forecasts in mind, and she turns with confidence south-southeast into the Ballard Reef Channel. In the old days this was one of the dangerous sections of the river. Silt and drift had accumulated on the rock bottom and reduced the depth of the main current to about ten feet. We slip along through a straight twenty-six-foot channel, headed toward the Upper Entrance Light where the Livingstone and Amherstburg Channels join. The river broadens between Grosse Isle and Amherstburg to a width of almost two miles. It is obstructed with islands and shoals. One-way traffic is maintained.

Upbound ships keep close to the Ontario shore and pass between Amherstburg and Bois Blanc Island. Downbound ships use the Livingstone Channel which cuts a straight line for seven miles through the shallows east of Stony Island and west of Bois Blanc.

We turn at the upper entrance and begin passage through the channel. We are now in one of the many marvels of channel-building on the Great Lakes waterways. It is not so spectacular as the locks at the Sault or on the Welland Canal, because the achievement is buried under water, the ships are not lifted and lowered, and the surface is serene as though the passageway had always been there. Until early in the present century this seven-mile strip of river from Ballard Reef to Bar Point was only eight to ten feet deep. Ships were crowded into the narrow passage east of Bois Blanc. William Livingstone, for whom the channel is named, was one of the prime movers to get this passageway cleared. The work has been expensive and has required years of constant labor. And the work is never done. As we have already observed, the development of lake commerce and shipbuilding has been so rapid from year to year that improvements are outmoded before they are completed.

The original Livingstone Channel was opened to navigation on October 19, 1912. Six miles of it go through a rock cut. A cofferdam had to be constructed so that holes could be drilled in the solid rock, filled with dynamite, and the rock blown loose. Over 25,000 holes were bored in one working year. By 1912 the channel was 300 feet wide through six miles of this cut, 800 feet wide from there to Lake Erie, and 22 to 23 feet deep. But if a ship ran aground or a collision occurred in so narrow a channel, there was danger of a blockade. When World War I ended, the Congress made a new appropriation to widen the channel to 450 feet through the cut. In 1922 another large appropriation was added, and at the close of the 1925 season the job was again complete, except for eight days of work. The enlarged channel was opened early in 1926. Additional improvements are made every year, and the end is not in sight.

A five-minute interval between ships must be kept in the Livingstone Channel. A semaphore on the light station signals that we have been in the passage for five minutes and that the way is clear for the next ship to enter. It happens to be the *Irving S. Olds;* she seems to fill up the space between the buoys, and her texas house seems to be skimming along on the edge of the dikes. We keep our space and distance. A dozen beacons mark the way. They rest on concrete piers, half of which were laid on the solid rock floor while the channel was dry in the cofferdam. Four others were built inside the cofferdam and later floated out and lowered to prepared positions where the rock had been dredged clean and stone and gravel were spread over it to make it level. The twenty-two-by-thirty-five-foot piers have icebreakers pointing upstream, and they are protected by steel platings against the terrific force of the ice jams.

We proceed at reduced speed, but the heavily laden carrier slides its 600-foot length along with as much ease and poise as a transatlantic liner hurrying through the Gulf Stream on a calm afternoon. We glance across the trees and summer homes on Bois Blanc to the steamers going up past the Amherstburg water front. The Westcott Agency reports us as we go by. The master has been standing calmly on the bridge observing casually the rows of buoys that line the channels. The buoys on these shipping lanes, with all their sizes and shapes and all their red and black and white colors and stripes, are confusing to the landsman. But each has its meaning. The fundamental regulations governing them were passed by the Congress back in 1850. As you come into a channel the red buoys with even numbers are to starboard, the black ones with odd numbers are to port. Those with red and black horizontal stripes are the "fairway buoys"; they indicate shoals with deep channels on each side. Those bearing black and white vertical stripes are planted right in the channel. Iron buoys, set at important points, have distinctive shapes to make identification easy. The red cone-shaped ones, often with a red light on their top, are the nun buoys. The black cylindrical ones with a white or green light on their flat tops are the cans. Taller shapes that stand high out of the water are now in general use. They are intricately constructed and are compartmented to withstand damage and remain afloat. Many of them are equipped with whistles or with bells for fog warning; the slightest movement of the water sets them ringing. The Livingstone Channel is marked with spar and gas buoys through its entire length—a gas buoy, then a spar, each quarter of a mile along the route. Gas for the lights is stored in a container within the buoy and is piped up to the burner. The Lighthouse Tenders service them—take them out, re-

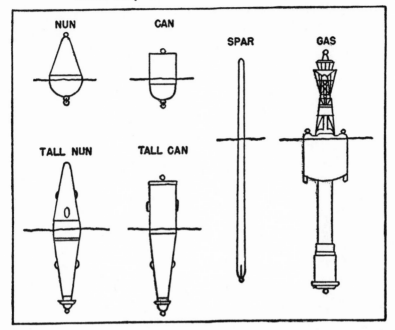

paint them and repair them at regular intervals through the year.

Opposite Bar Point we ease out of the Livingstone Channel into the common shipway that leads to Detroit River Light. Upbound ships, light or loaded with coal, are spaced to port, and are swinging in, one behind the other, to enter the Amherstburg Channel. We head for the light. The water outside the dredged channel is only a few feet deep because this part of the river was used as a dumping ground when the main channel was improved, and deepened through the widening mouth until it reaches the corresponding contour in Lake Erie. Detroit River Lighthouse stands in the middle in a normal twenty-two feet of water. Its light is visible from the wheelhouse for fifteen miles out on the lake. The radio direction finder guides the bulk fleet in the darkest night, and the master can tell at any point how far he has traveled. We swing to port at the lighthouse and follow the marked course that leads out to the twenty-six-foot contour of the lake. And at last we are in free deep water. We turn to port once more and set course almost due east for Pelee and the wharves in the crooked Cuyahoga at Cleveland.

Chapter 30

Ships for World War II

To the superficial view Lorain, a city of 45,000 people, is not
much to look at; its homes are plain and its business houses
are not impressive. The thin gash of the Black River estuary
appears deceptively insignificant. It is only 250 feet wide and about
three miles long. By night the vast acreage of the National Tube,
where the pipe for the Big Inch was rolled and bored, sends up into
the sky a flaming red glow like a sunset over Inferno. It makes a
fantastic backdrop for the dark river bed between the plant and
the Erie Street Bridge. And just above the bridge, glowing with a
thousand lights, are the yards of the American Ship Building Company, largest on the Great Lakes, where from 3,000 to 4,000 men and
women worked day and night to turn out ships for the war. Admiral
King himself came to this war port in August 1942 and again in
March 1944 to attend the launchings. And on Sunday, September
17, 1944, the city celebrated Ship Builders' Day.

The U.S.S. *Embattle* was launched under the spray of a bottle of
Lake Erie champagne. Twenty thousand people jammed the yards
to watch this 180-foot mine sweeper slide sideways into the slip.
The wife of a shipwright who had been with the company for forty-
seven years christened the ship. A septuagenarian French Canadian,
Joe Couture, salty and proud, supervised the launching. He too had
been with the company for almost half a century. I went below the
platform to talk to him and see the four guillotines fall on the re-
straining hawsers. Couture's face was aglow. As the battalion of
workers drove wedges under the *Embattle's* hull to shift her weight
from the timbers to the ropes, she quivered and moved an inch and
a half on the greased ways, pulling against the four big hawsers.

"She's alive She's crawling!" Joe Couture exclaimed in excited
accents. "That's the way I like to see 'em. Rarin' to go. I don't
let 'em loose unless they are alive and pullin'."

She was indeed alive. On signal from the launching platform an electric button was pushed, four big knives fell on the hawsers, snipping them like threads, and the ship raced down with a beautiful splash into the water.

"That's where we like to see them," said William Douglas, shipwright and head of the electrical engineering department. "A ship is like a person to us. We work at her for months. Then comes the big day when she slides down into her natural element. To see her rolling free in the slip is just like seeing a newborn babe. She is a live thing. It's hard for other people to understand how a shipbuilder feels about his ship when he sees her afloat for the first time and knows what all he has put into her."

In the afternoon of Ship Builders' Day the frigate U.S.S. *Lorain,* completed, tested on Lake Erie and now tied up in the Black River harbor, was formally turned over to the Navy and received officially by Vice-Admiral Vickery, "the greatest shipbuilder since Noah."[1] Admiral Vickery then turned the ship over to Vice-Admiral Waesche of the Coast Guard. The shipwrights who had built the warship paraded through the city. The Hungarians and the Poles among them marched in groups past the reviewing stand and joined their 20,000 fellow citizens who crowded the bank of the river to witness the ceremony. Most of them had bought war bonds which gave them permission to go aboard the *Lorain* in special recognition of the city. Lorain inspected its ship and was pleased. Like the other Lake Erie towns, it was conscious of the fact that it was no longer an inland port, but a war-coast city.

For that trim gray warship, so neat and graceful under the bright September sun, which Lorain had built and which bore its name, would depart within a few hours across the peaceful expanse of Lake Erie for the war on the high seas. These builders knew that she was carrying among her crew 161 boys from Ohio. They felt a solemn responsibility for the ship that was peculiarly their own.

There are fourteen important shipyard towns on the Great Lakes and five of them are on Lake Erie. The scene at Lorain might have been Buffalo, in the harbor at Ashtabula, in the long narrow yards

---

[1] Robert Godley's phrase. Vice-Admiral Howard L. Vickery is also a Lake Erie man, born in 1892 at Bellevue, Ohio, a dozen miles south of Sandusky. This great construction engineer and naval officer had the vision, the courage and the energy to see through the vast shipbuilding program of the U. S. Maritime Commission in World War II.

in the Flats at the mouth of the Cuyahoga at Cleveland, or on the River Rouge at Ecorse, Michigan. For the spirit and the determined achievement at Lorain are typical of all the shipbuilding cities.

When World War II finally reached America, we were desperately short on shipping. The fleet was inadequate and the Merchant Marine had been scrapped. But the nature of the war to be fought in Africa, Europe and the far Pacific demanded such a bridge of ships as the world had never before even thought possible.

Where were these ships to come from?

Many of them were to come from Lake Erie, where the Great Lakes Engineering Works with yards at River Rouge and Ashtabula, and the American Ship Building Company with yards at Lorain, Cleveland and Buffalo, had kept a flourishing shipbuilding tradition in season and out, serving the unrivaled Great Lakes transportation system. Careful and foresighted management of these companies had brought them out of World War I and through the idle depression years in a state of readiness for the national emergency. They promptly turned their resources to the urgent needs of war. Eight thousand men worked day and night in these yards to turn out the needed ships. They overcame the obstacles of winter blizzards, sub-zero weather, frozen lakes, slips iced over to a depth of four feet, and the constricted passages cut from the lakes to the sea. They built ships for Great Britain and Canada. They built and delivered the ships for the Great Lakes division of the Maritime Commission that was set up in Chicago in May 1942. They rushed to completion sixteen big freighters, as we have noted, to enlarge the ore fleet and help bring down the raw material from Lake Superior to Lake Erie to forge the weapons of war. By the end of 1944 the Great Lakes yards had produced about 350 ships of various types for the war and 200 knocked-down barges; a large proportion of them were built on Lake Erie. And the uncompleted contracts called for $100,-000,000 worth of ships yet to be delivered.

All through the summer and early autumn of 1944 these contracts were being fulfilled. Lorain and Cleveland were rushing ships to completion before the ice closed over in December. The Cleveland yard, for seventeen years not a building but a repair yard, converted quickly to the construction needs of the nation. The big Lorain yards surpassed themselves. The harbors and slips were bright with the yellow hulls of mine sweepers that had been launched and lay at anchor while they got their fittings. As soon as one was off the ways, another keel was laid. The yards built net tenders for the Navy. The small Buffalo yards turned out sixteen tugs and lighters. Cleveland built seven and Lorain built six handsome $3,000,000 frigates to fight the submarine menace on the Atlantic and to protect the convoys on the vast shipping lanes of the United States at war. The American Ship Building Company converted the *Seeandbee* and *Greater Buffalo* into the aircraft carriers *Wolverine* and *Sable*. Their yards welded ships and riveted ships and kept the ore fleet in repair. At the same time this company sent many of its best-trained men to New Orleans to create the Delta shipyards to build Liberty ships, tankers and colliers for the Maritime Commission.

It was a record that surpassed the great achievement of World War I when this Cleveland company built 236 freighters (including a dozen tugboats) on the lakes and voluntarily renegotiated its contracts with the United States Government to retain only a normal profit.

Smaller yards were doing their part in the stupendous shipbuilding program. The Matthews Corporation of Port Clinton, the Erie Concrete and Steel Supply Company of Erie, and the Bison Shipbuilding Corporation and the Richardson Boat Corporation of Tonawanda on the Niagara all engaged in building small craft for the Navy. The Stadium Yacht Basin at Cleveland built wooden-hulled mine sweepers for the Navy; expert wooden shipbuilders, who for years had practiced their craft only by hewing beams for recreation rooms and clubs, came back to the yards with ax and adz to turn out boats which the Navy prized highly for the beauty of their trim and their fine woodwork. The Toledo Shipbuilding Company built the Coast Guard icebreaker *Mackinaw* to help lengthen the shipping season by opening channels through the ice. In addition to its twin propellers aft it has additional screws forward to suck the water from under the ice which is to be crushed and broken. Although Frank Kirby of Detroit had suggested this Russian and Scandinavian type of icebreaker years ago, its radical design was not adapted to the Great Lakes until World War II. It cost several million dollars and required over two years to build. The need for barges and landing craft was so great that the Warren City Manufacturing Company some miles inland from the lake constructed them and shipped them to water on freight cars.

But the job was by no means over when the ships and craft were constructed. Getting them out of Lake Erie into the oceans is almost as much of an adventure as building them in the heart of America a thousand miles from the sea.

The warships leave the Lake Erie yards ready to fight. They are fully equipped right down the voluminous dossier of specifications from guns and ammunition to scrub brushes, dishcloths, paper clips, colored pencils and boxing gloves. The mine sweepers, 180 or 220 feet long, enter the Atlantic by way of the Welland and the St. Lawrence River Canals. Lorain-built mine sweepers helped clear the path for the landings in North Africa, Salerno and on the Normandy beaches. They are the little ships which go in first on a set course to open the mine field. They cannot maneuver or dodge shells and air attacks. They go straight forward—or not at all. The builders are proud of their record of accomplishment.

The frigates make a different journey to the sea—one that would have delighted Jolliet. They go down the Mississippi. They are 306 feet long and cannot, therefore, go through the small locks on the St. Lawrence River. That is what the St. Lawrence Deep Waterway controversy is all about. Instead they go out through the curving channel at the mouth of the Black or the Cuyahoga River, past the white Coast Guard station to the big lighthouse on the breakwater, then turn northward into Lake Erie. Three days they sail—up Lake Erie, the Detroit River, Lake St. Clair, St. Clair River and Lake Huron, through the Straits of Mackinac and down to Chicago. There they join the caravan that forms to make the ten-day run to the gulf via the Chicago Drainage Canal, the Des Plaines, the Illinois and the Mississippi Rivers. Traffic is rerouted in Chicago, up go the bridges, and down the passage past the Michigan Avenue skyscrapers, past the Merchandise Mart and across the plains go the Navy's ships under their own power. The masts are specially constructed to fold down on the deck to clear the low bridges, and the hulls are made to receive pontoons at Lockport where the draft is only nine feet. They lose only one day in getting their pontoons and shifting ballast. The pontoons are specially built steel drums twenty feet long and nine feet in diameter. They are welded and bolted to the stern, two on each side, to lift the ship to the required depth. Then a small river towboat is lashed to the frigate and pushes the ship into the 600-foot lock where it is lowered forty-one feet into the Des Plaines River. Then they begin their incongruous journey through the Illinois corn and wheat fields to the winding Mississippi near St. Louis, and down to the gulf. At New Orleans the pontoons are removed and sent back to Lockport to get another frigate. Fast, maneuverable and deadly, these frigates patrol the sea lanes, hovering over submarines, loosing depth charges on them or fighting duels with them with their deck guns. They played a brilliant part, along with their sister ships, the Canadian corvettes, in overcoming the submarine menace that threatened to strangle the life line between America and Great Britain.

By these ingenious methods, and through the labor and skill of lake shipwrights, the building resources of this region were linked to the total productivity of the nation. About sixty percent of all the materials entering into this vast construction—engines, winches, hatch beams, searchlights, radio equipment, ranges and a thousand other smaller items—came from the lakes in the form of raw materials, fabricated material or assembled units. They were the heart of the arsenal. The Lake Erie warships were but one more sinew in the fighting strength of these waterways.

At the top center of its Honor Roll of World War II on the public square, Lorain placed an autographed picture of Admiral Ernest J. King, USN, Commander in Chief of the Navy and Chief of Naval Operations. For the admiral was born in this lake-shore city November 23, 1878, and graduated from its high school in 1897. And this city, which has survived the battering of floods in its river and the furious devastation of a tornado to rise from its ruins a better town, has made of its Honor Roll a symbol of Lorain's achievement in the war and of its pride in helping in a small way to provide its native son with the largest and most powerful fleet ever assembled by any nation.

Chapter 31

The Canadian Shore

THERE are no important Canadian towns on the Lake Erie shore. The coast line itself is not so well favored there as it is on the American side, but that is not the primary difference. The American cities have spent millions of dollars to clear sand bars from their harbors and deepen them to accommodate their ships. Canadian cities could have done likewise if they had faced the same economic necessity or had had the same economic opportunities. They had no ore and no coal, and no future in steel. They were neither manufacturing cities nor terminal ports. It was different down on Lake Ontario where Hamilton and Toronto occupy a commanding position comparable to that of Cleveland and Buffalo on Lake Erie. The arrowhead of Old Ontario is a land of orchards and gardens, of tobacco farms and dairies, of woolen mills, canneries and small manufactures, not of heavy industries demanding transportation of bulk freight. Its needs are served by a network of railroads and trucking highways. Its centers of population are inland country towns serving a rural people. Its outlet ports are at Windsor and Sarnia on the Detroit and St. Clair Rivers and Hamilton and Toronto on Lake Ontario. Moreover, these two great cities on the Lower Lake are linked by short rail lines across the neck of the arrowhead with the Georgian Bay ports of Owen Sound, Collingwood and Port Nicoll, by-passing Lake Erie. The Canada Steamship Lines operates the largest single fleet in number of vessels on the Great Lakes—over a hundred ships of all kinds. Its home office is in Montreal. The passenger ships and package freighters of its Northern Navigation Division operate from Windsor north; they do not even enter Lake Erie. Its bulk freighters (and it has some mammoth ships) do not stop on Lake Erie, unless they have a cargo for an American port; they sail straight across the lake to Port Colborne and pass through the Welland Canal.

This quiet north shore, however, has its own scenic and human fascination. Old Fort Erie, joined to Buffalo by the six graceful arches of the Peace Bridge over the Black Rock Canal and the Niagara River, is a memorial to the era of strife that has passed and the years of peace that have come. The shore line from Erie to Point Abino is contoured into a series of pleasant bays and inlets. So many Buffalo people have summer homes along the shore that the region might almost be regarded as a suburb of the Gateway City. A half-dozen beaches, the amusement park at Crystal Beach and the Buffalo Canoe Club under the protection of Point Abino provide a recreation ground for Buffalo citizens whose own beachless water front is lined with industries. Commercial Port Colborne is the Lake Erie entrance to the Welland Ship Canal, that twenty-seven-mile, $120,000,000, water bridge around Niagara Falls. Over 7,000,000 tons of cargo pass through the port each year, and the ships that carry it through this main street of the town and the lift bridge that rises in front of them and lowers behind them lend color and stirring movement to the little town of 6,500 souls.

You would never suspect by looking at the Grand River at Port Maitland that it was once a waterway for steamships as far up as Brantford. The timber on the thin, sandy land has been cut off, and the river bed has filled up and choked to death with eroded soil. The feeder for the Welland Canal cuts east from Port Maitland. The irregular shore on west to the charming fishing village of Nanticoke and Port Dover on the Lynn River is escalloped into a series of promontories: Grand Point, Evans Point, Miller Point, Hoover Point and Peacock Point. The conservation-minded Ontario government has one of its game sanctuaries on Nanticoke Creek, utilizing this wasteland for one of the largest heronries in the country. Huge flocks of these long-legged birds wade about in the refuge ponds, crane their long necks, flap their large wings and reproduce their kind.

The Lake Erie shore is high to the west of Nanticoke. It is barely visible from the shipping lanes on the lake, and the King's Highway 3 keeps a few miles to the north; but a scenic road, known locally as the Lake Shore Road, runs along the high shoulder commanding a beautiful and quiet view of the lake all the way into Port Dover. Dover's nine-mile-long beach—wide, sandy and safe, and one of the few inviting beaches on Lake Erie—has become a resort center on the north shore. Cottages line the lake front and children play in the sand. A cairn in the village park reminds visitors that Sir Isaac

Brock gathered his troops here for the attack on General Hull and the capture of Detroit. The white marble cross reminds us again that Dollier and Galinée wintered here in 1669-1670. We pay our respects to these great men of old, and feel sure that their spirits, if they ever revisit this favored spot, take the same pleasure we do in watching the ten steam tugs and the fifteen gasoline boats of the fishing fleet put out in the early morning, and in viewing the acres of Ivey's greenhouses when they are a fairyland of flowers in bloom; for Ivey's is one of the largest rose-growers in all Canada.

Port Ryerse, like so many of the Lake Erie shore towns, was prosperous during the first years of the nineteenth century. It was the head of the London District, it had a courthouse, a post office and many thriving businesses. The Americans burned the courthouse when they raided the Long Point region in the War of 1812, the timber was cut off, the land was poor, and the Canadians turned their backs on Lake Erie and moved inland a few miles. Port Dover's neighboring Normandale has survived in a modest way. Its handsome location on the lake has long attracted summer visitors. Ontario maintains one of its largest fish hatcheries here. (A bronze plaque on the building recalls the Van Normans and their iron smelter and foundry which we have already noticed.) People go to Normandale in the spring especially to see and smell the blossoms of the famous peach orchards of Grant Fox, the great horticulturist who demonstrated that this sandy soil would grow luscious fruit if treated scientifically. Other men have followed his example. They have converted much of Norfolk County into orchards—5,000 acres in apples. The school children go into the orchards in late summer to help gather the crop. The fruit is shipped to all parts of Canada, some to the United States, and quantities to England. Just back of the lake are celery and vegetable gardens, beet farms and extensive strawberry beds, and dairies of fine Holsteins, Jerseys and accredited Ayrshires. Simcoe, and to some extent Port Dover, live by processing this produce. The Canadian Canners of Simcoe is one of the largest in all Canada. High-quality jams from the St. Williams Fruit Preservers, and pickles from the Lealand Company are shipped all over the world. The Norfolk Fruit Growers' Association distributes thousands of barrels of apples and hampers of peaches, and quick-freezes strawberries. The American Can Company has an enormous plant in Simcoe to provide containers for the canneries. And the men in the far north woods, opening their cans of Simcoe vegetables, also praise this town for the "Alligators" built by the West-Peachey concern: steamboats for the northern terrain which travel on land as well as on water. Likely as not, the woodsmen are wearing Don-a-Brook jackets, made by the Brook Woolen Company, and gloves from the Simcoe Mitt and Glove factory, and are using Drimilk from the Simcoe City Dairy.

These same woodsmen, like many another Canadian, are probably smoking tobacco grown in this region and flue-cured at Delhi. Some 40,000 acres in the Delhi district alone are now planted in tobacco. It all began in 1923 when H. A. Freeman and W. L. Pelton, after much experimentation, planted twenty acres in tobacco on a farm near Lynedoch. The crop was excellent. The idea spread. Other farmers turned to tobacco raising. Within fifteen years over 60,000 Ontario acres were green in summer with tobacco plants, and thousands of farmers were praying that windstorms and hail would not scourge them and that Lake Erie would hold off the frosts until the crop was gathered. In recent years the small farms have been bought up and turned into big plantations under company control. Thousands of immigrants from Belgium, Holland and Hungary have come in to work in the fields. The Imperial Tobacco Company at Delhi receives, grades and packs most of the crop. This vast new industry is made possible by the peculiar geography of the Ontario arrowhead; for Simcoe and Delhi are actually farther south than Buffalo, the tobacco plantations are on the same parallel as the Connecticut tobacco district, and the presence of the Great Lakes tempers the climate.

Much of the land around Long Point was a desolate sight a generation ago. The thick stands of white pine were cut off and the sand lands were cleared for agriculture. The results were inevitable: the thin soil was quickly exhausted, sand blew over the fields, sifted out from the roots of stumps, exposed barren limestone outcropping and drifted over the roads. Farms were abandoned and the buildings fell into ruins. Ontario decided to educate its people in conservation and to reclaim its land. It created a Forestry Department at the Ontario Agricultural College at Guelph in 1904, and established a nursery to supply farmers with seedlings for replanting the waste portions of their farms. Within four years the nursery was distributing 400,000 seedlings each year. Then the government began searching for the best spot for a big-scale forest station. They found it in Norfolk County along the barren shore of Lake Erie. The climate was ideal, and the region all the way to Port Burwell consisted largely of abandoned or submarginal farms banded by the sand belt. A vast government forest station was established at St. Williams. From its seedling beds, under the direction of Frank Newman, millions upon millions of young trees, mostly evergreens, have been grown and shipped out for planting on the wastes.

It is now a big-scale industry, as spectacular in its way as a 640-foot ore freighter under the Huletts at Conneaut. This Norfolk Station has an area of 3,800 acres; over 100 acres are in nurseries, and the rest are demonstration forest plantations. The demonstration tracts of from five to a few hundred acres show how to protect city watersheds, how to reclaim waste areas along the highways and how to stop drifting sand. Special school plantations have been developed; several hundred schools now have forest plots of from one to ten acres; and the Boy Scouts have two large forests where they have planted over a million trees. This admirable work has transformed sand lots into parks, and deserted fields into magnificent cathedral-like forests of red pine. And it has made the Lake Erie shore from Turkey Point to Burwell a region of beauty. The Houghton Sandhills remain to contrast with the reforested fields. These hills rise 230 feet above Lake Erie. The southwest winds blow almost ceaselessly up over them from the lake, piling the sand higher on the ridge, and pushing it slowly over the remains of the original forest. Much of the forest is already buried under the dune, and as the sand filters farther to the northeast it stifles the trees, leaving their dead trunks and branches stark and pathetic against the evening sun.

This Long Point region is also a favorite haunt of sportsmen. From the reforested parks on Turkey Point you look out to the long arm of Long Point, with the bay at your feet, Long Point Park in the distance and flocks of migratory birds black over the marshes. Most of the Long Point marshes are owned by private companies, and the general public is excluded from shooting there. But the open water on the north side is free and duck hunters make use of it during the season.

The Lake Erie coast region from Port Burwell west has not altered significantly since we last viewed it in the days of Talbot. London and St. Thomas, Chatham and Tilbury—all from ten to twenty-five miles inland—are the trade centers and the manufacturing towns. They communicate by railroads and highways rather than by the lake, though a few bulk freighters come in to the improved ports with coal for the Ontario cities. Rondeau Park, Erie Beach Park and Point Pelee are recreation centers. People come to the cool beaches from the hot summer interior towns and from Detroit during the vacation season; they come by automobile, not by boat. The good land north of the shore is largely given over to orchards, dairies and some tobacco farms.

The Windsor peninsula was almost cut off from the rest of the tip of the arrowhead by Lake St. Clair. Forty miles east of the Detroit River, the neck of this peninsula is only about fifteen miles wide between Port Alma on Lake Erie and the bend in Lake St. Clair just north of Tilbury at the mouth of the Thames. The effect is to isolate Essex County somewhat and to gear it toward Detroit-Windsor. When the Prince of Wales made his triumphal visit to Canada in 1860, he crossed Old Ontario by special train (entertained by a German band from Buffalo) through London to Sarnia. There he rode in a carriage drawn by four bay horses and attended by gentlemen and ladies on horseback, and went sailing on the St. Clair River. But he returned by rail through Brantford to Port Colborne without visiting Windsor, Detroit or Essex County.

We note the geographical peculiarity of this southwesternmost tip of Ontario, and we recall to mind that Detroit was the city on the straits founded by the French, settled and developed by the French, and the center of their life in the West for almost a century. They cleared and planted farms along the river and the shores of Lake St. Clair, but Detroit remained, as a matter of course, their market town. When the British took over, little was changed except the flag and the administration. Detroit was still the key town in western Ontario. But when the British yielded it to the Americans, the river became an international boundary line, and the Ontario side was, for the first time in its history, cut off from the mother town. The British established headquarters at Amherstburg down the river, and built Fort Malden, but that town was a military convenience and not a commercial port or administrative capital. The Canadian bank of the Detroit River never competed against the giant city on the American side.

British and Canadian citizens lamented this fact. Everyone who sailed up the river commented on the contrast between the two shores. Joseph Pickering went up the river in a sailboat with some farmers with butter and cheese for sale. He described Amherstburg as a "smart, neat, French-built town. . . . The houses have long steep roofs, after the French fashion: some neat gardens round the town, enclosed with paling. . . . This place is well situated for trade, in the very mildest and southernmost part of the province . . . but it wants some enterprising spirits to make it flourish rapidly." Sandwich he found to be pleasantly situated, but "the town, on entering it, excites feelings of disappointment and disgust. There are some few good houses, surrounded by others that have the appearance of desolation and poverty, occupied apparently by a dilatory, listless set of beings; and such was the miserable state of the taverns, that we could not procure refreshments, or be accommodated with a room at any one of them." Present Windsor, then still known as the Ferry (though its official name was Richmond), was a few taverns, a few houses and a wharf.

Anna Jameson was more violent in her language and more exercised in feeling.

"I hardly know how to convey to you an idea of the difference between the two shores; it will appear to you as incredible as it is to me incomprehensible. Our shore [this is a loyal British subject speaking] is said to be the most fertile, and has been the longest settled; but to float between them (as I did today in a little canoe made of a hollow tree, and paddled by a half-breed imp of a boy)— to behold on one side a city, with its towers and spires and animated population, with villas and handsome houses stretching along the shore, and a hundred vessels or more, gigantic steamers, brigs, schooners, crowding the port, loading and unloading; all the bustle, in short, of prosperity and commerce;—and, on the other side, a little straggling hamlet, one schooner, one little wretched steamboat, some windmills, a catholic chapel or two, a supine ignorant peasantry, all the symptoms of apathy, indolence, mistrust, hopelessness!—can I, or any one, help wondering at the difference, and

asking whence it arises? . . . Is it remediable? is it a necessity? is it
a mystery? what and whence is it?—Can you tell? or can you send
some of our colonial officials across the Atlantic to behold and solve
the difficulty?"

We have suggested some of the reasons. The French population
was conservative, rooted in old traditions and content with its ways.
Detroit was filled with Americans on the make, and receiving on
its wharves each year thousands of immigrants seeking a better
world. Much of Essex County was still an Indian reservation.
Canada was controlled by the "Family Compact," a group of families
and speculators who granted themselves and their friends vast tracts
of land in Ontario. Isaac Weld, who crossed Lake Erie in 1796 and
wrote about it in a book of travels, admired the 2,000-acre estate of
"Captain E——" at Amherstburg: "it is cultivated in a style which
would not be thought meanly of even in England." Robert Hamilton acquired 200,000 acres. And we have already noted the great
estates of Talbot and Selkirk. These were samples. Poor folk found
it difficult to get enough land to make a living on. William Lyon
Mackenzie's Canadian Rebellion which broke out in 1837 (shortly
after Mrs. Jameson's visit) was designed to break this monopoly.
Detroit was a base from which the rebels (or patriots) made raids
against the Canadian shore. Their violence brought reforms. The
Earl of Durham came over from England, studied the situation and
made recommendations. Lord Elgin carried them out, broke the
Family Compact and gave Canada back to the people. The Huron
reservation along the river was purchased, the tribes moved west,
and that land was turned into farms, tobacco plantations and fine
orchards.

The shore and the towns, which pained Mrs. Jameson, improved,
though their growth has been slow. Amherstburg had a population
of 600 when she visited it; it is now a pleasant town of about 2,800.
Richmond became Windsor in honor of the accession of Queen Victoria to the throne. It was incorporated as a city in 1896, and by the
turn of the century it had a population of about 12,000. In recent
years Detroit has, as it were, spilled over the border into Windsor.
The two cities are linked by tunnels, a bridge and ferries. Windsor
is the automobile center of Canada; Ford and other American man-

ufacturers have factories there. Like its neighbor, it is noted for its great drug companies, for its paint, varnish, salt and chemical plants, for its breweries and distilleries, for its pleasant residential streets, and for the fruit, tobacco and agricultural region which it serves. In 1935 East Windsor, Walkerville and Sandwich were annexed to Windsor, forming a metropolitan city of 105,000 souls.

The most famous and most frequently visited spot on the north shore of Lake Erie is a 400-acre farm near Kingsville. As many as a thousand cars, most of them with American licenses, have been parked there along the roadside during a single day, and over 20,000 during the weeks of spring. When the first warm days of March and April come to this "Sun Parlor of Canada," as the neat town of Kingsville (population 2,300) is called, you can tell by the crowded traffic in the Detroit-Windsor Tunnel and on the Ambassador Bridge that a fascinating show is on, thirty miles to the southeast. People from all over the world have made pilgrimages to Kingsville. Prime ministers and statesmen, Henry Ford and Ty Cobb, railroad presidents and directors of museums, the famous and the humble have come here.

They come to see the world-renowned bird sanctuary of Jack Miner,[1] the man whom Irvin S. Cobb called "the greatest practical naturalist and bird-lover on the planet."

One day near the end of the last century a hunter came to Jack Miner's house. He told Jack that two flocks of wild geese, seven in one flock, eight in the other, were coming each day to feed on Cottam Plains about four miles north of Kingsville. No hunter had been able to shoot them. Perhaps Jack Miner, experienced hunter, north-woods guide and expert rifleshot, could bring one down. Miner carved some wooden decoys and went out to the field long before daybreak. He dug a foxhole in the wet ground, lined it with grass, set his decoys, lay down in the trench, covered himself with a blanket and waited. Shortly after dawn the geese came, flying high up from Lake Erie where they spent the night. Miner called, "A-honk! A-honk!" The leader of the flock answered, and flew in toward the decoys. When he saw that they were false, he shied away

---

[1] Jack Miner has written his story in his own homely language in *Jack Miner and the Birds* (Chicago, 1923).

straight over Miner's blind. Jack threw off his blanket, raised his gun and drove fourteen swan shot almost through the gander. Another shot brought down his mate. The rest of the flock flew back to Lake Erie, screaming in panic. Jack hunted geese for the next few seasons. In 1903 he saw a flock going over his house. He went out early next morning with his blanket and gun to shoot them. They stayed out of his range, but they showed no particular fear of two men on the next farm who were going out to ditch. The experience weighed on Jack's mind as he walked home empty-handed. He kept hearing the sharp, alarmed danger-cries of the leader of the flock as he recognized the hunter; he seemed to be saying, "That's our deadly enemy! Everybody get, for your lives!"

Jack had a Road-to-Damascus conversion. If these wild birds could recognize him as their enemy, would they not also recognize him as a friend? He studied the habits of the wild geese. Reading in his Bible, he came upon a passage in Deuteronomy which he thought was addressed directly to him: "If a bird's nest chance to be before thee in the way in any tree, or on the ground, whether they be young ones, or eggs, and the dam sitting upon the young, or upon the eggs, thou shalt not take the dam with the young." He put the two together, and added the experience of his years as a hunter in Ontario.

It was an unusual experience. Miner was born April 10, 1865, near Cleveland in the village of Dover Center. His father made pressed brick and tile. Jack, redheaded and freckle-faced, went to school only three months. He worked in his father's brickyard, hunted muskrats and mink, raccoons and opossums along the creeks and in the woods in the suburbs of Cleveland. He watched the great flocks of passenger pigeons fly over in the early morning. When Jack was thirteen, his father decided to move to the clay lands at Kingsville near the Detroit market. He loaded his family and their goods on two wagons and trekked round the lake to the north shore. Wild life was still abundant in the woods and among the marshes. Jack hewed white-oak railroad ties and made ax handles from second-growth hickory. He hunted far and wide. By the time he was seventeen, hunters came from great distances to get him to lead their parties. He guided expeditions into northern Quebec and Ontario. Between hunting trips he pressed brick on the old machine which they had brought from Cleveland, and which Henry Ford now has on display in his museum at Dearborn. Meanwhile the bird population declined sharply and steadily.

Then the alarmed cries of the Canadian wild gander warning his young against Jack Miner, their enemy, changed the celebrated hunter into the friend of the birds. In 1904 he bought seven wing-clipped geese from a man who had trapped them unlawfully. He brought them over to his small farm. Ten acres of it were an eye-sore, for he had stripped away the topsoil to get to the clay below. He graded up one end of this barren plot and made it into a pond, or mudhole. This was the home of the seven geese. Three years later one pair nested.

Jack had promised his neighbors that if they would not shoot at a wild goose for a while, he would bring them into his pond. They agreed. The spring of 1905 went by, but no geese came. The spring of 1906, and no geese. Spring of 1907, and still no geese. The neighbors began to laugh slyly, ask him when the geese were coming, and greet him with a "Honk!" Jack kept his peace, fed and tended his birds. But on the morning of April 2, 1908, eleven geese came down on the pond. Excitement spread through the neighborhood. The hunters came with their guns. Jack persuaded them not to shoot until the geese were settled, but then, true to his promise, he allowed them to kill a few for their tables. They shot five; the other six flew screaming back toward Lake Erie.

It was a triumph to attract this flock to the pond, but would the geese return? A year went by, and Jack scanned the skies. On Sunday morning, March 18, 1909, he was out by his pond talking to his pet geese. Suddenly they started honking and chattering. Miner looked up to the sky. There, flying in from Lake Erie, was a string of Canada geese. They answered the cries from the pond, bowed their wings, sailed over Jack's head without fear and set their black feet down in the mud of his pond. The six geese had returned, and they had brought with them twenty-six more. Jack allowed his friends to shoot ten of them; the other twenty-two remained until the end of April, then they circled high and flew off toward Hudson Bay. In early March 1910 the geese came again. For two weeks they flew in until the pond was swarming with over 400 of them. They remained through March and April and then went north. And on February 20, 1911, they arrived in such quantities over a period of three weeks that they were like a cloud over Miner's house and field and pond.

That was the beginning of the Jack Miner Bird Sanctuary and of a new career for Jack Miner. And the marvel which the thousands of visitors come to see is the spectacle of 25,000 of these shy and wayward wild geese flying over the Sanctuary, covering the sky like an umbrella and filling the air with their honking and the swishing pandemonium of their flapping wings.

The transformation of the mudhole into the present beautiful parklike Sanctuary did not occur of itself and overnight. It has been a labor of love over long years of sacrifice by a devoted man whose single-minded zeal persuaded help from others who caught something of his own vision.

It took quantities of corn to feed the wild life that came to Miner's farm. Jack raised it and fed it, and took his pay from the friendliness of the birds that ate from his hands. He spread it out on the ground at night, and the flocks came back each morning from their roosting grounds on the lake three miles away. As the news spread through the flocks and more thousands came each year, the demands on Jack's granary increased; at the height of the migratory seasons in April and late November, he spread 200 bushels of ears a day around his pond. He began to make talks about his project.

He lectured far and wide over Canada and in American cities about bird life and the work of his Sanctuary. Formally unschooled though he was, his lectures filled with birdlore and homely wisdom, and delivered with wit and the charm of his own character, won the love of children and the applause of sophisticated adults. He encouraged boys and girls to become conservationists. "If I can induce a child to build a birdhouse," he said, "that child at once becomes a conservationist, because he will naturally put up the birdhouse and not allow the bird to be harmed that is apt to build in it." He taught them the inward law of kindness. He invited them to visit his Sanctuary. He built a community playground for them, remarking, "Farmers provide exercise grounds for their hogs; I feel the world would be far better off if they had provided, instead, recreation grounds, right at home, for their boys."

He got trees from the forestry nurseries, thousands of them, and planted them around his 400 acres as windbreaks and a refuge for birds of all kinds. He enlarged and beautified his pond to a two-acre lake. His Sanctuary grew to the point where it was costing $15,000 a year to maintain it. The government lent a modest aid of $4,000 annually.[2] Friends sent contributions. And Jack Miner, his wife and his son Manly devoted all their time to caring for the birds. They even established a hospital where they treated wounds, and bound up broken bones; this news, too, spread mysteriously along the flyways, and wounded birds flew to Jack Miner, or walked miles through the fields trailing a pinion shattered by a hunter's gun.

Miner wondered about the flyways of his ducks and geese. In August 1909 he scratched his name and address on a band of aluminum with a pair of shears and placed it on the leg of a black mallard with whom he had made friends. The duck flew south. The following January Miner received a letter from a hunter at Anderson, South Carolina, saying that he had shot the mallard on Rocky River. That was the beginning of an exciting new sport for Jack Miner—banding birds to chart the course of their migrations. By 1944 he had banded over 50,000 ducks and 31,000 Canada geese. He devised a special trap for catching them—a chicken-wire frame which he could drop down over the flock as it fed on his pond. In the autumn of 1939 alone he caught and banded 2,875 ducks and 1,317 geese and sent them on their way. He and Mrs. Miner in their comfortable house, with its walls covered with photographs of famous people who have visited him and are his friends, stamped the bands with Jack's name and address, a number and a verse of Scripture: "I go away and come again"; "Preserve me, O God"; "A friend loveth at all times"; "Have peace one with another."

For nearly forty years hunters have been returning these bands with notes telling where the birds had been shot. An Indian hunter in the marsh edges of faraway Magdalena River in Colombia shot a teal duck. Its leg was banded. The hunter carried it to a lawyer in Barranquilla who read, "Write Box 48, Kingsville, Ont. Let us consider one another. Heb. 10:24." They wrote to Jack Miner. Thirty miles north of Eastmain, in the Hudson Bay region, Charles

---

[2] An editorial in the St. Catharines *Standard,* August 22, 1940, condemned the government for reducing this to $2,500, and stated: "The government has $35,000,000 invested in national parks and preserves, and yet those 400 acres at Kingsville, the Miner property, are probably more famous and more attractive than any public-owned domain in the Dominion."

Shashawaskum, a Cree Indian, shot a banded goose; at Cape Jones, Richard Fleming, an Eskimo, shot another. The district manager at Moose Factory sent them back to Jack Miner. And as the thousands of bands have come back to Kingsville, eighty percent from United States hunters, Manly Miner has written notes of acknowledgment and his father charted them each with a red dot on a large map of North America. They show with reasonable accuracy the flyways, the feeding and nesting grounds, of the migratory wild fowl. Most of the geese fly down from James Bay in the autumn, cross over Lake Erie at Kingsville, pass down over western Ohio to the river near Cincinnati, reach the Mississippi near Cairo and proceed south down the valley. The ducks range over Lake Michigan to Minnesota, the Dakotas and the western Canadian provinces, and scatter from Kingsville over all the Southern states. Yet they find their way back, with miraculous precision, to Jack Miner's pin-point pond, and the food and safety of his Sanctuary.

Jack Miner's seventy-ninth birthday was celebrated as an event in Canada. There was a great reception at the Sanctuary. The Boy Scouts came and their band played. School children exhibited birdhouses. Prominent men from all over the country came. A large delegation from Detroit and the state of Michigan arrived to do him honor. Kingsville gave him a banquet. A nation-wide broadcast carried the ceremonies to the homes of his friends. The *Essex County Reporter* issued a sixteen-page Jack Miner Edition devoted exclusively to the man and his work. Henry Ford and Her Royal Highness, Princess Juliana of the Netherlands, sent congratulatory messages and words of praise. And His Majesty, King George VI, conferred upon him the Order of the British Empire.

Jack Miner died in his eightieth year in November 1944. He and Mrs. Miner had deeded their home, clubhouse, community park and the Sanctuary to the Jack Miner Migratory Bird Foundation. He had plans under way to purchase the 1,600 acres adjoining, in which the provincial government had prohibited shooting, to give added protection to the Sanctuary. In spite of his fourscore years, he died in mid-career with many of his plans and visions unfulfilled. But he could survey his accomplishments with satisfaction. He had turned a mudhole into a world-renowned park. Geese and ducks had made it a way station, the rare white swans were coming in flocks to the Lake

Erie shore at Kingsville, and thousands of small birds made a morning and evening choir of the 40,000 trees which he had planted for
their protection. He had seen a steady increase in the flights of migratory birds, a growing interest among governments and sportsmen to restore the wild rice in the nesting and feeding marshes and
to give intelligent protection to the birds. As he himself used to say,
"A goose lays from four to nine eggs and they raise about four
young on the average. Let the hunter take two and leave two of those
young geese and the goose problem will take care of itself." The
protection of his Sanctuary added each year, he estimated, about
25,000 to the population of the birds. And when the duck hunters
crouch in the shooting blinds among the marshes between Sandusky
and Toledo, up the west coast past Monroe, around Lake St. Clair
and along the north shore of Lake Erie, they have cause to honor
Jack Miner and to remember the wisdom of his words.

Chapter 32

Along the South Shore

THE south shore of Lake Erie from Detroit to Buffalo is divided into spheres of influence, each dominated by one of the five large cities on the lake. Detroit's influence is felt all around Lake St. Clair, down the Detroit River, and along the west shore of Lake Erie as far as the nursery and papermaking town of Monroe. A few miles below this "Floral City" the domain of Toledo begins; it extends eastward to Sandusky Bay, pulling Port Clinton and Sandusky into its orbit. As you near Huron and Vermilion, you feel the sovereignty of Cleveland. It is a physical sensation. You are turned forcibly around from the zone of Toledo and faced eastward, just as though a powerful loadstone had been brought to bear upon a field of steel filings. The billboards announce Cleveland hotels and department stores, and citizens of these towns have charge accounts at the Halle Bros. Company. Cleveland's sphere of influence extends throughout most of the Western Reserve and reaches east along the lake shore to Conneaut. Erie exerts a counterpull in its own sector along the Pennsylvania shore and contiguous region. But in the vicinity of Westfield the orientation is again shifted and the unmistakable magnetism of Buffalo draws Dunkirk and Silver Creek into its circle.

We shall have one more brief look at these cities and the towns which are geared to them. Buffalo has spread out in all directions in the present century. It has not become the second city on the Great Lakes, yielding only to Chicago, as it had hoped in the 1880's, but the extent and quality of its growth should satisfy any reasonable ambitions. It is not that Buffalo has failed to live up to the expectations of its builders, only that the growth of Cleveland, Detroit and Chicago outran all expectations.

The process of harnessing the prodigious power of Niagara Falls began in the 1890's. The giant turbines, roaring under the pressure of the falling waters, generated electricity to light the city, drive its streetcars, lift its grain, operate its mills and turn the wheels of its varied industries. The Pan-American Exposition called attention to this miracle and attracted new enterprises. The steel interests moved in. The Lackawanna Company began construction on its plant and blast furnaces in 1902. They were taken over by the Bethlehem Steel Company in 1922 and developed into the present monster works at Lackawanna. Republic Steel of Buffalo is now the third largest in the country. Henry Ford erected a large assembly unit. General Motors built a huge plant four miles down the Niagara River below the Peace Bridge. E. I. duPont de Nemours & Company, and the Dunlop Tire and Rubber Corporation located their plants near by. The Black Rock Canal was widened and deepened to twenty feet from Buffalo Harbor to the north tip of Squaw Island, and the Niagara River was dredged to make a channel of equal depth down the east shore of Grand Island to the turning basin at North Tonawanda. The Semet Solvay Company, the Wickwire Spencer Steel Company, the Gulf, Richfield, Frontier and other oil companies, and the Tonawanda Iron Works all spaced themselves along this channel.

Buffalo moved northward with them. Thousands of immigrants arrived to work in Buffalo plants—dominantly from Germany, Poland, Italy and Hungary. They settled in communities where they have stamped the city with their racial solidarity. Black Rock, once a rival of Buffalo, and now an almost indistinguishable unit in the metropolis, is the chosen quarter of 15,000 Hungarians. The 100,000 Poles gathered into a community on the East Side. The 80,-000 Italians spread in a less cohesive group near the water front, and in the towns and vineyard region to the southwest. The Negroes (about 15,000) were segregated around Michigan Avenue in the downtown section. The Germans are no longer a distinct community; they have taken an active and progressive part in civic and commercial affairs and are assimilated into the city as a whole. This expansion of industry northward along the river and the influx of population have made the entire Buffalo-to-Niagara Falls district into one almost continuous unit.

Off to the east, near the Buffalo Airport, are the aircraft factories which were enormously expanded during World War II. Headquarters plants of Curtiss-Wright and Bell Aircraft are located here. They have drawn to Buffalo thousands of workers. Acres of new housing units have sprung up in the fields around the aircraft district. The elevators, flour mills, cereal and feed plants are piled up in massive concentration around the basin, the Buffalo River and the Buffalo Ship Canal. A maze of railroad tracks, air lanes, steamship lines, highways and the barge canal converge on Buffalo to handle its 20,000,000 yearly tonnage of commerce and the 2,000,000 visitors who pass in and out every year.

The wealth which all this activity brings to Buffalo is reflected in the skyscrapers of its business center and in the appointments of the city. Like all cities, it has its violent contrasts: the Buffalo Yacht Club and the hovels of the poorer Italians; its singing cathedral towers of business and the downtown slums; its grimy water-front buildings and its impressive residential streets; its ten great public parks with greensward, lakes and woods, and its grim and crowded foreign quarters. Its cultural interests, begun a century ago in the days of Millard Fillmore, have flowered in the present era. The University of Buffalo, founded under Fillmore's leadership in 1846, has been greatly enlarged in recent years with many new buildings on its rolling 174-acre campus. Its 4,000 students have the benefit of the magnificent library which Thomas B. Lockwood gave to the university in 1933; and if they care to examine such priceless treasures, they may see the first four folio editions of Shakespeare's plays which Lockwood bequeathed to the library, along with many other rare books and manuscripts. The Jesuit Canisius College, founded in 1870, the State Teachers' College, opened the following year, and D'Youville College of the Grey Nuns of the Cross, carry forward the higher learning in opulent Buffalo.

The interest in art which Lars Sellstedt stimulated, the exhibits which he worked so hard to popularize, have had their culmination in the vast, neoclassic white marble Art Gallery in Delaware Park, a gift of a Buffalo businessman, the late John J. Albright. It features a collection of old masters and modern painters and sculptors, and carries on art education among the school children. The Public Library, founded back in the days when bookloving people browsed at Steele's, now serves scholars and citizens with its 640,000 volumes; and the Grosvenor Library, founded in 1857 with a $40,000 gift from Seth Grosvenor, is one of the great reference libraries in the country, with 300,000 selected volumes in history, science and art. The active and scholarly Buffalo Historical Society, so prized by

Fillmore and his contemporaries, is now properly housed in its handsome building in a corner of Delaware Park, a gift from New York, which had erected it as the State Building for the Pan-American Exposition. Its exhibits of western New York history and its collection of books, manuscripts and newspapers are invaluable. The beautiful, modernistic Kleinhans Music Hall, seating 3,600, was a benefaction of the late Mr. and Mrs. Edward L. Kleinhans. The $1,000,000 Museum of Science, giving a visual history of every branch of natural science, was Buffalo's own civic gift to its citizens.

Joseph Ellicott would stare with amazement at the thirty-two stories of the City Hall towering above the McKinley Monument in Niagara Square and looking out over the river and the lake; Samuel Wilkeson would marvel at the engineering of the harbor, the basin and the miles of breakwater; Joseph Dart would gasp at the fortress elevators; Captain Job Fish simply wouldn't believe that the 600-foot freighters rounding the lighthouse were lake ships; but if they could view this city from a few miles out on Lake Erie, they would all agree that in choosing this spot on the bank above sand-choked Buffalo Creek they had indeed chosen wisely.

The shore between Buffalo and Silver Creek has no important towns or villages. The ship lanes are well offshore to the north, and the main highways keep to the south, affording only a few glimpses of the blue lakes. The remains of the Indian reservation which the Prince of Wied visited over a century ago, now 21,680 acres in extent, still contains about 2,000 Indians, all that are left of the once proud Seneca, Onondaga and Cayuga who dominated the area as members of the Five Nations. It is well back of the lake on U. S. 20. The Chautauqua grape belt, which we have already described in some detail, begins a few miles west of the reservation and continues to the edge of Erie's domain. Silver Creek, Fredonia, Brocton and Westfield are the vineyard towns. Dunkirk with its harbor on the lake, though within the grape belt, is an industrial city.

The forty-second parallel, which forms the northern border of Pennsylvania, intersects Lake Erie only about three miles east of the Ohio boundary. It looked for a time as though this scanty strip would be Pennsylvania's only frontage on Lake Erie. But at the close of the eighteenth century, the state acquired title to a small triangle of land between this parallel and the lake with a shore line of fifty miles.[1] The city of Erie, with a population of 116,000, is just halfway between the borders of New York and Ohio. The Lake Erie Belt is only about four miles wide here, and the ancient shore-line terraces, bearing upon their level shoulders the railroads and highways, are near the lake. It is a region of apple and cherry orchards, small vineyards, tomatoes and cabbages. There are only two villages of any size near the lake: North East in the northeast, where the Welch Company bottles grape juice and cans tomato juice, and the market village of Girard in the northwest. The cherry trees are seas of bloom in spring, lovely beside the blue water of the lake; the best of their red fruit is made into maraschino cherries.

The 3,200-acre sandspit of Presque Isle, much of it wooded, curves nearly five miles around the water front of Erie. The ceaseless waves beat against it. They have eroded it down to a neck only a few feet wide at the west end where it joins the mainland, and threaten to cut it off into an island like Long Point. Under the wave action and the lashing of the winds the sandspit has been moving northeast at the rate of about 500 yards each century. Since it was acquired as a state park in 1921, steel pilings have been placed along the west shore to impede this action and to preserve Presque Isle as a playground and a breakwater. If the action is not stopped, it will eventually carry the spit right on down the lake. A monolith in the well-kept park commemorates the heroic achievement of Perry under the protection of Presque Isle.

The presence of this natural breakwater dictated the location of Erie; it is the only harbor on the straight and uninviting Pennsylvania lake shore. The town itself is singularly attractive from a great air liner circling above its housetops and trees and the rolling farms and gardens on its outskirts. The sandy beaches of Presque Isle are yellow in the sun between the bay and the lake, and the blue waters break into whitecaps against its shore. The harbor is busy from April to late November with 4,500 arrivals and departures of lake

---

[1] Largely through the efforts of Benjamin Franklin, who termed the lake "the Mediterranean of the New World." Pennsylvania paid $151,000 for the triangle, and got a very good bargain for its money.

ships, bringing in wood pulp, ore and grain, and taking out coal. The ore goes down to the steel towns over a branch of the Bessemer & Lake Erie Railroad which serves the larger port at Conneaut. The pulpwood goes to the Hammermill Paper Company. The fishing fleet puts in and out of the harbor. It takes about $200,000 worth of fish each year in the Pennsylvania waters of Lake Erie.

The business section is largely concentrated down on the lake front. The residential section fans out along the lake and up the terraces. There are few of the grimmer marks of a factory town about Erie although it is an industrial city. Its specialty is metal products of all kinds from steam shovels and air hammers to delicate gas and electric meters. General Electric has an enormous manufacturing plant spread low over the fields on the edge of town. Other plants, also spread about Erie, make toys and games, rubber and coke. Yet, in flying over Erie, driving through it or approaching it from the lake, you see few smokestacks, no pall of smoke; it is neat, tree-covered, and prosperous-looking. And, incidentally, it ranks fourth in size among the cities of Pennsylvania.

It carries lightly the aura of its rich historical tradition. Several of its old houses, built in the early decades of last century, still stand. The Erie Historical Society has been diligent in collecting and preserving the heritage of the past; it has, among scores of interesting items, the Indians' duplicate of the deed by which they ceded their interests in the region for $32,000 in guns, ammunition, blankets and supplies; and the kettle in which the bones of Anthony Wayne were boiled clean for transplantation among the graves of his fathers. And Erie's great and venerable newspaper, the *Dispatch-Herald,* can display on its masthead the legend: "Established 1820."

Conneaut in the northeastern corner of Ohio, seventy miles east of Cleveland, has no mills or factories, but it has a fine harbor and it is close to Pittsburgh. That is the secret of its growth from an isolated village into its present position as U. S. Steel's largest ore-receiving port on the lakes. It is a way station, a transshipping point. Its docks can receive the largest freighters on the Great Lakes. The batteries of Hulett unloaders at the docks of the Pittsburgh & Conneaut Dock Company bite out the ore, dump it into larry cars to be transferred to the stock piles, or drop it directly into the weighing hopper and onto the railroad cars of the Bessemer & Lake Erie Railroad to be hauled inland to the steel mills. The cars return to the lake loaded with coal to be dumped into the freighters and carried back up the lakes. Huge Brown electric machines, each with a lifting capacity of twelve tons, pick up steel made in Youngstown and Pittsburgh, and lower it gently into the emptied freighters for shipment to Canada, and to Detroit and other American cities on the Great Lakes. Much of the work around the busy docks is done by Finns; hardy men, still preserving the tradition of the Finnish steambath and other customs of their fathers who came to Conneaut to unload ore with picks, shovels and wheelbarrows.

Only a dozen miles farther east in the Ashtabula Harbor the scene is repeated in almost every detail, but with the added flavor of many fishing craft, the United States Coast Guard Station, and the car ferry transferring loaded trains across Lake Erie to Port Stanley. And on the rolling, well-favored land back of the harbor, tempered by Lake Erie's water, gardeners cultivate, under seventy acres of glass, fine vegetables for the Cleveland market.

The scene is also repeated once again just twenty-five miles west at Fairport Harbor, even to the Finns and the Hungarians who man the docks, and the white Coast Guard Station where officers and men are on the alert twenty-four hours a day all the year round. Long breakwaters reach out into the lake to give protection to the freighters in the harbor. And a couple of miles back on the plateau above the Grand River is Painesville, home of Lake Erie College, debarkation point for thousands of immigrants to the Western Reserve, a city of over 12,000 people which has kept much of its old Connecticut atmosphere in an industrialized age of steel. The Rider Tavern, built in 1818 at the very beginning of the stagecoach days, still stands. Several of the old houses designed by Jonathan Goldsmith, the architect who came out from New England in 1811 to beautify the frontier villages, are kept in trim repair. And near by at Unionville in a rural setting not far from the lake is gracious Shandy Hall which has been restored, furnished with antiques and period pieces from the Reserve, and kept as a museum.

The influence of Cleveland, clearly evident in these lake-shore towns, becomes overpowering as you approach the municipalities which are governmentally independent of Cleveland, but would have no existence without it. For Cleveland has gone through the process now so familiar in American cities of moving out to suburban communities in order to escape the inevitable effects of its own industrial and mercantile pre-eminence. The opulent deserted Euclid Avenue and the once handsome residential section of downtown Cleveland, and built mansions in the country along the creeks and glens, in the low rolling hills of Shaker Heights, and at Bratenahl on the lake. Those who could afford it migrated or settled in Euclid, East Cleveland, Cleveland Heights, Lakewood and Rocky River, and now commute to the offices and factories in the mother city. The older sections declined and decayed into slums. The new suburbs are neat, wooded and pleasant.

The core of Cleveland's prosperity is the steel-and-ore-shipping business which we have already examined in considerable detail. But around this center have flourished all kinds of industry, for Cleveland makes almost everything, in whole or in part, which modern mechanical civilization wishes to buy. Rockefeller's Standard Oil Company, organized in 1870, began here and spread through the world. Six big companies—Allied Oil, Shell Petroleum, Socony Vacuum, Gulf Refining, Marine Oil and Standard Oil—have oil terminals and vast storage tanks along the river. Charles Brush's experiments with electricity, dynamos and carbon lamps, and the merger of his company with Thompson and Edison, led to General Electric and its plants in Cleveland. General Electric maintains an experimental laboratory employing 1,200 specialists in its eighty-five-acre Nela Park overlooking Lake Erie in East Cleveland. Westinghouse and the American Gas Association also have important research and testing laboratories here. Around 1880, Worcester R. Warner and Ambrose Swasey, expert machinists, located in Cleveland to manufacture machine tools, precision and scientific instruments. They built the thirty-six-inch refractor for the Lick Observatory in 1886. Organized into the now world-famous company of Warner and Swasey, they have made, through their inventions or designs, almost endless contributions to the automotive industry and the scientific laboratories. Their precision instruments are used everywhere, and at the Yerkes Observatory, the Naval Observatory, the Argentine National Observatory and elsewhere, astronomers formerly used

Cleveland lenses, and still use Warner and Swasey instruments to loose the bands of Orion.

Cleveland was in on the ground floor in the manufacture of automobiles. One of the first automobiles made in America was built by Alexander Winton and sold in Cleveland on March 24, 1898, and many of our citizens who are still young will remember riding in the big Wintons, or seeing them stalled on the roadside waiting for a mechanic during the period of World War I. The White Sewing Machine Company, one of the big concerns in Cleveland, built the first White Steamer in 1898. Alva Bradley used to drive one down Euclid Avenue, frightening the horses and amazing the populace. The Stearns Company began making cars at the same time, and the Baker Company turned out electrics. The Peerless bicycle plant, so prosperous in the 1890's, began making Peerless automobiles in 1901. The Royal appeared in 1903. By 1910 there were thirty-two plants engaged in making automobiles in Cleveland, and their products were worth over $21,000,000. Packard was operating in near-by Warren. It looked as if Cleveland might be the automobile center of the country with its neighbor Akron as the rubber capital of the world. Clevelanders say that it was timid capital which lost this industry to Detroit where Ford, Durant, Olds, the Dodges and their colleagues were making the right guesses, gathering financial backing and snuffing out the competition of other cities. Cleveland still makes trucks and busses, and sends bodies, batteries and all kinds of parts to Detroit; it has assembly plants, and General Motors Winton Division; but it is an auxiliary to that motor metropolis and receives its finished cars lashed to the spar decks of the lake freighters and delivered from Detroit to the docks in the Cuyahoga Flats.

All the Cleveland plants went to war in 1940. White's trucks became armored scout cars. General Motors Winton turned out millions of dollars' worth of Diesel engines for submarines. Other factories made everything from tractors to addressing machines. Forty-five factories made parts and equipment for airplanes. Cleveland had long been air-minded. Its great airport handled an average of nearly 1,000 passengers every day in the year, and it was the scene of the air races that attracted national attention in the decades between the two world wars. The United States Government located an airplane-engine research laboratory here. Cleveland industrialists and mechanics, long skilled in the manufacture of machine tools and precision instruments, and in making automobile parts, converted easily to airplanes. They fashion propellers and landing gears, wheels and engine valves, and the delicate instruments by which pilots have flown the planes through the skies over every country on the planet.

Moses Cleaveland's Connecticut town lost its New England character as its mighty steel industry rose and attracted hordes of people to its mills and factories. Few American cities present so diverse an ethnic pattern as modern Cleveland. The entire Great Lakes bowl has been for a century the supreme melting pot of the nation, and Cleveland got its full share, if not more, of the immigrants. Traveling about among the different sections of Cleveland is somewhat like making a tour of the world, for there are forty-eight nationality groups represented here. They have come so rapidly and in such numbers, and they have congregated so closely and individually that assimilation has been retarded. You may still hear more than a score of languages spoken in the streets and in the native restaurants of the various quarters. Two-thirds of the population are either foreign-born or children of immigrants who flooded into Cleveland from all parts of the world to unload its cargoes and operate its machines. They give Euclid Avenue and the Public Square an interesting polyglot atmosphere as the crowds flow by or jam onto the streetcars and busses at Ontario Street and Superior Avenue.

The Hungarians gather annually in University Circle for a patriotic demonstration in honor of their great countryman and hero, Louis Kossuth, whose bronze statue looks across the Circle at Saint-Gaudens' figure of Cleveland's Mark Hanna. The Yugoslavs and Lithuanians dominate a large area between Euclid Avenue and the lake just east of the business district. Greeks and Russians are congested south of Euclid around East 14th Street. The Jews are farther east. The Italians are somewhat scattered, but "Little Italy" is still farther east and south of Euclid. Certain aspects of their life have been recreated and interpreted by their native-son novelist DeCapite in *Maria*. The Czechoslovaks and the Poles, both heavily represented in Cleveland, are concentrated on the South Side. Other groups, including the Irish and the Romanians, have gathered on the west side of the Cuyahoga in a drab section which seems to extend almost endlessly to the south. There are many Germans here also, as well as in other parts of the city. Most of these groups published newspapers in their native languages until World War I, and some of them still do.

While these nationalities are slowly being assimilated, they have been encouraged to keep alive their peculiar heritages. The small triangle at East 12th, Superior and Payne is named Pulaski, and it bears a stone marker to this great hero, placed there by the Polish veterans of World War I. Rockefeller Park has a large plot devoted to "cultural gardens" in which a score of these groups have reproduced gardens characteristic of their homelands, planted them with native trees, flowers and shrubs, and honored their poets, artists and statesmen. They hold their folk festivals and display their native costumes. Their music, dances and pageantry were a special feature of the Great Lakes Exposition held in Cleveland in 1935.

The sudden, violent growth of Cleveland from a small town to one of the great cities of the world obscured for a time the cultural and civic interests of the citizens which its wealth made possible. Cleveland came late to civic improvement. Its rich men bought land on the edge of town and developed great private estates. J. H. Wade, the portrait painter and camera man who became the telegraph magnate, purchased a seventy-five-acre tract north of Euclid, employed landscape architects and beautified it into a park. He donated it to the city in 1885 on condition that Cleveland would spend $75,000 for improving it. The iron millionaire W. J. Gordon did exactly the same thing with a 120-acre estate fronting on Lake Erie. When he died in 1892 he willed this beautiful tract to the city to be kept open to the public as Gordon Park. John D. Rockefeller owned the estate between Wade's and Gordon's. In 1896 he donated 276 acres to the city, and $300,000 in cash to complete a boulevard between Wade Park and the park lands on Shaker Heights. These gifts provided Cleveland with a magnificent and continuous park belt from Shaker Heights to the lake, down winding Doan Brook Valley. The addition of Edgewater and Lakewood Parks to the west on the lake front, and the Metropolitan Park area along Rocky River,

Pearl Avenue and Big Creek, and Tinkers Creek has almost completely surrounded the city with a chain of parks and playgrounds unsurpassed by any in the country.

The downtown area, however, languished. The lake front was a utility entrance and an eyesore. The Van Sweringen Brothers, real-estate dealers, developed Shaker Heights. They acquired the Nickel Plate Railroad, a rapid-transit system between the Heights and Cleveland, and downtown real estate, and inflated the vast bubble of their financial empire. At the close of the 1920's they turned their attention to the Public Square and dreamed up the Union Station and the Terminal Tower buildings at a cost of $119,000,000. The 708-foot tower dominates all Cleveland. It is hard to remember what the center of town was like in the days before the Van Sweringens. The depression of the 1930's swept away the Van Sweringens and their empire, but their material improvements remain to grace the city.

The Mall, which almost joins the Public Square and the Terminal Tower, was dressed up during the 1920's. The great Municipal Auditorium,[2] the Public Library, the *Plain Dealer* building, the Federal Reserve Bank, the Federal Building, the Board of Education Building—all similar in design and grouped about the south end of the Mall—the City Hall and County Courthouse to the north, and the Municipal Stadium on the lake front at the foot of West 3rd, are a fine beginning, at least, toward making the center of Cleveland dignified and attractive. And the new bridges and the lake-front highways have revealed to Clevelanders the beauty of the lake which they have treated as a back door when it should be an impressive front entrance.

The cultural institutions have kept pace with these civic improvements. The well-patronized Cleveland Symphony Orchestra was organized in 1918, and John Long Severance presented it with a million-dollar home on University Circle in 1930. The famous Museum of Art is near by in Wade Park. Case School of Applied Science and Western Reserve University are among the ranking institutions of the country and their grounds are almost a continuation of the Doan Brook parks. The Western Reserve Historical Society,

---

[2] Cleveland music lovers gather here each spring as hosts to the visiting Metropolitan Opera Company.

with its museum and rich collection of books and manuscripts, has been diligent for a century in preserving the records of the past. And the great Public Library, with its 2,000,000 volumes and its specialized collections, serves its varied clientele with marvelous patience and efficiency.

Yes, Moses Cleaveland, the city which you laid out in the wilderness on the east bank of the Cuyahoga has somewhat outgrown Windham, Connecticut.

The spirited city of Lorain with its splendid harbor has already been the subject of much comment in this story of Lake Erie. It keeps its own identity, but it is closely linked with Cleveland, and crowded busses run every few minutes day and night between the two towns. The lake shore through the lagoons at Vermilion, the ore-receiving and coal-loading port of Huron, and on to Sandusky is low and varied, and is lined most of the way with cottages and summer homes and vacation camps. Sandusky on its bay in the center of Vacationland and Port Clinton on the wide, marshy mouth of the Portage River have also held our interest throughout the history of Lake Erie. Sandusky with its fisheries and wine cellars, its neighboring lagoons and duck marshes, its Cedar Point resort and the Lake Erie Islands to the north remains one of the distinctive towns on Lake Erie. And it absorbs the big Pennsylvania Railroad Coal Docks and their acres of adjoining tracks without damage to its beauty. You would hardly suspect that it is the second largest coal-shipping port on the Great Lakes. Between Port Clinton and the Maumee the lake shore is generally soft, marshy, subject to heavy erosion, and without harbors.

The Maumee River is the broad highway through Toledo which feeds its industries and bears upon its yellow waters the materials of its prosperity. Seven bridges link the East Side to the business section on the west. The spacious Maumee is a striking contrast to the narrow and tortuous Cuyahoga. The big ships move up and down the river with as much freedom as they sail the charted courses on the open lake. Wharves, docks and industries line the east shore and much of the west bank. Twenty-four railroads converge on Toledo like the center of a cobweb. Many of them drag endless cars of coal to miles of loading docks along the river. The process of unloading the coal into the freighters is as ingenious as that of emptying ore from the ships' holds to the stock piles. It is automatic. An endless chain pulls a car up under the giant steel-framed tower of the unloading machine. Steel fingers grasp it firmly, lift it up, turn it over and dump the coal down through a chute into the hold. The entire process takes about as much time as a man spends in stoking his furnace for the night. The car is set delicately back on the rails, is pushed off down an incline, runs by gravity up another incline, slows up and stops, then rolls back and is deflected by a switchoff into the yards to be reassembled and hauled back to the mines for another load. The biggest of these unloading docks, costing $30,-000,000, is down on the recently industrialized neck of land at the mouth of the Maumee which Toledo calls Presque Isle, to the annoyance of the citizens of Erie, Pennsylvania.

As the home of the Libbey-Owen-Ford Glass Company combine, Toledo is one of the biggest glass centers in the nation. Edward Drummond Libbey used a large slice of his wealth to found the Toledo Museum of Art and to provide it with the extraordinarily beautiful building in which it is housed. Incidentally it has among its treasures the finest exhibit of glass from all the ages to be found anywhere in the world. Toledo Scales are used by shopkeepers of all nations. Miles of the Presque Isle water front are crenelated with the domes of the oil-refining companies, and the elevators of the milling companies. Willys-Overland held out precariously against the competition of the automobile makers of Detroit; and in the manufacture of generators, speedometers, steering wheels, horns and other parts, Toledo is almost an industrial annex to the automobile city.

Like the other lake cities, Toledo has looked to its parks and its cultural institutions. The families with wealth or with good incomes have deserted the downtown sections for the pleasant suburbs. Fine buildings in the business district rise up beside others grimy with age and decay. The nationality groups, almost as varied as those in Cleveland, are gathered into distinct but smaller "Little Poland," "Little Italy," "Little Hungary," in the business region and around the mills and factories. They all make use of Toledo's splendid new library. It is downtown among the department stores and office buildings and looks very much like them. Its street windows are display cases, as smart and artistic as Lamson's. They exhibit books and announce lectures and educational programs. And the modernistic interior is as pleasant and efficient as any I have ever worked in either in America or in Europe. The University of Toledo, supported by the municipality, is out in the more rolling country adjoining Ottawa Park.

Toledo is still far from beautiful, but it has come a long way in the century that has elapsed since its citizens were catching frogs in the vicinity of the Commodore Perry Hotel and writing in the *Blade* about the mud of Hog's Back on Summit Street. It is a vital nerve center in the intricate pattern of the nation's industrial life.

Lake Erie between the Maumee and the Detroit Rivers is shallow. Ships may not venture near the shore. A dozen rivers and creeks flow into the lake, but only the River Raisin, dredged out into the lake and carefully marked with lights and buoys, affords a harbor. Monroe is the only town on this coast, and it is four miles up the river. Its nurseries spread north and south near the shore. It has paper mills, and its glass factories make use of the Monroe sands. It was once a debarkation port for immigrants moving west. Thomas Mooney, an Irishman in Wisconsin, recommended it to his cousin Patrick Mooney in Ireland who was planning to migrate to America. In a series of amusing letters written in the late 1840's[3] he warned Patrick against the "set of wretched grog-sellers and low boarding-house keepers in Buffalo (many of them Irish) whom the Irish stranger should avoid as he would a cholera house. Better sleep out all night in the parks than enter one of them." But Monroe on its "tumbling river," with its four mills and 4,000 people was, he said, "rather an elegant place." And Mooney's description is still appropriate.

Our journey down the Detroit River unfolded much of the spectacular industrial might of the automobile capital of the world. At the turn of the century Detroit was a comfortable city of 285,000, shaded with trees, making wagons and carriages, working in wood and steel for the horse-and-buggy era. Ford, Olds, Durant and the other young experimenters and visionaries put America on rubber-

---

[3] Thomas Mooney's *Nine Years in America* (Dublin, 1850).

tired wheels turned by gasoline engines, transformed the pattern of living in the nation and rolled Detroit out into a sprawling, nervous, raucous city of over 1,500,000 people from every state in the Union and every country under the sun. The story of that transformation is long and complex and it takes volumes to recount it in any detail. Many volumes have recounted it. Every literate man, woman and child in the country, and in most of the world, knows it in general outline. The episode of Henry Ford tinkering with a homemade gas-pipe engine clamped to the kitchen sink while Mrs. Ford fed gasoline into it, is on its way to becoming as familiar as the picture of Benjamin Franklin and his kite. In the summer of 1896 Ford's first car appeared on the streets of Detroit.

Step by step, Henry Ford elaborated and simplified his engine, built it into a car that would run, improved the car until it would sell, and planted in the mind of every man the desire to own one. Early in his career he fixed upon the two principles of controlling his own finances and of making dependable and economical cars in the low-priced field. Ransom E. Olds of Lansing was also tinkering. He got backing from S. L. Smith of Detroit, formed a manufacturing company and went into business in 1899 at Detroit.

Possibly it was accidental that Ford and Olds, Durant and the rest were Detroit men; perhaps if they had been Chicago or Buffalo men, one or the other of those cities would have become the center of automobile manufacture. Certainly if somebody with a fully developed plan for making cars had just been casting about for a location, it is possible that he might have overlooked Detroit. But Detroit had the men of genius, it had the men of daring and vision, and it captured the industry from all other competitors.[4] It had a nucleus of skilled mechanics. It was an important center for the building of marine engines. It already knew how to build fine carriages, and it was immaterial at first whether they were drawn by a horse between the shafts or a Ford engine under the seat. Detroit men had accumulated great wealth with their varied industries and the exploitation of the timber and minerals of Michigan. They were adaptable and venturesome and ready to back the young inventors as Cleveland, for example, was not. And the ghost towns in the exhausted pineries provided a hardy reservoir of young men to

---

[4] In Ohio alone 161 companies have made automobiles.

operate the new factories. Once the industry got going in Detroit, it was natural for Dodge and Chrysler and General Motors and the rest to set up shop and pool the advantages of concentrated operation.

Under the combined impetus of all these vast new enterprises the growth of Detroit was simply fantastic. Expert engineers came in to find a way to meet the demands for increased production. There were not enough skilled workers to turn out the cars, for the record-breaking output of one season was only a beginning on the quota for the next. They developed the assembly line and taught each man how to do one single segmented detail of the total operation. Word spread through the world that workers were wanted in Detroit. They swarmed in from Germany, Poland, Hungary, Italy, Yugoslavia, Canada, Lithuania—from everywhere. Young mountaineers from Tennessee, Kentucky and West Virginia worked beside other young mountaineers from Albania and the Tyrol. The Negro population skyrocketed to 126,000 by 1930, and during World War II reached approximately 200,000. Men came by the hundreds of thousands, filled up the old city, spilled out over the countryside around the motorcar plants. Thousands of flimsy houses were thrown up to accommodate them; houses that have decayed since the boom of the 1920's and now fill many square miles of Detroit with grim desolation. Fine old mansions of the gayer era became rooming houses, then degenerated into the slums that lie under the serene towers of the Fisher and Penobscot Buildings. New attractive suburbs sprang up miles beyond the city of 1890, and Detroit-made cars carried their citizens back into town to make more cars. One of the sights of the hemisphere is the spectacle of Detroit workers swarming like ants out of the factories at the close of a shift, piling into cars in the parking lots like cans on a grocer's shelves, and driving home in all directions under a cloud of thin blue carbon smoke. The congestion and the overcrowding and the problem of transportation grew infinitely worse as all these vast plants converted their resources to make airplanes, tanks, armored cars and the mobile weapons for the Allied armies on all the fighting fronts of World War II.

The tensions produced by this pattern of life set the stage for the explosions in the strikes and riots of recent years. The strikes also called attention to the fact that, while Detroit is the automobile center of the nation, it is dependent upon the steady flow of gears and batteries and spark plugs and tires from scores of interlocking cities, and that a stoppage at Goodyear in Akron, or Fisher in Cleveland can stop the assembly lines in Hamtramck. Despite the tensions, the ingenuity of management and the production record of labor both before and during World War II have compelled the admiration of all peoples.

Detroit still has far to go to make its cultural institutions commensurate with its wealth, but it has made a beginning. It is attempting to restore some semblance of plan to the sprawling city. It supports one of the great symphony orchestras. It is going forward with plans for a new campus and fine buildings for Wayne University. It has begun the development of a worthy Civic Center out on Woodward Avenue between Kirby and Putnam Avenues. On the west side in a beautiful setting is the magnificent white marble $3,000,000 Public Library opened in 1921. It houses, among other treasures, the Burton Historical Collection which is a mecca for scholars interested in the history of Detroit and the old Northwest. The Library is balanced by the $4,000,000 white marble Institute of Arts just across the street. It was not donated by any Detroit automobile magnate, but was the city's own gift to its citizens and its children. It has a choice and representative collection of art through the ages from the Fifth Egyptian Dynasty and Nebuchadnezzar's Babylon to Diego Rivera's "Making of a Motor." And in adjoining Dearborn, Henry Ford, ignoring the more sophisticated arts and culture, has been transplanting to Greenfield Village the prized homespun relics of the American tradition: colonial and frontier tools and utensils, an Illinois courthouse where Lincoln once practiced law; the birthplace and school of William McGuffey; the Menlo Park laboratory of Thomas Alva Edison; and such priceless items.

These institutions are oases in a mercantile city that lives on turning wheels in the tempo of whirring engines and is proud to be called Automobile Capital, Miracle City or Dynamic Detroit.

Epilogue

So FAR we have come with the story of Lake Erie. It has covered a long age in geologic time, though the tenure of mankind on Erie's shores has been brief. The fabulous development has been achieved by the efforts of only four or five generations—most of it by the last two or three.

We have seen this southernmost and last to be discovered of the Great Lakes gradually opened by the explorers. We have participated in the wars that raged round it, and in the statesmanship that finally restored it again to peace and equilibrium, and made it a demonstration of international concord. We have seen men first from New England and then from all nations streaming in to Lake Erie to seek homes and new opportunities round its basin. We have watched them while they hewed out farms and villages in the wilderness to plant lonely cabins, schools and churches in the clearings at the creek mouths, and we have watched the cabins grow to become the great cities that now rim its water front—and continue to expand and to mature. We have watched their lake vessels grow from small pirogues that hugged the shore to the leviathans of the ore, coal and grain fleets which crowd Lake Erie's busy sea lanes. We have remarked the vision, the energy and the courage of these men, and have marveled at their ingenuity in transporting ore and coal, sand and limestone to fashion around Lake Erie the products of civilized living.

We have studied the lake itself in all its varying moods: Now quiet and subdued, imprisoned under the thick ice of midwinter; now raging like a wild and living thing under the lashing of the storms; now merry under the gentle breezes and silver clouds of a June day; or serene in July or September under a bright and windless sky. It is a wayward, restless and temperamental body; a playground, a melting pot, a fluid highway marked with spars and buoys into intricate traffic lanes. Trains rush back and forth along its ancient beach lines, planes fly the air lanes along its rim, and the lake and the life that gathers around it are always in motion.

We have dwelt on the singular variety of Lake Erie: The isolated, Old-World atmosphere of the quiet Wine Islands, and the strident modern life of metropolitan Detroit, Toledo, Cleveland and Buffalo; the yachts and fishing boats idling on the lake, and the batteries of Huletts at the ports unloading ore from Mesabi; and the fragrant vineyards and the sulphurous steel mills and furnaces.

So far we have come, but the pulsating history which we have followed, great though it is in human achievement, seems to be only the beginning of an unfolding drama in which the action is still rising toward a climax.

ACKNOWLEDGMENTS,
BIBLIOGRAPHICAL NOTE
AND INDEX

ACKNOWLEDGMENTS

I AM in debt to many people for their help in the making of this book. D. L. Chambers, Harrison Platt and their associates in the Bobbs-Merrill Company have been very patient during a disturbed period, and have given me valuable counsel and suggestions. Milo M. Quaife gave the manuscript diligent reading, and his profound knowledge of the history of this region has saved me from error on several occasions. I extend to him cordial thanks for his aid, and at the same time absolve him from certain interpretations with which he does not wholly agree. Howard H. Peckham, Director of the Indiana Historical Bureau, very kindly read portions of the historical sections and made helpful corrections. The late Jack Miner was generous in supplying me with material on his work and about his Sanctuary. Robert Godley of Cleveland has gone out of his way and has taken considerable trouble to put material at my disposal, to open many important doors to me, and to make it possible for me to see the ships and the shipyards in action. I have spent many profitable hours with him talking about Lake Erie and its vessels. He has been kind enough to read portions of the manuscript. I wish also to thank W. H. Gerhauser, President of the American Ship Building Company, for making available to me information on the development of shipbuilding on Lake Erie.

Lieutenant Commander William L. Morrison of Erie aided me on the story of Perry's ships and other details and he has been a most helpful consultant. Alva Bradley gave me unpublished materials on the C. & B. Line, and I shall long remember the conversations with him in his Cleveland office about Lake Erie and its ships and men. My thanks are also due to L. C. Sabin of the Lake Carriers' Association; to William R. Crawford of the U. S. Maritime Commission; to Clarence S. Metcalf, Librarian, and Donna L. Root, Head of the Division of History, Biography and Travel, Cleveland Public Library; to Ray Evans and John B. Titchener of Columbus; to the Ontario Travel Bureau and the Department of Planning and Development of the Province of Ontario; and the Norfolk County Council.

I owe special thanks to T. H. Langlois of Put-in-Bay for his many kindnesses to me and for his generosity in supplying me with data from his inexhaustible storehouse of learning; and to George W. White for his guidance on geological matters and Lake Erie erosion. Marjorie Lowell Endter typed or supervised the typing of the manuscript and aided at various points in the research.

BIBLIOGRAPHICAL NOTE

A BIBLIOGRAPHY of the Great Lakes would fill a fat volume by itself. The notes appended to each of the other four volumes on the Great Lakes in this series have indicated the standard works and the wide variety of material of all kinds available for consultation or for further study. New data turns up constantly. The revival of interest in the lakes is bringing to light many heretofore unknown private and amateur collections relating to the region. The recent organization of the Great Lakes Historical Society and its magazine *Inland Seas* has helped to stimulate this interest. The society has made rapid progress in expanding its collection at the Cleveland Public Library. It is receiving gifts of MSS., old ships' logs, photographs, letters, scrapbooks, rare volumes and such items that add new information on many chapters in the story of the lakes.

Materials of all sorts have gone into the making of this book on Lake Erie. A goodly portion of them are not from books but from personal observation and experience, firsthand knowledge, and from interviews and conversations with authorities on various aspects of life and the activity on and around the lake.

From the rail of the spar deck, from the bridge and from the wheelhouse, I have watched the lake ships dock and get under way. I have seen them navigate in fog, and have pored over the navigation charts through the intricate channels. I have observed the fishing fleets in action, and the Hulett unloaders at work. I have been on the launching platforms and have talked with the shipbuilders. I have seen the scientists at work in the Franz Theodore Stone Laboratory, and have watched the erosion of the shore line. I have seen the vinedressers tending their vineyards and the wineries turning grape juice into sherry and champagne. I have been in all the cities and towns and have observed the complex activity of the lake ports. These are the sources to which an author turns with most satisfaction and remembers with gratitude to the scores of people who added, unconsciously, some rivulet to the main stream of the story.

But there are also the countless hours happily spent in the libraries studying the vast accumulation of printed matter. Historians all know the pleasure of plowing through a hundred dull pages for the reward of one small golden nugget that may make only a sentence or a paragraph in the work at hand—as when several hours of reading in the *Memoirs* of Lieutenant General Scott yield the vivid sentence about the panic of his doctor aboard the plague ship, and the *Travels* of Christian Schultz brighten with the brief passage on his visit to the grave of Anthony Wayne.

The publications of the various historical societies around Lake Erie have become an almost inexhaustible mine of raw material for a work of this kind. The *Buffalo Historical Society Publications* (1879——) cover almost every aspect of Lake Erie and Buffalo history: the lake itself, the wars, the ships, the commerce, the growth of the city, the rise of the grain port, and the hundreds of interesting men and women who helped to build the city. I have drawn heavily upon the documents of the society. The *Michigan Pioneer and Historical Collections* (1874-1929), which include the Cadillac Papers; the *Michigan History Magazine* (1917——); the *Ohio Historical Collections* (1930——); the *Canadian Archives Publications* (1909——); the *Ontario Historical Society Papers and Records* (1889——); the *Historical Society of Northwestern Ohio Quarterly* (1929——); the *Western Reserve Historical Society Publications* (1870-1929); the *Magazine of Western History* (1884-1893) all yield important source material relating to Lake Erie.

The voluminous *Jesuit Relations and Allied Documents* (73 volumes), edited by Reuben Gold Thwaites (Cleveland, 1896-1901), and *Early Western Travels,* by the same editor, touch frequently on Lake Erie. Father Hennepin's *A New Discovery, etc.,* published in London in 1699, was also edited by Thwaites. The works of Francis Parkman—*The Pioneers of France in the New World, The Jesuits in North America, La Salle and the Discovery of the Great West, The Conspiracy of Pontiac*—are still standard in material and literary distinction, though some new work is being done by historians which may alter the details in certain instances. Other important contributions have been made by Seymour Dunbar's *History of Travel in America* (New York, 1937); *Narrative and Critical History of America* (Boston, 1884-1885), edited by Justin Winsor; William B. Monro's *Crusaders of New France* (New Haven, 1918); George M. Wrong's *Rise and Fall of New France* (New York, 1938); Jesse Edgar Middleton and Fred Landon's *The Province of Ontario—A History, 1615-1927* (Toronto, 1927); C. H. Van Tyne's *The Loyalist in America* (New York and London, 1902, 1929); William S. Wallace's *The Family Compact* (Toronto, 1915); and numerous other works—for the field is still very much alive.

Complete data on the important Lake Erie ports are in the U. S. Lake Series: No. 1, *The Port of Buffalo, New York* (1940); No. 2, *The Port of Detroit, Michigan* (1940); No. 5, *The Port of Cleveland, Ohio* (1939); No. 7, *The Port of Toledo, Ohio* (1939); No. 8, *The Ports of Sandusky, Huron, and Lorain, Ohio* (1939); No. 9, *The Ports of Ashtabula, Conneaut, Fairport, Ohio* (1939). The *Annual Report* series of the Lake Carriers'

Association and the U. S. War Department's *Transportation on the Great Lakes* (1937) are full of valuable information relating to all aspects of shipping and maintenance on the Great Lakes. The *Great Lakes News,* published at Cleveland by Eugene Herman; the *Nautical Gazette,* the *U. S. Steel News,* and the newspapers of the port towns, running back through the years, are filled with news about the lake and the activity on and around it, and I have drawn frequently upon them.

The standard work on the Underground Railroad is Wilbur H. Siebert's *The Underground Railroad from Slavery to Freedom* (New York, 1898). Among an extensive list of volumes on this subject the most helpful are Levi Coffin's *Reminiscences* (Cincinnati, 1898), and James H. Fairchild's *The Underground Railroad* (Cleveland, 1895).

Other volumes that have been found particularly useful, or which may be recommended for further consultation on various aspects of Lake Erie are:

Atwood, Wallace W. *The Physiographic Provinces of North America.* New York, 1940.

Barry, John F., and Elmes, Robert W. (ed.). *Buffalo's Text Book.* Buffalo, 1924.

Beasley, Norman. *Freighters of Fortune.* New York, 1930.

Buffalo Common Council *Manual,* 1897. Buffalo, 1897.

Callahan, James Morton. *The Neutrality of the American Lakes and Anglo-American Relations.* Baltimore, 1898.

Catlin, George B. *The Story of Detroit.* Detroit, 1923.

Channing, Edward, and Lansing, Marion F. *The Story of the Great Lakes.* New York, 1912.

Chapelle, Howard Irving. *The History of American Sailing Ships.* New York, 1935.

Clowes, Ernest Seabury. *Shipways to the Sea.* Baltimore, 1929.

Colton, Calvin. *Tour of the American Lakes, etc., in 1830.* London, 1833.

Curwood, James Oliver. *The Great Lakes.* New York, 1909.

Cuthbertson, George A. *Freshwater.* Toronto and New York, 1931.

Disturnell, John. *The Great Lakes, or Inland Seas of America.* New York, 1863.

———. *Sailing on the Great Lakes.* Philadelphia, 1874.

———. *Upper Lakes of North America.* New York, 1857.

Downing, Elliot R. *A Naturalist in the Great Lakes Region.* Chicago, 1922.

Doyle, John H. *A Story of Early Toledo.* Bowling Green, 1919.

Duncan, Dorothy. *Here's to Canada.* New York, 1941.

Farmer, Silas. *The History of Detroit, Michigan.* (2 vols.) Detroit, 1889.

Foster, J. W. *Limitation of Armament on the Great Lakes.* Washington, D. C., 1914.

Freeman, L. R. *By Waterways to Gotham.* New York, 1925.

Garriott, Edward B. *Storms of the Great Lakes.* Washington, D. C., 1903.

Hall, J. W. *Marine Disasters on the Great Lakes.* Detroit, 1872.

Havighurst, Walter. *The Long Ships Passing.* New York, 1942.

Hennepin, Father Louis. *A New Discovery of a Vast Country in America.* Chicago, 1903.

Howe, Henry. *Historical Collections of Ohio.* (2 vols.) Cincinnati, 1900.

Mrs. Jameson. *Winter Studies and Summer Rambles in Canada.* (2 vols.) New York, 1839.

Kennedy, James Harrison. *A History of the City of Cleveland 1796-1896.* Cleveland, 1896.

Lake Erie Vacation Land in Ohio. Federal Writers Project. Sandusky, 1941.

Lazell, Warren (publisher). *Steamboat Disasters and Railroad Accidents.* 1843.

Leverett, Frank, and Taylor, Frank B. "The Pleistocene of Indiana and Michigan and the History of the Great Lakes," *U. S. Geological Survey,* Vol. LIII, 1915.

Levermore, Charles H. *The Anglo-American Agreement of 1817 for Disarmament on the Great Lakes.* Boston, 1914.

Lloyd's *Steamboat Directory.* 1856.

McDougall, Alexander. *Autobiography.* Privately printed, 1932.

McLaughlin, Andrew Cunningham. *Lewis Cass.* Boston, 1891.

Mansfield, E. D. *The Life and Military Services of Lieutenant-General Winfield Scott.* New York, 1862.

Marquis, Thomas G. *The Jesuit Missions.* Toronto, 1921.

Martineau, Harriet. *Society in America.* London, 1837.

Michigan, A Guide to the Wolverine State. New York, 1941.

Mills, James Cooke. *Our Inland Seas, Their Shipping and Commerce for Three Centuries.* Chicago, 1910.

Miner, Jack. *Jack Miner and the Birds.* Chicago, 1923.

Murphy, Raymond E., and Murphy, Marion. *Pennsylvania—A Regional Geography.* Harrisburg, 1937.

New York, A Guide to the Empire State. New York, 1940.

The Ohio Guide. New York, 1940.

Pickering, Joseph. *Inquiries of an Emigrant.* London, 1832.

Pollard, James E. *The Journal of Jay Cooke or The Gibraltar Records, 1865-1905.* Columbus, 1935.

Pound, Arthur. *Detroit, Dynamic City.* New York, 1940.

Putnam, George R. *Lighthouses and Lightships of the United States.* Boston and New York, 1933.

Quaife, Milo M. (ed.). *Burton Historical Leaflets,* Vols. I-X. Detroit Biographies. Detroit, 1922-1931.

——. *The John Askin Papers.* Detroit, 1928-1931.

Randall, E. O., and Ryan, D. J. *History of Ohio.* (5 vols.) New York, 1912.

Samuel, Sigmund. *The Seven Years War in Canada.* Toronto, c. 1934.

Schultz, Christian. *Travels on an Inland Voyage, 1807-8.* (2 vols.) New York, 1810.

Scott, Lieutenant General. *Memoirs.* New York, 1864.

Shepard, Francis P. "Origin of the Great Lakes Basins," *Annual Report, Smithsonian Institution,* 1937. Washington, 1938.

Spencer, Joseph W. *The Duration of Niagara Falls and the History of the Great Lakes.* New York, 1895.

——. "Origin of the Basins of the Great Lakes of America," *American Geologist,* Vol. 7, pp. 86-97, 1891.

Stone, William L. *Narrative of the Festivities Observed in Honor of the Completion of the Grand Erie Canal.* New York, 1825.

Thorndale, Theresa. *Sketches and Stories of the Lake Erie Islands.* Sandusky, 1898.

Trimble, George. *The Lake Pilots' Handbook.* Port Huron, 1907.

Urann, C. A. *Centennial History of Cleveland.* Cleveland, 1896.

Waldron, W. *We Explore the Great Lakes.* New York, 1923.

Wallen, James. *Cleveland's Golden Story.* Cleveland, 1920.

Williams, Ralph D. *The Honorable Peter White.* Cleveland, 1907.

Wittke, Carl (ed.). *The History of the State of Ohio.* (6 vols.) Columbus, 1942.

——. *We Who Built America; the Saga of the Immigrant.* New York, 1940.

Wood, William. *All Afloat.* Toronto, 1920.

INDEX